The Francophone film

The Francophone film

A struggle for identity

LIEVE SPAAS

Manchester University Press

MANCHESTER AND NEW YORK

Published by Manchester University Press
Oxford Road, Manchester M13 9NR, UK
and Room 400, 175 Fifth Avenue, New York, NY 10010, USA
www.manchesteruniversitypress.co.uk

Distributed exclusively in the USA by
Palgrave, 175 Fifth Avenue, New York NY 10010, USA

Distributed exclusively in Canada by
UBC Press, University of British Columbia, 2029 West Mall,
Vancouver, BC, Canada V6T 1Z2

British Library Cataloguing-in-Publication Data
A catalogue record for this book is available from the British Library

Library of Congress Cataloging-in-Publication Data
A catalog record for this book is available from the Library of Congress

ISBN 0 7190 5861 9 paperback

First edition published 2000 by Manchester University Press

First digital, on-demand edition produced by Lightning Source 2006

To Christina and Jessica

Contents

Illustrations

Preface

The aim of this book is to introduce the reader to the diverse film production of the French-speaking countries outside France, commonly called 'Francophonia'. The underlying premise is that a comparative study of significant films and their directors in these countries, taking into account distinctions of ethnicity, territoriality, religion and citizenship, yields vital insights into their separate quests for a specific identity within the context of a common Francophonia. To study films from a Francophone perspective allows us to group together films that might otherwise be divided by questions of race, gender, genre, period or nation, thus opening new insights for further comparative study of an unusually rich corpus of films.

The emphasis here is on the intersections between memory and history, narrative representation and social reality, with the intention of scrutinising the relationship between individual, social and political issues and colonial, postcolonial and neo-colonial problems manifest in Francophone cinema. The book is based on a historical reality which has shaped and continues to shape the individual and collective experience of a very large number of peoples throughout the world. It studies those countries of Francophonia that have had a sustained contact with France and, in the case of former colonies, that were French at the moment of independence.

The method followed is that of a mapping expedition in which individual films, film-makers and countries are treated separately in order to emphasise to the maximum their specific identities or that represented in their films; this method has also been chosen in order to offer a book that is readable, informative and accessible.

Maximum effort has been made to include the most representative and relevant films for a study of identity but the selection has, inevitably, also been guided by the films' availability. Care has also been taken in the filmography to be as accurate as possible but in some cases not all the information could be located and not all films had an English title. All references taken from French are given in English in the text and the original entered in a section at the end of the book.

Acknowledgements

I am indebted to many people and institutions whose support made it possible for this book to be completed. Kingston University and the Arts and Humanities Research Board granted research leave; the same Research Board and the Kingston European Research Centre awarded grants that allowed me to attend the FESPACO film festival in Ougadougou and to undertake research in various film institutes: the Cinémathèque Québécoise, Vues d'Afrique, the Cinémathèque Afrique and the Belgian Film Museum. In all of these places I have received the warmest welcome and support.

I am grateful to colleagues, friends and family: to Teresa Lawlor, Head of the School of Languages and Gail Cunningham, Dean of the Faculty of Human Sciences for encouraging me to undertake this project, to my colleagues in the School of Languages whose work load is inevitably heavier when someone is on leave.

I am especially grateful to Gloria Cigman who has lent unfailing support throughout the writing process of this book; without the innumerable faxes exchanged with her, this book would still be in the making. I thank Jacqueline Page for the painstaking work on the filmography and research assistance, Trista Selous for unstinting support and input into this book and Jenny Feller for her valuable editorial help and advice.

This book has made me discover, yet again, the generosity of many people: Françoise Pfaff and Frank Ukadike read and commented on the sub-Saharan section; Bill Marshall discussed Québécois cinema and graciously acted as a mini film library; Roy Armes for sharing his knowledge of North African film and Anne Judge for sharing hers of Francophone matters; Pat Corcoran lent me many African films. The late and much missed Bridget Jones was an inspiration for the Caribbean section. The following colleagues and friends read and commented on various sections of the book: Carrie Tarr, Arnold and Annick Saxton, Anne Showstack Sassoon and François Nectoux. In Montréal I received generous support from Josiane Boulad-Ayoub and Werner Nold, who also shared with me his vast experience of film editing.

Special thanks go to Diana Holmes, for her support and advice, and to Robert McNamee who helped both with the content and structure of this book and lent much appreciated technical help. I am grateful to Paul Mercken for reading, and commenting upon, the entire book.

Finally my warmest thanks go to my daughters: Christina who, when only three years old, pretended that she was 'doing footnotes', now decided – and rightly so – that this book, although it has no footnotes, could not be completed without her conscientious scrutiny while Jessica's constant support and vigilance contributed in no small measure to it. I dedicate this book to them both.

Abbreviations

ACCT	*Agence de la Coopération Culturelle et Technique/Agence de la Francophonie*
CCM	*Centre Cinématographique Marocain*
CRUA	*Comité Révolutionnaire d'Unité et d'Action*/Revolutionary Committee of Unity and Action (Algeria)
FEPACI	*Fédération Panafricaine des Cinéastes*
FESPACO	*Festival Panafricain du Cinéma de Ouagadougou* (Burkina Faso)
FLN	*Front de Libération Nationale*/National Liberation Front (Algeria)
FLQ	*Front de Libération du Québec*/Québec Liberation Front
IDHEC	*Institut des Hautes Études Cinématographiques* (Paris)
JCC	*Journées Cinématographiques de Carthage*/Carthage film festival
NFB	National Film Board/Office National du Film (Canada)
OAA	*Offices des Actualités Algériennes*/Algerian Newsreel Office
ONCIC	*Office National du Commerce et de l'Industrie Cinématographiques* (Algeria)
ONF	*Office National du Film*/National Film Board (Canada)

Introduction: Francophonia and identity

On 24 July 1967 General de Gaulle travelled from Québec City to Montréal, accompanied by the Premier of Québec. Wherever they stopped, the French President was cheered and celebrated. In Montréal, a large and keen gathering waited for him in the square in front of the Town Hall. De Gaulle, accompanied by his hosts, stepped on to the Town Hall's balcony to greet the enthusiastic crowd. He began, saying that what he felt at that moment was similar to what he had felt at the liberation of France after World War II. Pursuing the emotional rhetoric, he concluded with the words: 'Vive Montréal! Vive le Québec! Vive le Québec libre! Vive le Canada français et vive la France!'

The balcony speech may have been improvised but there was nothing surprising in the message. On the previous day de Gaulle had shouted similar slogans, although then he had used the old colonial name, 'La Nouvelle France', the colony lost to the English: 'Vive le Canada! Vive les Canadiens français! Vive le Québec! Vive la Nouvelle France! Vive la France!' On that same day, in a toast addressed to Québec's Premier, he explicitly embraced Québec's Frenchness by assimilating the two nations, addressing them as 'Français': 'nous Français, que nous soyons du Canada ou bien de la France' ('we French, whether we are from Canada or from France'), amplifying the sentiments by further flamboyant rhetoric, identifying the French from the two continents as belonging to the same family, sharing a single identity. De Gaulle even extended Frenchness beyond the boundaries of Québec, by referring to 'tous les Français où qu'ils soient' ('all the French people wherever they may be').

Undoubtedly, de Gaulle's hyperbolically rhetorical speech, with the ideal of a large French family and a universal French identity, was more a provocation to the North American continent (where he had just arrived) than a recognition of real family ties between all the inhabitants of the former French colonies. But addressed as it was to descendants of former French subjects, and delivered by such a historic and high profile media personality, this speech, however flamboyant, was possibly the most spectacular and militant proclamation of Francophonia ever uttered.

Throughout modern history, the French have seen themselves as owning a great and special culture, which it has been their duty to propagate. In his *Siècle de Louis XIV*, Voltaire did not hesitate to proclaim social grace as the natural quality of the French, which other nations felt themselves to lack – and indeed the insistence upon the universality and superiority of their language had been shared by a European elite in the eighteenth century. And that long tradition of disseminating French language and culture, upholding the ideal of a Francophone family, permeated France's colonial policies of 'direct rule and assimilation', founded on the idea 'that France and the colonies were a family, bound by the French language and culture' (Andrade-Watkins 1996: 113).

But where and what is Francophonia? The word 'Francophone' was coined in France in 1883 by a geographer, Onésime Reclus (Reclus 1883: 422–5). It has linguistic and geographic connotations, evoking the fact of speaking French and referring to the places where French is spoken. 'Francophonia' encompasses these two meanings. It was given official organisational status in 1970 at a conference in Niamey (Niger) with the creation of the ACCT (*Agence de la Coopération Culturelle et Technique*) whose function was to set up technical and cultural support to the former French colonies. In 1993, ACCT became *Agence de la Francophonie* though the acronym ACCT remained.

L'Agence de la Francophonie has become a world-wide organisation with fifty-two members from Europe, North Africa, Black Africa, Arabia, Asia and North America. The only criterion for membership is some degree of Francophonie, no matter how small, varying from more than 80 per cent for some populations to as little as 1 per cent.

There is no doubt that a neo-colonial ambition lurked at the heart of de Gaulle's insistence on a universal 'French family' and the subsequent creation of the ACCT: the old coloniser aimed at maintaining economic and cultural control over its former colonies. It was with this objective in mind that, under de Gaulle's government in 1961, the Ministry of Cooperation was created, with the function of setting up technical and cultural support for the former colonies. The French attempt to forge links with these new independent countries met with an initiative emanating from some African leaders themselves, who proposed formalising links with France. Although these leaders advocated a partnership of equals, they may well have been reflecting the success with which the French had seduced the colonised with their assimilation ideal. While these leaders were at times charged with neo-colonialism, they certainly ignited the Francophone flame. The most prominent of them, Léopold Senghor from Senegal, not only activated Reclus's forgotten notion of 'Francophonie' but also initiated the whole Francophone movement. It is, therefore, to Africa, as the proto-member of Francophonia, that we must turn to understand the Francophone phenomenon.

A striking aspect of the early Ministry of Cooperation was its interest in cinema. Within this Ministry, two channels were set up to deal with cinema: the *Consortium Audiovisuel International*, which produced news-reels and various educational films for the former colonies and the 'Bureau de cinema' which provided financial and technical support to African film-makers. The Bureau's assistance was instrumental in making Francophone Africa the most important centre of Black African Cinema. Before independence from France, not a single film had been made by an African in Africa, but by 1975 over 185 shorts and features were produced with the technical and financial assistance of the Bureau (Andrade-Watkins 1996: 113).

There is no doubt in the mind of Claire Andrade-Watkins that the primary objective was not the development of an African cinema, but the maintaining of 'the colonial legacy of assimilation, perpetuating and strengthening a Franco-African cultural connection through newsreels, educational documentaries and films of cultural expression' (1996: 112). France's attempt to control cinema produced in its former colonies is by no means surprising since cinema is widely believed to have the power to promote ideologies and blind people to their own oppression. Little wonder that cinema became the main cultural instrument to safeguard France's hold over the former colonies: colonisation of the territories was replaced by that of the screens.

The strategy used for this new means of colonisation was not unlike actual territorial colonialism: the French employed the Africans to do the job. This time, the Africans were given cameras instead of weapons, they shot images instead of each other and, still identifying with the French, they unwittingly colluded with spreading French culture and civilisation at the expense of their own. Throughout Francophone Africa, educational and cultural films were shown to inculcate French values and entice the Africans into a French universe. For the entire period of colonisation, the Africans had seen French films made by French film-makers. The assimilation policy became a clever ploy: the films were still financed and sanctioned by France, but now the Africans were making the pictures themselves. The ongoing promotion of Frenchness and the affirmation of a French identity through cinema would inevitably impede the development of an African identity.

However, the French, while still colonisers, had already instilled in Africans an interest in cinema even if they did not allow them at that time to make films in their own countries. Intellectuals and aspiring artists, who went to study in France, acquired technical skills and developed an *auteur* film-making approach that would later influence their own film-making. Cinema had always been a way for the French to define themselves; this too was transmitted. If initially the African film-makers espoused the French model, they soon came to see that they had to fight this model and its neo-colonial interest in Africa's film-making in order to project their own identity on screen. This required them to defend themselves against the French, to appropriate the screen and so to reflect Africa. In order to achieve this, it was necessary to resort to Francophone technical and financial support for many aspects of film-making.

One of the major aims of France's support for African film-making was to preserve and spread the French language but, as the Africans grew more and more confident in their film-making, they resorted increasingly to the use of their own languages. This led gradually to the paradoxical situation of Francophonia becoming the means for abandoning the French language and of a return to the pre-colonial situation with its traditional languages and African identity. While adhering to the medium, African film-makers rejected the idiom.

Africa's struggle for identity was well on the way when, in 1967, de Gaulle suddenly drew attention to Québec, where the French idiom, unlike the situation for Africa, constituted the very core of identity. The French language defined the Québécois and they welcomed the onset of the Francophone movement to support them in self-affirmation. When, in 1970, Francophonia became a proper organisation, linked by the use of French, it emerged that French could either confer an identity or obstruct it. In the case of Québec, as for Belgium, the French language was the fundamental attribute of identity; for Africa, and by extension the Caribbean, it was the opposite. However, for all the Francophone countries it was through the vehicle of cinema that this struggle for identity was expressed.

I EUROPE

European Francophonia is spatially characterised by its contiguity to France. Each French-speaking country or region is adjacent to France: Belgium, Switzerland, the principalities of Monaco and Andorra and Luxembourg (where the official language is *Luxembourgeois* but where French remains the parliamentary and judiciary language). But of this group, only two countries can boast a Francophone cinema: Belgium and Switzerland.

It would be difficult for either country to speak of a national cinema because of their linguistic divisions. Moreover, the countries' size stands in the way of making a viable commercial national cinema. The advent of sound further emphasised the language split and complicated the funding of films in different languages in one and the same country. These constraints have influenced the genre of films which flourished in both countries; film-makers, seeking a wider audience than that of their individual linguistic region, have turned to documentaries and art-cinema. Often too, they have opted for co-productions.

For both countries, the vicinity of France had and still has a major influence. On the one hand, the attraction of the more powerful neighbouring France remains strong and France frequently welcomes talented Francophone film-makers from the two adjacent countries. Luxembourg, although not a producer of Francophone films, plays a role in promoting the art of film through its well-stocked *Cinémathèque* and through its contribution to the establishment of the *Union des cinémathèques de la communauté Européenne*, an organisation which coordinates the work of Europe's film archives.

1 Belgium

Identity, Amin Maalouf argues, is not given once and for all; it is constructed and transformed throughout one's existence (Maalouf 1998: 33). This statement is particularly true for Belgium and its problematic national identity. Bilingualism divides the country between French-speaking Wallonia and Dutch/Flemish-speaking Flanders. Some Belgians extend this linguistic identity and feel affinity with France or the Netherlands. It was not until 1922 that Flemish gained official status and was accepted as a language equal to French. A few variations in lexis and accent aside, Flemish differs little from Dutch; the distinction between the two may be compared to that of American and British English. There is also a small German-speaking community in the Eastern Eupen-Malmédy region.

It has to be remembered that Belgium is a young country, created in the aftermath of the Napoleonic wars when, at the Congress of Vienna in 1815, Britain advocated the integration of the formerly French-controlled land into the Kingdom of the Dutch Prince of Orange, as a strategy to prevent military attacks from France. In 1830, a national uprising against the Dutch – in which the Catholic clergy played an important part in reinforcing the hostility towards the Protestant House of Orange – led to Belgium's independence.

While the French-speaking south benefited from Belgium's early industrialisation, the Flemish-speaking north derived its wealth from agriculture and commerce. In spite of its neutrality, which was guaranteed by Britain, Belgium was attacked by the Germans in 1914, drawing Britain and the entire British Empire into the war. The heavy fighting of both this war and World War II left deep scars in Belgian society.

Post world war Belgium underwent numerous changes. King Leopold III abdicated in 1951, accused of collaboration with the Germans. In this period the entire nation was divided as the population of Wallonia accused many Flemish-speaking Belgians of collaborating with the Germans. This Walloon/Flemish discord became increasingly problematic, moreover, when the crisis in heavy industry reversed the balance of wealth between the two parts of the country. Flanders, with its access to the sea, now attracted new industry and became more prosperous. Under Flemish pressure, the University of Leuven/Louvain, had to relocate its Francophone section to a newly built campus in the French-speaking part of Belgium (Ottignies). It was clear that Belgian identity was becoming increasingly complex.

The image of Belgian society also changed dramatically after World War II. Abandoning the principle of neutrality, Belgium joined NATO and the Benelux union. In 1960 it withdrew from the Belgian Congo. All these factors affected Belgian society: it was now a country that had entered the internationalisation movement and was part of the postcolonial world. Belgium's enthusiasm for the European Union reflects the Belgians' tendency to move towards a more European identity, although the internal problems by no means disappeared. The growing division between the two linguistic communities prompted the implementation of a three-stage process to create a federal state. This was completed in 1993.

In the light of the creation of a federal state, it is hard to identify what a Belgian identity might be. The abandoning of Belgium's neutrality has led to the influx of a great many people from a range of different countries, ethnic groups and social strata, each with their own legitimate identity. The large number of European civil servants adds a further foreign presence. Belgium has become an amalgam of peoples who bear the marks of postcolonial relocation, the Jewish diaspora and general post-war mobility: it is a mosaic of different groups of people, for whom Belgium is a place rather than a nation.

To what extent has this instability of identity influenced Belgian cinema? As in many countries, cinema in Belgium started as a fairground spectacle. The first showing of the cinematograph Lumière took place on 10 November 1895 before a small selected audience. The first public performance occurred on 1 March 1896 in the Galerie du Roi. The opening of a permanent movie-house in 1904 gave rise to the dream of creating a Belgian national cinema; however, from the start, this was to be a difficult notion.

One of Lumière's technicians, Alfred Machin, built a studio on the outskirts of Brussels, where he made a number of films. The best known, *Maudite soit la guerre* (1913 – *Damn the War!*), is a somewhat naive appeal for peace, especially in the light of the war that followed. This first Belgian film was supposed to herald the start of Belgian national film production, but the onset of the war halted this momentum. The end of the war did not improve the situation, as American, French and even German firms monopolised Belgian cinemas. Moreover, several talented actors and scriptwriters (Léon Mathot, Berthe Bovy, Charles Spaak, etc.) were attracted to France, leaving the embryonic Belgian film industry impoverished. Only after 1930, when sound had already been introduced, was there some development in Belgian film-making.

During this early period the distinction between Francophone and Flemish-speaking films was very apparent. The exodus of Francophone talent was not mirrored in Flanders. However, Flemish film-makers had to face the disadvantage of suffering from cultural insecurity in a very Francophone climate. Brussels, where decisions were made, was mainly French-speaking. Moreover, the Belgian authorities were short-sighted where cinema was concerned and official support for film production remained minimal and highly centralised in the French-speaking capital. However, this period did see some successful cooperation between Flemish-speaking Belgium and the Netherlands and the emergence of two important Flemish directors: Charles Dekeukeleire and Henri Storck.

It was not until after World War II that a Belgian film industry began to take shape. The distinction between Flemish and Francophone cinema became blurred, as versions in each language were often produced for the same film. Also, Flemish film-makers were usually fluent in French as well as Flemish and were able to produce films in both languages – which is why Dekeukeleire and Storck, for example, have come to be included as both Flemish and Francophone film-makers. Both these seminal figures of Belgian cinema have also attained international fame.

Early film production in Belgium consisted mainly of documentaries. These films are rooted in Belgian tradition, both Flemish and Walloon and, while displaying a sense of the real and the concrete, they also evince a fascination with the surreal and fantastic. These early film-makers also show strong social awareness and used film as a means to reveal and address social problems. This social awareness, however, does not seem to have been applied to the colony of the then Belgian Congo. Instead, the films inspired by the African experience display a fascination with the exotic and the natural beauty of the country rather than any social or political problems.

The film-makers who stand out and in whose work there is a discernible struggle for identity are the above mentioned Charles Dekeukeleire and Henri Storck, and also André Delvaux, Jean-Jacques Andrien, Chantal Akerman, Jaco Van Dormael and the Dardenne brothers, Luc and Jean-Pierre. The diversity of background and origins of some lesser known film-makers – Swiss-born Boris Lehman, French-born Marion Hänsel, and Palestinian Michel Khleifi – adds to a richness of voices which provide valuable reflections on identity.

Charles Dekeukeleire

Born in 1905, Charles Dekeukeleire became a cinema enthusiast and one of Belgium's foremost film critics. A socially committed film-maker influenced by Soviet writings on film, Dekeukeleire denounced the way the institution of cinema was ruled by money and mediocrity. Influenced also by Germaine Dulac, he proposed a real film-language, combining a sense of genuine cinema with social commitment. Although Flemish, he did not hesitate to demystify the Flemish nationalistic ceremony staged yearly in Dixmude in his 1931 film, *Dixmude*. He took a similar approach in his film *Lourdes* (1932), where he shows the mercantile side of the pilgrimage town in the French Pyrenees. Dekeukeleire excelled in the making of commissioned documentaries, such as the remarkable *Terres brûlées* (1934), a moving reportage on the Belgian Congo, which transcends any touristic or colonial approaches and captures the glow of the sunburnt earth it observes and reflects. His *Thèmes d'inspiration* (1938), which won the prize for best documentary at the Venice Film Festival, is a journey in time in which he blends the present reality of human faces and landscapes with paintings from the past by James Ensor, Constant Permeke and Constantin Meunier, who were themselves inspired by these faces and landscapes. It juxtaposes the imaginary world of the painters and the reality of everyday Flemish life. Dekeukeleire is undoubtedly one of the founders of Belgian cinema together with Henri Storck, who was two years his junior.

Henri Storck

As Cathy Fowler states (Fowler 1995: 38), 'it is to Storck that the promotion and development of cinema in Belgium can be credited'. What is striking is that Storck seems to have transcended the Flemish/Walloon division. With him there emerges a unique kind of identity, firmly rooted in Belgium's artistic tradition but also open to the influence of the outside world. Storck was Flemish, born in Ostend in 1907. In the city and its surroundings he was exposed to the three local avant-garde Flemish painters – whom he later befriended – James Ensor, Léon Spilliaert and Constant Permeke. Their social awareness and intense relationship with the materiality of the pictorial process had a strong effect on the young Storck. The later Flemish painters, Paul Delvaux and René Magritte, born nine and ten years before him, were virtually his contemporaries. There is no doubt that artistically and socially Storck's identity remained profoundly Flemish, like that of Delvaux and Magritte. Although they moved in international artistic circles, they were able to keep a critical distance from French trends and continue to give expression to their own specific Flemish identity.

From a very young age, however, Storck was fascinated by the inventiveness and development of a new art, the cinema. When only eleven years old, he acquired a *Pathé-Baby* with which he projected burlesque Chaplin films. He also bought a puppet theatre in which he performed his own creations. By the age of twenty, having already distinguished himself as a photographer, he began to use an 8 mm camera. He discovered the *Club de l'Ecran* in Brussels and soon founded a *ciné-club* in his home town. The work of Robert Flaherty was a revelation for Storck, confirming and encouraging his natural inclination to observe and evoke everyday life. He met French film critic Léon Moussinac in Paris and, encouraged by him, bought a portable professional camera. By the age of twenty-five he not only had acquired an unusually rich cultural knowledge but had developed a powerful artistic and social sensitivity. The artists Storck admired and the friends he made reveal both his artistic stature and his political inclinations. His acute sense of observation drew him to reportage and documentary films. His early films such as *Images d'Ostende* (1929) and *Trains de Plaisir* (1930) reveal a very personal style which captures the ordinary in a poetic and often humorous way.

In 1930, at the International Congress of Independent Film-makers in Brussels, Storck met Jean Vigo, Joris Ivens and Germaine Dulac, who encouraged him to go to France. In 1932 he became Vigo's assistant for *Zéro de Conduite*. However, the Paris studios did not really suit him and Storck returned to his home country in search of his own identity which, while being Flemish, also integrated a Francophone dimension. Storck's most notable work is the film *Misère au Borinage* (1933), made in collaboration with the politically committed Dutch film-maker, Joris Ivens. It is one of the most memorable documentaries in European cinema. Combining reconstruction and documentary footage, it denounces the intolerable living conditions of the miners in the coal-mining area of French-speaking Belgium between Mons and the Franco-Belgian border, known as the Borinage. The film, although dealing with a Belgian issue, was also an indictment of the capitalist system for its waste of human resources and angered both Dutch and Belgian authorities with its outspoken political criticism. In Belgium its projection was prohibited for a long time but, unlike Joris Ivens, Storck was not compelled to leave his country. He settled in Brussels in 1934 and went on to make a considerable number of films about Belgium, Flemish art, Paul Delvaux and Peter Paul Rubens, as well as a remarkable series of anthropological films about Belgian rural life, *Symphonie Paysanne* (1942–44).

Raising the question of identity in the case of Henri Storck leads to important insights. Storck is emphatically Flemish, but though he has a deep interest in Flemish history, art and folklore, his social aware-ness and artistic independence transcend class and ethnic boundaries. It may well be that the period in which Storck worked still permitted a kind of hybrid identity where, being Belgian, one could stay away from extreme nationalism and where it was possible to feel both strong affinity with one's place of birth and a sense of belonging with the other linguistic community. In his film *Misère au Borinage*, Storck identifies with the Francophone Belgians. As a founding member of the *Centre de l'Audiovisuel à Bruxelles*, a centre created in 1978 with French support, he is at once a Flemish, a Francophone and above all a European film-maker.

André Delvaux

André Delvaux, son of the painter Paul Delvaux, was born in Leuven in 1926. Although much younger than Dekeukeleire and Storck, he belongs to the same cultural and cinematic tradition. All three Flemish film-makers were unique in creating a dual Flemish/Francophone identity.

Delvaux's films, however, seem to be in a category of their own. Although difficult to place in a specific film movement or genre, the one label no one would dispute is Belgian. His inspiration is rooted in the cultural and linguistic heritage of both Flemish/Dutch and Walloon/French communities. Visually, his films are reminiscent of paintings by artists such as René Magritte, his father Paul Delvaux, Bosch and Bruegel. He derived his literary inspiration from both Flemish and Francophone literature. His first films were based on novels by Flemish author, Johan Daisne, later films on those of Francophone Belgian writers such as Suzanne Lilar and Marguerite Yourcenar. Aware that Belgian cinema lacked experience, Delvaux made the strategic decision of selecting well-established French actors and technicians, who then collaborated with young Belgian artists and emerging technicians. Yves Montand, Anouk Aimée, Anna Karina, Bulle Ogier, Jean-Luc Bideau and Marie-Christine Barrault all appeared in Delvaux's films. In this way, he guaranteed high professional standards while promoting Belgian cinema.

Despite Delvaux's Flemish family background, his early schooling was in French. He inherited his love and talent for music from his family, which included several professional musicians. Meeting Jacques Ledoux, director of the *Cinémathèque Royale de la Belgique*, was to have a major influence upon him. Ledoux's invitation to Delvaux to accompany silent films on the piano was his initiation to the world of cinema.

His first long feature film attracted the label 'magic realism', a label with which Delvaux's name was to remain associated. Originating in Germany in the 1920s, magic realism combined Expressionism and New Objectivity (*Neue Sachlichkeit*). Although the term refers to the literature and art of the fantastic, it is actually founded on the notion that images *appear* to be the reproduction of the real. Real and imaginary are perceived as part of the same Janus reality, rather than being antithetical. In the late 1940s and 1950s Flemish novelist Johan Daisne became one of its major representatives.

Magic realism is relevant when dealing with the notion of identity, for it is precisely the idea that one's own identity can be the object of knowledge which is being challenged. The core question in the work of both Daisne and Delvaux concerns perceptual knowledge: how do we know that what we perceive is actually there? And how do we know that what we remember is real? And, if we cannot be sure about the world we perceive, how then can we know ourselves? Delvaux's grappling with these questions through the medium of cinema has led to a highly original film language and style, in which images are often literally and symbolically shrouded in mist. In several instances a character is seen asleep or dozing off in a train; when he awakens, reality seems illusory and neither character nor viewer is able to disentangle the fragile border-line between reality and dream.

Delvaux's first two long feature films *L'Homme au crâne rasé* (1966) and *Un Soir un train* (1968) are both based on novels by Johan Daisne: the first one, *De Man die zijn haar kort liet knippen* (*The Man Who Had His Hair Cut Short*), a classic in Flemish literature, written in 1946, which remains one of the finest examples of magic realism. Uncertainty about our relationship with the outside world lurks at the heart of both Daisne's and Delvaux's fictional worlds. When the main protagonists awaken from their sleep, their disorientation is shared by the viewer. Events seem to appear with clarity on the screen, and yet doubt pre-vails. Is what we perceive really there? The characters in both films are portrayed mainly in their relationship with their object of desire. They are, as it were, enthralled by a vision and yet remain uncertain of what they see to the point of casting doubt on its very existence. The memory becomes blurred and the knowledge of events precarious. Daisne's novel is about interiority, about the secret space of a man's thought and emotions, about the experience of the imaginary. But how can this first person narrative and the character's interiority be rendered in a visual language? How can the interior monologue and the character's own uncertainty about his perceptions and experiences be expressed?

L'Homme au crâne rasé (1966)

L'Homme au crâne rasé (*The Man Who Had His Hair Cut Short*) opens with a sequence in which the main protagonist, Govert Miereveld, a solicitor in a small Flemish town, lies stretched out on a couch. There are domestic sounds in the background, a child brings a cup of coffee, and the viewer can hear Govert's interior monologue, rendered through voice-over, stating: 'One day, I shall convey what you mean to me.' The 'you' he addresses is a student, Fran, with whom he is secretly in love. This opening is followed by a sequence at the barber's shop, the camera showing a close-up of the back of Govert's head as he is telling the barber that he likes his hair cut short. The viewer then follows Govert to the graduation ceremony, where he observes Fran from a distance. Without ever uttering the words, he addresses her in the second person singular: 'Fran . . . look at me', experiencing a near-mystical bond with someone who has no knowledge of it.

Fran and Govert do not meet face to face until ten years later. Govert witnesses an autopsy in a small cemetery near the river. By chance he meets Fran, now a successful actress, who is staying in the same hotel. She and Govert express their love for each other. She also confesses her deep sense of failure and begs him to kill her. A shot is heard. Govert, accused by the court of intention to murder, is considered unaccountable for his actions and sent to a mental asylum. It transpires later that Fran was not fatally wounded and that she recovered.

But might these be the facts or is this a narrative told by 'the man who had his hair cut short' and was judged unaccountable? How can the viewer be certain of what he/she has learned? The trivial everyday events, such as the haircut which gives the film its title, the cup of coffee brought in by one of the children and, later, Govert buying new shoes and throwing the old ones away, seem to be the only facts that the viewer can know with some certainty. But these trivial moments seem mere punctuation marks highlighting the impenetrability of the character. Who is this man who asks for his hair to be cut short and is so determined to express the meaning of a relationship? The viewer is drawn into the man's quest for meaning, but the only certainty the viewer gains is that the subject sees but does not know the other. It is this gaze which Delvaux renders, but which remains uncertain for the viewer, kept at a distance.

An example of this is provided by the autopsy, which is juxtaposed with the encounter between Fran and Govert. The autopsy is carried out off screen, while Govert's horrified face remains on screen accompanied by the sounds of the instruments. In the hotel room sequences that follow, the 'lovers', almost motionless, express their feelings in a factual manner. Each is shown separately, there is no touching, no embrace; the only 'touching' will be that of Govert's bullet, but even that does not touch Fran fatally. To juxtapose the horror of an autopsy with the beauty of a young actress lends a dramatic tone to the film – or is it a reflection of Govert's disturbed mind? The discussion about Fran's sense of failure and her sense of the ephemeral quality of beauty, and finally, the sound of a shot, leave the viewer disoriented. There is an *effet de réel*: the viewer has observed the facts, has heard the conversation and has the impression that it is all real, but this 'reality' is not parallelled on the sound track: Frédéric Devreese's carefully composed music for flute, harp, piano and harpsichord – alternating between melodious moments and dramatic crescendo – makes an impression upon the viewer, but is not part of the narrative.

The interplay between dream and reality, the power of the imagined and the science of autopsy, beauty and decay, leaves the viewer at a loss. Govert's inner life slowly unfolds, drawing the viewer in an almost imperceptible way from normality into another reality, that of the imaginary.

Un Soir un train (1968)

Un Soir un train (*One Night a Train*), based on Johan Daisne's novel, *De Trein der traagheid* (*The Train of Slowness*), again confronts the viewer with reality and illusion and with Delvaux's belief that it is impossible to know the other or oneself. Anne, a French theatre designer, lives in Leuven with her lover, Mathias, a university lecturer in literature and linguistics. When Mathias is invited to give a guest lecture in another town, Anne decides to accompany him, but their relationship is fragile and communication difficult. Mathias dozes off during the train journey and relives various fragments of his life with Anne in a dream. However, when he wakes up Anne has disappeared and the train inexplicably stops in the middle of the countryside. Mathias and two travelling companions wander through the desolate landscape until they reach an inn, full of silent customers, where a mysterious woman, Moïra, is dancing. Eventually, the whistle of a train is heard. As Mathias steps outside, he sees the derailed train; in the wreckage he finds Anne's dead body. Again, the viewer, like Mathias, is caught in a web where illusion and reality are indistinguishable. Is this dream or reality? Is Mathias's dozing off into sleep, followed by the piercing noise of the accident, a sinking into the world of the unconscious?

These two films, based on Daisne's work, established Delvaux as an original film-maker. *L'Homme au crâne rasé* was shown at many film festivals and obtained several awards, including the best film of the year award by the British Film Institute. The film placed Belgian cinema on the map. There was, in general, total ignorance as to what might be specifically Belgian culture; but Delvaux succeeded in realising a Belgian cinema in which the two cultures coalesced to form a single Belgian identity.

This does not mean that Delvaux remained ignorant of the conflicts dividing Belgium. His *Un Soir un train* takes the politico-linguistic conflict in the country as its starting point. The main protagonist, Mathias Vreeman, expresses sympathy for the demands of his Flemish students and agrees to cancel his course at the university. Mathias is of Flemish descent, but has been brought up speaking French; his partner Anne is French but is living in Flemish-speaking Leuven, where she relates only to French-speaking people. When the film opens and Mathias has agreed to stop his class, Anne is involved in the creation of the sets for *Elckerlyc*, a Flemish play about death. Geographically and symbolically the characters are located at the boundary between two cultures and between dream and reality.

Delvaux's later films remain at the same threshold of doubt and uncertainty, real and imaginary, blending everyday concrete facts or events with fantasy and dream while evoking political realities in the background, as in *Rendez-vous à Bray* (1971) and *Belle* (1973).

Rendez-vous à Bray (1971)

In *Rendez-vous à Bray* (*Appointment in Bray*), Jacques, a musician in the Air Force, has invited his friend Julien, a young Luxembourg pianist, to meet him in the old family property during his leave from the Army. Julien goes to the rendezvous, where he meets an unknown, silent woman, played by Anna Karina. A long wait ensues and Jacques does not arrive. As he waits, Julien remembers his friendship with Jacques and his partner, Odile (Bulle Ogier). Night comes and the unknown woman and Julien make love. The following day, Jacques is still not there. Julien goes to the station to return to Paris. When his train arrives, he lets it go without him, leaving the viewer in the dark as to where he will go.

The film, a free adaptation of *Le Roi Cophetua*, a short story by French author Julien Gracq, was the first foreign film to win the prestigious *Prix Delluc* in 1972. It juxtaposes people with different cultures, who speak a different language. Music was the language which united the two friends: in the missed rendezvous, the 'other' is either silent (the woman) or absent (Julien). The identity of the woman in the house remains unknown and the failed meeting is only partly explained by a newspaper report that bad weather had grounded the planes. Against the background of war, Julien relives the past. The action lies in the minute observation of the wait, the recording of the woman's gestures and movements and the tinkle of the crystal ornaments that softly echo the canons in the distance.

Belle (1973)

In *Belle*, a similarly mysterious atmosphere prevails. The action is located in the Belgian Fagnes, a beautiful but frequently mist-covered marshy area in Wallonia. Mathieu Grégoire, a Francophone author (played by Jean-Luc Bideau), meets and falls in love with an enigmatic woman, whose language he does not understand and whom he calls 'Belle'. The passion he experiences for Belle is such that it disrupts his family and professional life. He arrives late at a public lecture on the sixteenth-century French poet, Louise Labbé, his shoes covered in mud, and is unable to focus or answer questions properly.

The beginning of this film once again creates a situation that instils doubt in the mind of the viewer. One dark evening, Mathieu is seen driving home in his white car, which suddenly spins around, leaving him dazed. Is the spinning movement a skidding into the imaginary, like Govert's sleep in *L'Homme au crâne rasé*, Mathias's dozing off in *Un Soir un train* or Julien's reminiscing while waiting for his friend? Is it also a tangible signal that the imaginary or the past is erupting into a present which, therefore, fails to appear as real, or, rather, only appears to be real?

There is more than an aesthetic value to this kind of cinematic magic realism, where images assume a dream-like quality. It also has implications as to the identity of the subject. Knowledge seems suspect: the protagonist is not a hero but someone who is uncertain of himself and is never free of that uncertainty. The 'I' doubts the existence of the other and hence his own existence. We have moved a long way from a Belgian identity, since, as Adolphe Nysenholc observes: 'The subject, once a self-assured hero, has been undermined by the philosophies of suspicion (Marx, Nietzsche, Freud). . . . "I" no longer knows if he exists, if he is himself' (Nysenholc 1985: 28, trans.).

The preoccupation with the search for identity takes on a different dimension, however, in Delvaux's films about two completely disparate artists, the Flemish painter, Dieric Bouts and the American film-maker Woody Allen. 'Who are you?' becomes the central question in *Avec Dieric Bouts* (1975) and *To Woody Allen, from Europe with Love* (1980). Although these two films may seem to have little in common, both question the task and position of the artist, the first in relation to a fifteenth-century painter, the second to an American director, the first distant in time, the second distant in space. Delvaux wants to discover the identities of these artists. Who was Dieric Bouts? Who is Woody Allen? Whom do they address? How do they communicate with the viewer? And finally, perhaps most importantly, how can the language of film convey the identity of a person?

Avec Dieric Bouts (1975)

In *Avec Dieric Bouts* (*Met Dieric Bouts*) Delvaux uses the medium of cinema to attempt an artistic understanding of the fifteenth-century painter through a single work, *The Last Supper*. Delvaux recreates Bouts's painting cinematographically. The aim is to achieve the same effect as Bouts did, with the actors in exactly the same positions as the figures in the painting, seen from the same height and angle. This re-enactment reveals how the painter, like the film-maker, had to negotiate space, stage a particular angle and give specific expressions or attitudes to the people in the painting. Delvaux thus experiences at first hand how the painter had to juggle space and positions within the constraints of perspective and, more importantly, religious ideology. By cinematically restaging the problems of production encountered by the painter, Delvaux enters into communion with Bouts and, like Bouts, places himself in the frame of the film, mirroring the painter's presence in the painting.

1 André Delvaux, *Avec Dieric Bouts*. The Last Supper.

To Woody Allen, from Europe with Love (1980)

The same procedure underlies the film about Woody Allen, made five years later, *To Woody Allen, from Europe with Love*. Again, Delvaux chooses a particular work, this time Allen's *Stardust Memories*, but unlike his engagement with Bouts, he now witnesses not just the end-product but the filming itself: he films the filming. Delvaux shows Allen giving instructions to the cameraman, actors and crew while a double temporarily takes his part. In the viewing room, Allen answers Delvaux's questions and explains the various problems he has encountered. Sequences from the film alternate with the viewing of the rushes. A close-up of a hand on a reel provides a sudden transition to another viewing room, this time that of Delvaux. As the sequences of Woody Allen watching the rushes unfold in front of Delvaux, it becomes clear that here too, as in the film on Dieric Bouts, Delvaux is returning to the artist's moment of enunciation, mirroring in his own cinematographic discourse those of Bouts and Woody Allen.

As has been seen from the films discussed so far, identification and identity are at the heart of Delvaux's films. Initially, he attempted to penetrate the uncertainty which haunts the human subject and to reflect the precariousness of any knowledge. Then he attempted a close

identification with two artists, a fifteenth-century painter and a contemporary film-maker, both removed from him in either time or space.

Femme entre chien et loup (1978)

More than any of Delvaux's other films *Een vrouw tussen hond en wolf/
Femme entre chien et loup*, translated in English as *Woman in a Twilight
Garden*, deals with the problems of Belgian identity. The initial idea was
Delvaux's, but the film is the fruit of his collaboration with his Flemish
contemporary, scriptwriter Ivo Michiels. The two men worked together
from the start. Both were aged about fifty and wanted to create a portrait
of Belgium from 1939 to the 1950s. The film resonates with their personal experiences.

Michiels, an established writer, reports how he had to work differently
on this film, in a non-continuous fashion. He had to anticipate Delvaux's
cinematic language and proceed in a more disjointed way, perhaps more
similar to the way that memory operates. The film captures a particularly
painful period in Belgian history, World War II and its aftermath, when
the conflict between Flemings and Walloons had become intense. It was
originally a Flemish film, but a French version, prepared with great care
by Claude Plougaro, was released soon afterwards.

The story is of a French-speaking Flemish girl, Lieve, played by French
actress Marie-Christine Barrault, who is about to marry an idealistic
Flemish nationalist, Adriaan, played by Dutch actor, Rutger Hauer. The
choice of actors emphasises the Latin/Germanic opposition which characterises and divides Belgium. As Belgium has declared itself to be neutral
in the war, this divide should be of little consequence. However, when
the Germans invade the country and Adriaan is sent to France to fight
the Germans, he comes to realise that his sympathies in fact lie with
Germany, from where he also expects support for the Flemish cause.

Lieve, now married to a collaborator, leads a secluded life until a
Walloon resistance fighter, François, fleeing a Nazi raid, forces her to
shelter him in her house. Her initial impulse to get rid of him gives way
to feelings of warmth and eventually the two become lovers. Lieve, who
is initially uninvolved politically, thus comes to represent the Belgian
situation: a French-speaking woman, bearing a typically Flemish name but
without speaking the language, has become the wife of a Flemish nationalist collaborator and the lover of a French-speaking resistance fighter.

As the war ends, Adriaan returns, disillusioned and unable to come to
terms with the accusations against him, while François regrets that he
failed to flee with Lieve. But she, the woman in the 'twilight garden', the
woman 'entre chien et loup', has slowly developed a consciousness of
her own identity. Having witnessed the blind fanatical commitment of
Adriaan to the Germanic race, the hypocrisy of the Catholic church and
other supposedly charitable people, the reprisals after the war, and the

corruption of those in power, she seems to awaken to a reality whose existence she had not previously suspected. As Adriaan tries almost tragically to justify his idealism and forces Lieve to listen to his laboriously written defence, she finally emerges from her apolitical, accommodating position and interrupts her husband's tirade asking angrily, 'Did you know about the Jews? Did you know about the Jews and all of that?' She then smashes the Catholic ornaments with which her husband has surrounded himself and has to restrain herself from hitting him.

Until then, Lieve seems to have had little interest in, or knowledge of, war politics. She has nevertheless painfully witnessed local post-war horror and terror, such as that of the pro-Nazi butcher who feared imminent retaliation from resistance fighters, his subsequent suicide after killing his two little daughters, the humiliation of the young women who had German lovers, and the general end-of-war mass thirst for revenge. Having sheltered a resistance fighter spares her from punishment for her husband's collaboration. The question about the Jews, addressed to her husband, becomes a kind of liberation for her and finally allows her to take an ethical position: she will leave her confined space and start a new life away from both her resistance lover and her Nazi husband in an unknown post-war space.

Shortly after the confrontation with her husband, Lieve is seen leaving the house with her son, carrying a small suitcase, then looking briefly back and dropping the key in the letterbox. She and her son walk away and mingle with the anonymous crowd in the street. The film closes by freezing on the image of the street, with lively music on the soundtrack, while on screen a text appears saying 'Fifteen years in the life of Lieve.'

While events unfold chronologically on screen, colour, music and objects, especially the frequent shots of the garden taken from different angles, convey almost as much as the events themselves. Images, sounds and seemingly anodyne facts evoke tone and mood which reflect Belgium's complex political situation in 1939.

Benvenuta (1983)

The north/south or Germanic/Latin divide, which so dramatically tore the country apart after the German invasion, underlies Belgian identity and continues to split the nation. A similar divide is detected on a wider level in Delvaux's subsequent films. In *Benvenuta*, based on the novel *La Confession anonyme* by Belgian Francophone author Suzanne Lilar, this divide is staged in the love relationship between Benvenuta, a Belgian pianist from Gent, played by French actress Fanny Ardant, and her lover Livio, a Neapolitan lawyer, played by Vittorio Gassman. This north/south love affair is portrayed as a fictional story written by Belgian author, Jeanne, which a film director, François, wishes to adapt. Jeanne's narration extends over several visits by François, and as the love between the novel's two protagonists, Benvenuta and Livio, unfolds, that of Jeanne and François emerges. When Jeanne reaches the point of recounting the end of the lovers' physical relationship and Livio's death, François learns that Jeanne herself has died in an accident. As fiction and reality meet, there is a disturbing twist: the film director is left with Benvenuta, not knowing whether this character is purely fictional or an autobiographical creation of Jeanne's, casting doubt on the identity of both.

Babel Opéra, ou la répétition de Don Juan de Wolfgang Amadeus Mozart (1985)

The European cities in which Benvenuta and Livio are placed reveal Delvaux's preoccupation with space. His subsequent film, *Babel Opéra, ou la répétition de Don Juan de Wolfgang Amadeus Mozart*, has a symphony-like construction in which all the themes dear to Delvaux are choreographed: solitude, the vanity of the author, the precarious situation of the couple, the anxiety of loss and the meanderings of artistic creation. The film attempts to find its own identity, that of cinematic language, without betraying the specificity of Mozart's music. For Delvaux, images and music precede the meaning of things, while words impose meaning and hence give the illusion of certainty. Fleeting images in a film leave the viewer fraught with enduring doubt.

The film was shot during the rehearsals of Mozart's *Don Giovanni* at the Belgian National Opera, the *Théatre Royal de la Monnaie*. It is, writes Delvaux, a *rêverie* set around Mozart's musical comedy. The singers, musicians, conductor and stage director interact while around them imaginary characters gravitate, who mirror the operatic situation: they meet, fall in love, separate and meet again at the opening night. Several languages are spoken, as in Babel and in Belgium itself. Fantasy and reality intertwine, geographically distant places such as the River Schelde and the Fagnes, which recall other Delvaux films, are juxtaposed and inserted in the operatic space, hence creating a tower of Babel on many levels.

L'Oeuvre au noir/The Abyss (1988)

It is no surprise that this director, initially so preoccupied with the identity of a people, wished to adapt a novel by Belgian novelist, Marguerite Yourcenar. Her literary oeuvre is a quest for people from her past, as in *Mémoires d'Hadrien*, and forms a collage of historical documents, complemented by fictions she developed out of fragments of reality found in archives. Delvaux undertook the difficult task of bringing Yourcenar's *L'Oeuvre au noir*, which won the *Prix Fémina* in 1968, to the screen. In this book Yourcenar creates the fictional character of Zenon, a sixteenth-century alchemist and philosopher, born illegitimately in Bruges, who travels across Europe observing the often tragic and cruel events of his time.

With regard to identity, a threefold development may be detected in Delvaux's oeuvre. In his early films his characters are haunted by a profound disquiet and the self's uncertainty concerning the very existence of the other; he then goes on to explore the identities of artists, Dieric Bouts and Woody Allen, in the light of the distinctive features of their chosen artistic medium. Finally, he extends the notion of identity, initially located geographically in Flanders and Belgium, to include the larger territory of Europe with the character of Zenon in *L'Oeuvre au noir*. The depiction of this illegitimate character travelling across the continent anticipates the construction of present-day Europe and a European identity. Delvaux, who used the metaphor of Babel to express the plurality of cultures rather than the divisions between them, has created an oeuvre which emphasises the importance of the struggle for cultural specificity in the face of a threatening 'globalising culture' (Sojcher 1999 II: 357).

Jean-Jacques Andrien

Jean-Jacques Andrien, who has been called the 'spiritual son of André Delvaux' (Sojcher 1999 II: 180), can be referred to as an *auteur* film-maker because of his discernibly personal style.

Le Fils d'Amr est mort! (1975)

Le Fils d'Amr est mort! (*Amr's Son is Dead!*) was awarded the first prize of the 1975 International Film Festival in Locarno. In this film Andrien starts with a search for a particular person's identity in the literal sense, then extends it to the identity of Belgium. The film relates the story of Pierre, a Belgian, who with a Tunisian accomplice engages in petty theft in trams and theatres. When Pierre finds his friend dead one day, he realises that he knows nothing about the man. The identity papers he finds on the body prompt him to go to Tunisia, to find the birthplace of his accomplice, Salh Ben Ahmed Erbayi, and discover something about his past.

But the search for Salh Ben Ahmed Erbayi's personal history leads to an exploration of his own background and country. Andrien, Sojcher argues, puts forward a metaphor of identification which refers to the Belgian community (Sojcher 1999 II: 181). Not only does the relationship between the two men represent the dual Belgian identity, but the many conflicts in Tunisia which Pierre discovers parallel many of the Belgian problems. In his accomplice's village the split between the pro-French policy and the more radical pro-Nasser politics is still tangible. These conflicts dividing the former French colonies also reflect the divisions that torment Belgian society.

Le Grand paysage d'Alexis Droeven (1981)

Andrien's 1981 film, *Le Grand paysage d'Alexis Droeven*, addresses two problems: the first is that of Belgium's Fourons region, site of a bitter conflict between Flemish and Walloon inhabitants, and the second that of the dramatic changes that have affected the agricultural world. When Alexis Droeven dies, neither his younger sister, who lives outside the Fourons in the city of Liège, nor his son, who has also left the region, wish to take over the farm. The very name of the main character, 'Alexis', which sounds French, and 'Droeven' which is Flemish, encapsulates the French/Flemish struggle. In the Fourons this conflict was particularly serious. The government was in the process of drawing up a map of Belgium, dividing the country into different geographical regions based on language. The six villages of the Fourons, with a total population of some 4000 people, were included in the Flemish part of Belgium. The language spoken was a Germanic dialect and thus closer to Dutch/ Flemish than to French, but it appeared that the many inhabitants favoured being part of Wallonia.

The film does not address this question politically, but questions the disempowering of people, not only when it comes to changing the juris- diction in which they live but also, as is the case for Alexis Droeven, when it concerns agricultural policies. Decisions made centrally, by the Belgian government for the Fourons or by the then European Common Market for the farmers, affect the lives of individual people. 'Andrien', Sojcher argues, 'subtly leads us into the problematics of identity, in an interplay of mirrors between past and present in which the memory of the father becomes an existential quest' (Sojcher 1999 II: 185, trans.).

Chantal Akerman

In Delvaux's film *Femme entre chien et loup*, the main character, Lieve, asks her husband, a German collaborator, whether he knew 'about the Jews and all of that'. Chantal Akerman's films begin where Delvaux's film closes: her characters are descendants of the Jews Lieve asks about. Delvaux drew his inspiration from Belgian society, politics, art and culture but, being born six years after the war, Akerman draws hers from the fragmentation of post World War II Europe, her Jewish heritage and her womanhood. Her films seem dictated by unconscious memories: her own, her family's and those of the Jewish diaspora. They raise an awareness of a different kind of identity, one which transcends that of nation or culture, which is paradoxically located on the border of homeland and exile, of here and elsewhere. Akerman's characters, driven by the loss of – or the quest for – an origin, are in search of an elsewhere or a home or both. If Jewishness is one marker in Akerman's films, gender is another: the intersection of the two underlies Akerman's cinema.

Akerman was not yet eighteen years old when she saw Godard's *Pierrot le Fou*. It was to be a decisive moment. Though not previously a cinephile, she suddenly decided to become a film-maker rather than a writer. At eighteen she made her first short black-and-white film, *Saute ma ville* (*Blow Up My Town*). One of the first established directors to recognise the talent in this early film was André Delvaux.

Saute ma ville (1968)

A young girl, Akerman herself, returns to her flat in a high-rise building, carrying a bunch of flowers. Impatient when the lift fails to function, she runs up the stairs humming a song, the rhythm of which grows slower the higher she climbs. A crane shot captures the speed of her ascent as if it were a lift. She arrives in her orderly flat, still singing, enters the neat kitchen and prepares spaghetti, which she eats voraciously. Then, something seems to crack: order turns to chaos as the girl empties the neatly ordered cupboards, flings cutlery, a meat grinder, pots and pans on the floor, starts to polish her shoes but soon polishes her entire leg, pours a bucket of water over the floor and attempts to mop up the created mess. She pours cleaning liquid over herself, dances in front of the mirror, then sets light to a photograph on the wall above the cooker, opens the gas burner without igniting it, takes the flowers and places her head down on the burner. As she lies there, clutching the flowers, the sound of escaping gas is heard, then suddenly the image is cut; an empty screen appears as a series of explosions is heard resounding like the blowing-up of an entire city. As the explosions end, the girl's voice is heard, humming the earlier tune.

Is this madness? Is this an adolescent crisis or a feminist statement? A 'housework metaphor for May 1968', as Jacqueline Aubenas puts it: 'métaphore ménagère de mai 68?' (Aubenas 1995: 20). The viewer knows nothing about this girl, there is no context other than the anonymous space of her high-rise flat. Who is she? It all looks playful – even the carefully prepared suicide. The cat is put out, the windows are sealed with tape. No music is heard other than the singing/humming of the girl and the playful 'bang bang' shouts as she sets fire to the photograph and turns on the gas. It is all a burlesque.

But behind the burlesque mood of Akerman's first film lies a fundamental question concerning the self and its representation. In a sequence that creates a mirroring *mise en abyme*, as may be seen in the following series of self-references, Akerman plays herself as herself. Underneath a photograph of herself pinned on the front door of the flat are the words *c'est moi* (that's me). Before committing suicide, she stares at herself in the mirror, then traces on it the same words, *c'est moi*. Finally, she kills herself after setting fire to a photograph (of herself?). It is her picture that is seen and her voice that is heard.

There is a breakdown, not just of the lift, but of the relationship between the person and her surroundings, between the self and the elements, water, fire, air: she floods the flat, sets fire to the photograph and seals out all air. There is a visceral quality to film-making here and to the exploration of the subject, whereas identification with the character is systematically undermined through the gag-like presentation of a series of apparently crazy gestures, foolish actions and meaningless sounds. The self seems to be striving for recognition (staring in the mirror, changing expression, seeking to identify herself, then writing *c'est moi*) and for self-expression before staging and carrying out her own death. No witnesses, no accomplices, no message for anyone, except for the viewer whose desire to identify is mocked and left unfulfilled.

While referring to the film as a 'story' (*récit*), it is clear that for Akerman a story is, in the first instance, autobiographical; not in the sense of telling events that happened, but a story inspired by the self and by the past without narrating either. This short film may be seen as prophetic in that it heralds Akerman's entire oeuvre, in which autobiography provides the creative motor.

Hotel Monterey (1972)

While *Saute ma ville* focuses exclusively on a character, the silent film made four years later, *Hotel Monterey*, fixes entirely on space – that of a hotel – and time – that measured by the movements the camera records. The camera is thus particularly attuned to and obsessed by space, movement and duration. This is a descriptive film of pure observation in which an immobile and frontally placed camera films the hotel's entrance, the corridors, the lift, the inside of the lift or a room, emphasising lines, shapes, frames and above all emptiness. The camera, as it were, stares at the lift as it slowly ascends and descends, at the depth of the corridors, offering an exploration of depth, height, width, verticality, immobility and slow motion. The viewer waits for the lift to return and for a glimpse of a corridor or of people standing in the lift, seen through the round glass pane in the door, reminiscent of the eye of the camera.

The lift's controlled, monotonous and slow movement seems to add to the spatial immobility in which the only real movement is that of the hotel's clients who come, go, wait, stand in the lift or are seated on chairs. None of them ever becomes an individual with whom the viewer can identify. They remain anonymous, passers-by. This is the common space people share, the place where identity is lost, rendered anonymous. These are empty shots, with characters who are not in a story, who do not relate to each other, who stare the viewer in the face without ever communicating. These are people who all have a story, who all have an identity, but who remain unidentified.

La Chambre (1972)

Made in the same year as *Hotel Monterey*, *La Chambre* (*The Room*) also explores filmic space, but this time the space is the room of an individual, that of the character film-maker, who is spatially and narratively central in the film. Through three circular panning shots, the camera renders what the centrally placed person perceives. Again, there is no story and no real action, just a figure lying in bed. Editing seems forbidden as the camera circles three times around the room without pausing at any particular object. It then makes swinging movements, limiting the field of vision and space.

These early films by Akerman set the style and mood for her exploration of identity. Identity is linked to space in its literal sense, the space immediately contiguous to the character, the objects, the walls, the doors, the lift, the room, the corridor as well as the attributes of space, verticality, horizontality, width, height, volume. The absence of editing emphasises the relationship between the subject and its spatial context. The film addresses the question of space in a twofold way: as a privileged context for the character and, experimentally, as cinema's primary essence.

Three further films conclude Akerman's initial experimental period. The first one *5/8*, referring to the date of the filming in 1973, captures the puerile and incoherent discourse of a young girl, heard in voice-over, while the camera follows all her movements. There is no story; the girl carries out trivial activities such as eating, staring out of the window, or organising her handbag. The film is at once documentary and experimental, a minute registering of ordinary movements and activities. The second one, *Hanging out in Yonkers* (1973) remained unfinished; it was shot at the request of a welfare organisation and follows the activities of young delinquents on a rehabilitation programme. Akerman listened, watched and recorded hours and hours of interviews. It reveals her as a meticulous observer of people.

Je, tu, il, elle (1974)

The last one of the three is *Je, tu, il, elle* (*I, You, He, She*). This film reveals her interest in the exploration of her own self at age twenty-four. Akerman enacts Akerman, intertwining reality and fiction. The film emphasises time, voice, space and emptiness, the temporal emptiness of waiting. 'Je' is the main character of the story (Julie/Chantal Akerman), who voluntarily isolates herself in her room and undertakes a kind of initiation journey: 'Je' rids the room of all its furniture and her body of its clothes, stripping herself bare as if to experience the limits of the self. The second person 'Tu' is the unknown addressee of the letters she writes, the third person 'Il' is a lorry driver who talks about desire and loss of desire. Finally, 'Elle' is Julie's friend, to whom she returns and upon whom she calls for her primary needs (*j'ai faim* – I'm hungry), but whom she leaves quietly in the early morning.

Jeanne Dielman, 23 Quai du Commerce, 1080 Bruxelles (1975)
In 1975 Akerman entered the world of cinema in a memorable way: she brought out a 200-minute film, *Jeanne Dielman, 23 Quai du Commerce, 1080 Bruxelles*, which was to shock the film world. In *Le Monde* Louis Marcorelles referred to the film as 'Undoubtedly the first masterpiece in the feminine in the history of cinema' (Marcorelles *Le Monde* 22 January 1976, trans.). The film captures the daily tasks of a Brussels housewife, Jeanne Dielman, over a three-day period. She is played by Delphine Seyrig, an icon of European art cinema.

It takes a bold film-maker to show a housewife peeling potatoes or preparing Wiener schnitzels in real time. One example will suffice to illustrate this. On the morning of the second day, the alarm clock rings, Jeanne puts on her dressing-gown, goes to the bathroom, then to the living room, also used as the son's bedroom, lights the gas heater, gets the son's clothes ready, goes to the kitchen, puts on the kettle, takes some shoes and carefully smears polish on them with one cloth, then, with another cloth, shines them. She then puts coffee in the electric coffee grinder, empties the coffee in a paper filter, pours water on the coffee, stands and waits – as does the viewer – for the coffee to drip into the pot. She finally sits down and drinks the coffee, returns to the living room to wake her son, then serves him breakfast. The entire sequence is filmed without music, only the sounds made by Jeanne, that of the coffee grinder or the kettle.

Who is Jeanne Dielman? The name combines Flemish (Dielman) and Francophone (Jeanne) elements, as well as female (Jeanne) and male (Diel*man*). She is a widow living with her adolescent son, whose comings and goings from and to school punctuate Jeanne's life. During his absence she undertakes some child-minding for a neighbour and also receives one customer a day, who pays her for sexual favours. Jeanne displays no emotion, carrying out her actions and movements in clinical and hygienic fashion. The viewer is left with questions but no answers regarding Jeanne's nature or identity, which seems to be defined by her punctual routine and the regularity of her actions.

All might have continued in this fashion if the alarm clock had not, one day, rung one hour too early. This disruption of the daily routine is most unsettling since none of the daily actions can be performed on time. While the day began too early, the arrival of an unexpected parcel causes further disruption in Jeanne's normally perfect timing. When her customer rings the doorbell, Jeanne has not yet put away the wrapping of the lingerie sent by her sister in Canada or the scissors used to open the parcel. She feels obliged to hastily hide the items. Unlike on the first

2 Chantal Akerman, *Jeanne Dielman, 23 Quai du Commerce 1080 Bruxelles.* Jeanne and her son having dinner (waiting for the main course to be ready).

and second day, the camera this time penetrates the immaculate bedroom and stays to capture Jeanne and her customer on the bed. The scene that is revealed is far removed from the conventional brothel scene. This is an orderly event, taking place on the towel on the tidy bed in a bourgeois bedroom, where both Jeanne and her customer experience pleasure. But Jeanne does not linger: as she stands near the dressing table she looks at the man still stretched out on the bed, face down. Suddenly, she takes the scissors, used for opening the parcel, and plunges them into his body.

Critics have speculated about this extraordinary action after which, with Jeanne seated calmly in the tidy living room, the film closes. Why this sudden impulsive act? Did the disruption of time throw her into a temporal void? Did the scissors being out of their proper place provoke this? Or had some deeper awareness been triggered by her son's earlier questions about her sexual relationship with her deceased husband, dismissed by Jeanne's comment 'one does not talk about such things', or by the letter, received from her sister urging her to remarry, or by the lingerie received just before the arrival of the customer? A few symptomatic incidents have indeed occurred before the fatal error in time. On the second day, Jeanne forgets to replace the lid on the soup terrine in the middle of the table (in which she puts the money received from her customers) and lets the potatoes burn. On day three, before she realises that she has started the day an hour early, she forgets to switch off the light in the bathroom, drops her hair-brush and, a little later, a knife. In a film in which nothing much happens and where the viewer has been called upon to watch that 'nothing much' – the domestic tasks of a Brussels housewife – a new way of looking develops.

The viewer has the feeling of watching a presentation of real life, not a representation of life. And this presentation has no interest other than the way it is shown and possibly a meaning which will be elucidated later in the film. This hyper-realist documentary mode of filming draws attention to the minute signs which begin to summon the viewer to speculate on the character of Jeanne and the nature of her existence, her past and her desires. In fact the excessive punctuality and regularity of Jeanne's daily existence are machine-like in their repetitive monotony, so much so that some feminists have seen the film as a manifesto exposing the alienation defining the condition of women whose identities are determined by men. The name/title reveals all too clearly a male-dominated society: Jeanne Diel*man*, reminiscent of the director's own last name Aker*man*. And, indeed, all the people Jeanne caters to are male: the son, the customers and even the baby, with the female neighbour kept outside, heard but not seen.

Jeanne speaks little and hardly looks at people. The dinners that she and her son take together are painfully silent. The baby cries when she takes him in her arms. It is as if Jeanne has eradicated any human warmth and desire. And just as Jeanne's desire is lacking, the viewer's habitual film pleasure is also lacking. Door upon door is closed, lights carefully switched off. The viewer is left with little to watch beyond the immediacy of the frame on screen. And yet, the woman's clock-like existence, her obsession with cleanliness and routine arouse the viewer's suspicion and lead to the film being seen as a symptomatic discourse of obsession.

Did the disruption in time also affect Jeanne's emotional life, apparently so perfectly under control, and leave her vulnerable to sexual pleasure? Is it possible that Jeanne suddenly recovers her emotional life, experiences pleasure and then commits an act about which the viewer can only speculate? Is the act revenge for the pleasure received, a punishment for the guilt towards the husband whose place was in the bed, not on the bed? The murder, committed with scissors, a predominantly female instrument, in the space which belonged to the husband, literally cuts off the relationship between the self and the other, between the self and the self's desire.

Jeanne Dielman was followed by a considerable number of films, two of which are particularly relevant for a reflection on identity: *Les Rendezvous d'Anna* and *D'Est*. Both films are about journeys. The first relates the journey of a film-maker, Anna, who has travelled to Germany for the premiere of her latest film; the second records a journey from Germany to Moscow, from the end of summer to the depths of winter, and captures pictures of Eastern Europe in the post World War II era.

Les Rendez-vous d'Anna (1978)

Les Rendez-vous d'Anna (The Meetings of Anna) refers to the encounters of Anna, a film-maker, who at the opening of the film arrives in Germany, then travels back by train to Paris, where she lives. The character and existence of Anna (Aurore Clément) are undoubtedly a reflection of Chantal Akerman's own persona. Like her creator, Anna is preoccupied with questions about Germany and Europe after Nazism. Through the personal confessions of the five people she meets, the viewer gains a view of post-war Europe. Geographically, narratively and emotionally central in Anna's encounters is her meeting with her mother in Brussels, on the second night of the three-day journey, preceded by one night in Germany and followed by one in Paris.

Each person carries his or her own memories and together they make up a social map of Europe. There is Heinrich, a German Anna meets at the premiere of her film, whose wife left him to go to live with a Turk, and who now lives with his child and his mother. There is Ida, a family friend from Brussels, who meets her at the station in Cologne. In a long monologue Ida tells about the past, the 'terrible things that happened', her husband whose character changed completely and who became obsessed with order, shouting angrily if something was out of place. Then in the train from Cologne to Brussels, Anna meets another German who after living in several countries has decided to go and live in France, which he calls 'the country of liberty'.

In Brussels, Anna and her mother at first fail to recognise each other, having not met for three years. Here also post-war problems are introduced: migration, the economic crisis, and the effect these have on people's personal relationships. Anna refuses the invitation to go to her parents' house and suggests instead that they spend the night together in a hotel. The following day Anna returns to Paris, to a bare flat and an empty refrigerator. The film closes with Anna stretched out on her bed, listening to the messages on her answerphone, one of them giving her the itinerary for her next trip.

It seems that in both Jeanne Dielman and Les Rendez-vous d'Anna the main characters inhabit, albeit in very different ways, a Europe of exile: Jeanne Dielman and Anna's mother both live in Brussels, the heart of Europe; Jeanne's son and Anna's mother both speak French with an accent, the mother's a reminder of the Jewish diaspora, the son's a sign of the divisions in Belgium. Also, both Jeanne and Anna's mother have financial difficulties. Jeanne's flat is too small for her and her son and her modest income forces her into prostitution. Anna's mother reluctantly admits business is very bad and security poor. Moreover, the stories collected by Anna somehow uncover those hidden by Jeanne: Ida's husband, who has become unreasonable and obsessive because of 'all these terrible things', evokes the viewer's suspicion about Jeanne's obsessive housekeeping. The viewer has no knowledge about Jeanne's past other than that her husband is dead and her sister is in Canada. The fact is that Jeanne's impeccable and meticulous housekeeping veils a dysfunctional and lonely person, unable to communicate. And while Jeanne is constantly seen preparing food, Anna does not consume any. Only once does she touch a morsel of left-over food on a tray outside a hotel room. Her breakfast, brought to her room, remains untouched. Also, when she is with Ida in Cologne, she states that she is hungry and yet does not feel like eating when she enters the restaurant. Akerman's films constitute a dietary continuum, from the bulimic girl in *Saute ma ville* to Jeanne, whose main task is to prepare food for the son who hardly appreciates it, and to Anna, who is never seen eating and returns to the security of an empty fridge.

All the films, except for *Hotel Monterey*, have focused on a single major female protagonist whose psychology is not explored and who is difficult to know. The characters display symptoms which the viewer can comprehend only in terms of the traces of memories left by 'these terrible things' which continue to haunt Europe. Akerman's camera most frequently captures images patiently and frontally. *Les Rendez-vous* has only 96 takes (a very low number for a film of 122 minutes). This makes the viewer aware of what cinematic experience usually involves, by opening a void in which one acutely feels the absence of action. Akerman forces the viewer to see the everyday, to watch the slightest movements of the characters and thereby to gain knowledge which differs from that acquired through conventional storytelling. And while this technique renders identification with the character impossible, the notion of identity emerges as a major theme throughout the entire oeuvre.

D'Est (1993)

The journey undertaken in *D'Est* (*From the East*) takes the viewer from former East Germany to Moscow. It is Akerman's most experimental film. More than a film, it is an event. It makes use of three different rooms: in the first, the film is shown uninterruptedly against one of the walls. The three rows of eight seats limit the number of viewers to twenty-four, a number which is equivalent to the twenty-four images projected per second on the screen. The same number is repeated in the second room, where twenty-four television monitors are placed like the chairs in the first room, three rows of eight. Instead of sitting down to watch the screen, the spectators walk between the rows of monitors and catch glimpses of the images appearing on the screens. These images, edited in sequences of four minutes, are identical to the film projected in the first room, but here they are fragmented in such a way that they visually echo from one monitor to the next. And finally, in the third room, is the '25th screen', referring to a twenty-fifth image, the one in excess of the normal twenty-four images per second. Here the spectator is seated on a cushion on the floor in front of a blurred picture, which is accompanied by a text in Hebrew read by Akerman. The text is taken from *Exodus* 20: 4 and gives the commandment not to make 'any graven image or any likeness of what is in heaven above, or that is in the earth beneath, or that is in the water under the earth'.

The images retrace the journey which began at the end of the summer in eastern Germany and terminates at the end of winter in Moscow. The film is neither a documentary (there is no commentary) nor fiction (there is no story). It shows crowds of people who either ignore the presence of the camera or do not actually see it, or are not directed to respond to the camera but left free to ignore or respond as they wish. No story is told; Akerman has filmed what attracted her eye or what happened to be in front of the camera. Nothing personal is shown of the people filmed, no anecdotal snapshots. Instead, the camera films people waiting, walking, moving. Summer alternates with winter, interiors with exteriors, faces remain anonymous. The spectators walking slowly between the monitors in the second room watch the endless walking of the people on the screen. The ongoing movement on screen erases individual identity, yet each one of the people filmed holds memories and harbours an untold story. Notions of exile, home and diaspora are evoked by the walking, which is reminiscent of the plight of the Jewish people: Chantal Akerman's grandmother never returned from the German concentration camps.

The film depicts Europe's tragic past and reveals the desolate map of people in post-war Eastern Europe. This post-war trauma underlies many of Akerman's films: the young girl wishing to blow up her town; the girl stripping her room or herself naked; Jeanne, not imprisoned in a camp but painfully incarcerated in her obsessive behaviour; Anna without demand or desire. Whereas *Hotel Monterey* showed the space and, within it, the customers of the hotel, in *D'Est* the people have themselves become filmic space, as they occupy the entire screen without, however, conveying an individual identity.

Sud (1999)

Akerman remains preoccupied with people's identities, her own Jewish one in the first instance but also those of other people, even if they are no more than passers-by, as was the case in her 1993 film *D'Est*, to which her more recent film, *Sud* (*South*), acts as a counterpoint. Whereas

D'Est dealt with a journey to Eastern Europe, in *Sud* Akerman travels to the south of the United States. She structures her film around a real event, the murder of James Byrd Jr., a black man who was lynched in Texas by three young white men. Akerman does not try to investigate the murder, but attempts to understand the nature and impact of the physical and historical environment upon the individual and upon such an event. Akerman is intrigued by the use and abuse of history: for her, murder and genocide are often perpetrated in the name of history or in the face of its absence: they are the ultimate negation of people's identities.

Boris Lehman

Boris Lehman, like Chantal Akerman with whom he collaborated, combines Belgian and Jewish identities. Three themes dominate his films: the *mise en scène* of the self, the city of Brussels, where he 'travels' and which is the location for most of his films and, lastly, the impossibility of meeting or knowing the other.

Lehman's interest in the self is evident in his early film, *Album I* (1974), made for a festival of super 8 films held in Brussels. The aim was to show the potential of the super 8 format. For a period of two months, in July and August 1974, Lehman had himself filmed by 150 people, including friends and passers-by he met in the street. This display of the self was a kind of therapy for Lehman, who states: 'My life became the screenplay for a film which itself became my life' (Sojcher 1999 II: 162, trans.).

In 1979 he brought out *Magnum Begynasium Bruxellense*, his film on Brussels' Old Béguinage district, an area where property speculation and office-building has led to the area losing its identity. The title of the film indicates its subversive nature. It is a subjective rendering of Lehman's perception of the district, showing its buildings – the Club Antonin Artaud for mentally handicapped people, the creche, the church – and people – people on the fringes of society, mentally handicapped people, people who are single, divorced or widowed, pensioners, artisans and above all old people. It is a film without a story line that aims to reveal the 'soul' of the old Béguinage district.

Lehman's main undertaking, *Babel, Lettre à mes amis restés en Belgique* (1991) is an autobiographical project that took ten years to complete. It concerns a journey from Brussels to Mexico and back and in it, rather than showing the viewer what he saw, Lehman shows himself. The film thus becomes a fictional documentary of the self, where a bizarre interplay unfolds between 'I am', 'I show myself' and 'I am seen'. The desire to be seen also explains Lehman's frequent presence at screenings of his films. This quest for his own self that dominates his films inevitably calls for a new cinematic language, in which the notion of *auteur* is taken to its very extreme: in the 'babelised' Brussels, the 'I'/eye of Lehman's camera articulates itself.

Michel Khleifi

Khleifi, who lives in Belgium, is a Palestinian from a Christian family, who grew up in Israel.

La Mémoire fertile (1980 – *The Fertile Memory*) illustrates Khleifi's concern with displacement and oppression. The film depicts the fate of Palestinian women who are doubly oppressed, first by Israel and secondly by the traditional Arab attitudes to women. By juxtaposing two women, one a fifty-year-old widow, Farah Hatoum, and a younger woman, Sarah Khalifeh, who was married at eighteen, Khleifi reveals the many dilemmas in which women are trapped. Farah, whose husband died in 1948 in Beirut, where he was in exile, faces the struggle of providing for her children's education and is haunted by the dream of recovering a plot of the land expropriated by the Israeli authorities. For Sarah, the problems are different. She is fighting for a divorce and custody of her children. Both women are confronted with the reality of the Israeli occupation, which deprives them of their territorial identity, and with the obstacles women experience in Arab society.

For Khleifi, memory is a necessary link with the past and with tradition. But the present situation of living in an adoptive country inevitably involves identity problems. Like other uprooted film-makers, the medium of film becomes an attempt to remember what and where one comes from and to integrate values from the past with the realities of the present.

Marion Hänsel

To place Marion Hänsel with film-makers who overtly address the question of identity may be questionable, as she does not explore individual identity. However, her representation of the claustrophobic dysfunctional family context in which the individual is trapped reveals important insights into the formation of identity. Her most famous film, *Dust* (1985) – which won the main award at the Venice film festival – presents a 'family' in South Africa (although filmed in Spain), consisting of Magda, her father and two black slaves, a man and a woman. The relationship between father and daughter is totally asymmetrical: Magda has a passionate and exclusive love for her father, while he seems to have no feelings for her. When she learns that her father is having an affair with the woman slave, she kills him and uses the man slave for her own first sexual experience.

Les Noces barbares (1987 – *Cruel Embrace*), based on Yanne Queffelec's novel, presents an equally tortuous family structure. Here, a woman,

Nicole, is raped and made pregnant by an American soldier. Unable to cope with the memory of the rape when the child, Ludo, is born, she locks him in the loft for years until she marries Micho, who has a child himself. For a short time Ludo lives some kind of a family life but, as he grows older, his presence becomes increasingly intolerable to Nicole. He is sent to an institution for retarded children, but runs away when told that he will be sent to a psychiatric hospital. From an abandoned boat near the sea, where he has taken refuge, he contacts Nicole. She comes to see him but, when she announces that she is divorcing Micho and remarrying someone else, Ludo kills her.

The viewer is confronted with tortuous psychological situations that seem to offer the key to an understanding of an individual's actions. The claustrophobic family of two – single parent and child – is so diseased that it destroys any transmission of values or feelings except for brute instinctual reactions.

Jaco Van Dormael

Jaco Van Dormael was no newcomer to cinema when *Toto le héros* (*Toto the Hero*) appeared. Between 1980 and 1985 he had directed seven short films, including a few documentaries. He studied film at the Brussels film institute, INSAS (*Institut National Supérieur des Arts du Spectacle et Techniques de Diffusion*), where his final project *De Boot (The Boat)*, a short film representing a Flemish musical comedy for children, earned a prize in Los Angeles for the best film made by a foreign student.

Toto le héros (1991)
Jaco Van Dormael achieved fame with this film, which tells the story of Thomas at three different stages of his life: childhood, adulthood and old age. These intertwine as the film moves from flash forward to flashback, from old age to birth, from adulthood to death and cremation, in such a way as to leave the viewer in doubt as to whether the events are real or imagined.

Thomas is convinced that, because of a fire in the maternity hospital, he has been confused with another baby at birth. In the panic of the moment the wrong mother grabbed him and he, Thomas, is in fact, someone else, Alfred, the neighbours' child. The two boys have identical birthdays but only Thomas 'knows' that Alfred has usurped his identity.

The film opens with all the signs of a murder – a broken window, a dead body in a fountain – then shows Thomas in an old people's home, getting ready for bed and stating that he wants to kill Alfred. He addresses the intended victim, saying: 'It will not even be a murder because I will only be taking what belongs to me, the life that you have stolen from me the day I was born: my life.' The film then cuts to the fire in the maternity hospital where the mistake is supposed to have occurred. The worst consequence of this theft, according to Thomas, is that his life has been empty, and the story to be told is, therefore, that of someone to whom nothing happened.

One might assume Thomas is afflicted by the psychiatric disorder of a delusion of the double – a failure to distinguish between self and other – or that this is a case of pathological jealousy, since Thomas is extremely envious of Alfred's rich parents and social success. But the film is clearly not trying to present a psychoanalytical case. Instead, the quest of the double reflects the tradition of magic realism, reinforced through the film's treatment of time and its conjuring with events and characters, located between memory, dream, fantasy and reality.

The events encompass a wide spectrum of moments in Thomas's life: early infancy (0–3 years); childhood (about 10 years old); his imagined future as a secret agent in which he will become 'Toto the hero'; adulthood (about 30 years old); the present time of the narrator (as an old man in an old people's home), and lastly, the planned murder of Alfred in the future. This linear chronology is discernible after the entire film has been seen, but throughout its length the narrative shifts back and forth over these six temporal phases.

The film creates a web of coincidences which cast doubt in the mind of the viewer, whose vigilance has been alerted from the beginning because of the murder shown and planned. The main coincidence concerns Thomas's sister Alice, loved equally by Thomas and by Alfred.

It is the murder that will ultimately resolve the question of Thomas's belief that he has been robbed of his identity. This happens when Thomas learns that there has been an assassination attempt on Alfred, linked to his firm's bankruptcy. Out of fear that some unknown murderer might rob Alfred of the life that belongs to him, Thomas decides to undertake this task himself. He steals the porter's gun, escapes from the old people's home and goes to Alfred's house. However, as Alfred opens the door, Thomas can only utter 'bang! bang!' as a child would do with a pretend gun. He leaves without committing the murder, contemplates using the gun to kill himself but throws it away instead.

Unarmed, he returns to Alfred's house, asks for a cup of coffee and locks Alfred in the kitchen. He then disguises himself as Alfred and, knowing that Alfred's life is in danger, reveals himself to the men who are waiting for an opportune moment to kill him. Thomas finally recovers his identity at the moment of his death. The murderers shoot 'Alfred'. As he falls into a fountain his head becomes enveloped in a transparent net curtain, which he drags with him creating the effect of a Magritte painting. At last the meaning of the film's opening shot becomes clear. In getting killed as Alfred, Thomas finally reclaims his identity and, for a short while, fulfils his dream of riding in a Chevrolet – even if it is to be taken to the crematorium. His laughter is heard, the laughter of victory at dying with his true identity.

However, the film closes with an ironic twist concerning identity. Alfred identifies the body as that of Thomas and the initial confusion is repeated: the ashes are labelled with Thomas's name. At the two crucial moments of Thomas's life, his birth and his death, he is identified by someone else, his mother at birth, Alfred at his death. Thomas's desperate attempt to assign his own identity fails: it appears that identity is given by others and cannot be acquired by the self.

Le Huitième Jour (1996)

One attractive feature of Thomas in Toto le héros is his bond with his brother, Célestin, who has Downs Syndrome. Van Dormael had already included characters with Downs Syndrome in two earlier films, Stade and L'Imitateur. Now in Le Huitième Jour (The Eighth Day), the Downs Syndrome character is one of the two main protagonists. The film is about Harry, a businessman, who is so involved in his work delivering motivating lectures to aspiring salesmen that he forgets about his family. His wife has left him and taken the two children with her. One weekend, when the children were supposed to be with him, he was so absorbed in his work he forgot to pick them up at the station. Now neither his wife nor his children want to see him again. Driving around aimlessly, close to despair, he nearly hits Georges, a young man with Downs Syndrome, who has run away from his institution because everyone else had gone home. At first Harry wants to get rid of Georges, but they slowly develop a bond; through Georges the ambitious businessman gains a different vision of the world, his life and family.

The film was selected for the Cannes Festival, where the two actors, Daniel Auteuil (Harry) and Pascal Duquenne (Georges) shared the award for best actor. The story line may not be of the greatest originality and the film is far less revolutionary than Toto le héros, but the slow identification that develops between two people who apparently have nothing in common constitutes an appeal to society for tolerance. 'Differences', Van Dormael says in an interview, 'frighten people and yet, they express the richness of society' (Sojcher 1999 III: 77, trans.).

Luc et Jean-Pierre Dardenne

The Dardenne brothers had been making films for more than twenty years when their film Rosetta won the coveted Palme d'Or at the 1999 Cannes Festival. It shook the film world: the film was made on a low budget and its subject and style are as far removed from Hollywood cinema as one can possibly imagine. Moreover, the leading actress, Emilie

Dequenne, who plays Rosetta, was not even a professional. The French press were full of outrage and, further insensed by the three awards made to an equally controversial film, Bruno Dumont's *L'Humanité*, they declared that Cannes 1999 had been the worst festival ever.

Luc and Jean-Pierre Dardenne began making films in the late 1970s. Jean-Pierre, born in 1951, trained as an actor; Luc, born in 1954, as a philosopher. They started with video documentaries. One early documentary, *Lorsque le Bateau de Léon M. descendit la Meuse pour la première fois* (*When Léon M.'s Boat Sails Down the Meuse for the First Time* – 1979) tells the story of Léon, an activist in the 1960 strike that shook Belgium, who now devotes his time to building a boat. But his memories of the strike have remained vivid. Instead of making a documentary of the strike, the film-makers start with Léon's memory and take an introspective approach. For them, memory is vital: it ties people to their past and to the events lived. The emphasis on memory characterises the Dardenne brothers' films from the late 1970s to the early 1990s.

Falsch (1986)

Whereas in the case of Léon M. the memory was individual and referred to a workers' strike, the Dardennes' first full-length feature film, made in 1986, concerns the collective memory of the Holocaust. The film is an adaptation of *Falsch* (German for false), by the Belgian playwright René Kalisky. The play is set in a New York bar where Joe, sole survivor of a Jewish family, meets all his close relatives who died in the Holocaust. The Dardenne brothers changed the location for this imagined encounter from New York, a place of exile, to an airport, a place where people are in transit. The choice of an airport offered several advantages: it was sufficiently confined to stage the gathering and it also offered the space necessary for shifting from theatre to cinema. The different levels and stairs inside and the runways outside are all used by the film-makers to achieve a blending of theatrical and cinematic effects, evoking multiplicity of locations and the comings and goings which vividly suggest the scattering of the Jewish people.

The only precise reference to time is that of the family's last Shabbat in Berlin, in 1938, before Joe flees to New York. It was the obstinate refusal of Jacob, Joe's father, to leave Germany which led to the extermination of so many of his family members. As they now meet again, it emerges that behind the family bond lurk old tensions, accusations, feelings of guilt and of hatred. This is not the united Jewish family one might imagine but a family which embodies the wars that have torn the Jewish people apart. While the Holocaust has created a belief in a monolithic Jewish people, the Falsch family breaks this illusion. As Jacqueline Aubenas writes: 'The family becomes a metaphor for the exterminated people and its diversity enables the playwright to explore the relationship between Jewish people and Germany and the inextricable ties of guilt that at once bind victims and persecutors together and radically separate them. But the central focus of the family itself brings a broader human resonance to this psychodrama of historical suffering, giving universal dimensions to this meditation on the Holocaust: the fratricidal struggles of Cain and Able, the necessary murder of the father and rivalry between sisters' (Aubenas 1996: 63, trans.).

Lorsque le Bateau de Léon M. and Falsch shed light on the difference between what is universal in identity and what is circumstantial. Léon's identification may be with the workers and that of the Falsch family with the Jews, but these are specific attributes of identity which can only be captured through memory, the agent for identity formation.

Both these films present fictional characters whose memories refer to real events, the holocaust and the strike. Such fictional recreations of historical realities break from, and yet at the same time continue, the tradition of the late Henri Storck, whose documentaries, rooted entirely in reality, had a lasting impact on many Belgian film-makers, especially those who, like the Dardenne brothers, share Storck's profound concern for social justice.

Je pense à vous (1992)

In Je pense à vous (I Think of You), the Dardenne brothers continued their creation of a fictional mise en scène of an existing reality. Rather than opting for a cinéma du réel (cinema of reality), they invented a fiction based on reality. The film focuses on the crisis in the steel industry that swept through Europe in the 1980s and affected Wallonia very deeply. The opening shot shows a bunch of flowers on the roof of a car; in the background is an imposing landscape of steel works. Though it is not clear if this is a funeral hearse, the image nevertheless signals the death of an industry. But an industry does not die a solitary death: a region dies with it and a society loses its identity.

With the market economy, paid work has become so much a part of human existence that it is difficult to sustain a feeling of self-worth without it. Yet, the relationships of individuals to their work vary considerably. The film depicts two of these: for Fabrice, a redundant steel worker, identification with work depends on the nature of the job, while for his wife the emphasis is on being paid enough to provide for their social and individual needs. Finding himself on the threshold of poverty is not sufficient reason for Fabrice to accept any kind of job. This raises the problem of the pressure economic hardship puts on the unemployed, especially in Fabrice's world, in a region that is characterised by an ethic and a tradition of a particular kind of livelihood. Fabrice's predicament cannot be seen as an individual case: it reveals the drama of a whole region that has always been identified with heavy industry. The loss of that industry leads to a genuine identity crisis where a social group loses its origins (Sojcher 1999 III: 92).

The Dardenne brothers acknowledge their indebtedness to the socially militant Armand Gatti and state their interest in history and philosophy; in *Falsch* they interviewed Emmanuel Levinas, for whom ethics underlies all philosophy. *Je pense à vous* conveys an ethical relation to the world expressed by the brothers' genuine concern with the contradiction that exists between the capitalist system and the threat of poverty, in this instance caused by the collapse of an industry and the closure of factories. Without being didactic or proposing particular political ideas, the films clearly display the film-makers' commitment to social change, hence their admiration for the playwright Armand Gatti, whose theatre merged with his militant social beliefs and with whom they collaborated.

While conceding the major influence of Gatti as a spiritual father, the Dardenne brothers also admit that at some point one inevitably wants to 'kill the father' and come into one's own. Their earlier Gatti influenced films are based on the premise that the magnitude and importance of memory is a vital constituent of identity. After *Je pense à vous* a break occurred: memory was abandoned. The following films, *La Promesse* (1996) and *Rosetta* (1999), use a new cinematic language to express a new paradigm, where identity emerges in the present as an ethical awakening in a face-to-face encounter.

La Promesse (1996)

La Promesse (*The Promise*) brought international fame to the Dardenne brothers. The film tells the story of a builder, Roger, who with his son Igor exploits illegal immigrant labour in the Liège region of Belgium. In the first part of the film, Roger wheels and deals and Igor adopts his father's ruthless and dishonest practices without questioning this behaviour.

One day, inspectors unexpectedly appear and Igor has to evacuate the site as quickly as possible. In the rush, Hamidou, an African immigrant worker, falls off the scaffolding. Realising he is seriously injured, he begs Igor to look after his wife and child, and Igor promises to fulfil his wish. As soon as the inspectors leave, Igor urges his father to take the dying man to hospital, but he refuses and buries the man in concrete instead.

The promise he has made to Hamidou brings about a change in Igor. Up to this point he had been continually running or speeding around on his motorbike. Now he slows down, keeps an eye on Assita, Hamidou's widow, and her baby, and helps her in indirect ways. Whereas his father is eager to keep Hamidou's death hidden from Assita and plans to deport her to Cologne, Igor prevents his father from carrying out this plan, thereby breaking away from him and putting an end to his own childhood. He now lends unfailing support to Assita, and in the process discovers different aspects of her culture.

Finally, when it has been arranged that Assita will go to her uncle in Italy, Igor's father interferes one last time and Igor succeeds in chaining him to a hoist in the garage. The immobilised father pleads with Igor, then tries to bribe him. After a moment's hesitation Igor leaves to take Assita to the station, and as they mount the steps admits for the first time that her husband is dead. Assita turns to him and their face-to-face encounter completes the change in Igor, who is clearly not returning to his former life. After this, Assita removes the headdress she has borrowed from the woman on whose passport she was planning to travel and walks back through the underpass with Igor following her. This short sequence provides the film's open-ended closure.

In *La Promesse* the characters seem to come from nowhere, to have no memories and to live strictly in the present until the moment when Igor makes his promise and finds himself propelled into an ethical system of which he previously knew nothing.

Rosetta (1999)

In *Rosetta*, the Dardenne brothers portray a struggle rather than tell a story. This is a young girl's struggle for survival, consisting of working, eating and sleeping. Rosetta lives with her alcoholic mother in a dismal trailer park. She cannot keep a steady job since she stands up to all the

3 Jean-Pierre Dardenne and Luc Dardenne, *Rosetta*. Rosetta.

bosses, who then sack her. When a young man called Riquet, who had befriended her, falls into the water, she contemplates leaving him to drown in the hope that she might get his job selling waffles. After a brief moment of hesitation, she reaches out and saves him, but this does not preclude her from betraying him later when another opportunity arises and she succeeds in having him fired and getting his job. Rosetta is driven by her instinct for survival and does not question or reflect on the morality of such behaviour.

However, faced with an increasingly difficult situation with her mother, who prostitutes herself for drink, Rosetta's struggle finally exceeds the primitive force generated by her survival instinct. The only one she can now direct her anger against is herself and her survival instinct switches into a death instinct. She phones her boss to say she is not coming to work any more, retires to the caravan and switches on the gas, but the bottle is empty. Violently angry and frustrated, she tries to lug another bottle to the caravan, when Riquet reappears, circling her on his motorbike. They both stand still, saying nothing but looking at each other in a face-to-face image that closes the film.

Rosetta has a minimal narrative with no complications of plot and was made entirely with a hand-held camera, without the use of heavy technical equipment. The story consists of Rosetta's movements; the camera captures what she sees, what she does, and where she hides her shoes. She is constantly on the move, scurrying around and pursuing her aims relentlessly. The film-makers have avoided aesthetic shots and picturesque location. The film is set in a bleak winter landscape (filming was stopped when the sun came out). The caravan is bare with nothing in it to remind Rosetta of her past and throughout the film no memories are evoked, no flashback recalls a past, no flash forward records a dream. Rosetta lives in the present and that present is the only story line in the film.

She is the kind of character/actress who belongs to the category that Deleuze refers to as a new kind of actor: not just non-professionals, but actors who are more able to see and do than to act or speak their lines (Deleuze 1985: 55). She is seen only by the camera. As Luc Dardenne explained in an interview, the film-makers avoided letting another person's potentially transforming gaze rest on Rosetta. She herself never looks at the camera but remains entirely absorbed in her activities: she sees and acts, unaware of anyone looking at her.

There is a preponderance of close-ups of faces in both *La Promesse* and *Rosetta*, revealing faces that never exchange a gaze and rarely look at each other. The shot/reverse shot is thus virtually never used. If the person whose face is seen in close-up speaks to another person, that other is most often off screen. There is, therefore, minimal identification between any two people, who seldom occupy the same filmic space. Because of the absence of any exchange of looks throughout the film, the closing face-to-face image which captures the looks exchanged by two people – Igor and Assita in *La Promesse* and Riquet and Rosetta in *Rosetta* – confirms the awareness of another person that the characters have developed. While any past is excluded from both films, in each something happens – promise or betrayal – that will remain etched on the minds of the two people for whom memory has hitherto seemed irrelevant. The reciprocal gaze with which the films end testify to the possibility of each identifying and possibly establishing a relationship with that other. It opens the way to an ethical relationship with the other and attests to the dignity of the human being.

The Belgian Francophone films discussed here show that there is certainly no simple opportunity for a unified national or linguistic identity. The films reveal that the absence of such a hegemonic potential leads to rich artistic possibilities when it comes to exploring the multifaceted nature of identity in a multilingual society. However, something more than purely artistic concerns are on offer here, the period under discussion – from the early 1930s to the late 1990s – is framed by film-makers who emphasise the social aspect of identity: from Storck (in the 1930s) to the Dardenne brothers (in the late 1990s) the films convey the idea that identity is a right which is all too often denied.

2 Switzerland

At first sight Switzerland and Belgium appear to have a lot in common: both are trilingual and both were declared countries of neutrality by the Congress of Vienna. However, Switzerland succeeded in safeguarding its neutrality in both World Wars and its present federal system, dating back to 1848, has provided political stability to the country. Its three linguistic regions are subdivided into twenty cantons, six semi-cantons and one federal city, Bern. The Swiss constitution has received much attention because of its unique system of direct democracy which encourages the use of referendums for major changes in the country or the canton on issues such as votes for women and the distinction between Church and State. It was not until 1971 that women's right to vote became nationwide.

In Switzerland, as in so many other places, the *Lumière Cinematograph* made an early appearance at fairgrounds. The country itself soon attracted many European film companies and film-makers because of its spectacular beauty, which provided a natural setting for those in search of pretty pictures. Swiss domestic film production is inevitably limited because it caters to a population of only 7.25 million and is, furthermore, divided into three linguistic regions, where either German (73.4 per cent), French (20.5 per cent) or Italian (4.1 per cent) is spoken.

It was not until the eve of World War II that a mainly Germanic-language cinema began to emerge in Switzerland, flourishing until the mid-1960s. It was inspired by a sense of national identity, especially in the aftermath of a war that had torn European nations apart. Proud of its neutral status, Switzerland considered itself a model of democracy. But it would be illusory to think that the Swiss model could be applied elsewhere: as Irving Massey, remarks, 'its conditions are unique and not capable of being transplanted' (Massey 1994: 163). The remarkable characteristic of Switzerland's multilingualism is that there is no conflict over language differences and even the fourth language, Romansch, which is spoken by less than 0.7 per cent of the population, has the status of a national language.

According to Freddy Buache, although in the late 1960s 'people talked a lot about Swiss cinema, it was mainly to complain about its non-existence rather than its quality' (Buache 1974: 53). Few fiction films were made, partly because Switzerland had a documentary tradition and partly because fiction films required larger budgets. Moreover, the federal aid that became available in 1963 was intended for documentaries and not for fiction. A boom in Swiss cinema finally came with the emergence of the 'new Swiss cinema', which was heralded by Alain Tanner, Claude Goretta, the late Michel Soutter and Yves Yersin. Of these four, the two whose work is particularly relevant for the notion of identity are Tanner and Goretta. Tanner's oeuvre stands out in its systematic use of the spatial metaphor to reflect on identity, while Goretta focuses more on the identity of specific individuals.

Some may note here the absence of the seminal film-maker Jean-Luc Godard. Although born in Paris, Godard does hold dual French/Swiss citizenship and his close association with Swiss photographer and film-maker, Anne-Marie Miéville, has strengthened the link with Switzerland, where he now lives. There may be a Swiss perspective that calls for attention, but it would be difficult to claim that he is a Swiss film-maker, since most of his films were made in France and he is undeniably an international icon of French cinema.

Alain Tanner

Tanner was instrumental in drawing international attention to Swiss cinema and obtaining equal funding status for documentaries and fiction films. He became the dominant figure in the 'new Swiss cinema', which was based in, yet freed from, the celebrated Swiss tradition of documentary. It was firmly rooted in Francophone Switzerland (*la Suisse romande*), and showed awareness of Swiss cultural complexity.

Tanner's film career spans over forty years and constitutes a kind of journey which is at once cinematographic, geographic and ideological. While studying economics at the University of Geneva, his interest in cinema prompted him to collaborate with Claude Goretta in a Cine-Club. His film-making took off while he was in England in 1955, when he succeeded in finding work at the British Film Institute, made a documentary, *Nice Time*, in collaboration with Goretta, became acquainted with the 'Free Cinema' movement and met Marxist author, John Berger, who became a close friend and the scriptwriter of four of his films.

Tanner's contact with the Free Cinema movement, his meeting with John Berger and his London experience in general were to lay the foundation for his cinema of commitment to social change. From London Tanner moved to Paris and became acquainted with the 'New Wave' cinema which, after the political commitment of the Free Cinema, seemed to him too much like right-wing anarchism.

Tanner's first two films depict societies that are not Swiss: the first, *Nice Time* (1956), is set in London, and the second, *Une Ville à Chandigarh* (1966), is about the building of the Indian city of Chandigarh in the

Punjab. Tanner is Swiss, but he is also a traveller who takes a critical look at his own and other societies. His approach is that of a native informant and an anthropologist.

Tanner's films emphasise the camera's eye and are characterised by long takes and 'empty shots', where the camera lingers on the country-side after the characters have left the frame. The camera captures the characters in their spatial context. Most of them are people on the edge: they seem at one remove from society – exiled or excluded – they do not inhabit the same space as the society around them. This tendency was already apparent in *Nice Time*. A dense crowd moves up and down, a classless and ageless group of people, who are in London's Piccadilly Circus by chance and whose activities are recorded by the camera. The film draws attention to peripheral members of society: a sailor spending a short time in the city, or a prostitute, who is socially on the fringes of society, but nevertheless central to it. In an embryonic way, this first film brings out Tanner's fascination with the centre/periphery dichotomy on the geographic, social and cinematographic levels. Already, space is an essential component endowed with a social dimension: the city becomes a metaphor of society in which transience and the marginality of specific individuals emerge as powerful themes.

Une Ville à Chandigarh (1966)

Tanner's manifest interest in social reality becomes more prominent in *Une Ville à Chandigarh* (*A City at Chandigarh*). This sixty-minute documentary was an East/West collaboration: a Western architect, Le Corbusier, was commissioned by Prime Minister Nehru to build the new capital for the Punjab. Two Western artists, Tanner and Berger, filmed the creation of this new capital and its emerging social structure. Tanner's images are commented on throughout by Berger, who also co-wrote the script. Berger's voice on soundtrack takes the viewer beyond the space of the screen and away from the centre of the new city under con-struction, suggesting another space, that of the builders and the gypsies excluded from the city. The geographical separation corresponds to an economic one: the people living on Chandigarh's outskirts, although economically essential to the city, earn much less than those living within it. The centre/periphery dichotomy is evident and emphasis is placed on the link between the topography of the city and its hidden socio-economic structure. The only people not *living* in the city and not on screen are those who built and are still building it and who are not known but only talked about on the soundtrack.

Charles, mort ou vif (1969)

Unlike the two early documentaries, Tanner's feature films do not take the city as their immediate object: nevertheless they maintain it as an essential component of the narrative. Far more than just a background against which a story unfolds, it is an historical, economic and cultural factor in a society with which the individual is often at odds. The most telling example of the individual's failure to relate to his social context is Tanner's first Geneva film, *Charles, mort ou vif* (*Charles, Dead or Alive*). In this film the main character, Charles Dé, suffers a mental breakdown on the very day of the centenary of the family business, a Geneva watch factory. The celebration, which is reported on television, endorses an ideology of free enterprise, the accumulation of wealth through a system of inheritance in which a business is passed on through the male members of a family, and an appreciation of traditional family values. The opening of the film, where a factory employee praises his employers, sets up a parallelism between factory and family and also the city, re-presented by the presence of the television company which is filming the event.

The Swiss city is shown to have provided Charles with a self-image and an identity which, at the age of fifty, suddenly fragments: a crisis erupts when the image, provided by Geneva and projected on Swiss television, fails to coincide with what Charles sees in the mirror of his bathroom. Suddenly this watch factory owner perceives how he has been fashioned by Geneva and its paternalistic system; he cannot relate to the ceremony being staged in the factory or to the flattering images projected by the television broadcast and feels compelled to reject the approbatory gaze he receives from both factory and city. Charles's identity crisis makes him abandon his family and professional position. In his journey away from watch manufacturing, from his family, from conventionality and paternalism, Charles goes through various stages, each time taking a different name: from Charles Dé he becomes Mr Schwartz, then Carlo, thus completing a mental journey through Switzerland's three linguistic regions as if they had contributed to his experience of a fragmented self.

La Salamandre (1971)

In *La Salamandre* (*The Salamander*), the emphasis is also placed on social marginality, on exclusion and the alienation of the individual, set against the background of Geneva. But here, unlike Charles, the main character, Rosemonde, is an outsider from the beginning. The youngest of a large family, she has gone to live with an uncle in the city, earning her keep as a domestic help in order to ease the financial pressure on her family. The pleasures usually associated with the city quickly make way for the tedium of living with her uncle in a small flat. Rosemonde makes the headlines in the local newspapers for shooting and injuring her uncle, who then accuses her of attempted murder. The film depicts the attempt of two journalists, Pierre and Paul, to prepare a script based on the case for Swiss television. As the two authors try to unravel the case and interview former employers and landladies – who describe Rosemonde as lazy, untidy, restless and disorganised – they see, through the young woman, the intolerance of society towards unconventional people. The camera corroborates this by on the one hand showing Rosemonde stuffing sausages in a dehumanising factory and being reprimanded for looking untidy, and on the other revealing the rubbish that has accumulated in the city's streets because of a strike.

Pierre and Paul, seeing the ills of society more clearly than Rosemonde's guilt, feel akin to her and begin to understand that she has come to see herself as society depicts her. At one point, when travelling in a tram, they playfully enact their own rebellion against society. Paul acts as a noisy Turk, Pierre as a self-righteous Swiss man reacting against 'invasions' of foreigners. It does not take long before co-travellers support Pierre's objections: 'This gentleman [Pierre] is right. We are no longer at home in our trams.'

The two authors themselves live outside the confines of society, both literally and socially. They too are unconventional and, like Rosemonde, they struggle to cope with housing. In order to avoid high accommodation costs, Paul lives in a kind of no-man's-land near the border, while Pierre is required to provide collateral equal to eighteen months' rent. Instead of completing their script for Swiss television, they reveal to the viewer of *La Salamandre* the narrowness of society's norms which brings about the marginalisation of some people. Paul has previously imagined a fictional character like Rosemonde, about whom a voice-over states that 'her desires were completely normal, and that consequently one had to look elsewhere for what was not normal'. The film closes by applying the notion of normal to the weather: 'December 20. The snow had not come yet . . . which, in fact, was normal.' In comparing human behaviour to meteorological variations, the film invalidates the judgements to which Rosemonde has been subjected.

Le Retour d'Afrique (1973)

Le Retour d'Afrique (*Return from Africa*) presents a Genevan couple, Vincent and Françoise, who have to leave their condemned flat. Horrified by the prospect of bourgeois life in dreary Geneva, they plan to leave for Africa. Vincent longs for primitive places, for an escape from Western bourgeois culture and its capitalism. However, their journey never takes place and, too embarrassed to tell their friends, they choose a self-imposed exile in their condemned flat. Having sold most of their belongings, they are reduced to a rudimentary lifestyle, and the self-imposed exile assumes the characteristics of a journey to Africa: the dream of a primitive Algeria becomes a fake primitivism in the heart of Geneva. As the couple 'returns to Geneva' from their simulated journey,

Vincent meets Emilio, an immigrant worker, who throughout the film has represented the theme of exile and who is finally the one forced to leave the country, presumably for political reasons. His expulsion occurs when Vincent's self-exile ends, revealing how the search for a primitive elsewhere is a romantic search for the self; a search that contrasts sharply with the position of people coming from these 'primitive elsewheres' due to economic need.

Le Milieu du monde (1974)

Le Milieu du monde (The Middle of the World) focuses on two people, Adriana and Paul. Adriana is an Italian waitress, Paul a Swiss engineer and a candidate for the local elections. They have an affair whose duration coincides with the 112 days of the election campaign. The 'Middle of the World', located somewhere in the Swiss countryside, is also the name of a restaurant where one of the first meetings between Adriana and Paul takes place. The 'Middle' becomes a metaphor for the entire film and for the society in the film. In the Middle, the world is divided in two, 'one side for the rich, one side for the poor', as Paul phrases it. Whereas Adriana refuses to stay in the Middle, Paul embraces it and is embraced by it. His middle-of-the-road politics are reduced to 'solving problems'. Adriana is the foreigner, he is the election candidate who expresses his Swiss identity by treating the Italian immigrant waitress to Swiss tourist presents, a musical cow, a watch, a camera. Paul's conquest of Adriana, set up like an electoral campaign, also fails just like an electoral campaign. The Italian waitress has unconsciously or subversively defeated the Middle-of-the-World candidate.

Jonas qui aura vingt cinq ans en l'an 2000 (1976)

In *Jonas qui aura vingt cinq ans en l'an 2000 (Jonas Who Will Be 25 in the Year 2000)* eight characters meet by chance on the periphery of Geneva, where two of the eight run a small organic farm. They come together eight years after May '68, a reference made explicit by all of them having a name that starts with MA. They belong to the same generation, all are in their late twenties or thirties, and have been affected one way or another by the May '68 events, references to which, both verbal and in the form of black-and-white flashbacks, interrupt the narrative. These are marginal people, misfits in society, employed in work which offers little if any profit. Many of them are ill at ease in their jobs, and hence opt out of them or lose them.

A certain 'spirit' of '68 characterises the eight characters. Each one rebels against an aspect of society, advocates a specific philosophical principle, attacks a social injustice, or holds a definite opinion on ecological or educational matters. In the Swiss society of the 1970s these beliefs constitute a peripheral way of thinking. Even among the eight

4 Alain Tanner, *Jonas qui aura 25 ans en l'an 2000.*

characters there is no common ground other than that of being on the fringes. May '68 has contributed to the specific identity of each one of them, but the film, with its location in Geneva, reveals other realities which inevitably influence these marginal characters: from land speculation, migrant labour and Swiss banking to Calvin and Jean-Jacques Rousseau, whose statue is shown at the beginning and the end of the film.

Messidor (1979)

In *Messidor* two girls set out on a trip through Switzerland. The geography of the country structures the narrative: the direction of the story is an arbitrary itinerary along the Swiss roads. The girls are hitch-hiking: one because she has lost her train ticket, the other because she wishes to escape the noise of the city. They meet as a car stops and picks them both up. What was to be a return home for one girl and a few days away for the other, becomes an endless, hopeless and ill-defined journey on roads that lead nowhere and present little or no safety. Most cars are driven by men who offer paternalistic advice to the girls about their safety, then ruthlessly try to take sexual advantage of them. Although the two girls were not marginal characters at the outset of the film, their journey through Switzerland, which is tantamount to an initiation into

Swiss society, leaves them resentful and ill-adjusted, and their identities, like that of Rosemonde in *La Salamandre*, are shaped by society's rejection and prejudices.

Les Années lumière (1980)

Tanner's first fiction film to be set outside Switzerland is set in Ireland. It is also his first film to be adapted from a novel. His characters are thus not pure inventions, yet they reveal kinship with characters from earlier films. Yoshka and Jonas, the film's two main characters, share characteristics with the characters from *Jonas qui aura vingt cinq ans en l'an 2000*. In fact, implied in *Les Années lumière* (*Light Years Away*) is the notion that this is a sequel to *Jonas*. Yoshka, an eccentric character, who lives by himself near his car cemetery in a desolate place in Ireland, spends all his time trying to realise his dream of flying. He is joined by Jonas, a young man whom he meets in a bar. The relationship between Yoshka and Jonas moves through various stages: from master/slave to master/pupil and finally to father/son. When Yoshka enacts his dream of flying, he tragically dies when an eagle pecks out his eyes, thus throwing him back to the earth. Jonas inherits the car cemetery and the derelict garage, and seems also to inherit Yoshka's spirit.

The spatial metaphor pervades: the dream of an elsewhere that emerges from a failure to relate to the here and the now haunts the characters. Whereas the characters in previous films lived on the periphery of society, Yoshka and Jonas live in a kind of nowhere, both physically and socially in exile. The scenery around the desolate place where Jonas has joined Yoshka is of a wild beauty which the film abundantly reveals. There is a strong affinity, not merely between the two characters, but also between the characters and nature around them.

Dans la Ville blanche (1983)

Although the sea was occasionally the object of dreams or longings of Tanner's characters, it remained absent from his earlier films. In *Dans la Ville blanche* (*In the White City*) the sea becomes the central focus both visually and narratively. The film opens with a wide view of a ship in the mist, it then cuts to the noisy and hot engine-room, where a sailor is preparing to leave the ship during the stop-over in Lisbon. As in previous films, the narrative thread is thin: a sailor-mechanic deserts his ship on a stop-over. Though he loves the sea, he spends eight hours a day in an engine-room, from where no sea can be seen. He has in a sense become alienated from the sea: the ship is a floating factory and his life on it cannot be referred to as travel. The notion of a journey has changed, and the journey really begins with the stop-over. It is not the travelling to the city, but the stay in the city, that constitutes the journey, at the end of which he feels he has 'surfaced' once again.

The city/sea polarity underlies the sailor's journey of descent into himself. His dream of a 'white city' in which everything is white (silence and solitude are white) is enacted in Lisbon, which assumes these symbolic characteristics. Trapped between dream and reality, between city and sea, between a woman in Portugal and a woman in Switzerland, between mobility and immobility, he slowly realises that the only country he really loves is the sea, but it is precisely from this open space with its apparent infinity that he has been alienated.

No Man's Land (1985)

No Man's Land is set in an area which apparently belongs to no one – a real no-man's-land – a place of pastures and forests between the Franco-Swiss border, carefully patrolled by French and Swiss customs officials. In it the four main characters imagine an elsewhere where they hope they can realise their dreams: Canada for Paul, who loves flying; Paris for Madeleine, who wants to sing; the countryside for Jean, and for Mali, the frontier worker, her home country Algeria. This no-man's-land is a geographical reality, but more importantly, it is also the metaphor for the state of mind that characterises these marginal characters.

La Femme de Rose Hill (1989)

For La Femme de Rose Hill (The Woman from Rose Hill) Tanner returned to his native Switzerland. 'It does not look like the Switzerland we know from chocolate boxes', one woman told him at the London Film Festival where the film was shown. 'No,' Tanner replied, 'I am not paid by the tourist bureau.' Indeed, a tourist Switzerland it is not, even though the classical Tannerian slow tracking shots give spatial prominence to the Swiss countryside. The light-drenched, wind-swept or mist-shrouded takes provide the setting for the social drama of Julie, the 'woman from Rose Hill', a black mail-order bride. She comes to Switzerland from a far-off island in the Indian Ocean, having seen a photograph of a much younger Marcel, the ageing, unattractive farmer-husband she is to meet in the Swiss canton of Vaud.

Tanner films the lonely woman walking along misty roads or takes her in off-centre close-ups, leaving space for the snow-covered countryside. Inside the house, the image of the husband's overpowering mother, her shadow literally projected on to the wall, captures the threat of this silent presence. Julie's meeting with Jean, a man to whom she feels emotionally close, leads to yet another drama when she becomes pregnant by him. Conformism, paternal authority and social laws intervene, causing Julie to be forcibly expelled from her new country.

Requiem (1998)

Tanner's subsequent film, Requiem, is particularly noteworthy in its near-spiritual approach to the quest for identity. The film is set in Lisbon, where a fictional author, Paul, is supposed to meet Portuguese author Fernando Pessoa (who actually died in 1935) at twelve o'clock on that day. The heat is intense and there could have been a misunderstanding about the time. Twelve o'clock could have meant midnight instead of noon. So Paul has twelve hours to wait. The film follows him wandering through the streets of Lisbon, a city he has visited before. As he walks, the past surfaces through different encounters, including one with the spectre of his father. The viewer is drawn into an uncertainty similar to that surrounding the rendezvous with Pessoa. The wanderings through Lisbon appear like a dream where an imagined meeting is to take place, at noon or at midnight, in the heat or in the dark, with the author for whom the 'habit of dreaming and the ability to dream are primordial'. Tanner's identification with Pessoa transpires in this film, which opens with the quotation: 'We dream our lives. We are children of destiny.' Throughout his films, Tanner has disclosed the personal quest of the individual who undertakes an ill-defined journey into the self or to an imagined elsewhere in order to realise a sense of identity. In *Requiem* the viewer gains the impression that in identifying with Pessoa, who wrote that 'to live is to be other', Tanner is revealing his own relentless struggle for identity.

Tanner's oeuvre reveals an insistence on the interaction between space and identity. In each one of his films the individual is placed in a well-defined spatial context, which often takes on an identity of its own. Yet the common feature that underlies these places is that of exclusion. From the building of Chandigarh in India to Geneva in the heart of Western capitalism the same principle operates: the distancing of the marginal people to the periphery of the city or beyond. Tanner's films reveal how cities are social entities which allow or deny the spatial anchoring of identity. Entire groups of people (the gypsies and the builders) are excluded from Chandigarh, while the periphery of Geneva abounds with marginal people and immigrants. Personal alienation and loss of self strike even at the very heart of Geneva's capitalist edifice, represented by the respected family man and owner of a watch factory.

Tanner's topography is an apt metaphoric representation of the individual's quest for an identity: from the arbitrary itinerary of two young girls travelling along the roads of Switzerland, to a man dreaming of flying from a desolate place in Ireland, to the sea that represents the unfulfilled dream of the sailor, and to the dream of Switzerland for the woman from a far-off island in the Indian Ocean. All these ill-fated journeys constitute the enactment of the individual's search for an elsewhere that would allow the self to be redefined.

It seems that Tanner's own personal search underlies these imagined journeys. His recent films are impelled by an urge to return to the past and to reflect on the ideologies that fashioned the 1968 generation. He returns to these marginal characters, whose otherness was ill tolerated by society, and shows how individual marginality such as that of Rosemonde in *La Salamandre* has been replaced by the marginality of the social group (*Fourbi* 1996). In another film, *Jonas et Lila, à demain* (1999), he re-evokes the child Jonas, the symbolic offspring of the ideologies of May '68, who would be twenty-five in the year 2000. He is now twenty-five, studied cinema and lives in Geneva with his black African lover. This return to the life of a fictional character, born in an earlier film, creates a fusion of fiction and reality, an interlocking of past and present and produces an illusion of the construction of Jonas's identity. It also reveals the changes in society whose own identity is now being constructed.

Claude Goretta

Alongside Alain Tanner, Claude Goretta is the best known of the 'new Swiss cinema' film-makers and like Tanner he began with documentaries, the first one being their jointly made *Nice Time*. Whereas Tanner develops a link between space and identity in a major way throughout his oeuvre, integrating numerous characters and showing a strong pre-occupation with Swiss society, Goretta's approach is more narrowly defined in that it focuses on specific individuals without attempting to comment upon Swiss society, with the exception of *L'Invitation* (*The Invitation*), Goretta's 1973 film which won the Jury Prize in Cannes. The three most arresting films with regard to the specific development of the identity of the characters are *La Dentellière* (1997), *La Provinciale* (1980) and *Les Chemins de l'exil* (1978). The first two present fictional characters, while the last focuses on Jean-Jacques Rousseau.

L'Invitation (1973)

Rémy Placet, an ageing bachelor, lives with his mother in a small and modest house. When his mother dies, Rémy inherits a considerable fortune with which he buys a magnificent property. It is in this property that the action takes place when Rémy invites his office colleagues to a lavish party. At first dumbfound by the magnificence of house and garden, they are soon distracted by the food and alcohol. Slowly the social constraints of this conventional Swiss society loosen and each of the guests begins to behave in ways that never would have come to light in an office environment: one colleague bursts into a wild dancing performance while another performs a striptease. Finally, when a theft is discovered, the party ends. In presenting the temporary collapse of a well-mannered Swiss society, this comedy reveals the discrepancy between personal idiosyncratic behaviour and social identity. It sets the tone for Goretta's exploration of identity in his subsequent films.

5 Claude Goretta, *La Dentellière*, François and Pomme.

La Dentellière (1977)

The main character in *La Dentellière* (*The Lacemaker*) is Béatrice, known as Pomme, a young employee in a hairdresser's salon. She lives with her mother, who is separated from her husband, and has befriended a colleague at work, Marylène. When Marylène's affair with a married man breaks up, she invites Pomme to go with her to the sea for a holiday; however, once there, she quickly finds a replacement for her former lover and leaves Pomme to her own devices. Pomme, now alone, is noticed by a young Parisian student, François, and a relationship develops between them. Back in Paris, they move in together, but the social and intellectual differences that emerge cause François to withdraw and to end the relationship. After this rejection, Pomme suffers a breakdown and ends up in an institution. The film closes showing her sitting by herself knitting – comparable, the voice-over states, 'to the lacemaker in a genre painting'.

Two of these three characters, Marylène and François, identify with and reproduce well-known archetypes in society and are very different from Pomme.

Marylène, who is considerably older than Pomme, is a beautician. She tries to look seductive and puts on poses, copying the many images propagated by the media. The large poster of Marilyn Monroe pinned to the wall of Marylène's flat personifies the image the beautician wants to emulate. Not only does she try to imitate the media images, her behaviour also copies the lifestyle of these models. When they go for a swim at the seaside, Marylène uses all the alluring gestures of swaying hips and leaping from the water that belong to the Marilyn Monroe register. She continually puts herself on display, posing naked on the edge of the bath in front of Pomme or studying her own image in the mirror, surrounded by photographs of herself. Similarly, at the disco they visit in the evening, Marylène follows the Monroe code of expressions and movements. Her only concern is to fashion an image that will attract men. The identity she seeks is entirely shaped by the dictates of fashion magazines and photos of film-stars, in short, the consumer world. However, time goes by and Marylène moves from man to man without any relationship leading to real happiness. In the course of the film she starts to show signs of becoming the tragic victim of excessive image consumption.

François too has accepted and internalised a model dictated by society which combines the discourse of pseudo left-wing French intellectualism and the social prejudices of the middle class. Because of Pomme's background and menial job, he is apprehensive about introducing her to his parents – François's father is a lawyer, breeds dogs, and lives with his elegant, well-read wife in a beautiful country house. And, although François's intellectual friends warm to Pomme, he is ashamed of her lack of culture: she should study, quit her dreadful job and do something more meaningful.

Pomme, who is about eighteen and a junior employee, taking on menial jobs in the beauty salon, is the exact opposite of Marylène and François. She has no physical or mental image in mind which she wishes to copy, no particular behaviour pattern to follow and no ideology to endorse. In contrast to Marylène, she moves somewhat clumsily and avoids looking at herself in the mirror. At the disco she sits by herself and refuses to dance, and when François's friends come over and engage in intellectual discussions, she stays quiet and uninvolved. She has not identified any models to follow, either for her appearance or for her patterns of thought. The viewer is told that the only image that bears a resemblance to her is that of the lacemaker.

We know little about Pomme's past, except that in the privacy of her bedroom she often spends time looking at photographs of her childhood. One might presume that she has stayed in that childhood and that her self-effacing character comes from a poor sense of self. Her self-effacement is so great that it leads to the negation of her self by other people as well. Two sequences portraying her with François are particularly revealing in this respect: in one she is blindfolded and forced to submit to François's will, in the other she is silenced by him.

The first sequence shows François and Pomme near a steep cliff. Pomme is blindfolded and, literally, entrusts her life to François: he tells her how many steps she is to take in each direction until she comes dangerously close to the edge of the cliff. François tells her to look while he stands ready to catch her in case fright makes her lose her balance. The second event happens at a dinner at the home of François's middle-class parents. They are eating fish when his parents ask Pomme what she does for a living. When François, anticipating his parents reactions, cuts her off from saying what her job actually is, Pomme has to 'swallow her words', chokes on a fish bone and has a coughing fit. Ashamed to acknowledge her class to his parents, he silences her when she was about to speak about herself.

There is irony in François's behaviour. His eager engagement in a linguistic discussion about phonemes – the minimal distinctive utterances of speech – with his friends, contrasts with the way that any utterance by Pomme is gagged. The dinner conversation is one example. After another discussion Pomme asks the meaning of 'dialectical', having heard the word repeated by François and his friends, but his only explanation is 'dialectical materialism', emphasising the gulf between his hollow phrase, borrowed from Marxist theory, and his contempt for Pomme's working-class and 'unintellectual' background. When he finally rejects her, one of his more enlightened friends summarises the relationship by stating that François has treated her the way employers treat workers: 'you used her, then fired her'. This leads one to deduce that Pomme, who ends up in a psychiatric hospital, represents the alienation of the working class exploited by their employers. The film implies a critique of capitalism, consumerism and the bourgeoisie.

The choice of actresses is also ironic. Florence Giorgetti as Marylène, who acts the glamorous woman, does not succeed as a Monroe lookalike, while Isabelle Huppert's stunning looks contradict the clumsiness of the supposedly ill-at-ease Pomme.

For film critic Gillian Parker, Goretta is 'attempting to reorder our perception', because the poster of Monroe reminds us 'that our vision has been trained at the movies: Marilyn is immediately both seen and known by the audience because her identity has been coded into the familiar language and values of the mass media' (Parker 1978: 52).

The last sequence shows François's visit to the institution in which Pomme is confined. Pomme seems to have lost all sense of identity and reality: she tells François that she visited Greece, but the camera reveals that the Greece she 'visited' is the poster of Mykonos behind her and that she can no longer distinguish between reality and imagination. François returns to his life, Pomme to her knitting. The film ends with Pomme staring directly into the camera and so into the viewer's space. One is left with the question of how a voice that has been deemed unworthy of social circulation can be regained. Perhaps a film is one of the places where an identity can be restored by giving expression to this voice, translated here into Pomme's final gaze which, unlike Vermeer's painting, *The Lacemaker*, openly challenges the viewer. It seems that voice and look are similarly expressive of self and that when the voice is gone, the look takes over and addresses the viewer directly.

Les Chemins de l'exil (1978)

Having created the fictional characters Pomme and Isabelle and depicted their malaise and sense of exile in certain social environments, Goretta turned to Geneva's foremost philosopher, Jean-Jacques Rousseau in *Les Chemins de l'exil* (*Roads of Exile*). In 1762, following the publication of his two most controversial works, *The Social Contract* and *Emile*, Rousseau suffered persecution and had to leave his home, remaining in exile until 1770. He first settled in Môtiers, in the Prussian principality of Neuchâtel, but left there when stones were thrown at his house. He then spent some time on the island of St Pierre in Lake Bienne in Switzerland, but was expelled by the authorities in Berne. He fled to Paris and from there to England at the invitation of the philosopher David Hume. After a quarrel with Hume, Rousseau returned to France where he lived in several places until 1778, when he moved to Ermenonville, north of Paris. He died there later that same year.

It is not surprising that Goretta was attracted to the subject of this dramatic exile, especially since it was during the time of his exile that Rousseau started writing his *Confessions*, the first major autobiographical work in modern literature, in which memory comes to constitute identity. Goretta based his film on the *Confessions*, following the author in a subjective manner, filming from his point of view and introducing flashbacks into Rousseau's consciousness. The film reveals the increasing persecution mania that beset the author.

Goretta appears to follow Rousseau's *Confessions* faithfully and chronologically. However, his treatment of Rousseau's companion and housekeeper Thérèse is particularly interesting. While the film overtly deals with Rousseau's exclusion, Thérèse is also excluded in a way reminiscent of *La Dentellière*, although she is present on screen throughout the film. Firstly, Rousseau only very rarely looks at Thérèse. In most of the instances where the viewer sees her, Rousseau does not. The many times she enters the room to announce a visitor or offer a cup of tea all happen without Rousseau looking at her. The same applies to the camera itself: while showing Thérèse, it hardly ever focuses upon an event from her point of view, despite the fact that she is quite outspoken from time to time. As was the case for Pomme, the viewer knows little about Thérèse's inner life. Each time Rousseau moves to a different place, the film features several brief takes showing Thérèse left behind. The person behind the great philosopher was herself exiled and excluded.

La Provinciale (1980)

Unlike Pomme in *La Dentellière*, Isabelle in *La Provinciale* (*The Girl from Lorraine*) is a sociable, well-adjusted and popular young woman. She lives in Lorraine, an impoverished industrial part of northern France, and has been unemployed for thirteen months since the company she worked for went bankrupt. An architectural draughtswoman, she has decided to move to Paris, where she hopes to use her skills in a rewarding job. A friend will lend her his flat while she is getting settled. The film follows Isabelle's journey from Lorraine to Paris, the problems she has when she gets there, and her ultimate decision to return to Lorraine.

The film takes a chronological approach, beginning in the small town of Homecourt in Lorraine, where Isabelle is on her way to choir practice for the last time. Her friends have prepared a special song for her: she is clearly liked very much and they are sorry to see her go. The choir also briefly sings the 'Internationale', the Communist Party's anthem, providing a vocal reminder of the social division between capital and labour and recalling that Isabelle, the unemployed who will be 'la provinciale' in Paris, may well have to contend with this dichotomy.

In practice the situation reflected in the tune of the 'Internationale' becomes an all encompassing reality in Paris, where exploitation underlies all forms of human interchange, whether professional, social or personal. Not only do Isabelle's efforts to find work as an architectural draughtswoman fail, her professional talents and feminine charm are systematically exploited or misused, from grotesque attempts to touch her breasts by 'accidentally' spilling juice on her blouse, to using her architectural qualifications as a guarantee to induce people to buy real estate. Wherever Isabelle goes, she is confronted with some form of exploitation, from her lover whom she leaves when she realises that she has been only 'une femme parenthèse', a woman in parentheses, inserted into his life with wife and family, to the man who gropes her when she is playing pinball in a bar.

The people with whom Isabelle comes into contact seem equally exploited or alienated. Her friend Claire, a single mother living on the poverty line, has to turn to prostitution to solve her money problems. Pascal Chatel, a potential employer who invites her out for dinner, has just been abandoned by his wife, gets blind drunk and later throws himself out of the window. It all seems far removed from Lorraine, where the quality of human relationships was preserved. Isabelle's journey ends when, unable to find a place for herself in the new environment, she rejects any further exploitation and returns to her old identity in Lorraine.

Neither of the two film-makers discussed present a specific Swiss identity. While many of Tanner's films are located in Switzerland, there is no attempt to herald Swiss values. To the contrary, Tanner is critical of Swiss society and uses the metaphor of the city to show how exclusion and marginality are created. In Goretta's films exclusion of the individual is equally important but is more class-related. Neither film-maker emphasises an ethnic or national identity, instead they focus on individual and social identity.

II NORTH AMERICA AND THE CARIBBEAN

North America was for a long time an international battleground for European nations, as well as a land of settlement. It was ultimately the 1763 Treaty of Paris, concluded at the end of the Seven Year War, that determined the destiny of the last French possessions in North America and the Caribbean: France lost its last Canadian territory and kept control over only two small islands in the mouth of the St Lawrence River, Saint Pierre and Miquelon; it also retained the Caribbean islands of Guadeloupe and Martinique.

Québec still claims an autonomous Francophone identity which is reflected in its separate status, alongside Canada (an officially bilingual country), in the international organisation of the Francophone world. Despite its distance (both geographically and emotionally) from France, Québec uses the Francophone label as a strategy to resist the influence of its giant Anglophone neighbours. Yet at the same time, it harbours a certain resentment against the French for their self-centred attitude and the dominant place they occupy in the Francophone world.

The Caribbean covers an interesting geographic area comprising a large number of islands off the North and Central American Atlantic coasts. Only a few of the islands are French-speaking and, only three of them, Martinique, Guadeloupe and Haiti, are involved in film-making. Of these, Haiti is the only island to be a member of the Francophone World Organization in an independent capacity. Since the other two islands are administratively French, they cannot be members of the Organization in their own right.

There is no film industry in the Caribbean and film production is, inevitably, limited. However, the biennial *Images Caraïbes* film festivals, initiatedby a Martiniquan woman Suzy Landau in 1988, 'aim at encouraging and promoting the development of a distinct and original Caribbean cinema by Caribbean people' (Cham 1992: 13). The festivals provide an impetus for Caribbean film-makers, many of whom work in Europe, to gain a sense of belonging and of being Caribbean.

3　Québec

Québécois cinema (there is no specific French-Canadian cinema outside Québec), perhaps more than any other 'national' cinema – despite it not being a 'nation', the concept is applicable – is permeated with the memory of its past. As centuries of accumulated sensitivities are reflected in the cinema of Québec, a brief summary of its history is called for.

Jacques Cartier's discovery of Newfoundland and the Labrador Coast in 1534 seems to be perceived by the Québécois as one of the pristine moments in French pioneering history. In the name of François I, Cartier took possession of 'la Nouvelle France', the name given to the French possessions in Canada. In 1604 the colony of Acadia was founded, while in 1608 Samuel de Champlain founded Québec. From this point onwards the immigration of French settlers was encouraged and in 1627 the Company of the Hundred Associates was created. They were rich merchants, who set up the fur trade with the Amerindians and also started the work of evangelisation. However, the Franco-British wars led to France's loss of its Canadian territories. In 1713 they lost Acadia, the more northerly part of what we now call Nova Scotia and Newfoundland and in 1763 they lost Nouvelle France. One particular event, referred to as the *Grand Dérangement*, which followed the loss of Acadia, has become the emblematic instance of English oppression. Thousands of Acadians who refused to swear allegiance to England were deported to other English regions along the coast; a number went to Louisiana and became known as the 'Cajuns' (a corruption of the word 'Acadians').

The English conquest left a deep mark on the French settlers and subsequent generations. Today the memory of this loss is still painfully alive: every car number plate carries the words 'Je me souviens' (I remember), referring to the French loss. This beginning of the Québécois' resentment towards the English later shifted to Anglophone Canadians and Americans and generated a feeling of solidarity with those other victims of colonisation, the Amerindians, who sided with the French against the English. Throughout the nineteenth century Québec remained a rather isolated agricultural province, which led to many people emigrating to other parts of Canada. The Depression of the 1930s was to bring even more poverty to Québec and in 1936, in the hope that the then opposition party would bring more prosperity to Québec, the National Union party was voted in and the long-governing Liberal party ousted: Maurice Duplessis became Québec's Premier and would remain almost continuously in power, until 1959. Duplessis believed in a set of values that would promote Québec's autonomy. They included return to the land, family values, religion and a work ethic. His oppressive regime was overthrown in 1960, when the Liberal Jean Lesage became Premier and heralded the so-called *Révolution tranquille* (Quiet Revolution). This revolution pulled Québec out of the dark Duplessis years by nationalising all energy production under the name *Hydro-Québec*. Education was also nationalised, reducing the power of the Catholic church. The slogan *Maîtres chez nous* (masters in our own house) captured the mood of that period, during which the FLQ (*Front de Libération du Québec/Québec Liberation Front*) was also founded.

There was undoubted resentment towards the Anglophone world and friction between Canada, the federal state, and Québec the province. As a province, Québec enjoyed a certain level of autonomy, with its civil law based on the French legal system and the retention of French as its language (although this was not official until 1974). There could not have been a better moment for de Gaulle to come and fuel burgeoning feelings of nationalism. Bitterness about English colonisation, memories of the French heritage, nostalgia for the lost *mère-patrie* ('maternal' fatherland), and Cartier's Nouvelle France and a feeling of Frenchness were suddenly fomented by General de Gaulle's visit in July 1967 and his famous cry, 'Vive le Québec! Vive le Québec libre!'.

A year later, René Lévesque founded the Parti Québécois, which promoted independence for Québec. In 1975, a federation was created for the Francophones outside Québec (*Fédération des francophones hors Québec*), the French Canadians who number about one million people. Hopes for an independent Québec were crushed at the 1980 referendum, when 59 per cent of the Québécois voters said 'no' to independence.

Cultural memory is kindled in Québec's cinema above all by two trends: one where memories, dreams and disillusion often prevail – from the recollection of Jacques Cartier's voyage and his imagined emotion upon the founding of Canada to the dream of an independent Québec; the other, since 1980 when the referendum shattered the dream of an independent Québec, where anger erupts and where traditional values are questioned. Québécois cinema also defies the dictates of Hollywood and prides itself on producing a more direct cinema, away from the studios and from special effects and post-synchronised sound. It has gained an international reputation in the genres it produces besides fictional features – the non-commercial short film, the essay-film, the documentary, the animation film, the popular genre and, more recently, a 'feminine camera' in which a new aesthetic emerges.

This is not to say that the history of Québécois film was an easy one. Francophone film was late in establishing its presence on Canada's prestigious National Film Board, the NFB – in French, the ONF (*Office National du Film*) – created in 1939 and located in Ottawa. It was not until the 1950s that a small Francophone film-making division came to be represented on the Board. This delay was partly due to the ONF's/NFB's first director, John Grierson, whose report on Canada's film production had resulted in its establishment. He believed that film must serve the nation as a whole and that dubbing films into French was sufficient to meet the needs of the Québécois and other French-speaking Canadians.

By 1941, however, the few Francophone members on the administrative board had succeeded in convincing Grierson of the importance of a Québécois cinema and the first Francophone film-maker was appointed. Two years later some fifteen more entered the ONF/NFB. Unfortunately, this success was short-lived. In 1945 Grierson's successor, Ross McLean, introduced budgetary restrictions, which were inevitably detrimental to the Francophone film-makers. There was little improvement under McLean's successor, Arthur Irwin, appointed in 1950. In the same year, the Board had stated its specific aim of using film as a means of promoting a knowledge and understanding of Canada among Canadians and other nations. Although there was perhaps no explicit objection to Francophone films being made, it was argued that not only were the Francophone film-makers not inclined to promote a knowledge of Canada, their films were too expensive for the limited audience they attracted. *L'Homme aux oiseaux* (1952 – *The Man with the Birds*) proves this point. Its directors, Bernard Devlin and Jean Palardy, had to struggle to complete their film for these very reasons.

In 1953, Studio F was created, with the aim of producing films in French for television and the following year Pierre Juneau was appointed as special advisor for Francophone film production. Two years later he became executive director. Irwin, though he did not advocate a strong Francophone film production at the ONF/NFB, was to be instrumental in the later blossoming of Francophone film. His appointment, as Yves Lever points out, occurred at the height of the anti-Communist crisis, which made him keen to separate film-making from political issues. He therefore proposed moving the ONF/NFB offices from Ottawa to Montréal (Lever 1995b: 149). A large bilingual city with a strong artistic tradition, Montréal seemed an obvious choice and the move was made in 1956.

The presence of the ONF/NFB in Montréal captured the attention of journalists, who soon embarked upon a campaign for an autonomous French section on the Film Board. Lever enumerates the injustices the journalists revealed, including: lower salaries for bilingual Francophones than for their unilingual Anglophone colleagues doing the same job, poor representation of Francophone cinema at the ONF/NFB, which amounted to only 7 per cent of its overall output, and an obligation to present scripts in English because of the authorities' failure to understand French. The ONF acronym, Lever writes, came to be satirised by some intellectuals as meaning 'Organisation Non Francophone' (Lever 1995b: 151).

When Guy Roberge, the first Francophone director, was appointed in 1957, there seemed to be a glimmer of hope for a Francophone film production, but it was not until 1963 that Roberge proposed a new structure for the ONF/NFB, in which a Francophone section and an Anglophone section would coexist, each with its own autonomy and budget. Finally, on 1 January 1964, twenty-six years after its creation, the ONF/NFB adopted this proposal, which would reflect Canada's bilingual reality.

Three years later, one year before de Gaulle's visit to the province, under pressure from the influential *Cahiers du Cinéma*, a cinema in France showed a film by a young Canadian director, Gilles Groulx, *Le Chat dans le sac* (1964). These two events, Groulx's well-received film and de Gaulle's battle cry, drew the attention of the French and of the rest of the world to the fact that in North America there was a Francophone community with cinephiles and film-makers, who were, as de Gaulle would phrase it, 'cousins' of the French.

The early ONF/NFB film-makers, who had mainly made documentaries for television, left their mark on Québécois cinema. Their productions were highly successful and were to lay the foundations for a cinema in which the strong documentary tradition continued, underpinning fiction films as well. The search for what was specifically Québécois and the interest in social realities also remained dominant. The appointment of a number of very talented Francophone film-makers to the ONF/NFB heralded a golden age. As Marcel Jean states: 'The part played by the ONF in the evolution of Québécois cinema is so significant that it is true to say that very few major film-makers were not involved in it, either as full-time employees or, at least, as part-timers' (Jean 1991: 33, trans.).

The film mentioned above, *L'Homme aux oiseaux*, co-directed by Devlin and Palardy, illustrates the early ONF/NFB film-makers' interest in social issues, their attention to details from real life and to Québec's precious cultural heritage. A similar preoccupation characterises Bernard Devlin's 1958 film, *Les Brûlés* (*The Promised Land*), made in eight episodes for television. In it, he retraces the difficult colonisation of the Abitibi region, while also drawing attention to contemporary problems created by the recession and evoking the dream of a return to the land. The film illustrates both the close observation of the documentary film-makers and the social commitment which characterises many Québécois films. The early documentary style combined with the film-makers' social awareness would continue to remain a fundamental characteristic of Québécois cinema.

Women film-makers were conspicuously absent from Québécois cinema until the late 1960s and 1970s, when the feminist movement contributed to women's growing awareness of the need for self-expression. That this awareness came so late is not surprising, for it was not until 1940 that Québec women obtained the right to vote and, as Simone Suchet notes, it was not until 1970 that they had the right to enter drinking establishments. This last right may seem anecdotal but is, nevertheless, very meaningful, because it left women out of a place where social life and the exchange of ideas took place.

The Québécois feminist movement, which inspired many women film-makers, was active, militant, and cut across the barriers of social class, ethnicity and age. It is fitting and understandable that the first woman film-maker, Anne-Claire Poirier, should have held a degree in law and had a genuine concern with social justice for women. In 1967, after a few short films, she brought out her first full-length film, *De Mère en fille*, which dealt with motherhood and was representative of women's concerns to address issues important to them. In 1970 she was appointed co-producer for the series *En tant que femmes*, which aimed at making audiovisual techniques available 'to those citizens, groups or classes who are said to carry a minority culture (culture of poverty, rural cultures, hippie culture etc.), the majority culture being expressed by governments' (Suchet 1986: 83a, trans.).

This newly formulated objective was to open the closed quarters of film-making to those who until then had had no voice with which to express their identity. As expressed explicitly in *Médium-Média* 2 of the ONF/NFB, it was to 'allow women to break out of their isolation and to acquire a sense of solidarity, to learn to assume a specific identity and to redefine themselves' (Suchet 1986: 83b, trans.). The 1970s saw the release of a variety of films made by women and addressing women's issues. These included films by Mireille Dansereau and Paule Baillargeon, who is also a well-established actress. Dansereau's fable-like film *La Vie rêvée* (1972) deals with the strong influence of women's images in publicity and media which cause women to dream unrealistically about their future lives: two women try to free themselves from these stereotypical representations. In *J'me marie, j'me marie pas* (1973), the film-maker collects testimonials from four women in search of their liberation. Baillargeon's *La Cuisine rouge* (1979) starts with a marriage celebration in which the men remain seated at the table waiting to be served by the women – including the bride. At one point the women rebel, refuse to spend all their time cooking and cleaning in the kitchen, and in a reaction against the men engage in a pagan festival.

All these films aim at drawing the viewer's attention to the difficulty women have in asserting their identity. These film-makers seek to represent women on the screen in such a way that both the male and female viewer become aware of society's exploitation of women. While Dansereau and Baillargeon have contributed considerably to women's cinema, the three pioneering film-makers are Micheline Lanctôt, Claire Poirier and Léa Pool. But let us first turn to the early film-makers.

Michel Brault

One of the impressive number of ONF/NFB film-makers who gained international fame in the early period was undoubtedly Michel Brault. Before becoming one of Québec's foremost film directors, he was already well known in cinema in various technical capacities, his name frequently occurring in film credits as scriptwriter, cameraman or 'chef opérateur'.

Les Raquetteurs (1958)

Michel Brault's seventeen-minute film, *Les Raquetteurs* (*The Snowshoers*), made in association with Gilles Groulx, is frequently referred to as the manifesto of *cinéma direct*. In this kind of cinema, akin to *cinéma vérité* in France, the film-maker participates closely in whatever he is filming, thus adopting a subjective position which is fully acknowledged. Marcel Jean refers to *cinéma direct* as a revolution of the documentary (Jean 1991: 38), which aims to capture the human contact *en direct*, that is to say, through life reporting. This kind of cinema, influenced by two pioneers from the era of silent movies, the American Robert Flaherty and the Soviet film-maker Dziga Vertov, developed simultaneously in different countries. It was made possible by the development of new filming equipment, in particular the lightweight 16 mm camera.

Cinéma direct is particularly relevant to the notion of identity in the sense that, by participating in the action filmed, the film-maker establishes a close relationship with the people he is filming. In the case of Brault, the people or places filmed are first and foremost his very own people. His films are concerned with Québec, its history, its land, its people and its conflicts. The event filmed in *Les Raquetteurs* is the yearly congress of Canadian and US *raquetteurs* in Sherbrooke. Brault spent the entire weekend at the heart of the action, his camera on his shoulder, filming *raquetteurs* and spectators. The sounds recorded are those of the street – not always recognisable, but authentic.

Shortly after making *Les Raquetteurs*, Brault met French anthropologist and film-maker Jean Rouch, who was to be the driving force behind *cinéma vérité*. Brault joined Rouch and Edgar Morin as cameraman for their 1961 ground-breaking film in *cinéma vérité*, *Chronique d'un été* (*Chronicle of a Summer*). The ninety-minute film sets out to discover what a few Parisians think about themselves and the world. It includes no professional actors, no background music. Rouch and Morin are present on the screen, they conduct the interviews and establish a rapport with the people the viewer will follow on the screen.

By 1961 Brault had worked on a great many films and had come to be considered as Québec's most accomplished cameraman, a man of the image, so to speak. His collaboration with Pierre Perrault for *Pour la suite du monde* (1963 – *For Those Who Will Follow*) was particularly fortunate because of the two directors' complementary views on film-making (image/sound) and their similar interests in Québec's people and history.

Entre la Mer et l'eau douce (1967)

Brault is the director of *Entre la Mer et l'eau douce* (Between the Sea and Fresh Water) but, as is the case for so many Québec films, many colleagues and friends collaborated with him, including Denys Arcand, Claude Jutra and Jean-Claude Labrecque. The title of the film comes from his earlier film, made with Pierre Perrault, *Pour la suite du monde*, that takes place on the island of L'Ile-aux-Coudres in the St Lawrence river. The original phrase was used by Jacques Cartier in his memoirs to pinpoint the location of L'Ile-aux-Coudres and to indicate the exact point where the porpoises gather in the Saguenay estuary – the point where the St Lawrence river meets the salt water of the Gulf of St Lawrence and the Atlantic Ocean. In *Entre la Mer et l'eau douce* Brault uses the expression to convey the rupture between the sense of belonging to a part of the country and the attraction to the adventures and promises of the city.

The film opens with a concert by the singer Claude Tremblay at the Place des Arts in Montréal. A flashback shows him as a manual worker in his region, Charlevoix, about to leave for Montréal, incarnating the metaphor of being between the sea and fresh water. He fails to find work and settles for a room shared with his brothers, who are similarly uneducated and taking on any odd job available. Claude falls in love with a waitress, Geneviève, but the relationship ends when he meets a television presenter who helps him launch his singing career. Disenchanted with city life, he returns to his village, but there too things have changed. His return to the city, where he becomes a successful singer, links the end of the film to its opening and to Claude's successful performance, at the end of which Geneviève, now a married woman with children, congratulates him.

On the surface, this is a story of the success of a village boy, Claude Tremblay, who becomes a famous singer. However, the real issues in the film relate to large-scale social problems such as unemployment and urbanisation. This was 1967, the year of the World Exhibition and the construction of the Montréal underground. Unemployment was rife: within a space of two months Claude has four different menial jobs – in an abattoir, on a construction site, as a cess-pool emptier, then a liftboy – ending up unemployed, while Geneviève needs to work in order to make ends meet. It was also the period of the Laurendeau-Dunton report on the economic inferiority of French Canadians, many of whom were nevertheless hoping to see the establishment of a Québec nation.

A discourse of independence underlies the film: 'I suppose you are French Canadian', an American asks Claude, but then, referring to independence, adds, 'but you'll never make it'. Claude Tremblay's success has socio-political importance. He has no say in what happens in his country, he feels like an immigrant in the city and suffers because he cannot speak English. Through the story of this 'immigrant', who becomes a successful singer, Brault literally lends a voice to the people who have no say in the running of their country.

Like cinema, the *chanson* has contributed to the spreading of an awareness of Québécois identity through the songs themselves and through the popular success of their singers. When interviewed during the TéléMétropole competition, Claude Tremblay introduces himself as being 'of Québécois-French nationality and proud of his soul'. If Brault's film is a success story, it is even more an expression of the transition from rural, traditional Québec to urban life in an expanding city, a new kind of film-making and the modern notion of Québécois identity.

Les Ordres (1974)

Les Ordres (Orders) evokes the October events of 1970, when a British diplomat and a member of the provincial government were kidnapped by members of the FLQ. In reaction to the kidnapping, the federal government implemented the War Measures act, allowing the police to arrest on suspicion any person who might possibly be linked with any of the 'illegal associations' that might have been involved with the kidnapping. On the night of 16 October nearly 500 people were arrested. In order to write his script, Brault interviewed some fifty of them, who reported to him in detail what happened. He then built his script on five of these people: a factory worker who belonged to a union, his wife, a social worker, a politically active unemployed father and a socialist doctor. The film uses a novel technique. The five people first identify themselves as they are in real life, then state who they are in the film in which, under fictional names, they enact what happened to them. This stylistic procedure, as film-maker Claude Jutra writes, 'insists on separating fact and fiction, but inverting our expectations. The actors project themselves as vehicles of the illusory, even though the events that they enact are true and take place in reality' (*Copie Zéro* 1980: 22, trans.).

Whereas Brault's earlier films captured Québec and its traditions, this one takes a political stance denouncing the authorities who so openly suspend the rights of people. The arrests are made with the utmost brutality, without any justification other than *les ordres*. The sequences of the five people in prison reveal the psychological abuse they received, aimed at eradicating any form of political action. To give but one example,

6 Michel Brault, *Les Ordres.*

Richard, the unemployed father, is told that he will be executed in three days. When the day arrives he is marched through endless corridors, then told to walk to the end of a dark area where he will be shot. A blank bullet is fired and the petrified Richard loses consciousness and collapses at the sound of the shot.

Prior to revealing the five people in prison, the film captures them at the moment of their arrest, the unemployed father changing the baby, the workman and his wife having to leave their young children unattended and the doctor leaving his wife in the last stage of her pregnancy. Yet, there is no melodrama in this film; the characters move with lucidity and detachment from their fictional characters to their real selves and, having enacted their characters, reflect upon the emotions and the anguish they have experienced. Their talking to the camera/viewer under their real identity has the effect of placing the viewer in a position of judgement, while the narrative structure also calls for a dual identification with these people/characters, who have endured such an ordeal. The length of their incarceration varied from six to twenty-one days. All were released without charge; they had been arrested because of *les ordres.*

No one takes responsibility, but the film closes suggesting that these authorities have been put in place by a system of democratic elections and that, therefore, there is a collective responsibility.

The film did indeed leave Québécois viewers with a feeling of unease. When it was awarded the prize for best direction (*réalisation*) at the Cannes Film Festival and the world hailed its great Québécois director, in his own country, Claude Jutra writes, they really did not want to know. As he points out, the essence of Michel Brault 'is to assert his Québec identity. It is this passion that pervades his every move, every film he makes' (Jutra 1980: 22, trans.).

Pierre Perrault

Pierre Perrault is at the heart of Québec's *cinéma direct* movement. Committed to capturing real life, he relentlessly travels with his camera throughout Québec, exploring his country and its people. His television series, *Au Pays de Neufve-France* (*In the Land of New France*), which grew out of his earlier radio programmes, was a voyage of discovery resembling the journey undertaken by French navigator Jacques Cartier more than three centuries earlier. Where Cartier's ambition was geographical, Perrault's is anthropological: he wants to discover people in their own environment and is preoccupied with the drives that compel them to work, survive, remember the past and relate to the environment around them. The *Au Pays de Neufve-France* series, consisting of thirteen instalments of 30 minutes, made in collaboration with the French editor-director, René Bonnière, revealed Perrault's ambition of portraying the authentic Québec. Its success was such that it prompted the ONF/NFB to ask Perrault to make a film about the inhabitants of L'Ile-aux-Coudres. That film, *Pour la suite du monde*, made in collaboration with Michel Brault in 1963, has become a classic of Québec's *cinéma direct*.

Perrault's aspiration to capture reality underlies his exploration of Québec, the land, its people and their traditions, especially those threatened with extinction. He observes people's daily lives, listens to them talking and records their voices and stories, so much so that he is often referred to as *le cinéaste de la parole* – the film-maker of the spoken word. Perrault pursued his anthropological journeys throughout the 1960s. He refers to these films as 'leafing through the family album', using the family metaphor to refer to the Québec nation and its link with France, as in *Le Règne du jour* (1966) in which he filmed the Tremblay family's trip to France, a return to their origins.

These films of the 1960s remain documents of primary importance for anthropologists, sociologists and film enthusiasts. All made in collaboration with colleagues, they offer an insight into the many aspects of traditional Québec culture and society: the importance of nature and of religious and mythical values, the heritage of art and crafts and the significance of festivals and celebrations. A wealth of material emerges from Perrault's patient recording and observing. Attention to the details of words and signs creates a world on screen that he wishes to preserve.

In the early 1970s Perrault's attention shifted to the theme of nationalism. In *L'Acadie, l'Acadie* (1971), the name of the lost land of the Acadians, for example, he captured the increasing linguistic awareness expressed in the student revolt at the university in Moncton, New Brunswick. A similar theme runs through the cycle of films about Abitibi, in which he celebrates the people who settled in the region in the 1930s and engaged in a struggle for their 'kingdom'. This nationalist theme emphasises the link between people and the land they inhabit and recurs some years later with *La Grande Allure* (1986). For this film Perrault and several travelling companions, including the French philosopher Michel Serres and the poet Michel Garneau, sailed from Saint Malo to Québec City. The film considers the importance of Cartier's discovery of the country and the legitimate claims this entailed for the settlers. As Pierre Barette argues, *La Grande Allure* may be one of the least political of Perrault's films, but it is one in which the nationalist claim to the land is expressed most clearly (Barette 1999: 8).

Of the films made in the 1980s the most memorable is *La Bête lumineuse* (1982 – *The Shimmering Beast*), a documentary in which a number of men from different socio-economic backgrounds gather in the Maniwaki region of Québec to hunt the *orignal* or Canadian elk. The hunting party seems to provide a pretext for these men to measure and affirm their virility through vulgarity, swearing, alcohol and masculine rituals. While ostensibly hunting the elk, these merciless men are also on the scent of a human victim in their own group: the poet among them soon becomes a scapegoat. Through the savagery he shows and the flood of verbal vulgarities he records, Perrault tries to grasp the character of the Québécois men.

In the large corpus of Perrault's films, two are particularly relevant for an understanding of Perrault's search for Québec identity: *Pour la suite du monde* and *Le Règne du jour*. In both films his characters are Québécois people who recreate an event for anthropological documentation.

Pour la suite du monde (1963)

Pour la suite du monde (*For Those Who Will Follow*) was the first Canadian film to be entered into competition at the Cannes Film Festival. It is a reconstruction of a fishing method used by the inhabitants of L'Ile-aux-Coudres to capture porpoises in the St Lawrence river. When the film was made porpoises had not been caught for years, but Perrault persuades the old fishermen to go on a porpoise-catching expedition once again.

Perrault succeeds in awakening the old fishermen's enthusiasm for this project.

The film opens with a reference to Jacques Cartier, who discovered the island of L'Ile-aux-Coudres in 1534: Cartier's description of the island is accompanied by tracking shots of snow-covered landscapes. The film then shifts to the islanders and their deliberations concerning the fishing expedition. Only a few old people remember porpoise fishing, last practised more than fifty years before, when it was a well-organised cooperative operation in which thirty-two individuals owned shares to the fishing rights in the St Lawrence river. Close-ups of the faces of old men who might still remember the fishing give an aura of authenticity, as do the activities and customs shown – such as religious processions and festivals – and the discussions recorded.

The island's daily routine is interrupted by the anticipation of this unusual event, which the younger people had never seen. The islanders' decision to go ahead with it is, they state, 'pour la suite du monde' ('so that the world goes on') – and also so that the young people can see in action the method devised by the old people. As they await the spring when the expedition will take place, the religious calendar continues to punctuate most of the islanders' social activities – all are related to religious celebrations. Finally spring comes, the event takes place and is filmed in detail. The images of fishing boats on the river and poles placed in the water, accompanied by folk music, are imbued with unusual poetry and leave a lasting impression on the viewer. When finally the gleaming white porpoise comes into view, the islanders are ecstatic. A thirty-eight-year-old man, who has never seen such an animal, declares that it must come from paradise. Having succeeded in bringing the porpoise aboard, they take it to the aquarium in New York.

One of the fishermen, specifically identified, is Alexis Tremblay, descendent of Léopold Tremblay, who was merchant and president of the New Society for porpoise fishing. In Perrault's 'family album' the Tremblays play a prominent part, as is seen in the sequel to this film, *Le Règne du jour*.

Le Règne du jour (1966)

The tracing of the past is pursued in a more explicit manner in *Le Règne du jour*, a film which Perrault made in collaboration with Bernard Gosselin and Jean-Claude Labrecque. Seventy-nine-year-old Alex Tremblay and his wife Marie, aged seventy-six, travel to France in order to trace their ancestors, in particular Pierre Tremblay, who emigrated to Québec and became the founder of the largest French family in Canada. Proud of the spreading of the Tremblays, Alexis mentions several times that he and his wife have sixteen children, seventy-two grandchildren and seven great grandchildren. Again, this is not a spontaneous journey the

Tremblays would have undertaken, but one suggested for the purpose of the film.

Alexis Tremblay becomes genuinely involved in what was initially the film-maker's suggestion. On the journey out he talks about France and Normandy, where the Tremblays come from, as the 'cradle of his ancestors'. It is a slow and moving discovery of a place Alexis Tremblay has heard and fantasised about. The film shows the couple meeting people, among them Françoise Montagne, who has written a book about the emigration to Canada from Perche, the Tremblays' region. Here too, Perrault captures festivals, customs and traditions. Human's fascination with the killing of animals, which will become dominant in *La Bête lumineuse*, is apparent here in the sequence showing the killing of a young pig during an annual event, *la fête du cochon* (the festival of the pig).

When the Tremblays go to church, 'less full than it used to be', the *curé* gives them a public welcome and praises the family that went to Canada but kept their attachment to France and to the faith of their ancestors. They are shown authentic documents relating to the Tremblays and taken to a farm that once belonged to the family. The woman who owns the farm now has little knowledge of its past occupants and certainly cannot testify to Pierre Tremblay's being born there. However, Alexis Tremblay, in a moment of spiritual affinity and deep emotion, feels with certainty that this is his ancestor's birthplace.

In the course of their journey the Québécois Tremblays encounter many different aspects of life in France, and in particular Normandy, including the impact of the war, class distinctions – those who emigrated were the workers, the people from the country – the work patterns on the farm and the changing attitudes of modern young people. Most of all a multitude of stories is told revealing the importance of Québec's oral tradition. The criss-cross talking of people telling stories, explaining, asking questions or making comments is so overwhelming that a great deal of what is said is lost. Before the Tremblays leave, the search for the real founding father reaches its climax with a visit to the Jacques Cartier museum and Tremblay's admiration for a model of Cartier's sailing boat.

Eventually they return home. Marie resumes her usual tasks and is often seen spinning and weaving. She was not born a Tremblay but, having been married to one for fifty-six years, she has come to empathise deeply with her husband without, however, giving up her independence of thought. She contradicts her husband's opinions several times in the film. The portrayal of this very united couple gives a special dimension to this film. There are hardly any women in Perrault's oeuvre and, of those there are, Marie Tremblay is the only one who is given any importance.

Although these two films belong to *cinéma direct*, Perrault preferred the term *cinéma vécu*, which implies the participation of the film-maker in what he is filming. His aim was to undertake a quest for Québécois identity that was free from fictionalising. The films depict events that have been staged, not in the sense of there being a complete pre-written script, but where the events – the porpoise fishing and the journey to France – have been instigated for the purpose of the film. This approach does not take away all spontaneity, since events develop naturally once a process has been triggered off. Nevertheless, many film critics question the authenticity of Perrault's *cinéma direct*. Yves Lever, for example, draws attention to the fact that it abounds in imaginative devices: the choice of decor, the *mise en situation* (staging of the event), editing styles and verbal or musical commentaries (Lever 1986: 36). The film *L'Acadie, l'Acadie* is, therefore, a more authentic document and a genuine *cinéma direct* experience, since the event was a genuine student demonstration not instigated by the film-maker.

What transpires in all of Perrault's films is a magnified belief in the possibility of capturing a Québécois identity. For Perrault, Québécois people are people whose tradition is oral, people who remember. In this respect, the discovery of the unforgettable Alexis and Marie Tremblay was most fortunate. They embody the two fundamental values of Perrault's cinema, the spoken word and memory. They are genuine people, proud of their French background and Norman ancestry, proud of the Tremblays' contribution to the human race. They believe in familial values, religion, a work ethic and tradition, as shown for example in Marie's spinning, spooling and weaving.

However, it also emerges from Tremblay's account of his beliefs about his origins that, while Perrault declares an aversion to fiction, Tremblay's account is based on fantasy. As philosopher Gilles Deleuze writes about Perrault: 'What cinema must capture is not the identity of a character, whether real or fictitious, through objective of subjective aspects; it is the development of a real person when he begins to "fictionalise", when he is caught in the act of creating a legend and thus contributes to the invention of his people' (Deleuze 1985: 196, trans.). Ultimately then, Perrault's *cinéma vécu* may signify being present when a character contributes, through his memory and fantasy, to the creation of his own origins and identity.

But there is another side to Perrault's Québécois character and that is the macho man, the hunter, the one who subjects animals to his power and kills them, the primitive man to whom the fisherman in *Pour la suite du monde* also compared himself when he revelled in repeating that primitive act.

Above all, there is also a very concrete and more political struggle for identity. Perrault did not cut the remark made by the French people the

Tremblays met on the boat on their way to France: after Alexis Tremblay's proud statement that he was returning to the 'cradle of his ancestors', a French woman adds: 'But the French abandoned you', suggesting the metaphor of the abandoned child. Perrault's quest for Québécois identity, expressed in his recapturing of lost traditions and search for origins, amounts to an ongoing fantasising about identity. Perrault's comparison between hunting and film-making is telling in this respect, since it leads him to state that, in the end, there may be no animal at all: 'When I make a film, I enjoy all the thrill of the hunt . . . There are tracks to follow . . . everything I do is determined by these tracks . . . At the end, there may be a creature to be caught, or there may not' (Lever 1995b: 486, trans.).

Gilles Groulx

Gilles Groulx entered cinema when he co-directed the earlier mentioned *Les Raquetteurs* with Michel Brault, which heralded the beginnings of Francophone cinema at the ONF/NFB. Groulx's editing of the film gives it a playful dimension. No effort is made to include only the best shots; instead, Groulx attempts to keep the spontaneity that inspired Brault's camera work. This concern with the authenticity of events also characterises Groulx's twenty-two-minute documentary, *Golden Gloves*.

Golden Gloves (1961)
The film opens with shots of boxers practising while a narrator reads the rules of the Golden Gloves competition for amateurs, which precedes entry to professional boxing. This early film reveals Groulx's ease with both camera work and editing. He carefully observes the movements of the two adversaries, Ronald Jones and Georges Thibault, from multiple angles alternating close-ups of boxers and spectators. He is clearly interested in boxing as a sport, but also emphasises its social context by getting to know the boxers as people – Thibault is a French-speaking Canadian, who works as a waiter in a bar, and Ronald Jones a young, black, unemployed Anglophone from a working-class family. Through Jones, Groulx draws attention to the plight of the black Anglophones in Montréal, who are at a disadvantage, not only because they are black but also because they don't speak French, and to the fascination that boxing exerts on the underprivileged. For them, the dream of attaining a more glorious future through boxing answers the need for recognition in a society that ignores them.

Le Chat dans le sac (1964)
Groulx's first feature film, *Le Chat dans le sac* (*The Cat in the Bag*), deals directly with the identity problems of young people in Québec in 1964.

The film, in a style reminiscent of Godard, portrays a couple, Barbara and Claude, who engage in interminable conversations and reflections on who they are, what they are searching for and how they think and feel. They have long discussions about life, love, society, feminism and nationalism, approached mainly from a totally subjective point of view, with only a few references to books. The search for the self preoccupies the characters so fully that their relationship is bound to end.

The film opens with the two protagonists introducing themselves directly to the camera/viewer. Barbara, looking like Godard's famous actress Anna Karina, is 'Jewish Anglophone and wants to be intellectual'; Claude is 'French Canadian and therefore seeking himself and in need of equilibrium'. He announces that the society portrayed in the film does not offer him what he needs in order to live his life. So, he concludes, 'I must find certain truths in myself. I am like *le chat dans le sac.*'

He has decided to work for a newspaper, because in that way, he thought, he would really be able to express himself. But when his articles are scrutinised, he has to contend with the criticism that they apply only to him and not to society in general. The words and thoughts of both characters concern mainly their own selves. 'Have I changed since I met Claude?', Barbara wonders. As she thinks about herself she makes vague plans for the future – 'I feel attracted by ethnic groups' – and she also wishes to go to Paris. 'Anyone learning French wishes to go to Paris', Claude retorts. He, too, is dissatisfied and feels he is not leading a real life.

As they try to find their place in society, they drift further and further apart. He questions Barbara's unfounded assumption that man is superior, the only reason she can give to substantiate her comment is simply 'because he is a man'. Torn between inherited principles and vague dreams about the future, they seem trapped. 'I have no ambition', Claude admits and they go on discussing themselves as the camera tracks across the table to capture first one then the other, endlessly speaking to each other without ever communicating. Not so much disillusioned as brooding and sulky, they seem far removed from any revolution. 'Journalists are not supposed to communicate revolt', states Claude the apprentice, a comment with which his colleague disagrees. Little by little each becomes disillusioned with the other's discourse about the self.

This film is set at the time of Québec's Quiet Revolution, which introduced much-awaited changes after the reactionary Duplessis government. But in *Le Chat dans le sac*, the couple's only struggle seems to be that of the search for themselves. As Yves Lever puts it, they live in 'sterile opposition' (*contestation stérile*) (Lever 1995a: 75). While Québec was finding a new identity for itself in the 1960s, the people Groulx portrays seem unable to establish theirs.

Au Pays de Zom (1982)

Au Pays de Zom (*In the Country of Zom*) takes Groulx away from *cinéma direct*, although the film is no less a social critique of an affluent bourgeoisie. Adopting the genre of opera, it is an ironic, lyrical fable, often falling into caricature: a bold film in which Groulx freely experiments with style, tone and *mise en scène*. It depicts the life of Monsieur Zom, a wealthy businessman with pretensions of being an art connoisseur, who sets himself up as a spokesman for the people. He reflects on his life, on society, on his feelings of guilt for not intervening sufficiently when public decency is lacking, but he takes heart at the thought that private schools are thriving. Monsieur Zom touches on many social and religious values, upholds tradition and denigrates the marginals and those infiltrators who poison society. In short, he represents religious, capitalist Québécois man, whose hypocrisy Groulx exposes through caricature. The experimental style of the film reflects Groulx's relentless search for a personal film language, which he uses to give an acerbic social critique of righteous Québec society.

Claude Jutra

A memory recorded by Michel Brault reveals Claude Jutra's early passion for cinema. At his boarding school Jutra would walk everywhere with a camera, taking photographs and experimenting with various kinds of shots (*Copie Zéro* 1980: 5). Brault spent many holidays with the Jutra family and remembers with fondness their precious years of 'cinematographic ebullience'.

The first contact with the ONF/NFB was an unhappy one for both filmmakers. The main problem was the preponderance of English-speaking technicians; for example, there was only one French-speaking cameraman. For his film about musical youth programmes, Jutra was assigned an English-speaking cameraman and, Brault recalls, 'it was hell for him'. According to Brault, the entire camera department was not only Anglophone but also Francophobe. However, ONF/NFB policy was to change and both Brault and Jutra benefited from this, though not continuously.

The film that brought fame to Jutra was *A tout prendre* (1963), which is regarded as the first feature-length film of *cinéma direct*. It is dedicated to two of his mentors, Norman McLaren and Jean Rouch. With McLaren he made a near-surreal short film, *Chairy Tale* (1957), in which the protagonist, played by Jutra, is engaged in a struggle with a recalcitrant chair. The theme of the power struggle between the chair and the actor who wants to use the chair is developed with great originality and technical dexterity. Jutra had worked with Jean Rouch on a project on Niger, *Le Niger, jeune république* (1961 – *Niger, the Young Republic*), which Jutra ended up making by himself, including the editing. In the film he endeavours to explore a new style of narration through the introduction of a commentary in the first person. Preceding and anticipating *A tout prendre* were two further short films, made in collaboration with Brault, *Québec U.S.A. ou l'invasion pacifique* (1962 – *Québec USA or the Peaceful Invasion*), an imaginative and ironic film about the invasion of Québec by American tourists, and *Les Enfants du silence* (1962 – *The Children of Silence*) which, using *cinéma direct*, sensitively deals with the plight of children who are hard of hearing.

Both these films are attempts on the part of Jutra to develop his own style and establish his own identity in Québécois film. *A tout prendre* is the moment of celebration in this search.

A tout prendre (1963)

The film tells the love story of Claude, a thirty-year-old film-maker, and Johanne, a black model; he is a bachelor, she is married and has a child. On seeing her one evening at a party, he falls in love. Their relationship develops until Johanne first makes Claude aware of his homosexual tendencies and then becomes pregnant. After breaking off the relationship and borrowing the money for Johanne's abortion, Claude disappears without telling Johanne where he has gone. In the Québec of 1963 to deal with homosexuality and abortion was an act of daring. Equally daring was the filming itself.

The *mise en abyme* created by making a film in which the main character and narrator is a young film-maker lends itself to experimentation. This is indeed an avant-garde film in which one recognises the stylistic influence of Godard: intersecting narratives and narrative voices, the abrupt launching of the story, syncopated editing, the blurring and freezing of images and interpolated photos or stills.

A playful, experimental style dominates the film and has been seen as the mark of an amateur or a newcomer to cinema. Rather than the result of inexperience or lack of proper equipment though, the film is a kind of indulgent exercise by a film-maker wanting freedom of expression in order to find himself, in the same way that the character in the film apparently sheds inherited bourgeois values by falling in love and having a relationship with a married black woman with a child and condoning abortion. If Jutra breaks with cinematographic conventions, Claude breaks with social and moral ones.

The film is seen almost exclusively from Claude's point of view. Claude mirrors the power of Jutra and is free to step in or out of the story and address the viewer, as he does at one point stating: 'For a good understanding of the narrative, I must introduce some facts.' He can call forth African images and music when imagining Johanne's African background. Since the voice-over is entirely his, Johanne's thoughts and feelings remain unknown.

Nevertheless, she displays remarkable insight, when she uncovers his homosexuality and also when she guesses his thoughts and loss of feelings, which are communicated only to the viewer. Early on in the film it seemed that she might have a voice when, at the beginning of their relationship, Claude says he wants to know everything about her. As she tries to convey her past – she was an orphan and there was an attempt to find black parents to adopt her – she struggles against the emotions this confession provokes and expresses her desire to be able 'to identify with something such as . . .', but before she finishes her thought, Claude has already cut her off by saying 'Really?' and has stopped listening.

Claude's power as protagonist in a love story, narrator and film-maker is almost absolute. When Johanne is pregnant he very briefly contemplates marriage, issues her with a list of his requirements – to leave him free to come and go as he wishes and not even be faithful – and she complies with them all. But she is dismissed anyway, with a payment of $200 for the abortion. As he walks out of her life, her pain erupts, but Claude has no awareness of it.

Black people are rare in Québécois cinema and in Québécois society. Johanne may have succeeded in entering Claude's life temporarily, but she is expelled from it. Claude's father warns his son that the pregnancy might be a 'lure on her part to penetrate your social milieu'. For him women are 'crafty and covetous', while Claude defines them as 'men without a tail and a head'. Gaining little respect as a woman, she gains even less as a black woman. The only identity she is entitled to is that of an immigrant, even in her love relationship. She is expelled for no other reason than the whim of the white, bourgeois Québécois.

Ultimately then Claude, the character who wants to find himself and rejects social and moral conventionality, displays a total lack of awareness of both gender and racial politics: the issues facing his black, pregnant girlfriend do not concern him. While Jutra invites spectator identification with Claude, he exposes him to criticism for his a-political, self-centred attitude. At the end of the film, the graffiti 'Québec libre' appears as a reminder of another ignored socio-political reality.

Mon Oncle Antoine (1971)

Mon Oncle Antoine (*My Uncle Antoine*), voted in 1984 by a group of some hundred professionals as the best Canadian film ever made, remains Québec's best known film. For Ian Lockerbie, it is 'the seminal film in Québécois cinema' ('l'oeuvre fondatrice du cinéma québécois') while for Yves Lever, the accurate portrayal of Duplessis' Québec is the film's most important asset (Lockerbie 1996: 46 and Lever 1995a: 162). The possessive pronoun in the title 'mon' (my) reveals the film's point of view, that of Oncle Antoine's nephew, Benoît. Oncle Antoine and his wife, Cécile, run the general store in the village and also provide a burial service with their assistant Fernand. They are childless, but care for their nephew Benoît and a young girl, Carmen. The film opens with a winter landscape in a mining village as backdrop to the legend: 'In the Québec asbestos region not so long ago'. The following two juxtaposed sequences introduce the two narrative strands of the film, one concerning a mining family, the Poulins, the other Oncle Antoine's shop, which is the heart of the village community.

The Poulins' story opens with Jos Poulin, the father, repairing one of the mine's badly maintained trucks at the top of the road. The English-speaking boss drives up and tells him off for parking dangerously near to the edge of a ravine. Although he does not know any English, Poulin does not fail to understand the boss's anger, nor does he hide his unspoken feelings of resentment. He decides to quit his job in the mine and go to find work as a lumberjack. The second strand of the film begins with the funeral of Euclid, one of the older villagers, organised by Oncle Antoine and Fernand and observed by Benoît, who is also an altar boy.

The Poulins represent Québécois family life, while Oncle Antoine's shop represents Québec's village life. The Poulins are a loving couple who work hard in order to bring up their five children. The father's decision to escape from the authority of the English-speaking boss and leave his family to find work elsewhere is tantamount to an abdication of paternal responsibility and draws attention from the outset to the ambiguity that surrounds fatherhood in the film. The film's cross-cutting from the mother to the distant father emphasises the awareness of his absence. At one point Poulin is seen chopping down a big tree in the forest, then the film cuts to the mother chopping down a small pine tree for Christmas. As she is doing this, she is called home to her oldest child, Marcel, who has fallen dangerously ill and who dies just before Christmas. In the absence of her husband, Mme Poulin telephones Oncle Antoine to take care of the burial arrangements. Benoît obtains permission to accompany his uncle to the isolated farm where he witnesses the family's grief.

From the death of the adult villager, Euclid, at the beginning of the film to that of the young Marcel Poulin, close to his own age, Benoît unknowingly undergoes a process of initiation that takes him from childhood to the threshold of adulthood.

A reflective mood characterises Benoît throughout the film, but from early on observation is accompanied by a sense of responsibility. This is seen in the funeral sequence, where he tells Fernand to adjust his tie, and later in the shop when he tells him off for not greeting him properly. It is clear that Benoît is not only developing a moral awareness, he is also showing a sense of responsibility which is lacking in many adults. This is particularly the case when, returning from the Poulins, he scolds his Oncle Antoine for his drunkenness, then discovers Tante Cécile's adultery with Fernand.

While two oppressive sources of male authority rule the village – the mine owner, who pays his workers too little, and the parish priest, who succeeds in obtaining offerings from the villagers and payments to say mass for the dead – the family lacks, as represented in the film, a reliable father figure: the father in the Poulin family is absent and the father substitute, the oldest son, dies; Benoît's father is never mentioned; Oncle Antoine, though kind, is an inveterate drinker; Fernand, who could be a father himself, seems to have little inclination to take on such responsibility; and Carmen's father, appearing only once with the sole aim of collecting the money she has earned, shows not the least interest in or fondness for his daughter.

Benoît comes to the end of his initiation when he has to return with Fernand to try and find the coffin that had fallen off Antoine's sled and which had been left behind on the road because Antoine was too drunk to help Benoît lift it on again. Benoît is not sure of the way and the coffin is nowhere to be seen. When they finally reach the Poulin house, they find that Jos Poulin has returned and the coffin has been carried back to the family. Earlier, Benoît had accompanied his uncle to the house to collect Marcel's body. This time he is outside the house, looking in through the window at the Poulin family united around Marcel's open coffin, the father grieving over the death of his son. Benoît's little mischievous face which observed the funeral of Euclid has now become the face of a young boy on the threshold of adulthood.

The film portrays a Québec that has lost a sense of purpose. All Poulin can think of is leaving and, in a way, abdicating his familial responsibilities, while Oncle Antoine, who wanted to buy a hotel in the States, complains of leading a meaningless life, especially since, as he admits to Benoît, he is terrified of corpses. But through observation and reflection, Benoît learns to judge what is good and what is not, what is admirable or of value. His decisive reactions on seeing people act against the moral principles they supposedly uphold reveal a young man who might contribute to creating a new identity for Québec.

Kamouraska (1973)

After the success of *Mon Oncle Antoine*, Jutra became an internationally acclaimed film-maker for whom it was no longer difficult to attract film finance. The well-established Québécois producer, Pierre Lamy, approached Jutra to make a film, *Kamouraska*, based on the Québécois writer Anne Hébert's best-known novel by the same name. Lamy found substantial finance for a co-production with France. The fact that this new project had a Québécois subject was more important to Jutra than the fact that it was an international film. The love story the film depicts could be located anywhere, but if it had happened elsewhere, Jutra has said, he would not have made the film (Jutra 1973: 19).

Changes are often imposed in co-productions and the film can lose its coherence. In this case, the final version of the film was considered too long by the French co-producer, who requested a re-edit. This tampering with the ending may well have contributed to some weakness in psychological credibility. The film failed to attract the same success or critical acclaim as *Mon Oncle Antoine*, in spite of the presence of the very talented actors, Geneviève Bujold and Philippe Léotard. The film depicts a powerful triangular passion in which Elisabeth d'Aulnières, married to Antoine Tassy, seigneur of Kamouraska, falls in love with an American, Dr Nelson. Although the love story and its dramatic development – Dr Nelson kills the husband – elicited interesting performances from Bujold and Léotard, the representation of Antoine as the father highlights yet again the ambiguity surrounding father figures in Québec: in this case, the father is a womaniser and an irresponsible drunk who is abusive to his wife. One particular sequence in the film encapsulates this kind of fatherhood. Elisabeth has given birth to their son and Antoine is, as usual, nowhere around. When the people gather for the christening, Antoine, drunk and abusive and looking wild in his big, fur coat, suddenly and spectacularly erupts on to the scene, to lay claim to his son. In *Kamouraska* male coarseness, the abuse of women and domination by

7 Claude Jutra, *Kamouraska*. The fatherhood of Antoine.

the absent yet tyrannical father represent the tragedy of the father's destructive impact on the family.

Gilles Carle

With a film-maker like Gilles Carle, who is an amusing storyteller, one might tend to forget the extent to which religion underpins the society he depicts and the individual characters he creates. In an interview with Jean-Pierre Tadros for *Cinéma Québec*, Carle explains to what extent religion has remained a major cornerstone of Québécois identity. '[I] have received all these religious ideas. I wanted my children to receive them because I believe that they are an important aspect of Québec.' And he goes on to say that, 'like all Québécois, I have undergone all the assaults of religion. I carry its traces in me; I do not want to hide or to disguise them' (Tadros 1972: 18, trans.).

To see only the religious underpinning of Carle's films would not do justice to his versatility. But when attempting to comprehend how film contributes to creating or reinforcing a Québécois identity, an exploration of the prominence of religion in his films exposes the indelible impact of the Catholic church. Religious traditions and beliefs inevitably play an important part in the shaping of people's identities and behaviour, but while they may constitute a valuable cultural heritage, the powerful words Carle uses to designate their impact include assault and religious alienation. A selection of four of his films, spanning a period of nearly twenty years, *La Vie heureuse de Léopold Z* (1965), *La Vraie nature de Bernadette* (1972), *L'Age de la machinfte* (1978) and *Maria Chapdelaine* (1983), reveals this religious persistence. Two of the four films, *La Vie heureuse de Léopold Z* and *L'Age de la machinfte* unfold against the background of the Christmas tradition while *La Vraie nature de Bernadette* and *Maria Chapdelaine* deal with the belief in sainthood.

Carle, the storyteller, has a sense of humour, and the religious themes are developed in a witty fashion and are linked in an original way to the specific personality of the characters. In a 1966 interview for *Objectif*, quoted by Yves Lever, Carle expresses the importance of casting characters that do not elicit full identification from the viewer. The public, he states 'does not always want to recognise the same facet of itself' (Lever 1995b: 211, trans.). Indeed, Carle's characters behave in surprising ways and, therefore, require the viewer to remain somewhat detached.

La Vie heureuse de Léopold Z (1965)

La Vie heureuse de Léopold Z (*The Merry World of Leopold Z*) was intended to be a documentary on a snow-plough operator, but it developed into Carle's first full-length feature film. It heralded a new tone in Québec cinema, which Marcel Jean describes as that of 'a storyteller who is able to look at society with fond amusement' (Jean 1991: 63, trans.).

It is an amusing film, where a series of funny anecdotes, skilfully edited by Werner Nold, reveal many of the ways in which Québécois men seek to affirm themselves. The snow-plough operator, Léopold Tremblay, is clearing the snow on Christmas Eve in Montréal. Not only does he have to cope with the emergency of a snowstorm, he also has to buy Christmas presents for his wife and son Jacques, collect a cousin, Josette, from the station, and help his supervisor and friend, Théophile Lemay, move his furniture, before going to midnight mass where his son is singing in the choir.

The film opens playfully with a documentary approach, exaggerating details that establish the identity of the city and the character. Not only is Montréal shown prominently in the film, but cousin Josette is also given a tour of the city. Details about the character include his precise address, the price of his house and the amount in his bank account. Léopold also seeks to affirm himself by trying out several signatures for Léopold Tremblay. Dissatisfied with all of them, he adds the distinctive feature of a 'Z', the first letter of his middle name, abandoning his distinctive French last name for a very non-French consonant. In all his films Carle attaches great importance to names and the Z that Léopold adopts, says the film-maker, is a means 'to valorise himself' (Tadros 1972: 18).

Léopold Z is a happy man: he loves his wife and son, and his job allows him to live in reasonable comfort, although he has to borrow money from the bank in order to buy a fur coat for his wife. Before returning home he spends time with his friend, Théophile, who gives Léopold his opinion on man's identity: a man does not have the right to live in a situation of inferiority, Léopold must assert himself, in marriage the man must dominate and be like General de Gaulle, who has obtained 75 per cent of the French vote. Yet Léopold is satisfied with his life, and whether his wife dominates him or not seems of little importance to him. After an evening with Théophile, he arrives just in time at the packed church, where his wife has kept a seat for him. He places the fur coat over the pew and the film closes showing the happy couple stroking the fur coat like a pet animal.

Léopold's search for identity ends with the introduction of the initial Z and his friend's words have little effect on him. Léopold Z, Yves Lever writes, has 'managed to devise for himself a life in keeping with his ambitions, which are not very great. He is probably', Lever continues, 'unaware that educated people are talking about a Quiet Revolution. It's his son who will reap the benefit' (Lever 1995a: 258, trans.).

La Vraie nature de Bernadette (1972)

In *La Vraie nature de Bernadette* (*The True Nature of Bernadette*), Bernadette Brown, née Bonheur (Happiness), a lawyer's wife, decides to leave her

8 Gilles Carle, *La Vraie nature de Bernadette*. Bernadette's back-to-nature move.

husband and the city and move to the countryside with her five-year-old son. Her relocation is a move back to nature. But before reaching her new home and village, the first of many obstacles confronts her when she finds the road blocked by a farmer, Thomas, in protest against food-processing monopolies. From the outset then, her lone back-to-nature movement unfolds against the background of Thomas's equally solitary political action.

Neither the roadblock nor the subsequent difficulties that await Bernadette crush her unfailing optimism and generosity. Her arrival in the large dilapidated house triggers both her energetic enthusiasm and the hospitality she extends to all in need – including an old man, a crippled young man and an abandoned, mute and paralysed child. All find a welcome and in one way or other contribute to creating Bernadette's 'family', in which she becomes not only the caring mother but also a willing provider of sexual favours to the needy old men.

The viewer cannot fail to see the religious parallels in the family structure: the three old men who come with presents and the three wise men who visit Jesus; or Marie-Madeleine, mother of the abandoned child, and the woman with the same name whom Jesus befriended. The latent religious themes come to the fore in Bernadette herself when the mute and paralysed child suddenly recovers his ability to walk and to speak and the news of a miracle spreads. Popular belief turns into veneration, projecting the identity of Bernadette Soubirous (St Bernadette of Lourdes), upon Bernadette Brown. Crowds of pilgrims descend upon the village. But the situation turns into a nightmare when two young men, who were earlier welcomed by Bernadette, turn out to be violent criminals. They steal all Bernadette's money and kill the crippled man. When Bernadette sees her crippled friend killed and her politically active neighbour Thomas attacked by pilgrims, she abandons her role as Bernadette Soubirous for a role reminiscent of Irish militant Bernadette Devlin. As Lever writes: 'Bernadette, nee Bonheur, then Brown through a Catholic marriage, will be taken for Bernadette Soubirous then for Bernadette Devlin, who is on the radio at the moment of the final demonstration' (Lever 1995a: 267, trans.). While these associations are not made in the film, the other Bernadettes would inevitably be familiar to Catholic Québécois audiences. In the final sequence, Bernadette joins Thomas's protest against the government's agricultural policies, grabs a gun and begins to shoot into the crowds, shattering her dream of a peaceful return to nature.

Although there is a well-developed narrative thread in the story, the film is composed of short sequences which often seem anecdotal but nevertheless fit into the saga of haphazard events in Bernadette's life, built on her naive belief in 'natural' values. Her seeking a new identity and lifestyle is based on the vague ideologies of the late 1960s and early 1970s, which advocated free, communal living and exalted the value of close contact with the earth. But the new life Bernadette chooses is based more on an emotional rejection of her bourgeois life than on a well-defined choice.

There is no clear Québec identity expressed in this film. Instead, fragments of identity are evoked, mimicked, referred to, made fun of, questioned, reversed or rejected. There is no interweaving of themes related to Québec society, only a build-up of many particles which lack ideological coherence. A spectrum of different ideologies, social dictates and government policies merge without ever integrating into a coherent vision. While denouncing many of Québécois society's afflictions, such as the religious bigotry, the collusion between the police and big business, the narrow-mindedness of many villagers and the hypocritical moral dictates that prevail, the film offers a playful, mocking spectacle of the inescapable presence and yet rejection of familiar Québécois themes and values infused with late 1960s and early 1970s ideas.

It is impossible, as Carle explains in an interview with Jean-Pierre Tadros, to take distance from Québec: '[I]f I try to deal with a subject, which has no relevance to Québec, life itself tends to eliminate it' (Tadros 1972: 19, trans.). But the most striking aspect of Québécois identity in this film is the inescapable religious foundation upon which both individual and collective identity rests. The religious dimension of the different characters in the film reaches further than the viewer might at first perceive. In this interview Carle himself makes it clear that the characters are incarnations of saints: the two thieves, he explains, are in fact St Luke and St Mark. What happens seems absurd, as these pleasant characters become killers. Carle admits that logically he should be able to explain this complete reversal from good to bad: but he refuses to do that. These two characters arrive in the film and occupy centre stage for ten minutes; the only way to explain the reversal, he concludes is 'a kind of moral misery' (Tadros 1972: 19). The main reality underlying each one of the characters, therefore, is their own profound internal contradiction.

L'Age de la machinʈe (1978)

While *La Vraie nature de Bernadette* is a very complex story, *L'Age de la machinʈe* (*The Age of the Machine*) has a moving simplicity. It tells the story of a policeman, Hervé Cantin, who on 24 December 1933 is sent to the Abitibi region (near the Ontario boarder) to fetch a female prisoner, the young orphan Claude Lachance. Caught in a snowstorm they spend Christmas with other travellers in the train station. One of their fellow-travellers, Octave Melançon, is a typewriter salesman through whom praise of 'the age of the machine' is introduced. While waiting for the weather to change, Claude practices typing on one of Octave's machines. The spelling of 'machinʈe' in the film's title reflects Claude's attempt to learn how to type. It is also the typewriter salesman who instigates the impromptu Christmas party, where an increasingly jolly Claude dances and celebrates as she had never done before and for the first time has the feeling of being part of a family with which she can identify. Rather than taking her to the police station in Montréal, Hervé takes her off to start a new life with him. He becomes a typewriter salesman, marries Claude and together they have three children.

This touching Christmas story is used to denounce social attitudes including the racism of the bus driver, the hypocrisy of the clergy and the incompetence of the police. It also gives an insight into many aspects of Abitibi society in the 1930s, such as the cost of living, migrant workers, Amerindians, illiteracy and prostitution. It is a tale that gives an insight into the mosaic of Québécois society in the 1930s rather than depicting the romanticised 'authentic' Québec past in which so many Québécois still believe.

Maria Chapdelaine (1983)

The story and character of *Maria Chapdelaine*, based on the novel written in 1916 by Louis Hémon, have often been seen as epitomising Québécois identity. Maria Chapdelaine stands for Québécois values: she is hard-working, religious and has an exemplary sense of duty. However, it is not so much the story that is relevant here but the illusory nature of the authenticity of this model, since the author was French and spent only a few months near Lac St Jean in New Brunswick. Yet the novel, for many years believed to be Canadian, continues to stimulate discussions and raise questions concerning collective identity (Laverdière 1983: 36). Hémon observed the land-clearers in Québec from a French point of view. His accurate and minute portrayal of mores and customs of the Québécois settlers was used as a comparison and contrast with the European way of life. While initially Hémon intended to offer an ethnographic study, he ultimately chose the novel form to depict the rigours of the lives of a French Canadian family in an isolated settlement.

According to film critic Suzanne Laverdière, Carle's *Maria Chapdelaine* hinges on the very question of identity: although Hémon was French, he seems to have grasped more fully than Carle the settlers' struggle with both the Indians and nature. Furthermore, she argues, Carle fails to show the role of religion, when in fact a trust in God was vital for these early settlers, whose daily lives were fraught with so many life-threatening dangers. It is particularly interesting that Carle's film is criticised for not sufficiently respecting Québécois identity, which the French author is regarded as having captured so much better (Laverdière 1983: 37).

Jean-Pierre Lefebvre

Unlike the film-makers who preceded him, Jean-Pierre Lefebvre did not start his career in documentary films or in *cinéma direct* but in film criticism and creative writing. His most popular film, *Les Dernières Fiançailles* (1973), brings an unexplored dimension to the notion of identity, that of the influence of love on the identity of a couple.

Les Dernières Fiançailles (1973)
Les Dernières Fiançailles (The Last Engagement) exemplifies what Lefebvre himself believes cinema should be: 'a sign and not a representation' (Coulombe & Jean 1991: 334). The film portrays a couple, Armand and Rose, who have been together for fifty years. They share everything and together they tend to their garden and house. The film captures the signs of their bond and their close affinity with each other. Rose prays never to be separated from Armand and, even when he has a heart attack, Armand refuses to go to the hospital, preferring to stay home with her. When Armand quietly dies, two small angels come and, taking Armand and Rose by the hand, carry them off to the life beyond, where they know they will be united for eternity, their *dernières fiançailles*.

9 Jean-Pierre Lefebvre, *Les Dernières Fiançailles*. Rose after the death of Armand.

Their life together with their emotions, beliefs, love and suffering – their only child was killed in the war – is expressed in their minute gestures, expressions, glances and sparse words. Everything reflects the fusion of these two people, who identify so strongly with each other that the death of one is also the death of the other.

Denys Arcand

Initially Denys Arcand belonged to the tradition of 1960s' documentaries, where the viewer could recognise the past depicted or re-created. Arcand began making films in 1962, while still a student of history at the University of Montréal. Following an early film on student life, he made three short documentaries: *Champlain* (1964), *Les Montréalistes* (1965) and *La Route de l'Ouest* (1965). They form a historical trilogy. The first gives an account of Samuel Champlain's military career and colonising expeditions in Canada; the second explores the difficult work of early pioneering women – the Montréalistes, as they called themselves – such as Jeanne Mance, who arrived in Québec with French aristocrat Maisonneuve and who contributed to the founding of the first Canadian hospital; the last film of the trilogy examines the arrival from the West of the early Amerindians and the discovery of the New World, from the Viking period around AD 880 up to Jacques Cartier.

These three films, made for the ONF/NFB, show how Arcand's film diverges from the mainstream Québécois documentary tradition. He does not draw upon recent Québec history, but delves into the events of a distant past and the lives of those who contributed to creating a French New World. In 1970 Arcand brought out a socio-political documentary on the textile industry, *On est au coton*, a controversial film whose release was banned by Sydney Newman, the recently appointed President and Commissioner of Cinematography of the ONF/NFB. This censorship reveals the political split at the ONF/NFB: Newman's policy was pro-Canadian and pro-capitalist; Arcand's film dealt with the politically sensitive issues of textile factory closures, working conditions in the factory and the illnesses these caused and the struggles and strikes of the workers. In that same year Newman also censored Gilles Groulx's film *24 heures ou plus* (*24 hours or more*), which offered a strong critique of consumer society.

As one might expect, the decisions of the censor encouraged solidarity among Québécois film-makers and had little effect upon independent-minded people like Arcand, a trained historian who by then had already acquired considerable skills as a film-maker. Arcand was to continue in the same militant vein in his nearly two-hour long documentary, *Québec: Duplessis et après . . .* (1972 – *Québec: Duplessis and After*). In it he drew a parallel between the electoral campaign of 1970 and that of Maurice Duplessis in 1936. Through skilful editing, the film combines real-life footage with historical documents and reflects on whether the Quiet Revolution really changed anything.

From his early historical films to those analysing social situations or present-day politics, Arcand has systematically tried to portray a full picture of how Québec has come to be what it is today. Arcand's combined interest in history and politics has contributed to his critical overview of what constitutes Québec. His own altercation with the Commissioner of the ONF/NFB over his film on the textile factory highlights the ideological divisions that beset not only that organisation but also Québec at large. The opposition to the inclusion of French-speaking Québécois film-makers on the National Film Board stimulated their solidarity and determination to assert a Québécois identity.

In his subsequent work, Arcand's film-making was to develop in an unexpected direction. He continued to set his films in Québec and to present Québec characters, but whereas in his earlier films he would juxtapose present-day Québec and a more remote past, now he began to evoke a past or an elsewhere unrelated to Québec. His 1973 *Réjeanne Padovani*, for example, begins with an actual instance of corruption, involving the construction of the motorway between Ville-Marie and Montréal.

At a dinner for VIPs, the motorway contractor, Vincent Padovani, learns of the return of his estranged wife, who had left him to marry a Jew. While continuing to entertain his guests, he arranges for her to be killed and her body moulded into the concrete of the motorway. It is a tragedy of corruption and, indeed, a link is evoked between this tragedy and that of Messalina, wife of the Roman emperor Claudius, who was executed by him when she was unfaithful (Jean 1991: 73). A similar historical link is established in Arcand's later film, *Le Confort et l'indifférence* (1981), where Machiavelli's *The Prince* is invoked to analyse the political games that took place during the 1980 referendum.

In these films, Arcand takes a twofold approach to Québec: he both exposes the many levels of corruption and deflects the notion of this being specific to Québec by establishing comparisons and references that show how prevalent corruption is. Arcand denounces the corruption but does not take a militant position: 'I'm not a militant film-maker because that implies that you know which direction society should be going in and, in the case of North American society, I've got no idea which way that society should be taken. A militant film-maker is someone who shows the way . . . my films are observations, observations of failure and alienation' (Arcand 1976: 21, trans.).

There is a deep pessimism here, and yet Arcand remains a Québécois film-maker who systematically locates his films in Québec, portrays Québec people and creates narrative situations which are exclusively Québécois. Even when he is deeply critical of that society, as in his main films, *Gina* (1975), *Le Déclin de l'empire américain* (1986) and *Jésus de Montréal* (1989), the systematic choice of Québec as the geographical point of reference must be seen as an ongoing questioning of Québec's identity as well as of his own.

Gina (1975)

The film's opening shows a station wagon with the caption 'Office National du Cinéma'. In 1975 Arcand's film about the textile industry, *On est au coton*, made for the ONF/NFB, immediately springs to mind, especially since at that time the ban placed on that film had not yet been lifted. The link becomes even more explicit when it appears that the subject of the ONF/NFB film to be shot within the film also deals with textile factories and will also be censored and its shooting stopped by ONF/NFB authorities.

The film relates the story of Gina, a dancer and striptease artist, who performs in the hotel Château Berthelet in Louiseville, where the ONF/ NFB film crew is also staying. Arcand uses cross-cutting, reminiscent of gangster movies or westerns, to great effect. This cross-cutting reveals the concurrence of events involving Gina and the film crew, but unlike in gangster movies they remain unrelated.

The main example of this is provided by the events following Gina's striptease performance. The members of the film crew and a factory worker, Dolorès, attend Gina's show. Afterwards, one member of the film crew withdraws to his room, where he reads and listens to classical music; Dolorès, accompanied home by the film director, tells of the violent 1952 strike during which the union's premises and private houses were systematically broken into and trashed by the police; Gina has also returned to her room, where she is brutally gang-raped by *motoneigistes* (unemployed people hired to clear tracks with their snowmobiles), while in the background the national anthem, 'O Canada', can be heard on the television. The juxtaposition of these events has a powerful effect. The film-makers, who are attempting to capture real life, remain ignorant of what is actually happening near them, while the country, despite a feeling of nationalism being encouraged by closing the day's television with the national anthem, is equally blind to its own violence.

The film closes with further cross-cutting to the different outcomes for each story. After their return to Montréal, the film-makers shoot a fiction film featuring well-known actors; Gina, avenged by her boss's strong men who have been sent to kill the *motoneigistes*, leaves for a holiday in Mexico and Dolorès marries her fiance from Louiseville. The cynicism of these three endings is obvious. Does the new project of a commercial feature signal the end of politically committed cinema? Is the merciless avenging of a brutal crime a mockery of legal justice? And finally, is the happy ending for the working-class girl a travesty of film endings and a glossing over of the life of the working classes?

The film no longer identifies a cause to fight for or a role model to identify with; one is left to wonder what sense of purpose might be discovered. A cynical attitude underlies the film in its doubts concerning social values and moral aims. This uncertainty about the identity of a society is reflected in the film's aesthetics and its ill-defined genre, located as it is at the crossroads of the gangster movie, the *auteur* movie – where the director uses the film within the film to comment on film-making itself – and the star movie, where the star, Gina, occupies the central place in the film. The film subverts all these genres: the gangsters in the film are brutes who have no understanding of strategy, the film crew opts for commercialism rather than *auteur*-ship, and the stardom of Gina is a satire of the striptease dancers, sent to isolated provincial hotels, where working conditions are similar to those of the textile workers. As Arcand says in an interview, he did not decide ahead of time on the structure of the film according to a specific aesthetic (Arcand 1976: 21). It is not surprising then that it is, as Yves Lever puts it, a film that marks a turning point – *film charnière* – in Arcand's oeuvre (Lever 1995a: 122).

Le Déclin de l'empire américain (1986)

When *Le Déclin de l'empire américain* (*The Decline of the American Empire*) came out in 1986, it was an instant success, especially in France where it was seen by more than a million people. The title establishes a link with the decline of the Roman Empire and gives a historical and comparative dimension to this film. However, it is perhaps a surprising title for a film from Francophone Québec and set in a scenic spot near Memphrémagog lake. The action takes place in autumn, when the scenery is at its most beautiful. Four men gather in a chalet: they prepare a gastronomic meal for four women, who have met at a Montréal sports centre. The topic of conversation is the same for both groups: sex. They are all well-established professionals and have reached a stage in life where epicurean pleasures, sex and individual happiness have become paramount.

For Michel Coulombe and Marcel Jean the film is 'a cynical observation of post-referendum Québec, the observation of the death of politics "of the crumbling of the Marxist-Leninist dream" in favour of immediate gratification' (Coulombe & Jean 1991: 11, trans.). As was the case for *Gina*, the film does not belong to a particular genre, although it has most often been described as a comedy. Janis Pallister rejects the comedy label and sees it 'as a morality play in the purest sense of that word' (Pallister 1995: 258).

In the light of Arcand's earlier difficulties with the ONF/NFB, it is worthwhile mentioning that he made *Le Déclin de l'empire américain* as a co-production with that organisation. Arcand had no project at the time and, after considerable reflection, hit upon the idea of making a film with shocking dialogue. Cinema, he felt, had always shown shocking events, but these had rarely been conveyed solely through dialogue (Arcand 1986: 28).

This emphasis on dialogue may have contributed to the film's success in France, where dialogue in film has always been important. Yet the French reception of the film was particularly interesting because it revealed that country's perception of Québécois identity. Denise Pérusse observed that many of the critical reviews emphasised the Québécois nature of the film: its views of the lake and the red, autumnal colours of the maple trees gave substance to the French fascination with Québec's vast, unspoilt spaces. The beauty of the land, the grandeur of the chalet and the sybaritic pleasures pursued by these affluent Québécois were a far cry from the hostile nature and poverty depicted in *Maria Chapdelaine*.

But it emerges from Pérusse's survey that the critics made a distinction between the director, who was 'Canadian', and the diegetic universe of the film (the fictional reality), which is referred to as Québécois – as are the characters who are referred to as Québécois intellectuals. Pérusse is surprised at this distinction, especially in 1986, when the French were familiar with the position of Québec and its desire for independence. Lever sees an allusion to Québec's predicament in the opening of the film where it is mentioned that the only valid law in history is that of numbers. It is, Lever writes, as if Arcand 'wanted to establish from the outset that the struggle of the Québécois minority in America is without hope' (Lever 1995a: 89, trans.).

In his portrayal of a Québec in decline, Arcand depicted a society where material aspirations had become overwhelmingly important: he also aimed at an international audience with an innovative *mise en scène* heralding a new film aesthetic of dialogue. Although the French public noticed a Québécois accent, the French was quite acceptable to them.

Jésus de Montréal (1989)

Both *Le Déclin de l'empire américain* and *Jésus de Montréal* (*Jesus of Montreal*) won prizes at Cannes and brought celebrity to Arcand and international recognition of Québécois cinema. *Jésus de Montréal* tells the story of an actor, Daniel Coulombe, who is asked by a Montréal parish priest, Father Leclerc, to modernise the yearly Passion play. In order to do this Coulombe consults a theologian, who mentions to him that new archeological evidence has come to light concerning the life of Jesus. Coulombe researches the material and recruits four actors to collaborate with him. The result is a script that breaks with aesthetic conventions and religious orthodoxy, but finds immediate success. Praised by the media and hailed as a play that must be seen, it shocks the religious authorities, who prohibit it. In the course of the last unauthorised performance, a row between the police and the audience erupts in which Coulombe is fatally injured. However, his death benefits other people since his heart and eyes are used in transplants.

For Ian Lockerbie, *Jésus de Montréal* is of particular significance for an understanding of identity. In his incisive article 'Québec Cinema as a Mirror of Identity', he argues that

> Québec cinema is helping to crystallise the pattern of sensibility and sense of identity needed by a society which is both 'distinct' and rapidly evolving. Traditional values are being safeguarded but also reshaped. Long-standing traumas from a difficult past are being overcome but still form part of imaginative experience. No single film offers the perfect synthesis of all the forces at work. . . . If one film were to be chosen . . . it would have to be *Jésus de Montréal*. No subject could offer a more striking combination of the sombre and the tragic sublimity of the Passion. . . . The *mise en scène* draws on all the elements of grandeur in the Biblical story but turns them to general symbolic and imaginative ends . . . the film has the particular characteristic of offering a blueprint of the pattern of imaginative experience that defines Québec identity at the present time. (Lockerbie 1991: 307)

There is also a further dimension in the film's topography which is significant for the understanding of identity. The very title draws attention to the link that exists between space and identity: a person is identified with a space; if there is a Jesus in Montréal, it must be someone who has adopted his identity. This is indeed what happens. Through playing the part of Jesus in the play, Coulombe comes to identify with him and finally lives similar events. If there is here a merging between two spaces and two identities, a similar intertwining occurs on a cinematic, aesthetic level between the film and the theatrical play within it. The viewer shifts from relating to characters in a film to seeing these same characters become actors in a Passion play.

One particular incident shows a shift of identification for one spectator of the play. At one point an off-screen female voice is heard shouting: 'Jesus, I belong to you . . . Forgive me, I have sinned. Speak to me.' A black woman comes rushing towards Jesus/Coulombe, grasping his clothes and begging him to speak to her. Both the viewer of the film and the spectators of the play are temporally confused as to the identity of the woman who, with her long dress and scarf, could well be one of the actors in the play. Then the police intervene and drag the woman away.

Throughout the film a shifting of spaces and identities occurs, leading to the final merging of Jesus/Coulombe, which reveals that 'being a self is inseparable from existing in a space of moral issues, to do with identity and how one ought to be' (Taylor 1989: 112). Coulombe interiorises Jesus and the moral values he stands for. In a very literal sense, Coulombe, like Jesus, will extend far beyond Montréal, as his heart will save the life of an English-speaking Canadian from Sherbrooke and his eyes are transplanted into an Italian woman. The film is rooted in the reality of Québec and denounces many of its prevailing aspects: the hypocrisy of the clerics (highlighted through the parish priest Leclerc's affair with one of the actresses); the narrow-mindedness of the Catholic church; the sensation-seeking media; the repugnant practices of marketing and publicity and the appalling situation of the city hospital emergency services. But while exposing these concrete situations, the film symbolically transcends the local Québécois identity and suggests a new, positive interpretation of values that remain relevant.

Arcand remains Québec's emblematic film-maker of the 1980s, the period where the baby-boomers of the 1960s reached maturity. His films reveal the individual torn between forces of good and evil.

Francis Mankiewicz

Mankiewicz's short film career – he died in 1994 before he had turned fifty – was a fruitful one. He was born in China, but his parents emigrated to Montréal shortly after his birth in 1944. After studying geology he went to England, where he studied at the London School of Film Technique from 1966 until 1968, then worked as a cameraman on six documentaries and returned to Montréal in 1969. His five feature films are characterised by a remarkable thematic coherence in which the focus rests on the family and, in particular, the child. Two of these films are particularly relevant for the understanding of a child's identity formation: *Le Temps d'une chasse* (1972) and *Les Bons Débarras* (1980). The script for the latter was written by Réjean Ducharme, a well-established Québécois script-writer, that of *Le Temps d'une chasse* was Mankiewicz's own. Michel Brault was the cameraman for both films.

Le Temps d'une chasse (1972)

The preoccupation with childhood, paternity and family, so recurrent in Québec cinema, dominates *Le Temps d'une chasse*. The story takes place over a weekend in the autumn, when three friends, Willie, Lionel and Richard, and Richard's ten-year-old son, go hunting. The film opens with a long shot lingering over a street lined with cars on each side. As Willie and Lionel drive up to Richard's house, they display all the clichés of macho behaviour – aggressive blowing of the horn, drinking at the wheel and generally adopting the 'we must have fun' approach. Richard's wife, equally clichéed in dressing gown and hair curlers, shouts angrily from the window at the arrogant arrival of these two men, 'waking up the entire neighbourhood'. Richard's young son, Michel, arrives with luggage and gun and soon they all set off. Willie, the oldest of the three, entertains the young Michel with boastful hunting stories. They get lost and end up staying in an anonymous motel, forcing themselves to 'have fun', drinking and trying in vain to attract the attention of the waitresses.

The next day, nothing happens: the boy engages in imaginary hunting scenes, while the adults aim their guns at empty bottles. While Willie and Lionel have a prolonged siesta, Richard and his son enjoy a moment together during which Richard shows him how to hypnotise frogs. On this second evening, Richard has an amorous encounter with one of the waitresses, while Willie persuades a waitress to do a striptease for him and Lionel, a dismal and failed performance without music, accompanied only by Willie's childish sniggering. Finally, on the third day, they sleep until lunchtime, then the so-called hunting happens. Willie, still drinking continuously, is trying to track the animal; the camera stays with the boy. A shot is heard, followed by Willie's victorious shouting. The boy dashes at great speed towards the others: he discovers Willie has shot his father by accident. The film closes showing the men and Michel standing near the body.

The shooting of Richard, supposedly mistaken for a wild animal, in front of his son, reveals the ludicrous nature of these men's attempts to assert their manhood. What they perceive to be masculine pleasures – talking about women or cars, drinking excessively – ends in the killing of the only one of the three who had some notion of fatherhood. Here again, as in Jutra's *Mon Oncle Antoine*, the child is a witness to the inadequacies and immaturity of the adults, who totally fail to provide him with an identifiable framework of values worth striving for. Unlike Benoît in *Mon Oncle Antoine*, who constantly observes and takes note of the adults, Michel, perhaps too young to do this, has engaged more in imaginary games on his own. Whereas in *Mon Oncle Antoine* the film ends with a close-up of Benoît's face, looking thoughtfully into the room, in *Le Temps d'une chasse*, the camera shows Michel from the back looking down at his dead father. The film takes on the tone of a documentary in the style of *cinéma direct*. These characters, who as Gilles Marsolais notes are all in search of an identity, in the end learn nothing about themselves. The only hope for a change in the future lies with the child who witnessed the sad spectacle (Marsolais 1994: 19). But the viewer cannot begin to speculate as to what the future might hold for this young boy and for Québec's youth or what values they might identify in the adults around them and strive to emulate.

Les Bons Débarras (1980)

Les Bons Débarras (*Good Riddance*) also places the child at the centre of the story. For Marie-Claude Loiselle, it is one of the last worthwhile films to appear before the production in Québec of a plethora of empty films seeking purely aesthetic effects (Loiselle 1994: 20). The film opens with a zoom, showing a small settlement where Michelle lives with her mentally retarded brother, Tit-Guy, who is drunk most of the time, and her precocious pre-adolescent daughter, Manon. The three earn their living delivering firewood to well-off customers.

While Michelle divides her love between her brother, her daughter and her lover, Maurice, a policeman, Manon's love is fixated exclusively on her mother. Her incessant reading of Emily Bronte's *Les Hauts de Hurlevent* (*Wuthering Heights*) feeds her imagination and she loves her mother with a passion reminiscent of that of Heathcliff, wanting her all to herself. She dreams of being killed on the road with her mother and of their blood mingling so that a flower will grow through the asphalt. She resents her mother's caring for Tit-Guy and her love for Maurice, and becomes especially irate when she discovers that her mother is pregnant. Her aim is to eliminate those who lay any claim upon her mother. She succeeds in breaking up the relationship between Maurice and her mother by falsely accusing him of sexual advances towards her, and pushes Tit-Guy to suicide: finally, triumphant, she has achieved her aim.

The film cannot be seen solely as a portrayal of a fragmented and incomplete family, where yet again the father is absent and there are no adult role models to guide the young people. It represents the most wretched people in society – a tendency which often characterises Québécois cinema – and inveighs against a social disorder which the chaos of the hunting scene in *Le Temps d'une chasse* also highlighted. Whether the film deals with the identity problem of the individual – Tit-Guy, mentally handicapped, or Manon, endowed with primitive criminal urges – or that of the family or of Québec at large, is difficult to assess. There is here an instinctual drive so strong that it pushes a young girl, suffering an 'immense foetal nostalgia', in Vincent Ostria's words, into eliminating everyone who stands in the way of her idealised and exclusive society, created by the fusion of mother and child (Ostria 1985: 55).

The film, Loiselle comments, came out three months before the 1980 referendum. The coincidence is too beautiful, she writes, 'to resist the temptation to read in it a superb metaphor of Québec and her people'. She admits that this kind of interpretation is hazardous, yet she sees in Manon's refusal to accept what life offers her – some fragments of love, a bicycle, a new little brother – the seed of the intense energy that characterises the film. The refusal, Loiselle feels, may be seen as a metaphor for Québec's aspiration to grow and rise above its little ordinary misery (Loiselle 1994: 22).

Jean Beaudin

Jean Beaudin's background combines Fine Arts (Montréal) and Design (Zurich). He joined the ONF/NFB in 1964.

J. A. Martin, photographe (1976)

The film, set in the nineteenth century, depicts a couple, Joseph Albert Martin and his wife Rose-Aimée, who live a quiet, orderly life with their three children and the paternal grandmother. An uncomfortable silence has set in: the husband has become taciturn, the wife short-tempered. She carries out her domestic tasks, he is fully absorbed in his photographic work. Although the couple have grown emotionally distant, they are always in close proximity as Martin does all his work in the house. After fifteen years of marriage, their relationship has become a silent spying on each other. Their family life is stern and silent. There is no laughter.

The film is about seeing and observing. Rather than presenting these and subsequent facts in a linear storytelling mode, the film offers a series of tableaux in which composition, light, colour, texture and framing are of the utmost importance as in a photograph; the end of each tableau fades to black.

Every year J. A. Martin travels for five weeks to see his clients. This year, Rose-Aimée decides to go with him, overcoming objections and material difficulties. From the enclosed space of the house, in which the viewer has observed only the symptoms of a declining relationship, the film becomes a Québec road-movie about a couple travelling in a horse-drawn wagon, through whom the symptoms of an alienated French-Canadian society become apparent. Two juxtaposed and related sequences give a particularly acute insight into the plight of the French-speaking Québécois: the photo session with Mr Wilson, a well-to-do Anglophone miller, and the session with his French-speaking workers.

The first sequence opens with a long shot of Mr Wilson's manor house and surrounding grounds. Martin is to take a photograph of Mr Wilson, his wife and their son. All three are elegantly dressed; Mr Wilson is seated, his son kneeling to his left, his wife behind him. Martin gives instructions in English with a French accent. As he prepares to take the picture, his wife comments on the beauty of the place and expresses a wish to live somewhere similar. Martin replies, 'For that you would have to speak English.'

The session ends. From an open space the scene shifts to a group of men all huddled together at the mill, sitting wherever space can be found. All are eating avidly, no one speaks and all look towards the camera, next to which the Anglophone 'boss' is standing. Young boys and yet more men and children are revealed through pans and tilts. When the boss tells Martin that the photograph can only be taken during the lunch-break, he angrily packs his bags, saying he does not wish to use up five of their fifteen minutes. However, two things make him change his mind: first, his wife, looking at the large group of men, says he will be disappointing a lot of people, then Martin notices a young boy standing by a horse, who smiles faintly in his direction. He prepares for the photograph and the workers assemble in rows, all except the boy by the horse. Martin tells him to join the group, but the boy is stopped by the boss who explains that he was sacked a few days earlier. Ignoring this, Martin leads the boy to the front row. The session closes with a static shot of the workers.

The contrast between these two sequences is telling. In the first, a wealthy family of three is photographed in front of their mansion; each person is addressed individually by name and the space around the threesome is vast. In the second photo session, there is no space around the people, the group fills the entire screen, the camera has to move to find them all and Martin has to place them tightly together in rows to fit them into his photograph. The Anglophone boss watches from a distance and, immediately after the camera's click, exhorts 'the boys' back to work.

The individualised identities of the Wilsons contrast sharply with the collective identity forced upon the workers, who are simply Mr Wilson's workforce; the only one to be singled out is the boy who has been sacked, implying that only rebellion can give them some form of individual recognition. However, the images reveal all too clearly the workers' passive acceptance of their lot and, as Ian Lockerbie states, 'passivity is the outer sign of social alienation' (Lockerbie 1991: 303).

If Beaudin's use of Martin's photography constitutes an incisive social commentary on the identity of the francophone Québécois, it also leads to astute observations concerning the representation of identity by revealing the history and context of each photograph. In one session pans are used to show the different groups who have assembled in an inn to be photographed. Having captured each little group, the pan is halted for a moment so the viewer can clearly see the staging of the event. The last in this series is a couple being photographed in front of a screen showing white, snow-covered scenery. These images show how photography can be a means to create an imaginary identity which hides the real one.

Furthermore, while the social commentary inherent in the photograph of the mill workers – resigned faces and the prominent presence of child workers – cannot escape the viewer, the film provides a context that still photography can only suggest. In the mill sequence the film extends beyond the bounds of the photograph to show how men and children alike are made to work an inordinate number of hours with virtually no breaks under the control of an anglophone boss and a wealthy, anglophone proprietor.

Such an extension of meaning is also made possible through the juxtaposition of sequences. The photo session with the affluent Wilsons and their one child is preceded by a scene in which Rose-Aimée Martin has a miscarriage. The couple's behaviour during this event suggests that it is by no means Rose-Aimée's first miscarriage: she is on her own in the wagon, her husband sits near the lake, casting a glance at her from time to time. When she finally signals that everything is over, he fetches a shovel from the back of the wagon, without their ever exchanging a word. The off-screen sound of digging blends with a few notes of a stringed instrument, adding to the silent acceptance of their misfortune. These seem like routine gestures, reflecting the numerous pregnancies of Catholic Québécois women (Rose-Aimée already has three children). This is further emphasised in the mill sequence by the numerous child workers and the sacked boy returning home to his dying mother.

The film emphasises the loss of individual identities in a collective, oppressed body of workers and the isolation of women silently living by unalterable dictates. Yet Rose-Aimée Martin decides to distance herself from her traditional role by accompanying her husband. Her attitude has justifiably led critics to perceive a feminist theme in the film. Rose-Aimée's action awakens an old self, a fun-loving and extrovert person, long forgotten by both herself and her husband. Furthermore, in the course of their journey the two gradually discover the reasons for the decline of their relationship: an obsession with the children on her part, an 'absent' presence on his. By the time they return home their attitudes towards each other have changed and the distinctive features of their individual personalities have re-emerged. The film closes with a tender love scene which, this time, is not interrupted by a crying baby. All the same, the last image reminds the viewer of the power of what Ian Lockerbie calls 'the life-denying force of the Catholic Church' as the camera tilts up to reveal the crucifix hanging centrally above the marital bed (Lockerbie 1991: 303).

Jean Yves Bigras

Jean Yves Bigras is a versatile talent. He started acting at the age of five, studied civil engineering, was in the air force during the war and worked for the radio and in theatre. Finally, he chose to enter the ONF/NFB, where he directed and edited films, among which his most successful one, *La Petite Aurore, l'enfant martyre* (1951), is about a cruelly abused child.

La Petite Aurore, l'enfant martyre (1951)

The story of Aurore, an already well-known legend in French Québec, was bound to draw large audiences and attract widespread attention. It concerned the tragic death in 1920 of Aurore Gagnon, a little girl who was physically abused by her stepmother and biological father. The events leading up to the girl's death were particularly repugnant and widely reported in the newspapers. After the death of Aurore's mother, in January 1918, the father married Anne-Marie Houde, who had been living in the house and had nursed the sick mother. Two years later a neighbour reported the debilitated state of the girl, but by the time an inquiry began Aurore had already died. The coroner found fifty-four wounds on her body and witnesses revealed that the second Mme Gagnon had burned the child's scalp and hands, had beaten her, deprived her of food and made her eat slices of soap. While the stepmother was found guilty of murder, the father was found guilty of involuntary manslaughter.

A play re-enacting the story and the trial ran to full houses from 1921 until Bigras's *La Petite Aurore, l'enfant martyre* (*Little Aurore, the Child Martyr*) appeared in 1951. Aurore's father, still alive at the time, asked for an injunction on the film. A temporary injunction was granted, but the film was released in April 1952. Although it had been made in twenty-three days with a very modest budget, it became hugely popular: in less than a year the returns exceeded $100,000. It is not surprising that such a profoundly distressing case stirred the Québécois deeply, but the fact that the interest in the story lasted for decades raises the question of Québécois' identification with the Aurore case. The story raises so many fundamental issues: family life, marriage and remarriage, paternal authority, the Catholic religion, and suffering – one has the impression that not one fibre of Québécois identity was left untouched.

Christie McDonald, who studied the trial and the powerful legend which grew up around it, argues that the stepmother has been systematically demonised while the father figure has been factored out, exonerated so to speak, and yet, he too was guilty of beating the child brutally. Looking at the play and the novels that were written about Aurore, McDonald observes that in most retellings of the story the evil stepmother remains central while the father is seen as absent, morally weak or as someone who abdicated his paternal authority. If the case held such fascination, McDonald suggests, it may be largely related to a vision of paternity – and its lack: 'What conception of fatherhood can be gleaned throughout the different versions of Aurore, as the blind spot or unthought area of a legend which raises questions not only about martyrdom and the evil of false maternity, but also the exoneration of abusive and abdicating paternity?' (McDonald 1998: 57).

McDonald sees a link between the strong reaction to the Aurore case and three aspects of the changing socio-political conditions of the time. These are the lack of a strong male model within Québec (World War I had forced many men to leave their families), the new political strength for women outside Québec (women were able to vote in federal elections after 1921 but Québec did not grant voting rights to women until the 1940s) and, finally, the spectre of changes in society and family life (heated debates on divorce were going on and Québec opposed the proposed divorce law in Canada) (McDonald 1998: 57–8).

The film, based on Emile Asselin's novel, *La Petite Aurore: L'Enfant martyre*, became Québec's emblematic film of the 1950s, when Duplessis' government was still promulgating strong religious values and family life and idealising the virtues of the countryside. The Aurore case demystified those ideals and dreams and Bigras's film did little to reinstate them. Its excessive emphasis on Aurore's acceptance of her suffering and the village priest's advice to place her trust in God, whose eternal happiness awaited her, was symptomatic of a society that had come to see suffering as a virtue: belief in God and eternal life justified all earthly torment. As for the stepmother, her sadism was so blatant that one wonders how thousands of people could tolerate watching it, were it not, as Réal Ouellet pointed out, that the continued representation of Aurore indicates 'a sadism within society about which it is necessary to speak out' (Ouellet quoted in McDonald 1998: 59). Aurore's father, in abdicating his authority and failing to assume responsibility, forecast the place the father would occupy in numerous Québécois films.

Jean-Claude Lauzon

In Québécois cinema the figure of the father is most often ambiguous, unknown, absent, or as in *Le Temps d'une chasse* killed in front of his son. The father has almost systematically failed to be a model for a son to identify with. In *Un Zoo la nuit* (1987 – *Night Zoo*), in contrast to this common portrayal of fathers, Jean-Claude Lauzon celebrates a reunion between father and son.

Un Zoo la nuit (1987)

After two years in prison for dealing in drugs – which had been procured by corrupt policemen – Marcel Brisebois, called 'Poignard' (Dagger), is released. He is almost immediately confronted with police corruption, violence and homosexual aggression. Marcel is a musician and all he wants is to find his girlfriend again, locate the drug money left behind when he was arrested and leave with her so that they can make music together.

As Marcel returns to his warehouse-style flat overlooking the river, all seems to have been left untouched. He removes the large sheet from the window to let in the early morning light. The hi-fi equipment is still there and on the answer-phone is a message from his father, Albert, wishing him *bonne fête*.

Two juxtaposed, yet intertwined narrative strands unfold: there is the thriller depicting the threats and violence used by the police to extort the drug money which they know was in Marcel's possession; but there is also the father–son story which tells how they rediscover each other.

Lauzon handles the totally different styles required by each story almost equally well: violent conflict with the police is depicted through accelerated rhythm, created through quick, short sequences, while Marcel's encounter with his father is filmed in long sequences with unusually poetic images of the beauty of Québec.

Through the elimination of several characters – the girlfriend no longer wants Marcel and the policemen threatening him are killed – the father–son story is foregrounded. Initially Albert seems to fall into the same category as all the other disappointing Québécois father figures: his marriage and family life break down and all that interests him is hunting the *orignal*, the Canadian elk. But little by little another father figure emerges: it was the father who secretly rescued the drug money after his son was arrested and also admits he used to listen to his son's answer-phone just for the pleasure of hearing his voice.

A strong bond develops between father and son, reaching its finest moment when they go fishing together. The father rediscovers a youthful pleasure and the intimacy they share leaves a lasting impression especially as the early morning over the lake is of unusual beauty. As they return to Montréal another heartwarming surprise awaits the father. The Italian immigrants, whose life he shares, have prepared a surprise birthday party for him. Whatever hostility Marcel may have had towards his father disappears, their reunion and his father's approaching death give Marcel the desire to help him make peace and fulfil his dreams, if only in his imagination. This leads to the unusual hunting scene in which Marcel takes his father in a wheelchair on an 'elephant hunt' in the zoo at night. A photograph of the 'killed' elephant – a large stuffed elephant in the entrance hall of the zoo – is the 'proof' his father shows to Tony, his friend and rival, when he tells him he went hunting with Marcel.

This is, then, an unusual film in the history of Québécois cinema. In the midst of the drug culture, police corruption and violence a son, after two years in prison, makes peace with his father and tells him: 'I am your son, you are my father and that still means something to me.' Albert dies of a heart attack, but as Lever puts it: 'Marcel, who no longer feels contempt for him, no longer needs him in order to create a new life for himself' (Lever 1995a: 252, trans.).

Micheline Lanctôt

In the 1980s Lanctôt, herself an actress, brought out *Sonatine* (1983) which deals with two adolescent girls, Chantal and Louisette, who are trying to discover and express themselves. Failing to gain understanding or attention from the adults close to them, they relate best with un-known people who intuitively understand them better. Set in Montréal, the film has a tripartite structure. It first shows the friendly collusion between Chantal and a bus conductor, the bus's wanderings through the city and the comings and goings of passengers, giving a lively micro-picture of Montréal society; the second part follows Louisette, who hides on a Bulgarian ship but is discovered by a lonely sailor – she too develops a playful conspiracy with the sailor. The final part takes place mainly on a Montréal underground train. The girls, now really wanting to be noticed and taken seriously, decide to kill themselves in the underground; they have managed to steal sufficient drugs but still fail to draw attention to their plight of adolescents lost at the threshold of adulthood. They place a large notice board behind them: 'Indifferent World: We are going to die. You must stop us. Do something.' Many people come and go, enter and leave the train. Hardly anyone notices the girls, a few do and read the board but do not react. Finally, the girls swallow a large amount of drugs and drink their chocolate. The train comes to the final stop for the night, the girls have not been noticed, they have collapsed and lie dead on the floor of the train.

Anne-Claire Poirier

Anne-Claire Poirier is the doyenne of women's cinema, a highly committed film-maker for whom films are founded in social reality. Her aim is to give a voice to women. She exposes the history of women's servitude in Québec in her film, *Les Filles du Roy*, while her 1979 film, *Mourir à tue-tête* (*A Scream from Silence*) denounces rape.

Mourir à tue-tête (1979)

The French expression *à tue-tête* (literally 'one's head off') means at the top of one's voice and usually accompanies either the verb to shout or to sing. Used in combination with the verb *mourir* (to die), it gives a powerful poignancy to the title, 'Dying at the top of one's voice'. The film is a screaming indictment against rape and against the legal and judiciary authorities dealing with rape. While it focuses on one particular rape, that of Suzanne, a nurse at the Saint-Luc hospital in Montréal, it places her case in the larger context of the many, often widely accepted, forms of rape. The film also denounces the laws and general attitudes that condone rape. The case of Suzanne reveals how her identity is demolished to the point of annihilating her very being. The rape leads to her suicide.

One evening, at midnight, Suzanne returns home after her shift at the hospital. Very near the hospital she is attacked by a young lorry driver who drags her into his lorry where for several hours he beats her, insults her, humiliates her and rapes her, pausing briefly from time to time to drink a bottle of beer. The film shows the assault at length and makes for painful viewing. Upon her return home, she phones her boyfriend but can hardly speak.

The film then cuts to large-scale rapes, those committed and condoned in wars, such as the Vietnam war, and other forms of violence against women's bodies that may be seen as forms of rape. Among these, the film-maker includes clitoridectomy, still widely practised in Africa.

The police enquiry and medical examination that follow Suzanne's ordeal seem like a prolonging of the rape scene – she has to lie down for the examination by a male doctor and for the photographs taken by a male photographer. Poirier ensures that the ordeal itself and the confrontation with the investigators are filmed in the same way in order to emphasise the similarity between the two. Moreover, the interrogation tends already to question her integrity: 'Why did you not scream?' – she was too frightened – 'Why did you call so late?' – the ordeal lasted so long but she had lost all notion of time, to her it seemed all night – 'What time did you come home?'

All Suzanne wants is to get rid of the traces of the rape, take a bath and tidy herself. Combing her dishevelled hair proves to be particularly difficult. As the question, whether she wants the hair cut, triggers off panic in her, the film cuts to what must have been the immediate association for her, historical European footage of the humiliating head-shaving of the women who had fallen in love with German soldiers during World War II. The women are shaved, then placed in a row where they all sit silently in the same position while the sound track emits a high-pitched harsh sound.

Poirier combines fictional sequences with archival footage, three fictional debates between the film-maker and the editor who discuss Suzanne's case, and also staged court appearances. The film-maker meets Suzanne and talks with her. 'What in particular do you remember?' Poirier asks. And Suzanne replies: 'It is not the pain, not even the rape itself but the fear and the shame, the shame of being raped.' The wish to eradicate this shame, located on the wrong side of the crime, is what makes this a militant, feminist film.

The court sequence also corroborates this feminist message. It shows groups of women and young girls forming a kind of Greek chorus facing the camera/judge. It is a powerful, stylised and theatrical scene in which, in a controlled way, the women discuss the widely prevalent practice of rape and denounce the dismissive attitude of the courts whose almost systematic effect is to reverse the situation so that the raped woman is considered responsible for the rape. As the women address the judge, who remains invisible, and make point after point invoking theories of woman's fundamental masochism or death instinct that supposedly instils in them a desire to be raped, the judge's voice replies: 'Mesdames, don't confuse matters. The law is the law and Canadian law defines the crime of rape as unwanted sexual intercourse with a woman who is not your spouse.' The list of grievances continues. Young girls speak up who were abused by their fathers, but the crime of incest is systematically denied in the name of 'the rights of the family' or placed in a so-called cultural context that justifies it.

Considerable time is allocated to the staged court case, leaving no doubt as to the film's militant position. But the emphasis remains on the specific case of Suzanne, and it is through her that the destruction of the person's selfhood is exposed. The film conveys this through two evocative uses of the mirror. The first one occurs after Suzanne has managed to return home. In the bathroom a mirror reflects her bruised face and dishevelled appearance. She stops to look, approaches and stares at a woman she hardly recognises. She opens her mouth in horror, and finally succeeds in screaming at her own horrific image in the mirror. The second occurrence is much later, after her boyfriend has expressed his frustration at her prolonged withdrawal and inability to resume their sexual relationship. After he has left, she goes to the bathroom and again looks at herself in the mirror. The visible scars of the rape have gone.

She examines her image, then opens her mouth as if to scream, but this time she cannot emit a single sound and is left with the vision of her silenced screams. She takes an overdose and, dressed in white, dies *à tue-tête*, screaming silently at the top of her voice. The film closes on the white image of Suzanne dead and dignified on the bed and fades to white.

Mourir à tue-tête confronted Poirier with the difficult task of showing the unshowable. She was also determined not to arouse voyeurism or fall into sensationalising. For Poirier, there is an ethical dimension to cinema: as a film-maker she has the moral responsibility to create a cinema that is true to herself.

Tu as crié, 'Let me go' (1998)

Poirier's most personal film, *Tu as crié, 'Let me go'* (*You Shouted, 'Let Me Go'*), is the moving account of a mother's attempt to identify closely with the daughter she lost. As such it posed an even more testing challenge than *Mourir à tue-tête*, because it dealt with the film-maker's own experience. Poirier's daughter, Yann, a drug addict and prostitute, was murdered in 1992, shouting at her murderer, 'Let me go'. Devastated, not only by Yann's death but also by the years of her daughter's drug addiction, Poirier decided to make a film about this personal and painful event.

The film is structured like an odyssey that allows its maker to rediscover her daughter's world and to identify with her. Throughout the film the mother's voice-over addressing Yann intensifies the identification conveyed through the images. Although she speaks in the first person in the film, Poirier wants to extend and share her experience with the many viewers/parents who, perhaps, have to deal with the same tragic reality of their children's drug addiction.

The odyssey takes her to many places, tracking down long corridors as if seeking the person no longer to be found. She shows the places where her daughter once went, visits the seedy alleys, the streets, the morgue; she goes to the courtroom and points out the spot where the murderer sat. She talks to drug addicts, parents, friends, doctors and social workers in order to come closer to her daughter whose off-screen presence dominates the film and who is so often named in it. As she did in *Mourir à tue-tête*, Poirier extends the individual experience to investigate the general problem of drug addiction to which society closes its eyes. Only a society that does not want to know itself can remain blind to such a large group of people in its own midst, trapped in their marginality. People tend to think that drug addiction is elsewhere, yet it invades all classes. And again, Poirier takes a militant point of view, pleading for decriminalisation of drugs and for the lifting of the hypocritical silence that surrounds addiction.

The film opens with a shot of huge icebergs and closes with the same icebergs. When they reappear on the screen, the mother addresses her daughter and, in an ultimate attempt to identify with her, uses the words Yann screamed at her assassin, 'Let me go'. She uses them as if Yann had addressed them to her: 'I must let you go Yann, I do let you go.' A certain violence lurks in this appropriation of her daughter's last scream, represented visually by the breaking of the icebergs and their crashing against the waves. On the one hand, the film deals with the intense identification of a mother with her daughter and, on the other, with that of Québécois society refusing to see its own changing identity.

Léa Pool

When it comes to reflecting on identity in Québec and Francophone cinema, Léa Pool opens up new horizons. Born of a Polish father and a Swiss-Italian mother, she moved from one Francophone region, Switzerland, to another, Québec. Her move to Montréal in 1978 was to be the start of a successful film career. The following year, having made several videos and a few short films, she embarked on a feature film in black and white, *Strass Café*. Made with a budget of $6,000, the film appeared when Pool was only thirty. It encapsulated the themes that would characterise her later work: exile and wandering (the French term 'errance' captures this better), desire and memory, solitude and insularity, and above all a search for identity – the identity of both the characters in the film and the film-maker's aesthetic self.

From 1978 until 1983, in addition to her filming activities, Pool taught cinema and video at the UQAM (*Université de Québec à Montréal*) and worked for the Montréal festival of world cinema, the *Festival des Films du Monde*. Her concerns and interests were also reflected in her work for Radio-Québec where she directed ten programmes on cultural minorities. In 1984, she brought out *La Femme de l'hôtel* (*A Woman in Transit*) which drew the critics' and the public's attention and won several prizes.

La Femme de l'hôtel (1984)

The film is set in Montréal and is structured around three women: Andréa, a film-maker in the process of making a film; an actress/singer selected to be the character in that film; and Estelle, a strange woman wandering aimlessly by herself in and out of the hotel. Andréa, trying to complete the story for her film, reaches a point where the identity of her fictional character escapes her. As she desperately struggles to get out of this sterile limbo, she meets Estelle, whom she had seen briefly at the hotel reception upon her arrival. An unconscious recognition and powerful attraction between the women lead to Estelle becoming the inspiration and model for Andréa's fictional character, and the newly created character, in turn, plays a vital role in enabling Estelle's liberation from a painful past. The film is reminiscent of Chantal Akerman's films, the identity of Pool's women being equally founded in space. The opening sequence reveals this.

A long shot of Montréal fills the screen, slowly tracking from right to left, with the voice-over of Andréa confirming that this is Montréal, where it rains, snows and is cold. It is a poetic text that reinforces the images and stresses the importance of space for self-discovery: 'I look and listen to a city that I inhabited for eighteen years; I thought this was my home [chez moi] but I am no more at home here than anywhere else. This is perhaps why I have chosen to film here, to rediscover within myself the stranger I have become.' These crucial words are recited while the camera tracks through the city, showing its buildings, bridges and skyline.

The first preoccupation of Andréa, the film-maker character, is space: we see streets, a hotel, a theatre, a station, temporary places (lieux de passage). These, she says, are places where she was herself but when 'I was someone else' (j'étais une autre). After this long opening, the two main characters, Andréa and Estelle, meet at the hotel reception. Estelle, hearing Andréa addressed as 'Mme Richler', asks her whether she is Jewish. The direct question concerning her identity surprises Andréa, who does not reply.

The entire film delineates the question of identity which concerns Andréa's fictional character; she realises, as Léa Pool herself states, that 'one makes personal films, films that resemble oneself' (Pool 1986: 54). In this case the identification fails. As she drives through Montréal and takes photographs in order to recognise the places from her own past, she realises there is no resemblance between what she remembers and what she revisits. Andréa has to rediscover everything in order to finish the story of her fictional singer. But only the actress can give that character the gestures and gaze that make her come alive. However, the crucial expression of that singer's identity has to be the song for her star performance, and that Andréa has not been able to find.

Ever since Andréa saw Estelle at the hotel reception, the memory of her has haunted the film-maker. When she finally sees her again in the hotel, she immediately approaches her with the words, 'I have been looking for you'. The film has intimated that Estelle's experience is similar to that imagined by Andréa for her character and so Estelle becomes the necessary mediator between the two.

Intuitively Andréa feels compelled to talk about her character's madness. 'Why do you tell me all this?', Estelle asks. 'Because I have the impression that you understand,' is Andrea's reply. And indeed, Estelle, as revealed already in the opening sequence, understands the character's indifference as to whether she is here or elsewhere. 'Here' she can forget who she is and what she wants. Little by little the signs of the opening sequence shift to the film in the making: the sequence in the psychiatric hospital features a resident who, when the actress-singer is about to leave, asks her to phone just 'to hear you there and me here'. And while all this is communicated through a kind of symbiotic relationship, Andréa can only admit to Estelle that she knows nothing about her. 'Who are you?', she asks, 'and why are you in this hotel?'

It emerges then that the fictional character has not been invented but that it needs the deep identification between Andréa and Estelle to endow her with an identity from real life. The song will become the ultimate emblem of the singer's recovery and the film-maker's closure of the story entitled *Absence prolongée*. Pool uses the song 'Touch Me' as an integral part of the story: it occurs several times in the film and each time it marks a stage in the development of the story. Louis Goyette examines the central place the song occupies in the narrative (Goyette 1989: 53–6). For Andréa, it refers to the problem of the creative process and expresses her desperate quest for a character; she is the first to sing it, when by herself in the bath tub, insisting on the line 'I want you to touch me, I want you to feel me'. The second time it is rehearsed by the actress but, incapable of uttering a single sound, she comes close to a breakdown. Finally, the words of the song become the expression of the liberation of all three women.

Through the mediation of the singer, Andréa has also confronted Estelle with her double. When Estelle becomes the spectator of the sequence in which the singer bangs her head violently against the closed glass doors of the psychiatric hospital, a pan shows Estelle recognising herself in this fictional character and regaining a sense of herself. The three weeks' involvement with Andréa and her film have thus restored Estelle's own sense of identity – an identity which, in the opening sequence, was without location or direction. Uncertain as to whether to go to New York or to Toronto, she finally opts to go nowhere and stay in an anonymous hotel, most suited to cope with her sense of loss of self. The film closes, the actress-singer faces the audience and starts to sing. Estelle eclipses herself from the group and disappears, leaving only a message for Andréa, thanking her for 'having heard what could not be said'. She is last seen in the train, finally able to anchor herself again in space.

Anne Trister (1986)

'An identity', Victor Burgin notes, 'implies not only a location but a duration, a history. A lost identity is lost not only in space but in time' (Burgin 1996: 36). *Anne Trister* is the story of a woman who tries to locate herself through her art, using her particular history. As she places layers of paint on the surfaces of her large Montréal studio, extending space by creating perspectives on walls and juggling with hues, lines, shapes, adding fragments of collages and light washes, Anne Trister tries to escape from the geographic boundaries that frame and limit people's identities.

After the death of her father and his Jewish funeral in the desert, which leaves her with vivid memories, Anne decides to leave her native country, Switzerland, for Montréal. She is an artist but has come to feel limited by the standard size of canvasses, her creativity blocked by their frames. In Montréal she contacts a friend of her father's, Simon Lévy, who finds a large studio for her, and an old friend, Alix, a doctor in a children's hospital, with whom she can stay.

Two main locations occupy the film's centre stage and in each of them a healing and self-discovery will happen. These places are the studio where Anne produces works of art concerned with distance and near-ness, space and memory, and the therapy room where Alix helps a little girl, Sarah, act out her feelings and relate to others with the help of a toy bear. In each place female bonding occurs, marked by a longing for intimacy. The parallelism between the two places is striking: in both Alix has to impose limits on the intimacy desired, she stops Sarah from touching her breasts and Anne from kissing her on the mouth. While Sarah withdraws angrily, Anne splashes white paints over her murals, stopped only by Simon's unexpected visit.

As the artwork develops into a huge coherent creation which fills the empty studio, it becomes clear that these monumental frescoes, for which a scaffold on wheels is needed to reach the walls and ceiling, are the site of Anne's coming into being in a way similar to how Sarah's work with the bear allows her feelings to surface and to discover herself. However, one day Anne fails to secure the scaffolding properly and falls off it, lying unconscious on the floor until Simon comes by and has her taken to hospital. But the real catastrophe happens when she recovers from her fall to find that the studio has been demolished for a new development. Simon has managed to keep a few fragments of the frescoes, but all that remains are stones and pieces of walls, leaving Anne with a fragmented sense of self. The film closes with Alix projecting a film sent by Anne, who left without telling her. It shows the tomb of Anne's father in the desert – in front of it, Anne moving in and out of the screen, the frame never holding her fully, enacting the underlying and necessary displace-ment of an identity that no location can contain.

Emporte-moi (1999)

Pool's latest film, *Emporte-moi* (*Set Me Free*) yet again places the focus on identity and identification. The film is dedicated 'to my mother and to my daughter', stressing the female bonding of three generations. The story concerns a thirteen-year-old girl, Hannah, growing up in Montréal in the 1960s. Her Jewish father and Catholic mother have a stormy relationship. Like Anne's father in *Anne Trister*, who wanted to be but never became a writer, Hannah's father also wants to be a writer and terrorises the entire household with his writing ambition, asking his wife to type the texts he dictates after she has done a full day's work.

There is little that Hannah can relate to at home; but she is close to her brother and has developed a deep affection for one of her teachers. However, the real identification happens in the cinema when she sees Anna Karina, playing Nana, in Godard's *Vivre sa vie*. From that moment on she identifies fully with the actress, who reminds her of the teacher she likes, and tries to model her life on her. A crisis at home makes Hannah run away and seek refuge with the teacher. But the teacher, who first channelled Hannah's infatuation for Anna Karina, now gives her a movie camera before the summer holidays. The camera provides Hannah with the ultimate tool to help her find her place in the world.

In all of Pool's films identity comes to the fore. Many of the characters are Jewish, which inevitably poses the questions of exile and displacement, and shows a special affinity with the films of Akerman. In Pool's films, as in Akerman's, the search for identity is related to women for whom it is, in the first instance, expressed through space: stations, (psychiatric) hospitals, the studio in which the frescoes become impressive *trompe l'oeil*. But then, for Léa Pool, as she admits, cinema and *trompe l'oeil* are somewhat the same (Pool 1986: 56). In Pool's films, spaces are emptied and filled, are represented or evoked through letters, films and objects. It seems that the location on the screen with which one identifies is, in fact, a *trompe l'oeil*.

The images of itself that Québécois cinema projects on the screen reflect an ongoing construing of identity. The initial conscious endeavour to use memory as the foundation for the creation of identity accounts for the urgency that has prompted many film-makers to retrieve and recreate the past and to capture its still visible remnants in the present. Their fascination with the history of the Québécois people and the depicting of their nature and daily lives have left a valuable corpus of films.

It became apparent very early that political and economic forces were instrumental in Québec's identity formation. Increasingly, film-makers revealed the social problems of modern Québec and displayed a political awareness that shed a new light on its perception of itself. Identity is not just construed from the memory of the past; it is an ongoing process in which internal and external forces interact.

Inevitably, a nation has a self-image founded on shared traditional values with which an individual can identify. However, it is precisely in these shared values that ruptures occur which lead individuals to disengage from their social context. The celebrated institution of the family, for example, in which the child seeks its models to follow, appears to be fraught with conflict. The model of the father, in particular, is beset by difficulties because of his frequent absence or strained relationship with the son who is left without a positive masculine model to emulate. Adolescents, in the process of seeking a role and an identity, find themselves confronted with a society that pays little attention to them and is blind to its own failings.

While there has been an emphasis in Québécois film on the interaction between memory, society and identity, there is also an emerging interest in the individual whose personal experience is located outside Québec as is, for example, the case with Léa Pool's characters. The journey from the nostalgia of Acadia to present-day Québec is a long and interesting one. On the way we see the convergence of social problems, personal existential dilemmas and new external forces that contribute to the ongoing conflictual dialogue between individual and social identity.

Finally, the intersection between film and different art forms, painting, music, theatre – and including in particular the appearance of film-making in several of the films – reveals art as an essential and creative means for establishing one's identity.

4   Guadeloupe and Martinique

When in 1946 Guadeloupe and Martinique were given the status of French Departments, the new French West Indians found themselves in a hybrid situation: from colonised people, many of them descendants of slaves, they became fellow-citizens of the colonisers. Those in favour of the new status believed it would mean the end of colonialism and discrimination and the establishment of equal human rights. More than fifty years on, there is still no real perception of equality nor has French citizenship contributed to healing the wounds of the earlier expropriation of identity. Although slavery was abolished nearly a century before the granting of departmental status (1848), it was indelibly inscribed in the memory of the black people. They had been forcibly and inhumanly transported from Africa to the Caribbean islands, whose native inhabitants had been exterminated by the colonisers in 1635.

A common identity implies the sharing of a common history and a common experience; after the slaves' original African identity had been obliterated, all they shared was common slavery and the memory of a cruel loss. Becoming a French *département*, and later a region, did not end the struggle for identity of the Caribbean French. Instead, the newly acquired status led to a haemorrhage of the islands' population, which Aimé Césaire has called 'genocide by substitution': more than one in two Caribbean people now live in France.

It is often through artistic production that a people voices its struggles and attempts to reappropriate its history. Caribbean theatre, as Bridget Jones has shown, expresses 'a vigorous desire to transmit a distinctive cultural tradition' (Jones & Littlewood 1997: 12). More recently, cinema has offered an important new channel of expression for the Caribbean quest for a specific identity, but inevitably the technical skills and financial requirements make it a far less accessible medium for the artist than theatre.

Early cinema was used principally as a colonial tool, a means to 'educate' people into accepting the values of the colonisers and to show them the great country of France. The two main channels of distribution, as older Caribbean people recall, were the priest and the teacher. Reels and reels of French films introducing Caribbean children to winter sports, Versailles, the Eiffel tower and Lourdes still fill the shelves of the *cinémathèque* of the overseas' *départements* and *territoires* (Silou 1991: 25). When French film-makers became aware of the beauty of the Caribbean islands, they began to make documentary films about them with telling titles such as *Les Antilles, vieilles provinces françaises* (1961 – *The Antilles: Old Provinces of France*). This tendency was followed by an interest in the islands as the setting of feature films such as for Howard Hawks's *To Have and Have Not* (1944).

In 1968 it seemed that a Caribbean cinema had been born when, at the Tunisian *Journées de Carthage*, France was represented by a thirty-minute film from Guadeloupe, *Lorsque l'herbe* (*When the Grass*). It was made by the twenty-nine-year-old Christian Lara, a trained journalist, who was then working for the French daily paper *Le Figaro*. The film pleads for a return to the land and criticises the mechanisation of labour. But it was not until 1979 that Lara brought out his first feature film set in the Caribbean, *Coco la fleur, candidat* (*Coco-the-Flower, Candidate*). It shows an electoral campaign in Guadeloupe in which Coco la fleur is asked to stand for election for strategic purposes. However, when he discovers how much publicity the campaign offers, he seizes the opportunity to voice the people's grievances.

Coco la fleur, candidat was the first commercial Caribbean feature film to be shown locally; the dialogue is mainly in Creole with French sub-titles. Filming in Creole was crucial for Lara, who explains that it was a discredited language, despite it being spoken by 8 million people: 'I refuse to produce a so-called international version, because I want the whole world to hear people speaking Creole' (Silou 1991: 52–3, trans.). Although Lara's later films usually deal with Caribbean issues, they have failed to retain the early aesthetic authenticity. His most recent *Sucre amer* (1997 – *Bitter Sugar*), a historical fiction, borrows its style from French theatre rather than from the Caribbean oral tradition.

While *Coco la fleur, candidat* was set in Guadeloupe, most films made by Caribbean film-makers in the 1970s were set in France and dealt with Caribbean immigrants there. This was the case in Gabriel Glissant's *Le Pion* (1972 – *The Pawn*), which depicts the plight of an uprooted Caribbean in Paris. In 1981, Michel Traoré, a graduate from the French film school IDHEC (*Institut des Hautes Études Cinématographiques*), also brought out a film on the life of Caribbean immigrants in Paris, *Mizik, rez-de-chaussée Neg*, Creole for *Musique au rez-de-chaussée des nègres* (music on the Negroes' groundfloor). The Negroes' 'groundfloor' is, in fact, the notorious *chambre de bonne*, a minute attic room, usually found on the sixth floor of buildings without a lift. The film depicts the nostalgia of a Caribbean immigrant in Paris who, after a day's hard work, returns to his room, which he has transformed into a piece of the homeland under a Parisian roof. Other exiles join him there and together they listen to the 'mizik' from their own country with which they can identify. For Silou, the 'mizik' becomes the 're-tying of the umbilical cord' with the mother island (*île matricielle*).

It is hardly surprising that neither Guadeloupe nor Martinique have a flourishing cinema. In the 1980s the two islands together had less than 1 million inhabitants between them and many of their artists and intellectuals had settled in France. It was difficult to imagine that any one could succeed in making a Caribbean film. Yet, that is what happened: in 1983 *Rue Cases-Nègres* brought Caribbean cinema to a world audience.

Euzhan Palcy

Euzhan Palcy obtained a degree in literature from the Sorbonne in Paris and a doctorate at the Louis Lumière Institute. She made a number of short films before bringing out her successful feature film *Rue Cases-Nègres*.

Rue Cases-Nègres (1983)

In 1983, as a young film-maker, Euzhan Palcy placed Martinique on the map of world cinema with *Rue Cases-Nègres* (*Sugar Cane Alley*). The film, based on Joseph Zobel's novel *Black Shack Alley* (1953), won many international awards including the Silver Lion for best feature at the Venice Film Festival, while Darling Légitimus, by then a well-established actress, won the prize for best female actress for her role as the grandmother, Amantine.

Set in poverty-stricken Martinique in the 1930s, the film tells the story of José, a twelve-year-old orphaned boy, who lives with his grandmother Amantine in Rue Cases-Nègres, next door to an old man, Monsieur Médouze. Both Amantine and Médouze work in the sugar cane plantations for a meagre wage, which barely allows them to survive and, in the case of Amantine, to care for her grandson. The film depicts the daily lives of the people in Rue Cases-Nègres, which is a microcosm of Caribbean colonial society with its old and young, its children, its white colonisers and its many different kinds of black Caribbean people. The simple story told by *Rue Cases-Nègres* is a powerful allegory of Martinique's history, represented by José's journey to adulthood.

The film opens showing postcards of Fort-de-France and various local views, which French colonials were in the habit of sending overseas. They are picturesque, sepia photographs revealing nothing of the poverty in which the little José is growing up. The child is at the centre of the narrative; his remarks, voiced in the first person, comment on events around him and punctuate the story, while the camera focuses mainly on what he perceives, observes, learns and internalises. Like the novel on which it is based, the film is an attempt to represent the understanding of identity: that of the little boy and, through him, that of Martinique and other colonial countries.

José is a particularly gifted child, who acquires an unusual command of the French language and is extremely keen to learn. The Catechism classes where children are told to learn the answers to the questions by heart seem to have had little impact on him. When he goes to the French state school the lessons about the French administrative system (*préfectures et sous-préfectures*) make him and his grandmother smile. The values he learns as a young child are passed on to him by the two elders: Médouze, who carries the memory of the past, and Amantine, who holds a vision for the future. Both also instill in him a sense of moral values and an abhorrence of injustice.

Through Médouze's retelling of the past, José's identity will be grounded in an imagined, yet real place of origin: Africa. Médouze's story starts with 'Once upon a time . . .', then tells about his father, who was brought from Africa as a slave. The story is now passed down by Médouze to José, whose grandfather was also a slave from Africa. The stories refer to the loss of a homeland and an identity that can never be recaptured. Médouze recalls his father telling him every day about his country 'Africa'. His father wept and wept and never understood what had happened when the white people came. People were caught by lasso, then forced to march for days, before being loaded on to ships, then unloaded in Martinique to work in the sugar cane fields for white people, who stood over them with guns.

Palcy uses the camera to powerful effect: in fast reverse angle close-ups, she shifts from the indignant face of the old man telling the stories with intense passion to José, listening avidly and never missing a word, as confirmed by his prompt 'Krak' in response to Médouze's 'Krik', the opening and acquiescing formulae in oral narrative performance in many Caribbean societies. Médouze is not very precise about the country; he speaks simply of 'Africa'. The first layers of identity – family, village and country – have been lost, the descendants of the slaves have all become 'Africans'. Africa the lost land also has the aura of a promised land for José: 'If you go to Africa, I'll come with you', he promises Médouze, who is too realistic for such a dream: 'Alas, Médouze will never go to Africa, there is no one left from my family. When I am dead and buried, I'll go to Africa but I cannot take you', he concludes. 'One day we'll all go.' While he is talking, Médouze is sculpting a small African figure in wood, which will become the token of the rich heritage he leaves for José.

Then Médouze tells the story of the blacks' revolt against the white people: one day all the black people came down to Saint-Pierre. They burned the houses of the whites and 'that is how slavery ended. The whites trembled with fear'. The liberated slaves were now 'free' to go all over Martinique: 'we were free but had empty stomachs'. No longer slaves, they were nevertheless forced to come back to the same place: 'whites had all the land and paid very little'.

These words, spoken by an emaciated black man, son of an African slave, still forced to work in the sugar cane fields for minimum wages, is

10 Euzhan Palcy, *Rue Cases-Nègres.* José and Médouze.

a moving indictment of neo-colonialism, where 'free' people remain economically dependent. Equally telling is the representation of the grandmother who, like Médouze, is old and tired and should not be working in the sugar cane fields. The ultimate irony is revealed when the children are looking for sugar in José's house and search every possible place where Amantine might have hidden it until they realise there is none: those who work in the sugar cane fields cannot afford to buy sugar.

Where Médouze's anger explodes when recalling his father's history, Amantine erupts when she pictures the future. When the children get into serious trouble for creating havoc during the school holidays, they are sent to work in the sugar cane fields. But Amantine refuses to let her grandchild go to work with his friends and vows that she will not condemn children to misery like all these 'gutless black people'. José also remembers her words on hearing of a woman's second stillbirth: 'at least one more poor devil has escaped the cane fields of the whites'.

While Médouze praises the precious gift of life, 'more important than your name', he says, Amantine fights for justice and quality of life. The old man endows José with a spiritual awareness and transmits the narrative of the past, the grandmother looks to the future with insistent political awareness. Médouze represents the African heritage, Amantine embraces French values and transmits these to José – he is taught good table manners and proper behaviour. Education becomes the means of giving him the freedom that was denied to his grandmother and so she carries on with her excessively demanding work, not even contemplating how she is going to find her obligatory contribution to José's tuition fees. For Amantine, the road to this freedom is through identification with French values.

Monsieur Médouze and Amantine, who both die in the course of the story, endow José with human, spiritual and political values that form the foundation of his identity. This, it has been suggested, consists of 'the names we give to the different ways we are positioned by, and position ourselves within, the narratives of the past' (Hall 1992: 224). Médouze provides this narrative, while Amantine is instrumental in instilling a Frenchness in José. These two elements come together in a new cultural identity that integrates the African past and the French future. This explains the two different promises José makes: to Médouze he says, 'If you go to Africa, I'll come with you'; and to Amantine, exhausted by work, he promises to earn enough money to look after her.

These two parent figures become the determining influences on José, who will nevertheless also develop a sense of self through his own peers and other members of society. There is the group of children who discuss zombies and witches who turn into animals; there is the little girl, bright like him, who is not allowed to continue at school but has to start earning money. There is Léopold, the nearly white, second-generation mulatto boy who is not allowed to talk to the 'black' children, but who is himself not white enough for his father, a French aristocrat, to recognise him officially: only 'white' people can inherit a name like de Thorail. Here Jones identifies a use of 'the rhetorical oppositions of *négritude*' in associating de Thorail with the factory and machines in contrast to the Edenic image of a bathing scene which 'suggests a harmonious natural order before the incursion of the whites' (Jones 1993: 8).

When José obtains a full scholarship to study in Fort-de-France and prepares to leave Rue Cases-Nègres, Amantine dies. Médouze is already dead. For José, they will now both return to Africa while he will go to Fort-de-France, 'taking Rue Cases-Nègres with him'. In its merging of the past, through Médouze, with the present and the future, through Amantine, the film reveals that cultural identity is not only a matter of 'being' – but also of 'becoming' (Hall 1992: 223). The contract between Médouze and Amantine suggests both a balance and a dichotomy in identity formation: while Médouze conveys a black consciousness and an anti-colonial discourse of *négritude*, Amantine anticipates the hybridity of Caribbean identity. As Hall puts it: 'Across a whole range of cultural forms there is a "syncretic" dynamic which critically appropriates elements of the master-codes of the dominant culture and "creolises" them' (Hall 1992: 235).

In identifying the link between *Rues Cases-Nègres* and *négritude*, Jones raises another important concept of Caribbean identity. The concept of *négritude*, coined by Martiniquan poet Aimé Césaire in 1948, encapsulates the cultural antagonism between Europe and its colonised countries. The *négritude* movement, endorsed by Martiniquan author Frantz Fanon in his book *Peau noire, masques blancs* (*Black Skin, White Masks*), emphasises the dehumanising aspect of colonialism. While *négritude* is frequently seen as reversed racism, in 1988 Césaire reconfirmed his belief in it, seeing cinema as a great vehicle of *négritude*. *Rue Cases-Nègres* certainly is a case in point (Césaire 1992: 369).

No other film captures so powerfully the past losses and historical rupture of the Caribbean peoples or restores what has been called an 'imaginary fullness'. For the viewer from Martinique *Rue Cases-Nègres* represents a major event: 'By bringing to the screen this novel which is at the same time a novel about roots and about education, the film-maker tackles what is maybe the most intimate part of the Antillean consciousness' (Ménil 1992: 168). The film was hailed as the start of a new cinema of the diaspora. But this was not to be. The promise the film generated has remained unfulfilled. Palcy herself went to Hollywood to make films. Recently she made *Siméon* (1992) with French funding, yet even in this film, where she attempts to celebrate the Afro-Caribbean culture, the elaborate style and excessive use of special effects do little to encourage hopes for the future of Caribbean cinema.

Nevertheless some film-makers are attempting to create Caribbean cinema in the face of huge financial difficulties. One of these is Guy Deslauriers, Palcy's assistant on *Rue Cases-Nègres*. His 1989 short, *Les Oubliés de la liberté* (*Forgotten by Freedom*) deals with 1789 and the spreading of the news of the French Revolution in Saint-Pierre. In 1994 he brought out *L'Exil du Roi Béhanzin* (*The Exile of King Béhanzin*) a film which, though it may not be remembered for its cinematic qualities, nevertheless reveals the core dimension of Caribbean identity through the character of King Béhanzin, last King of Abomey, exiled by the French to Martinique.

Jones sees the film as 'an ambitious attempt at a historical romance, combining a fictitious love-story with a fable of *créolité*', and emphasises its importance as testimony to the melding diversity of the developing creole culture (Jones 1998: 19). Even if the king is presented more as a caricature than as an African dignitary, the phenomenon of creolisation is clearly introduced and raises the question of Caribbean identity.

For these Caribbean islands, writing and theatre have clearly expressed more fully the legacy of the experience of displacement and the cultural effects of the slave trade than film. As Loomba argues, for Senghor *négritude* means that 'racial difference and consciousness are part of the human reality' (Loomba 1998: 211). However, the characters of Amantine in Palcy's film and Deslauriers' King Béhanzin embody the cross-over of ideas and identities brought about by colonialism and now known as creolisation. This phenomenon is captured by Edouard Glissant: 'What has happened in the Caribbean over three centuries is literally this: a meeting of cultural elements from places that are absolutely different which have become truly creolised, truly enmeshed and which have melted into each other to produce an absolutely unforeseeable, absolutely new thing, which is Creole reality' (Glissant 1996: 15, trans.).

5 Haiti

Of the other Francophone islands, only Haiti has produced film-makers but most of them live and work elsewhere. Haiti's history was initially very similar to that of Guadeloupe and Martinique: discovered by Christopher Columbus, its indigenous people were exterminated and replaced by imported slaves. But the island took a different path from the others with a fierce slave revolt in 1791, out of which Toussaint Louverture rose as the new leader. The island gained independence in 1804, though in more recent history, it has long suffered under dictatorship.

Haiti's two main film-makers, Elsie Haas and Raoul Peck, work abroad. Elsie Haas's films are noteworthy for their sustained use of Creole. They depict the lives of ordinary people, through which she explores the themes of colonialism, economic exploitation and the ever-present humiliation of black people.

Raoul Peck

Raoul Peck was born in Haiti, brought up in Zaire (now the Democratic Republic of Congo) and educated in Germany. He divides his time between Europe and America. The social centre of his 1988 *Haitian Corner* is a New York bookshop of the same name, where a young immigrant regularly meets other Haitians. But even with them, he endures a sense of exile and alienation, because of the memory of the seven years he spent in prison. Peck's best-known film remains *L'Homme sur les quais* (*The Man by the Shore*).

L'Homme sur les quais (1993)

The film is set in Haiti in the 1960s after the dictator Duvalier has seized control and a period of violence and persecution has set in. The film's power stems from the fact that the witness to the violence is an eight-year-old girl, Sarah, whose parents have had to flee to escape execution and have left her and her two sisters in the care of their grandmother. The film is structured around Sarah's memory and uses intricate editing. The time frame switches back and forth between the present and events that took place in the past, when Sarah saw her father and godfather beaten and tortured. These are images that will never leave her and will mark her for the rest of her life. However, they are counter-balanced by the grandmother, whose calm, confident manner commands respect and reassurance.

The film denounces the brutality and torture that characterised the Duvalier regime; it also shows how young children who witness such inhuman behaviour on the part of adults are haunted by what they have seen for the rest of their lives.

It is clear that film practice in the Caribbean is an ongoing struggle. The absence of resources and of an adequate infrastructure are major factors in the limited film production. Attempts to encourage film-making have been made by individual islands, such as Martinique where, in 1976, Aimé Césaire, President of the Regional Council, founded the SERMAC (*Service Municipal d'Action Culturelle*) with the aim of promoting all kinds of cultural productions in Martinique. Martinique is also the home of the biennial *Images Caraïbes* film festival, established in Fort-de-France by a Martiniquan woman, Suzy Landau.

All these efforts to encourage Caribbean film-making are crucially important, since cinema plays a vital role in constituting people's identities. As Hall writes: 'I have been trying to speak of identity as constituted, not outside but within representation, and, hence, of cinema not as second-order mirror held up to reflect what already exists but as that form of representation which is also able to constitute us as new kinds of subjects and thereby enable us to discover who we are' (Hall 1992: 235).

III AFRICA

At a conference in Berlin in 1884–85, the European empire-building powers agreed to recognise the colonial *status quo* in Africa and to further divide those countries as yet uncolonised without fighting among themselves. The African peoples concerned were, of course, not involved in these discussions. Many tried to resist the invaders but the Europeans 'were too strong in technology and organisation, especially in the use of rifles and machine-guns; and the partition was almost complete by about 1900' (Davidson 1997: 5).

The colonisation of Africa was a brutal affair. At first European troops invaded the different countries, but soon soldiers from other colonised countries joined the European forces. 'After 1900', as Basil Davidson notes, 'African troops under European officers did most of this work' (1997: 6). Once Africa was colonised, its fate became inevitably linked to that of Europe and, through Europe, to events in the rest of the world: including World War I, the Great Depression, World War II and the Indochina War.

The two large areas that came under French rule were the Maghreb and sub-Saharan Africa. The name 'Maghreb', as Anthony Pazzanita explains, comes from the Arab *jazirat al-maghrib* which means 'island of the west'. It refers to its position as a kind of island, separated from Europe by the Mediterranean and from sub-Saharan Africa by the vast wastes of the Sahara. He further notes that, as a result of this isolation, it remained an outpost of Berber civilisation and language that proved resistant to Arab inroads. The three countries of the Maghreb – Algeria, Morocco and Tunisia – have often been perceived as a unit in spite of their separate histories. All three were colonised by the French but, while Morocco and Tunisia were able to keep regional languages and patterns of religious and local authority, Algeria experienced an extreme form of colonialism (Pazzanita 1998: xvii). The Maghreb countries are linked by a common religion, Islam, and a common language, Arabic. Although the language may vary considerably, it still offers a common idiom which is a great advantage for Maghreb cinema.

Of the countries south of the Sahara that became French colonies or came under French domination in other ways (Mandate of the League of Nations or United Nations' trusteeship territories), eight have a credible film output. They are Senegal, Mali, Mauritania, Niger, Côte d'Ivoire,

Guinea, Cameroon and Burkina Faso. They are usually referred to as 'French West Africa'. While it would be inaccurate to say that the countries not mentioned here, such as Gabon or Togo, make no films, their film output is either insufficiently representative or unavailable for inclusion in the present study. However, one country, the Democratic Republic of Congo, not part of the old French colonial empire but now a member of the Francophone organisation, has recently drawn international attention by winning the 1999 FESPACO Stallion with *Pièces d'identités* and is, therefore, included here. Unlike the Maghreb, the countries of sub-Saharan Africa have no shared religion or language other than French, which has remained distinctly foreign and implicated in colonialism.

Although the countries within these two Francophone regions each have their own distinct characteristics, several historical and linguistic criteria and their shared colonial experience justify grouping them when exploring their film production. While French is by no means the language spoken by most people in these countries – 23 per cent in the Maghreb and only 2.6 per cent in the sub-Saharan countries (*Le Monde*, 4 September 1999: 2) – it remains the *lingua franca* which links them internally in their own continent and, beyond that, with other Francophone countries and with France itself. They all belong to the *Organisation Internationale de la Francophonie* and although some, such as Algeria, shun the organisation for political or ideological reasons, it is nevertheless a channel for communication and for the promotion of the cultures of the individual countries.

It was not until independence, however, that these African countries began to make their own films. Most of them had been exposed to film from an early date, but it was film that belonged to the coloniser, who used it for the purpose of 'civilisation' or harmless 'entertainment'. No black people were shown in these films: the screens themselves were colonised. But when independence came about, sub-Saharan Africa was left impoverished. Colonisation had set up structures intended to preserve the colonial regime rather than to foster national autonomy. Those countries with natural resources did not have the expertise to exploit them and were left unequipped for economic survival without support from the former colonisers.

Film-making was not a priority for most African governments; it is, therefore, remarkable that such an impressive body of African films has been created, particularly since the problems facing African cinema were enormous. Economic infirmity, lack of technical expertise and training and the absence of government support in most of the countries left the film-makers with the dilemma of depending on an almost unobtainable medium, cinema, to give expression to the problems of their countries and to raise African awareness of the dangers of neo-colonialism (characterised most noticeably by greed and corruption).

Francophone African countries quickly became aware of cinema's potential for expressing autonomy and liberty. They realised that in spite of their abhorrence of colonialism, the 'Francophone' label was useful and probably necessary for promoting African cinema in general. It should be noted that in this context Francophone Africa has been much more successful than Anglophone Africa in film-making. As Manthia Diawara writes, 'Films directed by Africans in the former French colonies are superior, both in quantity and in quality, to those by directors in other sub-Saharan African countries formerly colonised by the British, the Belgians, and the Portuguese' (Diawara 1992: 21).

Cinema, it was believed, offered a means to educate people and to present the audience with images they could relate to and which would develop an African identity, as opposed to that forced upon them by the former coloniser or that projected on to their screens by the capitalist countries that continued to dominate African cinema distribution even after independence. Many African countries turned to Marxist nations, with whom they were more in tune ideologically; inevitably, these countries also offered models for the development of their film industry. It led some African countries to nationalise their cinema production, which in many cases also led to censorship.

In 1966 the first world festival of Negro art, the *Premier Festival Mondial des Arts Nègres*, was held in Dakar. At this festival, as Manthia Diawara records, film-makers had many recommendations concerning different aspects of film, such as the creation of an inter-African film office that would gather and disseminate information about African cinema; the transfer to Africa of production and post-production facilities; the restructuring of the film market (film catalogues, exhibition statistics, inventories of production equipment, and the creation of funds to sustain African film production). The festival also emphasised the need to create schools and institutes for film training. It was a near-exhaustive inventory and an ambitious programme for the development of African film (Diawara 1992: 38).

The Dakar festival brought out Francophone Africa's determination and motivation to build a rich and educational film industry. The festival paved the way for a meeting, that same year, in the historic Tunisian city of Carthage, to which Tahar Cheriaa invited a number of people most able to reflect on the development of a specifically African cinema and on its place in world cinema. The Carthage meeting led to the creation of what is known as the JCC (the 'Journées Cinématographiques de Carthage' – the Carthage film festival), a gathering of critics, film-makers and film lovers from all over the world. The winners of the golden Tanit (the Carthage festival's key prize), such as Ousmane Sembene's *La Noire de . . .* (1966 – *Black Girl*) and Med Hondo's *Les Bicots-Nègres, vos voisins* (1976 – *Arabs and Negroes, Your Neighbours*), reveal the militant stance of the

JCC in supporting politically committed films, often censored in the film-maker's country of origin. The JCC also offers fruitful contacts between the Maghreb and the sub-Saharan countries as well as with countries outside Africa.

Three weeks after the second session of the JCC, in February 1969, a week of African cinema was organised in the capital of Burkina Faso, Ouagadougou: the *Semaine du Cinéma Africain de Ouagadougou*, which was attended by many West African film-makers who had recently returned from the Carthage film festival. This 1969 event was to become the much-celebrated FESPACO (*Festival Panafricain du Cinéma de Ouagadougou*), which thirty years on has grown beyond all expectation.

The Carthage and Ouagadougou festivals created the need for an official organisation that would bring together film-makers from different parts of Africa. This would give the events official status, while itself remaining a non-governmental organisation (NGO). This new organisation, FEPACI (*Fédération Panafricaine des Cinéastes*), was created in 1970 and remains an important NGO. In his *African Cinema: Politics and Culture*, Diawara devotes a full chapter to an overview of the history of FEPACI, while Cheriaa, in his chapter 'La FEPACI et nous' (The FEPACI and Us), re-examines its impact and further direction. FEPACI is above all a body that aims at lending active support to its members (Diawara 1992: 34–50 and Cheriaa 1995: 253–68).

When the 'Week of African Cinema' took place in 1969, in Ouagadougou, eighteen African films from five countries were shown. In 1970, nine countries were represented and thirty-seven films shown. At the thirtieth anniversary of the Ouagadougou event, the 1999 FESPACO, 150 films were shown. In addition to the films, interviews take place and various debates and seminars are organised. FESPACO has become an institution that is now twinned with other film festivals such as the FIFF (*Festival International du Film Francophone*) in Namur, Belgium and Vues d'Afrique in Montréal.

The main theme of the FESPACO festival in 1987 was 'cinema and cultural identity' and the Yennenga Stallion (the prize for the best full-length feature film) was to be given to 'the film that gave the best understanding of the cultural identity and racial realities of Africa'. In awarding the Stallion to Med Hondo's *Sarraounia* (1986), the jury stated that this film had been selected because, firstly, it restored the historical realities of Africa; secondly, it had been made successfully as a co-production (Burkina Faso-Mauritania) with no distortion of its message; thirdly, it was the entry that best corresponded to FESPACO's fundamental goal of expanding and developing African film as a means of expression, education and consciousness-raising and, finally, it was the film that best reflected the theme of the tenth FESPACO: cinema and cultural identity.

Although there is now a very credible corpus of African films of excellent quality, as proven by the many international awards several of these films have attracted, it is difficult to speak of a unitary African or Francophone-African film industry, as one might for example of India. As film-maker Moussa Touré points out, 'Francophone' and 'African' are classificatory labels designating an ensemble of cinematic output. When it comes to a film-maker's specific identity, it is essential to refer to the context of that director's country and, where relevant, to its ethnic subdivisions.

Therefore, when considering the notion of 'identity' in relation to the African continent it is important to remember that in addition to common features inherited from a shared negative heritage of Western invasions, colonialism and slave trade, the Francophone African countries comprise a very wide variety of cultures, languages and religions. To speak of an 'African identity' would be to ignore the specific character of each ethnic group and country. However, as André Gardies observed in 1989, it is still difficult to identify national cinemas in Africa, in spite of the political determination of the 'new' countries to assert their own identities.

Ten years on, stronger national identities are emerging and studies on specific countries and individual film-makers are appearing. Yet, because of the distribution problems of African cinema, which cause African films to remain unknown to a larger audience, each country still needs the over-reaching groupings of being 'African' and 'Francophone'. Although French has been losing support in most of these countries and is spoken less and less, identification with the Francophone world remains advantageous for film-makers, because Francophone grouping provides a wider channel for distribution. Despite the increasing use of Arabic and local languages throughout the African continent, reference to Francophone African cinema continues to be valid; it views African cinema in its historical context and is a means of promoting the films of these individual countries more strongly. It also provides a counter-balance against an increasing incursion of Anglophone cinema.

6　Algeria

Algeria's rich and ancient civilisation began in pre-historic times, when the Berber peoples occupied North Africa. It was later transformed by the arrival of the Arabs, who established Islam in the country in the seventh century. The French invasion of Algeria in 1830 marked the beginning of a large-scale and oppressive European colonisation. The settlers not only took over the towns and confiscated the most fertile pieces of land, forcing Algerian farmers into the mountainous barren plateaux, they also crushed the cultural heritage, repressed Islam and discouraged the use of Arabic.

Muslim leaders and Berber groups initially tried to resist the colonising forces, but the French brutally suppressed any sign of rebellion. The repressive colonial system led to immense discontent. But French oppression was such that it was not until the 1940s that nationalist leaders, such as Ahmed Messali Hadj, began to campaign actively for equal rights. World War II brought more pressure for change. In 1945 serious riots broke out in a number of Algerian towns and in 1947 an Algerian Assembly was set up – though the elections were rigged to ensure that nationalists were kept out.

Peaceful campaigns for increased rights for Algerians led to more repression. So political manoeuvring gave way to violence. Ahmed Ben Bella, who later became the first president of independent Algeria, fled to Cairo in 1952 and set up the body which was to plan the revolution – the CRUA (*Comité Révolutionnaire d'Unité et d'Action*/Revolutionary Committee of Unity and Action). Its nine members are regarded as the historic leaders of Algeria's independence. The CRUA launched the Algerian Liberation War on 1 November 1954, having established the FLN (*Front de Libération Nationale*/National Liberation Front) to fight in central, coastal and urban Algeria and the ALN (*Armée de Libération Nationale*/Army of National Liberation) to fight in the almost inaccessible Aurès mountains. By 1956 France had sent nearly half a million troops to Algiers and had succeeded in capturing Ahmed Ben Bella and other FLN leaders. French retaliations were as brutal as the guerrillas' attacks and France itself was divided by the Algerian question. But it was a war France could not win and on 5 July 1962, Algeria became independent.

Cinema had been introduced into Algeria shortly after its invention in 1895, when the Lumière *opérateurs* organised their first screenings.

During the colonial era the Algerians themselves played no part in cinema, although Algiers and its casbah became a popular setting for French films, such as Julien Duvivier's *Pépé le Moko* (1937), and there were many film theatres catering to the European settlers in the cities. During World War II the French authorities set up a distribution network and a production unit to take films to the rural areas of Algeria for propaganda purposes.

When the Liberation War broke out in 1954, Algerians were not then in a position to bring images to the screen. However, several French films refer covertly or overtly to the war. The most outspoken French film-maker was René Vautier, the first to document the war in his *Algérie en flammes* (1957 – *Algeria in Flames*), made at the request of Frantz Fanon. Camera in hand, Vautier joined the Algerian resistance in the Aurès mountains and was wounded. He was then taken to East Berlin, where he edited the film. *Algérie en flammes* was subsequently banned in France and not shown until May 1968, when it was screened at the Sorbonne in Paris.

René Vautier was by no means the only film-maker to refer critically to the war. It was the subject or background of many French films of the late 1950s and early 1960s, such as Godard's *Le Petit Soldat* (1960), Agnes Varda's *Cléo de 5 à 7* (1961), Alain Resnais's *Muriel, ou le temps d'un retour* (1962), Jacques Rozier's *Adieu Philippine* (1963) and, more recently, Bertrand Tavernier's *La Guerre sans nom* (1991).

Algeria's own cinema was 'born out of the war', to use Armes's expression (Armes 1996). The focus of most of the first Algerian films was, quite naturally, the liberation itself – the traumatic founding event of modern Algerian society. Efforts on the part of the government to set up film production centres included the short-lived CAV (*Centre Audio-Visuel*), under the auspices of Algeria's Ministry of Youth and Sport in 1962, and the OAA (*Offices des Actualités Algériennes*/Algerian Newsreel Office) under directorship of Mohamed Lakhdar-Hamina, set up in 1963 and dissolved in 1974.

In 1964 the Ministry of Information and Culture set up the CNCA (*Centre National du Cinéma Algérien*) with a vast brief that included responsibility for film distribution, the creation of a film archive, the *Cinémathèque Algérienne*, and the setting up of a new film training institute. In 1962 the television system was nationalised and contributed considerably to the reputation of Algerian cinema. In 1967 the ONCIC (*Office National du Commerce et de l'Industrie Cinématographiques*) replaced the earlier organisations and was responsible for virtually all Algerian feature film production. It was directed by Ahmed Rachedi from 1967 to 1973. It was dissolved in 1984 following serious financial difficulties and was replaced by two organisations with different functions under the umbrella of the CAAIC (*Centre Algérien pour l'Art et l'Industrie*

Cinématographique). However, in the late 1980s this newly formed organ-isation was also plagued by financial troubles, which meant it could no longer pay the foreign production labs it used.

After its beginnings in 1964, Algerian cinema had three distinct periods. The first, from 1964 to 1971, sought to preserve the memory of the Libera-tion War. Most of the films made in that period attempt to come to an understanding of the events which preceded the war and to develop a notion of a new Algerian identity. The main films of the 1964–71 period were made by the directors of the state organisations, Lakhdar-Hamina (OAA) and Ahmed Rachedi (ONCIC). The second phase, from 1971 to 1976, was influenced by the Agrarian revolution of 1971 and the nascent industrialisation under the Boumedienne government. The war was not forgotten by film-makers such as Mohamed Bouamari, but the post-war problems and the struggles of the individual became more important. The third phase of Algerian cinema, starting in 1976 and lasting until the early 1980s, introduced new themes hitherto unexplored, including the problems of young people, women and marginal groups. In this period there is a greater integration of cinematographic style and the social reality depicted. Important film-makers of the third period include Merzak Allouache, Assia Djebar, Mohamed Chouikh and Jean-Pierre Lledo.

Mohamed Lakhdar-Hamina

Mohamed Lakhdar-Hamina, one of the representatives of the first period of Algerian cinema, is often claimed to have dominated Algerian cinema both as director of OAA and as a film-maker.

Le Vent des Aurès (1967)

Le Vent des Aurès (*The Wind from the Aurès*) came out the same year as *La Bataille d'Alger* (*The Battle of Algiers*) by Italian film-maker Gillo Pontecorvo. While Pontecorvo's film is set in Algiers' casbah and portrays a trapped hero, Ali La Pointe, for whom there is no escape, *Le Vent des Aurès* takes place in the imposing Aurès mountains, an almost inaccessible region of eastern Algeria, where the struggle for independence originated. The region's geography prevented the French from winning an easy victory and its isolation enabled it to preserve its old Berber traditions and culture.

The film depicts the war through the life of an individual farming family. The beginning shows the family's everyday life, punctuated by clandestine resistance activities at night. A French air raid, which kills the father, prompts the son to take up the resistance struggle. After he is arrested by the French, his mother wanders from camp to camp looking for him. When she finally sees him and rushes towards him, she is electrocuted by the wire erected around the camp. This tragic film contrasts the minute details of a family's daily life with the destruction of that existence, followed by the mother's desperate quest. The tragedy she lives is emblematic of that of Algeria as a whole: it represents the country through the image of an impoverished old Algerian woman, suggesting both the country's long history and the colonisers' exploitation of the agricultural people.

While still director of the Newsreel Office in 1972, Lakhdar-Hamina made *Décembre* (*December*), which explores the issue of torture through the eyes of a conscience-stricken French officer. His *Chronique des années de braise* (1975 – *Chronicle of the Years of Embers*), produced with the ONCIC, was the first African film to win the Palme d'Or at Cannes. This epic traces the development of the different Algerian resistance movements from the beginning of colonisation until the insurrection in 1954. While *Le Vent des Aurès* symbolised the tragic aspects of the liberation war through the character of a single woman, in *Chronique des années de braise* 'a peasant family represents the Algerian as a whole, experiencing the three historical phases of colonialism, described in the films as the years of ashes, the years of the chariot, and the years of embers' (Shafik 1998: 176). Lakhdar-Hamina's films are now classics of the representation of the struggle for liberation.

Ahmed Rachedi

Ahmed Rachedi's career as a film-maker started with his documentaries on the early years of Algerian independence.

L'Opium et le bâton (1970)

Like Lakhdar-Hamina, Ahmed Rachedi used his position as director of the ONCIC to make *L'Opium et le bâton* (*The Opium and the Baton*), a story of the maquis resistance fighters in Thala, a village in the Kabyle mountains. It shows several members of the same family, who are both separated and united by the liberation war: one has joined the French military of the Specialised Administrative Section or SAS (*Section Administrative Spécialisée*); another, Ali, has enlisted in the resistance; a third, an urban doctor, has difficulty in shifting from *thinking* about the situation to becoming actively involved.

The film includes long battle scenes, where at times it seems the resistance could have won the battle. However, the French succeed in capturing Ali and execute him in front of his family before burning the entire village. The resistance fighters are depicted as unusually brave, near super-human beings, glorifying the image of the Algerian fighter or *Mudjahid*. The film's graphic battle scenes and glorified representation of the *Mudjahid* have been viewed as Hollywoodian in their use of the 'recipes' of the American action film (Hennebelle 1972: 116). The

al-rudjila signifies 'virility, honour and courage'. When exaggerated it approaches machismo. For the Algerian viewer, it denotes a familiar cultural characteristic and, therefore, generates a specific expectation (Hadj-Moussa 1994: 148).

While Omar is describing himself, his background and childhood memories, he is getting ready to go out, creating his character, so to speak. He carefully combs his hair, with no mirror other than the gaze of the camera/viewer. Omar's address to the camera invites the viewer to be an ally or a witness. This strategy of commenting to the viewer will continue, but it also shifts to a voice-over expressing his interior monologue. As Armes remarks, 'Omar's voice-over has the same basic functions as the commentary in a documentary: naming, describing, predicting', while the 'technique of interior monologue is borrowed from narrated fictional films' (Armes 1998: 13).

The combination of documentary and fictional modes casts an interesting light on the identity of the character. As he introduces himself and describes his immediate family and geographic environment, he comes across as a virile masculine character; however, it soon becomes clear that this is also a story in which Omar will be shaped by events and by the society around him.

Wherever he goes, he takes his small cassette recorder on which he records two kinds of music: popular Algerian *châabi* music and music from the many Indian films shown in Algiers. When he is mugged and robbed of this fetish object, he loses a whole world of voices and sounds. Hadj-Moussa suggests that the *châabi* music, which emphasises the absolute power of love, acts as a substitute for the absence of women in a society where the sexes are segregated (Hadj-Moussa 1994: 157). Armes sees this segregation as the main theme in the film: it is, he argues, 'a profound analysis of the impact of social segregation in society' (Armes 1998: 35).

Women are absent in Omar's social environment, but they abound in his home. In the overcrowded house there is hardly any segregation between the sexes: Omar shares his room with his younger sister and the children of his divorced sister. His mother and divorced sister share a room and the grandfather sleeps in the kitchen. Omar finds his sister's presence in his room particularly objectionable: 'She is a woman now', he says, as the camera shows her combing her long black hair.

The only privacy he has is provided by the music and voices of the cassette recorder. When, after the mugging, Moh, one of Omar's friends, supplies him with another cassette player, the voice of a girl to whom Moh had previously lent it has been saved by accident on a cassette. This is the turning point in the film: Omar is seduced by Selma's voice. Allouache's mastery of cinematic language is revealed in the interplay of voice and image, when the viewer sees Omar's reaction to the power of

Selma's voice. All Omar's efforts are concentrated on the finding of the embodiment of that voice: Selma becomes the object of Omar's quest.

Omar's escape from his family's poverty and his growing awareness of his need for women were initially anchored in the music of his cassette recorder, but have now shifted to Selma's voice. It makes him believe in a future, especially when, with help from Moh, he succeeds in arranging a meeting with Selma. On the morning of the encounter he feels reborn. He is wearing his smart suit, has missed work and gone to the *hammam* (the communal baths) instead. He has created a new persona, feels in control, and is determined to bridge the distance between himself, the machismo male, and Selma. All he has to do now is cross the road to meet her. Encouraged by Moh but taunted by friends from the office, he hesitates. The film, which until this point has shown only overcrowded places, now leaves a void between Omar and Selma, a square to cross. Omar, ill at ease in his tight black suit is near the camera; Selma, at ease in colourful clothes, is at a distance on the other side of the square. At the last moment, Omar lacks the courage to bridge the distance separating them. The film closes showing Omar locked in his old daily routine, showing his imprisonment in an inert society, in which people have given up the struggle for change.

Bab el-Oued City (1994)

If *Omar Gatlato* depicts a character who fails to step out of his old persona, Allouache's more recent films, such as *Bab el-Oued City* and *Alger-Beyrouth pour mémoire* address another kind of inescapable social prison: that of Muslim fundamentalism, which does not allow room for individual decisions or non-conformist modes of behaviour.

In these two films, the characters also carry the memory of past violence: in *Bab el-Oued City* it is that of the serious riots of October 1988, while in *Alger-Beyrouth pour mémoire* the memory of violence concerns two cities, Algiers and Beirut. Here again, Allouache chooses to tell the stories of individuals, revealing how their identities and lives have been marked by the violence they experienced and witnessed in these cities.

In *Bab el-Oued City*, the October riots of 1988 are still very present in people's minds. They erupted because of resentment against the austerity programmes introduced by the government after the economic crisis caused by the collapse of the oil price and the devaluation of the American dollar in 1986. Prices rose sharply, unemployment increased and social benefits were reduced. In October 1988, the tensions erupted in widespread rioting. This was brutally suppressed by the army, which was called in when the police proved unable to cope. While Islamic militants did not start the riots, they were the only organised movement to voice the frustrations of the people. The Islamic movement that subsequently developed and the consolidation of the FIS (*Front Islamique du Salut/*

Islamic Front for Salvation) are seen by Lawless 'as a belated reaction to the continuing subordination of Islam to the FLN state' (Lawless 1995: xxvi). Allouache notes that since the October riots an important social structure of the city has been lost, that of the *quartier*. In an interview he mentions that the *quartier* 'has always been a place of refuge, where you can find yourself and be at home' (Allouache 1995: 34). When this social haven was destroyed, the family structure itself became threatened and the individual lost a sense of safety.

Allouache's stories always allow for identification with specific characters. *Bab el-Oued City* shows how a minor incident leads to violent revenge and ultimately to exile. The main character, liberal-minded Boualem, works the night shift in a bakery and sleeps during the day. One morning, irritated and unable to sleep because of the noise from loudspeakers broadcasting Islamic rules of conduct, he climbs on to the roof and tears the speaker down. Said, the leader of a group of young Muslim fundamentalists, sees this incident as an explicit provocation.

The film thus opposes two groups of young people, Islamic fundamentalists, represented by Said, and liberals, represented by Boualem. The problem of identity comes to the fore in this split. The Muslim identity is a collective one, as suggested by the way Said is always seen as part of a group in which everyone acts and thinks alike. The liberal-minded Boualem, on the other hand, is seen more often by himself or in conversation with Yamina (his girlfriend and Said's sister), or with another woman-friend – both covert relationships. The aggression escalates and in the end Boualem can only escape into exile. The film closes where it began: three years after Boualem's departure, Yamina is writing to him, her voice conveying the sadness she has felt since his departure.

Alger-Beyrouth pour mémoire (1998)

Alger-Beyrouth pour mémoire (*Algiers-Beirut: a Souvenir*) also focuses on exile, this time that of journalist Rachid. Rachid has fled from one war zone to another, from Algiers to Beirut. He is plagued by guilt because, when in Algiers, he colluded with the murder of one of his friends and co-collaborators. He has lost his commitment to any cause, leads an aimless life and has become an alcoholic. One day he has a chance meeting with a former colleague and friend, Laurence. Laurence's father died in Beirut and she has come to make a video for her ageing mother. The past feels distant to her, but for Rachid past wounds remain open. His act of cowardly betrayal continues to haunt him. His meeting with Laurence and their brief love affair finally give him the courage to return to Algiers. However, death is ever-present in this film. The final sequence shows Laurence, back in France. She is watching television, her mother has died and the news broadcast reports the death of yet another journalist in Algiers.

The stories in Allouache's films are intricate and at times difficult to unravel. They spin a web of the conflicting values which beset the individual in the Arab world, with its religious and political conflicts. In *Bab el-Oued City*, corruption also underlies the extreme religious fervour, as racketeers keep control over the city and over Said and his group. Some seek to escape while appearing to adhere to the Muslim principles; some, like Boualem, are unable to accept the senseless rules imposed by the extremists. The struggle for identity seems a lost battle: the individual either, like Omar Gatlato, lacks the courage to change, or, like Boualem, must face exile, or, like Rachid, sees his life wrecked and returns to the past, possibly to face death.

For Allouache himself, the struggle has become an artistic one. If the characters in his films fail to reach out for change and freedom, the films themselves typify a trend of decolonisation of both content and style, juxtaposing space, time and events in an unconventional way. Flash-backs, dreams and voice-over convey individual experience, casting it against a background of social stagnation, economic decline, political oppression and religious intolerance.

Assia Djebar

Assia Djebar, a well-established Algerian writer, succeeded in obtaining financial backing for her first film, which remains her best known.

La Nouba des femmes du mont Chenoua (1978)

La Nouba des Women du mont Chenoua (*The Nouba of the Women of Mount Chenoa*) interweaves documentary footage with staged reconstructions of actual events. The word *nouba* designates a traditional type of music. Its use in the title suggests that the film is constructed as a musical suite made up of different fragments, rather than a logical or chronological narrative; a device Djebar also uses in her novels. The film tells the story of Layla, an educated woman who returns from abroad with her paralysed husband and their child. In the course of her journey she visits and interviews women, who talk about daily life and about the past. The stories told by these women have hitherto not been listened to. Djebar's aim was to let women speak, to end the silence in which they are trapped. The film interweaves all these stories, using an intuitive musical structuring where voices and background music intertwine, creating a work of reminiscence, an evocation of past themes rather than accurate documents concerning the French occupation and the war of liberation.

Djebar makes a genuine attempt to emphasise the feminine, to give a prominent place to the female narrator-traveller and to make women's voices audible, supporting them with the music of the *nouba*. The film is dedicated to the Hungarian composer Béla Bartók, and includes pieces Bartók composed during his stay in Algeria, where he recorded thousands of folk songs. Djebar's task is similar: her recording of the voices is a strategy to let memory surface. The musical metaphor becomes important as a means of retrieving memory and so reaching a sense of self.

Djebar's feminism, rooted in a profound sense of justice, is brought out in two films about her made by Kamel Dehane: the documentary *Assia Djebar entre ombre et lumière* (1992) and *Femmes d'Alger* (1993), an exploration of the lives of Algerian women through Djebar's work. For Djebar, French, the language of the coloniser, became an instrument of the principle of freedom, on which she founded her identity and her art.

Mohamed Chouikh

Chouikh began his career as an actor in some of the most important Algerian films including *Le Vent des Aurès* by Lakdhar-Hamina, on whose film *Vent de sable* he worked as an assistant director. The same year (1982) Chouikh directed his own first film *Rupture (Breakdown)*, which deals with the protagonist's escape from prison and struggle with the colonial system. This debut was followed by three remarkable films *La Citadelle* (1988), *Youcef ou la légende du septième dormant* (1993) and *L'Arche du désert* (1997).

La Citadelle (1988)
The film opens with a long torch-lit procession winding down from the ridge above a village. This is the procession for newly married men, who are being escorted towards wives who are awaiting them. The future spouses do not know each other. The film shows the dramatic and decisive moment when, upon lifting his bride's veil, a disappointed husband's fury is unleashed. The procession's long, slow descent is like a descent into an abyss, in which the characters are trapped by a tyrannical social structure. In this harsh society, marriage is portrayed as the central despotic unit.

The film discredits this despotism by introducing an outsider, Kaddour, who is not integrated into society. He is the servant of a fabric merchant, who has four wives, while Kaddour is too poor to have even one. Kaddour seeks help from the marabout to gain access to the neighbour's wife, to whom he is attracted. This involves his stealing fabric from his master to pay the marabout. Kaddour then proceeds to carry out the marabout's subsequent request and cuts off a strand of the woman's hair. When his master learns about the incident he decides to marry Kaddour off that very day. There are no women available in the village, not even in the brothel.

Kaddour becomes the victim of a cruel joke, a pseudo-marriage in which he too is escorted to the room where an unknown veiled woman awaits him. Deeply moved, he enters the room and talks gently to the woman. When she fails to react, Kaddour seeks advice from the elders who tell him to beat her. Reluctantly he hits the woman, then lifts her veil only to find a mannequin-dummy. He is seen coming out of the room, carrying his 'bride', then walking through the sniggering crowd. Finally he comes to a sheer drop at the mountain's edge, throws his 'wife' over and jumps after her. A young girl who wants to jump after him is restrained. The film closes with a long, lasting freeze of the girl shrieking 'let me go'.

This film denounces the abusive power of an ideology that imposes a monolithic identity on all members of society. Those individuals who are unable to accept the compulsory values and customs have no place and are mercilessly excluded, in this case through a most cruel public humiliation.

Youcef ou la légende du septième dormant (1993)

Youcef ou la légende du septième dormant (*The Legend of the Seventh Sleeper*) also deals with the problem of an individual's failure to find his place in society, in this case, Youcef's return after years of imprisonment. Everything is blurred for Youcef, who is suffering the lasting impact of war and imagines himself back in the resistance. Using a rusty old radio in the forest, he tries in vain to link up with his old resistance group, unaware that the colonisers have left and the country is free. A victim of years of imprisonment, he can no longer relate to the world around him; he recognises nothing, is permanently at odds with the people he meets and fails to comprehend how it is that his fellow-fighters in the liberation war now live in the luxurious houses that once belonged to the colonisers.

He is baffled when he meets the free-spirited woman who fought alongside him for Algeria's liberation. Instead of the woman with the wind-swept hair he remembers so well, he finds a veiled woman, married to a husband who inflicts more violence than she ever endured in the war. Youcef is lost and disoriented in a world with which he can no longer identify. The film shows the painful state of being other, displaced in time and space.

L'Arche du désert (1997)

Chouikh's more recent film, *L'Arche du désert* (*The Ark in the Desert*), again portrays an outsider, this time a child. Unlike Kaddour, this boy is integrated into society; however, he is the young observer of adult behaviour and cruelty that he cannot relate to or identify with. Although the narrative is not structured from his point of view, he is present from the beginning as a silent observer and witness of everything that happens.

The film opens with images of happiness and harmony: people working and singing together in the fields, accompanied by drums. The boy observes how the atmosphere is suddenly shattered by the meeting of two young people, Myriam and Amin. The two have hidden from the villagers and are frolicking and laughing, when several of the girl's male relatives notice them and call for vengeance because they have been dishonoured. They brutally drag Myriam over the sand and beat Amin very badly. He is carried back to his house, blood running down his back, with his mother hysterically crying behind him. The little boy watches the scene from the distance.

The violence triggered by this incident escalates to real warfare. The once peaceful and harmonious society, in which several ethnic groups cooperated, fragments into different groups, filled with unrestrained hatred and brutality. Myriam and Amin are from different ethnic groups. He is poorer than she is and Amin's mother pleads in vain to let the two marry, saying that their poverty does not make them less honourable. But Amin is exiled and Myriam chained until her uncle comes to pronounce his verdict.

The little boy remains the silent, intense observer of the events. He is seen in close-up or medium shot, usually alone. Once he is seated with a little girl, both witnessing the treatment of Myriam. 'When I'm grown up,' the little boy tells the girl, 'I shan't chain my wife. Only animals are chained, not humans.'

Ultimately Myriam and Amin succeed in finding each other again, but only after Myriam escapes from a forced marriage. In the 'wedding' scene, Myriam emerges from the hut where the marriage is to be consummated in a blood-stained dress, but what was to be her own blood, proving her virginity, is that of the husband she has stabbed.

Some time later Amin and Myriam leave their hiding place and return to the village, where they are confronted with the effects of ethnic hatred: the houses have been set on fire and most of the people have been killed. The little boy has been spared. Carrying a small bag, he walks away through the palm oasis into the desert. He looks around, not certain which direction to take before setting out purposefully. A little further on he sees an ark in the sand, from which a man shouts that the waves will engulf everything and urges the boy to come in. The film closes showing the little boy shouting to the man: 'Grown-up people have gone mad and so have you. I'm not going into a boat in the sand. I will go somewhere to be in peace. I'm leaving for another land where children aren't killed and houses aren't burnt.' This almost surreal image of the boat in the sand epitomises the madness of the intolerance provoked by an excessive sense of ethnic identity.

In all three films, Chouikh depicts the conflict between individual identity and group identity. In each case, an individual, – Kaddour, the returning prisoner Youcef, and the little boy – fails to find a society with which he can identify. In each case the monolithic model proposed – respectively ill-conceived tradition, muslim fundamentalism and ethnic intolerance – is self-destructive. Chouikh films powerfully express the paralysing trauma such monolithic models cause.

Jean-Pierre Lledo

Jean-Pierre Lledo is himself an exile. In 1993, realising that intellectuals and artists were the main target of assassinations then occuring in Algeria and being directly threatened himself, he decided to leave. He now lives in Paris, yet Algeria remains the focus of his art and thoughts. In spite of the danger that filming in Algeria poses, he returned to make his *Chroniques Algériennes*, capturing the Algerian situation in 1994.

Chroniques Algériennes (1994)

These *Algerian Chronicles*, consisting of observations and interviews, were filmed by three film-makers, of whom Lledo is the most important, using small hand-held camera's over a three-week period. They document the killing of Khedidja, a thirty-five-year-old police woman, in front of her seven-year-old child; that of Ahmed Asselah from the Algiers' art school, and that of Abdelkader Alloula, a playwright whose daughter is also prepared to sacrifice herself, although 'sacrifice' has lost its meaning. How can these murders be 'justified' other than by blind belief in the Fatwa that explains them. A lawyer explains how a Fatwa killing is tantamount to taking the place of God and how he is in constant fear for his own life. A village committee of elders explains to the film-maker that everything hinges on the failure to distinguish between politics and religion.

The film-makers began filming on 16 June 1994. On the 29 June, they secretly filmed a demonstration organised to commemorate the killing of President Mohammed Boudiaf two years earlier. In the midst of the demonstration, a bomb exploded; rather than stop filming, the film-makers captured fragments of images: the faces of injured people and people reassembling to continue the march. Underlying their determination is a powerful desire to return to normal life and everyday pleasures. Islamic values and Algerian politics that fashion identities recede and are replaced by the universal thirst for pleasure. The film closes away from demonstrations, politics and funerals of murdered people, on a beach where people are enjoying the everyday pleasures that have become reasons for killing. A thirst for life dominates, while the Islamic fundamentalists continue to try and impose a monolithic Muslim identity.

These final beach scenes depict normal everyday life, the pleasure of swimming and a sense of freedom which, as one woman puts it, they are not willing to compromise. The search for a new self underlies these scenes.

Lledo's documentary on autistic children, *La Mer est bleue, le ciel aussi* (1990), contains a telling metaphor on the oppression by Islamic fundamentalism. Lledo shows a child drawing a set of traffic lights where all three lights are red. He then cuts to juxtaposed documentary stills showing the riots of 1988, making a link in this way between autism and a fundamentalist society, where the only order seems to be 'stop'. Such a society, the film implies, is an autistic society.

In Algerian cinema, history and memory intersect; the films are narrative representations of social realities, often contrasting the self-assured collective identity of the settlers with the ongoing struggle of the impoverished indigenous peoples to find some fragments of their lost past and lost identity. For these people the fight for more basic survival tended to reduce any sense of identity to the level of simple physical existence. These films provide significant insights into social and political issues and reflect on colonial, postcolonial and neo-colonial problems. While the early films dealt with memories of the war, the focus has shifted to the struggle for a new Algerian identity.

7 Morocco

While Algeria has for the most part been ruled by leaders from its war of liberation, Morocco returned to its status as a kingdom after gaining its independence in 1956, despite its long colonial history. The monarchy, an institution both secular and religious, survived the colonial period, giving it genuine historical legitimacy. Compared with Algeria, Morocco seems a politically problem-free country.

As in many African countries, films were produced in Morocco well before the African people themselves started to make them. The Lumière brothers shot a number of films there in 1896 and the first screening was held in the royal palace of Fez in 1897. Félix Mesguich filmed the start of the French attack against Morocco. In 1919, seven years after Morocco had become a French protectorate, some fifty films were made under French colonial rule. The films made by French directors during that period include André Zwoboda's *La Septième Porte* (*The Seventh Gate*) and *Noces de sable* (*Desert Wedding*). The most famous were Jacques Becker's *Ali-Baba et les quarante voleurs* (1954 – *Ali-Baba and the Forty Thieves*) and Alfred Hitchcock's *The Man Who Knew Too Much* (1955). The first film laboratory, *Cinéphane*, was set up as early as 1939, and, in 1944, the CCM (*Centre Cinématographique Marocain*), was established to make documentaries. From 1953 onwards, newsreels were made in collaboration with a French production company.

Production of truly Moroccan films did not start until the late 1960s. In 1968 the first festival of Mediterranean cinema took place in Tangier. The same year (1968) saw the production of the first Moroccan feature films, co-directed by Moroccan film-makers and produced by the CCM – *Vaincre pour vivre* (*Conquer to Live*), co-directed by Mohamed Abderrahmane Tazi and Ahmed Mesnaoui, and *Quand mûrissent les dates* (*When the Dates Ripen*) by Larbi Bennani and Abdelaziz Ramdani. Some independent film-makers came close to creating an *auteur* cinema, such as Hamid Benani with his 1970 film *Wechma* (*Traces*). However, it was with Souheil Ben Barka's *Les Mille et une mains* (1972) that Moroccan cinema reached international fame. The film won the Yennenga Stallion (the prize for best full length feature film) at the 1973 FESPACO.

Many Moroccan film-makers deal with social themes such as delinquency and polygamy. Hamid Benani's *Wechma* (1970), for example, addresses the problem of delinquency which is linked to the difficulty young people have in relating to the world around them. The young Messaoud, feeling oppressed by both family and society, seeks self-affirmation in delinquency, which leads to his tragic end. Moumen Smihi's *El Chergui* or *Le Silence violent* (1975 – *The Violent Silence*) addresses the custom of polygamy. The film is set in Tangier on the eve of the country's independence in 1954. It depicts Aïcha's efforts to stop her husband from taking a second wife. The film ends with Aïcha's drowning, an act which was supposed to be a ritual immersion to prevent her husband's wedding.

The film rejects traditional film structure, which Smihi defines as 'a product of Western bourgeois society'. Western film, he argues, is based on Western art forms such as the novel and the play. Smihi's film, structured around variations on themes, reflects his view that though the cinematograph is a Western invention, it should be able to generate new modes of thinking and filming (Smihi 1994: 26).

In the late 1970s a new trend developed in Moroccan cinema which was the adoption of a more ethnographic approach, as exemplified in Ahmed el Maanouni's *Alyam Alyam/Oh les jours* (1978 – *The Days, The Days*). The director captures the reactions of the members of a farming family when one of them leaves. The story is set in a traditional village. Abdelwahd, a young worker, feels in conflict with tradition. He dreams of a better material life and wants to leave, although, since the head of the family is dead, his mother is reluctant to let him go. However, nothing can stop the young man, who is determined to find a better job. The characters discuss their own lives; they talk about their sense of exile, about Europe to where so many people migrate and the break with traditional life this brings about.

Social mutations mark the work of several film-makers. The situation of women in Islamic society constitutes the main focus in the films of Jilalli Ferhati and Farida Benlyazid, while Mohamed Abderrahmane Tazi, in his 1981 film *Le Grand Voyage* (*The Big Journey*), offers an insight into the Moroccan underworld. The film tells the story of a lorry driver who transports a load of dates. The film has many of the features of a road movie, depicting events and meetings on the journey from Inézgane to Tangier. The main events is the theft of the dates. Too frightened to face his boss, the driver sells his lorry and tries to escape to Spain. But his allies, who are supposed to help him enter Spain illegally abandon him on the open sea. Souheil Ben Barka's *Les Mille et une mains* also shows how social conditions drive people into criminal behaviour.

Souheil Ben Barka

Ben Barka has an interesting film background. He was trained in Italy and worked for five years as an assistant to several film-makers, including

Pier Paolo Pasolini. His film, *Les Mille et une mains* (*A Thousand and One Hands*) attracted and continues to attract considerable acclaim in European festivals – recently the *Institut du Monde Arabe* included it in its festival of Moroccan cinema. In Morocco, however, the film had little success, which led Ben Barka to try and cater to the European rather than the Moroccan market.

Les Mille et une mains (1972)

The story takes place in Marrakech. An old wool dyer, Moha, and his son Miloud, transport large loads of yarn for Moha to dye for carpet-making. Moha takes genuine pride in his highly skilled work, which gives him both satisfaction and a sense of accomplishment, as it allows him to support his family. The camera lingers on Moha at work, displaying with photographic pleasure the many rich colours he obtains.

Religion plays an important role in the life of the wool dyer's family and they undertake a long pilgrimage to one of Islam's sacred sites. But when misfortune strikes and Moha is killed in an industrial accident at the carpet factory, a brutal reality is revealed. Neither religion nor any traditional structure can offer support, and no protection is provided by the employer. Through the accident, the film denounces the exploitation to which artisans are subjected. It highlights the painful contrast between the family's poverty and the wealth of the carpet factory owner.

When Miloud tries to see the owner to ask for a job, he is excluded at every stage. Frustrated by this rejection, he forces his way into the house. The sight of the luxurious interior and the magnificent carpets that are contingent to his father's fatal accident, triggers his seething anger. He violently wipes his muddy shoes on the carpets to soil them as much as possible. Powerful close-ups of his feet moving backwards and forwards express the response to oppression, finishing on a pessimistic note when Miloud ends up in prison.

Viola Shafik writes: 'Capitalist society is depicted as a ruthless machine in which only the rich and powerful are able to survive' (Shafik 1998: 160). But not only is material survival impossible, any sense of self is eroded in a system where poverty takes away the dignity of the human being.

Jilalli Ferhati

Like Tazi's *Le Grand Voyage* (1981), Jilalli Ferhati's *Poupées de roseaux* (1982 – *Reed Dolls*) was made with a small budget. These films testify to the film-makers' independence and determination not to work in France or the Middle East. *Poupées de roseaux* tells the story of A'cha and her move from country to city, from her parental home to that of her husband. A'cha complies with all the rituals required for her to become a wife and a mother. But when she is later widowed she refuses to accept another imposed husband. Doing so she learns that an adult woman remains a minor in the eyes of the law.

La Plage des enfants perdus (1991)

In *La Plage des enfants perdus* (*The Beach of Lost Children*), individuals come again into conflict with society's rules. Here Mina, a twenty-five-year-old girl who lives with her father, grandmother and stepmother in a remote fishing village, has an affair with a taxi-driver. When he refuses to marry her, she accidentally kills him and buries his body in one of the salt piles on the beach.

However, Mina is pregnant, and when her father finds out he wants her to stay hidden in the house. A very complex situation emerges at this point, affecting all members of the family. Mina and her stepmother are close in age, and while Mina is pregnant with an illegitimate child, her stepmother is infertile. The father tells the village that Mina has gone to spend some time with relatives and persuades his wife to pretend that she is pregnant. From the father's point of view, this solution avoids two shameful situations: the birth of his daughter's fatherless child and his wife's failure to give him a child.

Ferhati avoids depicting the situation as an exclusively conflicting one. Mina's father shows genuine warmth for his daughter, but is torn between a socially unacceptable situation and the compassion he has for her. Ferhati also shows the ambiguity underlying the difficult relationship between the pregnant Mina and her infertile stepmother. In the background, the taxi-driver's disappearance and the finding of the abandoned taxi near the beach add a dramatic narrative strand to the film, heightening Mina's sense of imprisonment.

An inevitable anxiety prevails when the police try to unravel the mystery of the abandoned taxi and when children play near the salt pile. The weight of secrets dominates the film, which ultimately does not reveal Mina's fate to the viewer. The child is born, but Mina is unwilling to give it to her stepmother. Instead, she takes it and escapes.

Farida Benlyazid

Farida Benlyazid, who came to cinema through writing, uses film to reflect on the liberation of women.

Une Porte sur le ciel (1988)

In *Une Porte sur le ciel* (*Gateway to Heaven*) Benlyazid reflects on female emancipation. She examines how Western-style liberation often underlies emancipation, but pleads for a freedom from within Islamic culture. For Benlyazid 'female self-realisation is not achieved by submitting to a national project, nor by destroying traditional structures, nor by escaping abroad' (Shafik 1998: 206).

The film tells the story of Nadia, who returns from Paris to Fez where her father is dying. Because he was married to a French woman, his now adult children are split along cultural lines. Nadia's brother Driss feels entirely French, while her sister Leyla has settled into a conventional Moroccan bourgeois marriage. After their father's death, Driss declares to his brother-in-law that Leyla has chosen Moroccan culture while he and Nadia have chosen to be French, but Nadia replies, 'I have chosen nothing. I want everything.' The film then becomes Nadia's interior journey of self-discovery. The camera slowly follows her through many ornate rooms and courtyards, offering glimpses of the outside world and at times observing the enclosed world of the women.

The first manifestation of Nadia's change occurs when her French boyfriend comes to see her. Tormented not only by the distress of her father's death but also by the Islamic values she is discovering, she sends him away. The sequence of their meeting is representative of the cinematic style through which Benlyazid attempts to show the division between the Western and Arab worlds. Nadia arrives at the very Western-looking hotel where her boyfriend is staying. When he sees her, he rushes towards her, but she recoils from his public embrace. Shocked by her reaction, he suggests they talk in his room. The meeting there is filmed from the balcony through the window. The viewer thus hears all the noises of the street while watching the couple talk. He is seated on the bed, she is standing against the wall, with the window casting a slightly hazy veil over the scene. Finally, Nadia comes towards the balcony, opens the door and removes the inside/outside opposition.

On their father's death Nadia's brother inherits two parts of the house, Nadia and her sister the other two. However, the brother also has the right to sell. Nadia questions her legal exclusion. 'What right?', she asks indignantly. 'We are giving away all that is best in our own culture and keeping just the traditional constraints stripped of all meaning.'

As she learns more about Islam and religious values from an older, wise woman, Kirana, Nadia feels more and more captivated by what she observes and discovers. She breaks with her boyfriend in France, for whose job she now has little respect. She has already reproached him for knowing nothing of her origins, his interest in the Arab world being limited to its folklore and exoticism. 'You are so Parisian', she says. Now she writes that she does not need his television pictures to discover *la misère* (poverty), and indeed, poverty penetrates her enclosed world in the form of a pregnant woman, a street child who has been beaten up and another woman running away from her oppressive husband.

Nadia succeeds in transforming the house into a place of refuge and contemplation. Through her work, Kirana states, 'the door to the sky will open', a reference to the title and to the future Nadia tries to build. Nadia's search for identity, as Viola Shafik writes, 'concentrates on metaphysics': through the overarching symbolism in the film, the problem of 'identity is solved by immersion in a spiritual sphere that in its core is common to all cultures' (Shafik 1998: 207).

The films discussed here give a threefold picture of Moroccan cinema's search for identity. With Ben Barka, the individual, in spite of being trapped in an exploitative system, nevertheless finds fulfilment in being able to care for his family and being able to use his artisanal skills; Ferhati shifts to the female point of view and to the problems concerning feelings of identity when, in the patriarchal structure, the woman is given no authority over her own decisions and actions. Finally, Benlyazid reveals the identity conflict in one and the same family divided over allegiance to French or Moroccan values and explores the combination of women's liberation and Islamic values.

8　Tunisia

Tunisia's history runs parallel to that of Morocco and Algeria. As in the neighbouring countries, its earliest population was Berber. The Roman occupation, imposing Latin and Christian influences, did not lead to the development of a Romance language. And as in Algeria and Morocco, Arab invasions erased the traces of Latin and Christian influences. After the Turks conquered Tunisia, the country flourished under Husayn Ibn'Ali's rule and the Turkish element became a definite part of Tunisian identity. Husayn Ibn'Ali was an enlightened ruler, who emancipated the Jewish people, abolished slavery and authorised the opening of Christian schools. In 1881 Tunisia became a French protectorate. The struggle for independence began in the 1930s with the Destour (the party of the Constitution). Its leader, Habib Ibn'Ali Bourguiba became an active fighter for independence, which was finally granted in 1956.

Tunisia boasts a long tradition of film-making. According to Paulin S. Vieyra, it began as early as 1924 with Chénama Chikly's short film, *Chezal, la fille de Carthage* (Vieyra 1975: 203). It was also at the forefront in creating its own infrastructures to encourage and facilitate Tunisian film-making and promoting the internationalisation of African cinema through the successful biannual African cinema event, *Journées de Carthage*.

Several studies by Vieyra and Victor Bachy provide surveys of the development of Tunisian cinema from its beginnings to the 1970s, when Reda Behi brought out *Soleil des hyènes* (1976 – *Sun of the Hyenas*), a film which calls attention to the crucial problems caused by the modernisation of the country. The film exposes the shortcomings of the government's policy on tourism; in this instance the creation of several holiday resorts, which resulted in the destruction of a fishing village. The villagers have their historical livelihood taken away and are driven to begging or selling souvenirs to tourists. Bachy's study covers Tunisian cinema from 1956 to 1977 (the date of Behi's film, which he analyses at length), concluding that it reflects a divided country 'a prey to internal contradictions, confronted with crucial problems, moving towards something better. But that "better" still remains ill-defined' (Bachy 1978: 328, trans.).

In the early 1980s a new kind of cinema was to emerge. Nouri Bouzid explains that there was a group of Tunisian film-makers, all from the same generation, who, 'without getting together, without coming to any prior agreement, went in almost the same direction and, for the most part, worked in a similar way. What they have in common is that they decided to make films that were like themselves' (Bouzid 1994: 48). The main representatives of this group are Férid Boughedir, Nacer Khemir, Nouri Bouzid himself and Moufida Tlatli.

The film-makers of the 1980s, while still concerned with social and political issues, place the emphasis on 'bringing an audience into a discourse that is new, aesthetic, cinematic, stylistic and dramatic in its totality' but in which the ideological dimension occupies a secondary focus (Bouzid 1994: 49). This generation of Tunisian film-makers were influenced by the ideology and cinema of the 1960s, from which they learned without attempting to imitate or remain within it. The fact that most of them delayed making films until a more mature age (they were all born in the 1940s, Khemir in 1948, Bouzid in 1945, Boughedir in 1944, Tlatli in 1946) may have contributed to the unique style each developed. Many of them had formal training and worked in the field of cinema before making their first film. They all recognised and respected the work of earlier African film-makers, studied them and wrote about them.

Férid Boughedir

The interest in earlier African film-makers was particularly marked in the case of Férid Boughedir who, after studying philosophy and literature in Tunis, Rouen and Paris, wrote his doctoral thesis on 'African cinema and decolonisation', then continued his seminal work on the history of African and Arab cinema bringing out two documentary films on the subject, before making his popular fiction film *Halfaouine*.

Caméra Arabe (1987)

In 1987, Férid Boughedir completed *Caméra Arabe*, his sixty-minute documentary on Arab cinema, covering the thirty years of its development from 1967 to 1996. The film includes interviews with film-makers and shows excerpts of their films. The credits are preceded and followed by images which, in the minds of many people, exemplify the two poles of Arab society – Islamic religion and exotic eroticism – represented by two women: one singing forcefully about Islam's power and exhorting the audience to join in, the other performing a belly-dance and attracting a different kind of audience. Very often films promote or create clichéd images of a country's identity and of specific societies, as was the case with Egyptian cinema.

For forty years, Boughedir comments, the Arab films most people knew and saw were Egyptian: a commercial popular cinema catering to large audiences. Youssef Chahine was the first Egyptian film-maker to break away from commercialism and to deal with subjects which were

normally taboo in Egyptian cinema. His influence on the new generation of Arab film-makers was considerable and Boughedir pays tribute
to Chahine's innovative work. His early *Gare Centrale* (1958 – *Central
Station*), a far cry from the sentimental Egyptian melodramas, depicts the
story of the limping, sexually frustrated Kenaoui, played by Chahine
himself. With this film, Chahine reacted against the commercial Egyptian
cinema by introducing social and psychological problems.

In his 1973 film, *Le Moineau* (*The Sparrow*), Chahine turns to politics.
In *Caméra Arabe*, Boughedir includes a sequence from this film, which is
set at the moment of Nasser's resignation. The sequence shows a small
group of people watching the television broadcast of Nasser admitting
the Arab defeat after the Six-Day War (5–10 June, 1967) and announcing
his imminent resignation. The reaction in the room is powerful; one
woman runs out shouting 'we'll continue the fight'. The scene shifts to
the outside, from the television to the street, showing a large building
whose lighted windows are all opened as a wave of indignation at Nasser's
resignation and the Arab defeat spreads.

Boughedir records the comments of his fellow Tunisian film-maker,
Bouzid, on the film in general and especially on the Nasser broadcast
scene. For Bouzid, this moment exemplifies the main characteristic of the
Arab nations: a feeling of defeat. Boughedir also included a clip from
Bouzid's 1986 film, *L'Homme de cendres*, made nearly twenty years after
the 1967 war. Bouzid's film and Boughedir's clip of it shocked audiences
by showing a moving friendship between an Arab boy and an old Jewish
man. In the aftermath of the Six-Day War, this was a bold narrative
episode, deconstructing the Jewish/Arab conflict.

From the Jewish/Arab conflict Boughedir shifts to the Algerian war
with the dominant figure of film-maker Mohamed Lakhdar-Hamina. His
prize-winning 1975 film, *Chronique des années de braise* (*Chronicle of the
Years of Embers*), shows the massacre of a crowd, trapped in a square,
who are slaughtered by Arab men on horseback wielding swords. The
camera moves from high-angle shots showing the panic-stricken crowd
trying to escape, to eye-level angle shots revealing the individuals being
massacred, before panning to the French generals, under whose orders
the massacre is carried out.

Leaving these tragic historical events, Boughedir turns to the problems within Arab culture itself, in particular those which preclude the
proper development of society and the building of its own identity. The
major social problem he addresses is that of the continued sequestration
of women. Many male film-makers take a strong position against the
treatment of women; one of these is the Tunisian Adbellatif Ben Ammar.
In his film *Sejnane* (1974), he creates a situation in which a young girl is
placed under the surveillance of a blind man, portraying such unjust
male power as a form of impotence. When interviewed by Boughedir in

his film, Ben Ammar expresses his anger about the situation of women. The world cannot evolve without their active participation. 'Woman', he feels, 'should re-invent the world.' He records that when his mother died he had the impression that her intelligence had been left unused.

Tunisian woman film-maker Neija Ben Mabrouk, whose film *La Trace* (1982) was banned by the authorities for several years, is also interviewed by Boughedir. She draws attention to the fact that, no matter how admirable the goodwill of the male film-makers may be, not only do they remain extremely privileged, but they cannot escape from the male point of view, leading them, as she sees it, either to idealise or 'miserabilise' women.

Boughedir also briefly introduces several films all of which, in one way or other, deal with contradictions in society. The Algerian film *Omar Gatlato* (1977), by Merzak Allouache, portrays a typical impoverished young Algerian man whose situation is representative of that of many young Arab men.

Boughedir shows how, at the end of the 1970s, memory became increasingly important in Arab film, as is the case in Chahine's *La Mémoire*, in which he abandons politics for a meditation upon his own past. 'If you do not accept who you are and, if you do not communicate with yourself', he states in an interview, 'how can you communicate with others?'

Halfaouine (1990)

In 1990, after having made his important documentary on Arab film and one on African film, Boughedir brought out his very successful *Halfaouine*, considered a landmark in Tunisian cinema. The film 'broke all box office records in Tunisia, including records for Hollywood movies' (Ashbury, Helsby, O'Brian 1998: 96). It is set in Halfaouine, the old quarter of Tunis and portrays the private world of a family and its immediate neighbourhood through the eyes of Noura, a young boy on the threshold of adulthood.

The opening sequence takes place in a women's bathing house to which little boys are normally taken. Noura is still considered young enough to go along, but the sequence reveals his awakening sexuality. Noura is placed centrally in the shot from where, intrigued, he stares at the women's bodies. His gaze expresses his sudden awareness of his sexuality. He resents his mother touching him and washing him which clearly distracts from what captivates him: the female body. He cannot keep his eyes off these semi-nude female bodies in their diaphanous underwear. At a subsequent visit to the bathing house he is expelled for looking too intensely at a naked woman

Not yet admitted into the world of men and excluded from that of women he finds he belongs nowhere. Moreover, he has to cope with the

11 Férid Boughedir, *Halfaouine*. Noura.

absolute power of his despotic father, who at one point, chastises him for hanging around the women. A couple of specific friendships replace momentarily the social integration which is awaiting him. They reveal different dimensions of Arab society: the young male adults who attempt to chat up young girls and the cobbler who uses his charm to seduce women. A powerful sexual atmosphere pervades the strongly segregated male and female societies. In both, songs and jokes are imbued with eroticism and sexual innuendo.

It is also at the time of Noura's sexual awakening that the circumcision of his little brother takes place which increases Noura's confusion with regard to sexuality. At the moment of circumcision, Noura lies in bed, suffering with the crying little brother which perhaps triggers his own memory of the pain of circumcision. Noura is attracted yet repelled by both male and female worlds. Expelled by the women and not yet admitted by the men, he seeks to be in touch with his nascent sexuality. When he finally has what seems to be a sexual encounter with a female servant, he emerges with a sense of self-assurance that allows him to stand up to his father.

The film gives a close-up portrayal of a young boy's discovery of himself. The closing sequence of the film shows the boy triumphant on the roof tops, defying his father, who in vain calls upon the boy to submit to his despotic authority. But the film itself asserts an artistic independence seldom encountered in Arab cinema. Boughedir does not hesitate to give a frank portrayal of the private and intimate world of families and, similar to Noura in the film, he defies the old film-making where such frank representation would have been censored.

The vitality that emanates from newer Tunisian films stems from a desire for self-expression using a personal language and style. Bouzid observes that these film-makers sometimes 'went as far as to reject plot and anecdote, considering that it was too easy to tell a story' (Bouzid 1994: 49). They nevertheless retained central characters, whose development they trace and who are frequently at odds with society. This conflict leads them to reflect on themselves and on society. One of the earliest films in this productive decade for Tunisian cinema is Nacer Khemir's *Les Baliseurs du désert*, a desert film, bathed in mystery, which reveals the force of memory and dream and where the search for the self ultimately leads to self-destruction.

Nacer Khemir

Nacer Khemir is a versatile artist and autodidact, who published short stories before turning to film.

Les Baliseurs du désert (1985)

Les Baliseurs du désert (*The Drifters*) tells the story of a teacher (played by the director himself). It opens with a long tracking shot of the desert taken from a moving bus, accompanied by a deep, male voice singing an Arab song. A brief close-up reveals the face of a handsome young man before the camera cuts back to the desert and a dedication, against the background of sand, appears on the screen: 'To my grandmother, the Andalousian.'

As the man takes his suitcase and prepares to leave the bus, the driver asks: 'How old are you?' The man does not answer. 'And what are you doing in the desert?' When the young man tells him that he has been appointed as a teacher in the village, the driver claims that there is no village. Although the other passenger, an old bearded man, confirms the existence of the village, the driver remains adamant. The camera then shifts from the teacher's startled face to unidentifiable greyish figures in the distance, struggling through the dusty sand. Next the teacher is seen walking through the desert, carrying his suitcase, and approaching a man digging a hole in the endless sea of sand. When he asks the man if he is planting a palm tree, the man runs away and returns, seemingly from nowhere, with other villagers to welcome the teacher.

This opening sequence leaves the viewer with an unusual sense of mystery: images of an infinite desert with only traces of a human presence – an abandoned jeep and men who look more like shadows than people – combined with dialogue in which the first unanswered question relates to time, the person's age, the second to space, the village, which apparently does not exist. The viewer is thus placed at an unknown time in an unidentifiable place, bereft of any sure sense of reality. One place is identified in an almost desultory way in the dedication to the grandmother, Andalousia, the centre of Arab culture in the eleventh century. However, the desert place is clearly not Andalousia, so the few pointers given leave both place and time enigmatic. The sense of enigma is heightened by the incongruous images which create a surreal atmosphere: the man, Assam, digging a hole in this huge desert; the teacher with his suitcase, thinking he might be planting a palm tree; the villagers appearing from behind the waves of sand.

The village is what remains of an ancient city where luscious vegetation once grew. The teacher, Adasalam, is welcomed by the villagers and invited by the Sheik to stay in the room of his son, who 'left for the desert'. There are only old men, women and children in the town; the young men have all left with the *baliseurs* (drifters or wanderers), whose followers never return. The villagers have waited for years for the teacher's arrival. But there is no school and the teacher never teaches, although, when asked by the children what he is going to teach, he mentions 'grammar and history'.

The story that unfolds is an allegory, an exemplary sequential narrative whose events and details are given over-determined meanings, creating a sense of mystery that continues throughout the film. The teacher slowly becomes enmeshed in this surreal and enigmatic world where the materiality of life remains invisible. In one sense, 'grammar and history' underlie the existence of the village, as the inhabitants live their coded lives determined by their collective memory and by the blind force that propels the young men into the desert, where they disappear one by one. Their absence is made tangible by the sporadic distant reappearance of the procession of greyish men, bent down under some unseen weight. One wonders, says Brahimi, whether they are 'convicts or praying mystics marching towards their God' (Brahimi 1997: 102, trans.).

12 Nacer Khemir, *Les Baliseurs du désert.* The children's garden in the desert.

The men in the village genuinely believe in the legendary existence of treasure hidden in the desert. And when the young rebel Houssin tricks them into believing that a gold coin was found, the entire village rushes into the desert with shovels and starts digging frantically. The children of the village also try to reconstruct the past by creating a garden. Though they fail to find out what a garden is and how it should look, they carry on with their work, stealing mirrors, breaking them into pieces and taking them to their 'garden'. 'If we speak of a garden or a palace,' said Khemir in an interview, 'it is translated mentally into park and castle' (Shafik 1998: 55). Not so for the desert children: when they finally finish their garden, made with pieces of broken mirrors, it looks like a big round sun with glittering rays, embedded in the sand.

The legendary Andalousia inhabits the town's collective memory, which is passed on to the children. As legends continue to be transmitted, both Adasalam the outsider and Houssin the rebel become caught up in them. When the teacher also vanishes, reality suddenly erupts: a policeman in modern uniform appears to collect testimonies from the villagers, who tell him inexplicable or incomprehensible stories. The policeman, a grotesque caricature of the modern police officer, understands nothing of the society he is investigating and, deciding that they are all dangerous tricksters, leaves. The film closes with Houssin preparing to set out for Cordoba, a little *baliseur*, about to follow the teacher and disappear in the desert.

This is a town without fathers, where the women are virtually invisible, with the exception of a few old women. There are also no little girls, only little boys. The only 'real' man who appears is the grotesque policeman. This leads Brahimi to argue that today's Arab society seems to be faced with a choice between two extremes: that represented by the mediocre policeman, a cretin who lacks vision, the other by the *baliseurs*, who are attracted to grandiose dreams, reject daily reality and leave for an ideal but who are, in fact, nihilistic and suicidal (Brahimi 1997: 102–3). For Shafik, the film depicts a protagonist, the teacher, who seems to find it impossible to integrate his cultural heritage into daily life. 'The journey becomes an odyssey during which the individual is entirely lost' (Shafik 1998: 196). Above all, the film portrays the Arabs at the crossings of untraced paths, a mood that also underlies the films of Nouri Bouzid.

Nouri Bouzid

Bouzid's films explore many aspects of identity, such as religion, sexuality, politics and the community one relates to – or fails to relate to. In taking this approach, Bouzid violates certain taboos in Arab cinema. This is very marked in his first and most famous film, *L'Homme de cendres*, which, as mentioned above, alludes to the Arab/Jewish question by depicting a warm and positive friendship between an Arab and a Jew, but more prominently focuses on male homosexuality, a subject shunned in Arab society and cinema.

L'Homme de cendres (1986)

L'Homme de cendres (*Man of Ashes*) centres on the trauma suffered by two young apprentice wood sculptors, Hachemi and Farfat, who, at the age of ten, are raped by their foreman, Ameur. Marked by the memory of their ordeal, the boys' entry into adulthood is seriously hindered. They feel unable to adjust to society around them which, in turn, perceives them as strange.

The film is bold in its explicit rendering of sexual taboos and its rejection of censorship, for example, in the rape scene. The trauma has a profound, yet different, effect on the boys and on the way they are perceived by the people around them. Farfat, accused by the other boys of being homosexual, is thrown out by his outraged father. Farfat may well have homosexual tendencies, to which the rape may have contributed. As for Hachemi, he is likened to a girl by his friends and has a deep fear of sexual experiences with women. Unable to come to terms with the marriage his family has arranged for him and which is about to be celebrated, he first hides from his family and guests, then, taking advantage of the chaos created by a sand storm, flees.

Haunted by the memory of the rape, Hachemi attempts to revisit the past and goes to see his old Jewish neighbour, Lévy, who has been a spiritual father to him. They spend the evening reminiscing together, while Lévy plays his lute and sings old familiar songs. Encouraged by the warm atmosphere Hachemi is about to confide in his friend, when Lévy, who is old and tired, falls asleep.

The normal transition into adulthood is hindered by trauma, and the community by which the boys would traditionally define themselves fails to understand their behaviour. What was supposed to be a close-knit family circle turns out to be a place of conflict. The problem centres on the fathers' authority: Farfat's father rejects his son, following the rumours of his homosexuality, while Hachemi's father awaits his return with the intention of beating him. Later, exorcism and an initiation ceremony are used to try and force the boys into conformity, but the rituals fail to have the desired outcome. Farfat, having to face up to his sexuality once again, resorts to physical force: aided by Hachemi, he confronts Ameur, the foreman who abused them, stabs and kills him, then disappears.

The two major themes (which recur in Bouzid's subsequent films) are those of patriarchy and defeat. There are three father figures in Hachemi's life, the biological father who brutalises him, the foreman who is to teach him the art of sculpting but who abuses him sexually and Lévy the Jew, the good father, who is, however, too old to listen and dies. Farfat's biological father is ruthless and leaves his son to fend for himself, re-inforcing his marginality. Bouzid comments on the problems with fathers, explaining that in the Arab world the father is not associated with the Oedipus complex but with the myth of Abraham (Bouzid 1994: 54). 'The son submits to the father and serves him.' In Arab society the individual is nothing, 'it's the family that counts, the group'. What this film-maker is trying to do is to 'destroy the edifice of the family and liberate the individual (Bouzid 1994: 54).

Les Sabots en or (1988)

While *L'Homme de cendres* focuses on adolescents, *Les Sabots en or* (*Golden Horseshoes*) presents a mature man of forty-five, someone who is no longer involved in identity formation and in discovering who and what he is. The protagonist, Youssef Soltane, is a political prisoner, who returns home after several years in prison. Viola Shafik records an interview with the film-maker, revealing that the story is based on the experience of Bouzid himself, who 'spent five years in Tunisian prisons because of his political conviction and, like his protagonist, was humiliated and tortured' (Shafik 1998: 194). The film is almost entirely in a chiaroscuro, visually and stylistically reinforcing the shift from ill-lit reality to blurred memories.

The film opens slowly with the return of the prisoner, the camera's eye gliding over places, objects, events at the pace of the released prisoner, who has to rediscover his environment and reassess his relationships with the family and the village he left. This careful and slow capturing of things, in contrasting light and darkness, is apparent from the opening of the film, even before the credits appear. The first shot is a close-up of a horse's mouth being examined. The horse, no longer fit to run, will have to be killed. Its shoes are taken off. A young girl strokes it; she is having great difficulty in accepting the verdict. Youssef Soltane witnesses the scene and says to himself: 'Mr Youssef, you are a conscripted citizen and that is what you will remain.' The credits appear over the tracking shot of walls in light and darkness, moving down narrow alleys, where the street lights suddenly come on. Evening is falling; children are lighting the fire for Ashoura. They are playing and dancing as Youssef drives into the town: the rain is pouring down. The memory of the condemned horse lingers despite the festivities.

Youssef Soltane moves slowly through the dark and narrow alleys of Sfax, which only now and then offer a glimpse of a lit opening or space. This dark atmosphere pervades Youssef's return to his home, where he tries to recognise loved ones and familiar places and to locate his former self. But his journey of discovery is intertwined with memories from the past, with traumatic flashes of the torture scenes in prison and occasional visions of horses. The line between past and present is blurred. Soltane recognises one of the children playing around the Ashoura fire. It is his daughter Raja. As he calls out to her and she recognises him he is overjoyed. Is this a memory from a past Ashoura celebration or is Raja really there? Little by little, the journey to the past unfolds and reveals the distance that has grown between him and his relatives.

Youssef returns as a son and father. An uncanny atmosphere awaits him: children are hiding behind the walls, clearly ill at ease in the presence of the returning father. Close-ups of details reveal the intensity with which Youssef looks at everything. A close-up of his mother's hands precedes that of her face. In between the mother's thoughts and comments, the clock ticks noisily, accentuating the prolonged silences. She reminds Youssef of his past and, through her, remembered scenes from his childhood well up. She refers to Youssef's deceased wife – 'Even at Fatma's death, you did not come' – and to his brother, Abdullah, whose visits are rare. But then she rejoices that Youssef is able to taste her special Ashoura dish. Apart from Fatma, the people Youssef used to know are still there, but most of them are estranged from him; they avoid or resent him.

The Arab architecture, with its interior courtyards and windows and effects of light and shade, becomes the perfect setting for Youssef's difficult journey into his inner self. The condemned horse of the opening sequence, which is linked to the title *Les Sabots en or*, becomes a recurrent motif that, together with Youssef's thought processes, structures the film.

Objects, details, gestures become meaningful when emotions are as intense as they are for Youssef when he meets his three children. There is Marien, who brings him red roses for his forty-fifth birthday, but is aloof and estranged; there is Raja, who embraces her father spontaneously and then asks about his torture in prison adding, without waiting for his answer, 'I cried because of that'; and there is his son, Adel, who does not really want to see his father any more. They all seem to resent the pain his absence has caused.

The film follows Youssef's mode of perceiving and remembering as he becomes aware of all that has gone on without him. The world around him has become estranged, as has the ideology for which he fought and because of which he was imprisoned and tortured. His memory forces him to relive the scenes of torture so that he becomes the spectator of his own pain, watching himself suffer and feeling it all over again. These are formally constructed scenes, at times even a little contrived, but some are very hard to watch, as when the torturers burn the soles of his feet which, when he is forced to walk, leave traces of blood on the prison floor.

Youssef receives no admiration for his ideology and subsequent imprisonment from anyone other than from one bizarre character, Sgaier, the eccentric weaver, who lives in the cellar and steals quietly through the house. 'Bravo for the years in prison,' he exclaims, 'some resistance!' But Sgaier too has fought, he remembers the war in Indochina. The scars left by the war, imprisonment and torture in the name of ideology, are carved deep in people's bodies and minds.

Finally, Youssef confronts his brother Abdullah at his place of work, the abattoir. Reality, ideology and emotions all merge. As the animals are being slaughtered, Youssef's beliefs are killed off one by one by Abdullah. Against a background of blood-covered carcasses, a fratricidal row explodes. 'You and your revolutionary lot: Marxists, Leninists, Trotskyists, Maoists, nationalists, Destourniens, Nasserists, Arab-nationalists . . .' rages Abdullah, the integrationist. As the row goes on, the horse is pulled into the abattoir to be slaughtered. Then Youssef's feet are seen in close-up in a shower; they move in a similar way to the horse's hooves. His hands scratch the walls, leaving bloody traces on them. The horse and Youssef are both going to die. The film closes with a sequence of a white horse frolicking in the sea. A voice-over is heard: 'Did you know that the irons and nails of your shoes are always golden?'

Although Youssef Soltane has tried to relocate himself as a son, father and brother, his imprisonment has had an effect upon him, similar to that of the rape of the two boys in *L'Homme de cendres*. These characters have touched upon fundamental taboos, sexuality and politics, and the traumas they have suffered set them apart from family and society, where difference and non-conformity are condemned. Yet their defeat is avenged in films which find a new language to penetrate these forbidden territories.

Bezness (1991)

Like *L'Homme de cendres* and *Les Sabots en or*, Bouzid's subsequent film *Bezness*, also set in Sfax, deals with defeat. Again this film deals with a taboo subject, this time prostitution. The title, *Bezness*, refers to the 'business' of young Tunisian boys who work as male prostitutes for female tourists. Through this subject, Nouri Bouzid again examines Arab society, traditions and religion, and this time also considers their conflict with the aspirations and contradictions of Western tourism. Here, as in the earlier films, the theme is explored through specific individuals, who communicate their thoughts in voice-over: Roufa, the most successful *petit bezness* person who, with unusual flair, singles out women likely to fall for his Arab charm; the French tourist and photographer who is never without his camera; and Khomsa, Roufa's fiancée, to whom the photographer is also attracted, and who is desperately trying to make sense of her female identity and destiny.

Both male characters are associated with an object: for Roufa, it is a Honda motorbike, the essential asset for seduction; for the photographer, it is his camera, which is his means of approaching the world around him. He seems to find it so difficult to look at people other than through the camera's eye that Khomsa asks him whether he has eyes to see.

The film begins by showing the photographer walking with his camera in the narrow, shady streets of Sfax, a small Tunisian town which has recently expanded through the development of tourism. 'There were no hotels when I was your age', Roufa tells his little brother, Navette. Western-style leisure establishments now flourish; many tourists are seen and the beach is full of topless bathers. There are also some post World War II settlers, such as the German homosexual who cannot shed the guilt he feels at having been born in Berlin at the beginning of the war. In Sfax, he claims, he has found some peace. There is also a Tunisian bartender, who emigrated to Sweden, but was deported. The film thus offers a picture of an Arab society that is both small enough to make it possible to highlight individual relationships and large enough to attract tourists and some settlers and to act as a window on the larger society beyond it.

Roufa is a victim of the dichotomy between Western and Arab women. He has no problem offering his services to Western women and clearly also enjoys what he does and being paid for it. Moreover, he makes no moral judgement about these women, 'they just are curious about our customs'. But when it comes to Arab women, his attitude changes completely. At one point, when he enters the women's quarters and sees them making sexy garments for the market he works in, he flies into a rage, tears the fabric out of their hands and accuses them of making indecent clothes.

Clearly, Roufa has been able, if not very successfully, to compartmentalise his life: one part takes place in the Western area of the city and one in the Arab. But Roufa himself is unable to keep a clear boundary between the two, since some of his earnings are for his Arab family. His failure to keep the two sides separate is poignantly expressed when he gives his fiancée Khomsa an engagement ring bought from his 'bezness' earnings.

The photographer also has to grapple with contradictions. He uses his camera in an attempt to find what is invisible to the naked eye. He realises that, in the Arab world, much is veiled. He has come to lift that veil, but soon learns that an invisible one remains. 'Behind each closed door,' he reflects, 'lies a city, a world that escapes me.' When he tries to photograph Arab women, he incurs the wrath of Arab men, and his attempts to take pictures of Roufa also present danger, for Roufa is afraid that they might end up in male homosexual magazines.

The film's setting and decor highlight the complexity of relationships, which all imply a conflict within the self and with the other: sunlit beaches contrast with shadowy city alleys, interiors with many mirrors reflecting multiple images of the characters, unexpected openings encourage voyeurism, offering sudden glimpses of unknown and secret events. As the German man confesses to Roufa, whom he tries to seduce: 'Nobody succeeds in winning the other.' In *Bezness*, relationships fail before they even begin; individuals are thrown back on themselves and left with dilemmas which ultimately lead to defeat.

Bent Familia/Tunisiennes (1997)

After having dealt with the taboos of the male universe in his earlier films, in *Bent Familia,* Bouzid approaches the question of women in his society. His oeuvre shows an increasing awareness of the plight of Arab women. In *Bezness*, Khomsa was disturbed by differences and contradictions between the lives of men and women and between Westerners and Arabs. In *Bent Familia*, Bouzid investigates the inability of Arab men to accept the modern Arab woman. The film deals with three women who are all going through a crisis. Each has a specific problem: Amina feels oppressed by her husband; Aida is divorced and suffering from society's contempt for divorcees; the third, a young Algerian, has fled from her country and is awaiting a passport and visa to go to Europe.

There is great solidarity and support between the women, but little can be achieved in a society that remains dominated by a tradition of machismo. The laws regarding women may have been relaxed, as with the prohibition against women appearing in public places, but deep down little has changed. When Amina rejects her husband's sexual advances, the remarks he makes reveal the man's supremacy in all areas of life: 'Don't make me mad; I am a man, it is my right. My own wife tells me not to touch her!'

In *Bent Familia*, Bouzid exposes the false modernity of the Arab world, a falseness which affects women more than men; however, he claims that he did not set out to make a feminist film, nor to please women: 'I just wanted to make a film made by a man from a woman's point of view.' This, argues his fellow film-maker Moufida Tlatli, is an impossibility.

Moufida Tlatli

When Moufida Tlatli brought out her first feature film, *Les Silences du palais*, she was no newcomer to the world of cinema. She had worked with established Tunisian film-makers for a considerable time and already had a reputation as a film editor. For this first film Tlatli collaborated with Nouri Bouzid, with whom she worked on the script and who wrote the dialogue. She edited the film herself. It was an instant success, further enhancing the already rich film corpus of post-1980 Tunisian film.

Les Silences du palais (1994)

Les Silences du palais (*The Silences of the Palace*) is set in the Tunisian palace of the pro-French governing beys in the early 1950s, on the eve of the country's independence. It focuses on the childhood and adolescence of Alia, the illegitimate daughter of a palace servant.

Until the young nationalist teacher Lofti comes to the palace and Alia learns to write, her world is one of oral discourse, of speech and sight. A playful child at the beginning of the film, after the onset of menstruation she becomes aware of womanhood and loses her playfulness. She speaks little with her mother, but observes her silently, spies on her and, finally, witnesses her mother being sexually abused by Sid' Ali, one of the beys, to whom Alia always felt close.

The first sequence of the film, set in the present, features Alia and Lofti, now a couple. Alia, a singer in an elegant establishment, discovers she is pregnant. She wants to keep the child but Lofti, having no intention of marrying her, insists on an abortion, stating that 'a child needs a name, a family, a marriage'. As they argue, Lofti suddenly remembers to tell her of Sid' Ali's death and she leaves immediately for the palace. Her interior monologue is heard in voice-over: 'I thought myself buried with my mother on that terrible night.'

It is from here that the story in the past unfolds, while Alia sits on the bed of Khalti, the old servant, now blind and bed-ridden, whom Alia loved so much. Oral storytelling is astutely entwined with the reconstruction of memory. As Khalti talks to Alia about her past, Alia visualises the places of her childhood and relives the trauma of 'the terrible night'. This evocation of the past happens in fragments, separated by the consciousness of Alia, the young woman, in the present.

The film is skilfully edited into three strands, telling the stories of Alia's mother Khédija, her country and herself. Tlatli creates a film which reflects a broad range of experiences, from the personal to the cultural and including social, political and historical events. Her film language combines elements from the oral tradition of storytelling and from Arab music (voice, lute and drums), integrating them into a narrative where the visual remains paramount. A few important examples of visual narrative moments illustrate this.

One scene reveals Alia's deep attachment to Sid' Ali. While he is asleep in the garden, Alia bends over to deposit a gentle kiss on his temple, but he wakes up just before her lips touch his face. This brief moment introduces three key events in Alia's discovery of her mother's life.

The first of these is an evening celebration in the palace. Although her mother has forbidden her to attend, Alia watches the party and discovers that her mother is the belly-dancer performing for the beys and their guests. Confused, she rushes off and enters the room of one of the beys' wives, where she puts on make-up and one of the woman's gowns and clumsily attempts to imitate her mother's belly-dancing.

The next discovery concerns her mother's relationship with Sid' Ali's brother. When Alia sees this man enter her mother's room, she secretly observes the couple's sexual encounter, apparently enjoyed by both, and her mother subsequently fulfilling the servant's duty of washing the man's feet. Even more confused than when she discovered her mother belly-dancing, she runs off, racing around the garden until she collapses. Sid' Ali finds her, unconscious or asleep, and carries her into her room.

Alia's final discovery happens when she awakens and witnesses her mother, who had come to look for her, being raped by Sid' Ali. The camera cuts to a sequence in which Alia sees herself running towards the iron gates of the castle, grasping the bars with her hands and trying to push her head through the opening: then in close-up, taken from the other side of the gate, the camera shows the girl's screaming face.

This 'screaming point', which Michel Chion sees as '[t]he point of the unthinkable inside the thought, of the indeterminate inside the spoken, of unrepresentability inside representation . . . embodies the fantasy of the *auditory absolute*; it saturates the soundtrack and deafens the listener' (Chion 1982: 68, trans.). However, Alia's scream has no voice; it is entirely visual, neither uttered nor heard, and gains its power from its very silence, the ultimate silence of a palace where women are condemned to silence.

Alia is taken ill after this event and remains silent. But the music she plays on her lute and her singing form an outlet for her restricted personal situation (Shafik 1998: 107). During the period of her recovery, political unrest in Tunisia increases, the nationalist anthem, broadcast over the radio, is banned in the palace and a curfew is imposed. This news only heightens the women's awareness of their permanent sequestration: 'Our whole life is a curfew!'

For Alia, the outlet of music intensifies and culminates at the end of the film when, at Sarra's engagement party, she rebels by singing the Tunisian nationalist anthem. As she sings, the scene shifts to her mother's abortion, the singing voice of the daughter in synchrony with her mother's screams. As people leave the hall in protest against Alia's singing the forbidden anthem, the women servants rally around her mother. Alia runs downstairs to find that her mother has just died.

The scene then shifts back to Khalti's bedroom, where Alia is saying that she did not even attend the funeral. She left with Lotfi, whom she thought would save her. The film closes showing Alia by herself, absorbed in an interior monologue: 'I am not saved. Like you, I have suffered and had a series of abortions . . .' In this spiritual encounter with her mother she comes to realise how much she has repeated her mother's life, in spite of not living in the palace. Throughout the film, she has tried to find a model to identify with – she has no name, no father, no family, and was told that she could not be like her friend, Sid' Ali's daughter Sarra. She tried in vain to find out who her father was and then realised that her mother was also unknown to her. 'But where do you come from?' she asked, and learnt that her mother was sold to the beys when she was ten. The child inside her suddenly becomes the link with her dead mother. The film closes with Alia stating: 'I hope I'll have a girl. I will call her Khédija.'

While Tunisia achieved identity as a nation, women still do not have their own. According to Shafik, the film disconnects national liberation from women's liberation. She deduces this from Lotfi's refusal to marry Alia 'because of her social and moral status' (Shafik 1998: 206). However, a distinction has to be made between Lotfi and Alia. For Lotfi, who taught Alia to write and advocated her emancipation, the liberation of the country is indeed disconnected from that of women. For the woman film-maker, and for the protagonist, that is ultimately not the case, since Alia chooses to keep the child, and in doing so vindicates both herself and her mother. While at first this film seemed to present the female situation as an inevitable defeat, it ends with a promise. This ending may also be seen as symbolic of Tlatli's own struggle as a woman trying to enter the world of men.

What has been at stake in the 'new' Tunisian cinema of the 1980s is the very question of individual identity seen from a twofold perspective: the protagonist's quest for identity, which reflects that of the film-maker in search of a personal language and style. To cite Bouzid:

> This question of identity keeps recurring: Are we Arabs? Are we Tunisians? What does it mean to be Arab? What is being Tunisian? Where do I come from? Why have we always been ruled? Are we Berbers? Are we a mixture? And these films search for identity, especially cultural identity. It's not a national identity, it's very often a cultural identity. We are forced to take this step, especially coming from a Francophone culture; we have gained our knowledge through the medium of a language which is not our mother tongue.
>
> (Bouzid 1994: 53)

In all of these films, memory plays a crucial role. It defines how people perceive themselves and how they map out their future. The teacher in Khemir's *Les Baliseurs du désert* does not share the collective memory of the village, yet slowly becomes absorbed by it and disappears into the desert. In Bouzid's *L'Homme de cendres*, Farfat, unable to forget the trauma, vanishes after killing his abuser, while Youssef Soltane in *Les Sabots en or*, burdened by his past, must also accept defeat. Perhaps only Tlatli's film leaves any glimmer of hope for the future of Arab society and cinema.

9　Senegal

Of all the sub-Saharan countries, Senegal was the first to produce films and the first to have its films attract international attention. In 1963 a film entirely conceived and created by an African won a prize at the International Film Festival in Tours. That film was the Senegalese film-maker Ousmane Sembene's *Borom Sarret*.

Coincidentally, the country to produce the first African film to win a prize, and a European prize at that, was also France's first colony in Africa. Becoming part of French West Africa in 1854, it became a French Overseas Territory in 1946 and then, after a short-lived federation with Mali, gained independence in 1960.

Senegal may be considered the founding country of African cinema because of the towering presence of Ousmane Sembene, as noted, the first African film-maker to gain international recognition. He is the only example, Roy Armes writes, of the 'cross-fertilisation between European language-writing and African film-making' (Petty 1996: 15). However, it was another Senegalese film-maker, Paulin Vieyra, who, together with three fellow film-makers in 1955, made the film which became the embodiment of African film-making aspirations, *Afrique sur Seine*.

Recently, Djibril Diop Mambéty, Sembene's junior, has been recognised as one of the most original of African film-makers. His premature death in 1998, at the age of fifty-three, contributed to the reassessment of his work and a recognition of his endeavour to decolonise African cinema. The innovative talent of the first African woman director, Safi Faye, has added yet another dimension to Senegal's cinema, while emerging new film-makers such as Moussa Touré ensure its future.

Paulin Vieyra

The late Paulin Vieyra is one of the pioneers of African cinema. He was the first African to graduate from the IDHEC in Paris and his *Afrique sur Seine* was the first African film made by Africans.

Afrique sur Seine (1955)

In 1934 the French promulgated the Laval Decree (*Le Décret Laval*), named after the then minister of colonies. This decree controlled the content of films made in Africa and discouraged Africans from making films. It imposed censorship and allowed for the confiscation of films considered to be subversive. Because of this decree, *Le Groupe Africain du Cinéma*, headed by Paulin S. Vieyra, was refused permission to film in Africa and obliged to set its film, *Afrique sur Seine*, in Paris.

Afrique sur Seine is an essay film that examines the situation of a generation of African artists and students in search of their civilisation and culture. It pictures Paris through African eyes and deals with the illusions the Africans have about the much-idealised city, centre of hope and promises.

The film begins by showing children in Africa playing freely in the water, then cuts to Paris, while keeping the continuity of African music. The transition from Africa to Paris emphasises the break with their native land and childhood happiness. This is a film about the estrangement experienced by Africans who arrive in a city they feel they already know through years of colonisation. This kind of false 'mother'-land betrays the fascination Paris exercises on the French-African imagination, between the imagined Paris of promise and its bitter reality.

Ousmane Sembene

Sembene has become the 'statesman' of African cinema as a whole and in particular of Senegalese cinema. He has an impressive film record and has been the subject of many critical studies. Born in Senegal in 1923 into a Muslim family, at age eight he was sent to Koranic school and then continued his education in a French school in Dakar. He left at fourteen and worked at odd jobs, but later took evening classes where he had his first contacts with labour union leaders. He served in the French colonial army in World War II, after which he became a docker and trade union leader in Marseille. Sembene's personal life experience and his work in the trade unions made him sensitive to the plight of the individual struggling for survival. Out of that sensitivity and his awareness of the colonial legacy and postcolonial exigencies in Africa, he developed his commitment to the cause of social justice. He decided to become an author and by 1960 had published three novels. Realising, however, that few Africans would be able to read them, he then turned to film, and spent a year studying in Moscow under the director Mark Donskoy.

Sembene is a film-maker with a sense of responsibility, whose aim is to expose the abuse of power, reveal what governments keep hidden, and speak to the Western world about its oppressive power and to his own people – and Africans in general – about their oppression. His films have become vintage material in African cinema. They are often parables with a didactic aim: *Borom Sarret* (1963) depicts a day in the life of a Dakar cart driver; *La Noire de . . .* (1967) is the story of a Senegalese girl who accompanies her white employers to France; *Mandabi* (1968

– *The Money Order*) tells of the misadventures of an illiterate Muslim when he receives a money order from Paris; *Taw* (1971 – *The Oldest of the Family*) is about the despair of a twenty-year-old Senegalese who looks for work in the Dakar docks; in *Emitai* (1971 – *God of Thunder*), the women of a village clash with French colonialists; *Xala* (1974 – *The Curse*) shows the paralysing effect of some of Africa's own traditions as well as that of Western oppression, prolonged by the Senegalese government; *Ceddo* (1977 – *The People from Outside*) focuses on Islamic structures of subjugation in the early period of Islamisation; *Camp de Thiaroye* (1988) is based on the 1944 massacre of Senegalese *tirailleurs* (African soldiers) by French forces; *Guelwaar* (1992) evokes Muslim–Christian conflict.

Sembene's entire oeuvre is relevant to an understanding of the development of the notion of identity. But since his work has attracted considerable critical attention and has become the subject of several excellent full-length studies, just three of his films are given fuller treatment here: the two early ones from the 1960s, *Borom Sarret* and *La Noire de . . .* , and the late 1980s' *Camp de Thiaroye*. These films, made more than twenty years apart, offer meaningful insights into Sembene's representation of Africa's struggle with and for identity.

Although Sembene's films are Senegalese, they provide a take-off point for the recognition of an African cinema. His early films portray African society and are of particular interest in that they focus on individuals who would not be film material in Western cinema: people whose voices are not heard and whose faces are not seen, but who represent the African in general. It is not surprising then that *Borom Sarret* and *La Noire de . . .* have come to be accepted as early icons of African cinema.

Borom Sarret (1963)

The title of the film is Wolof and designates 'the owner of a cart'. This nineteen-minute film is heralded by Ukadike (1994: 72) as an 'African masterpiece' which deals, 'in embryonic form, with important issues that later became dominant themes of black African cinema'. The film is about Ly Abdoulaye, a Dakar cart driver. The single day's experience of this humble Senegalese man condenses and reflects the sequence of human life, from birth to death. His journey through the two parts of the city of Dakar, one indigenous, the other Western, and the portrayal of the different people needing transport, give a moving account of urban African life. There are the regular customers, then a man with breeze blocks, a pregnant woman who urgently needs to go to the maternity hospital, a man with a dead child who asks to be taken to the cemetery, but is told he has to get the right papers, and finally a well-dressed man who has climbed up socially and wants to go to what used to be the Western quarter in prior colonial times.

Those who do not request transport, but are glimpsed through tracking shots or identified along the road, add further to the picture of society: the disabled beggar who, unable to walk, drags himself along over the ground; the griot (African storyteller) who charms the driver and extorts all his earnings; and the policeman who arrests him for having entered the Western quarter, forbidden to cart drivers, and who subsequently confiscates Abdoulaye's cart. The driver returns home with only his horse, walking first through the modern forbidden quarter, reflecting on the rich who live in the city and on the misfortunes that have led to his predicament. On arriving in the medina (the indigenous part of town) he regains a feeling of well-being, despite having lost his cart. Finally, when he admits to his wife that he has come back with neither food nor cart, she calmly hands the baby to him, walks out and promises to come back with food, leaving her husband and the viewer wondering where she is going at this late hour.

These sketches, taken from daily life, draw attention to the many forms of abuse which prevail in Dakar and throughout Africa. Through the characters in his film, Sembene criticises the many ways that oppression is maintained: from the policeman who confiscates the cart, to the cemetery employee who shows no compassion for the father with his dead child. He also abhors the attitude of social climbers, such as the Westernised African who claims to have powerful friends and reassures Ly Abdoulaye that he will be able to enter Dakar's former Western quarter, only to vanish when the policeman stops them. Sembene's depiction of these everyday events and problems instils in the viewer an awareness of the legacy of colonisation and calls for an African awakening.

Throughout the film, the viewer empathises with the central character, Ly Abdoulaye, a religious and family man, seen first kneeling in front of the mosque asking for Allah's protection, then leaving the house and greeting his wife who gives him some cola nuts to take along on his journey. His day would have been good had the griot not charmed him by invoking his supposedly illustrious lineage, which contrasts with his present status as a humble and impoverished cart driver. Sembene also uses this individual claim as an allegory for an Africa whose illustrious past does little for present-day life, as the following sequence illustrates.

Ly Abdoulaye is waiting for customers, lying back in his cart with his feet sticking up over the side, apparently oblivious to the town's hustle and bustle. An African guitar leitmotif is heard, while the camera shows the driver and cart from a slightly low-angle medium long-shot as a beggar enters the frame from the lower right corner of the screen, dragging himself along. The camera stays immobile, showing the beggar from the back as he approaches the cart, head and body first, then his deformed legs. He pulls himself forward along the side of the cart to where the resting driver's feet are sticking out, and appeals to him 'For the love of God, for the love of God . . .' As the beggar turns towards the cart and looks up at the driver's feet, the camera cuts to his point of view. The beggar pursues his appeal, 'Have pity upon me . . . have pity upon me.' While he is saying this, the camera cuts to a position near Ly Abdoulaye and shows the beggar from a high-angle position, then cuts to the feet as seen from the beggar's point of view, emphasising the dehumanised nature of this begging. When no response is forthcoming, the camera pans to the left, following the beggar who crawls away while Ly Abdoulaye reflects to himself, 'What is the point of replying? There are so many beggars. They are like flies.' The beggar leaves the frame and a new customer, arriving from the right, asks for transport. This long, carefully filmed sequence puts the plight of Africa into perspective, drawing attention to the continent's poverty and crippled economy which the beggar represents.

Religion and the traditional belief in past greatness are often read as paralysing forces in African history. No less paralysing are the new African aspirations to adopt Western values, as exemplified by Ly Abdoulaye's last customer, the African civil servant who wants to be taken from the African to the Western side of the city. In order to do this, as Férid Boughedir (1987: 67) puts it, he must also 'disguise himself as a European', and behave like the former colonial, that is to say, exploit the African. This very short film powerfully expresses Sembene's commitment to the struggle for an African identity. Despite independence, the continent remains caught between the dream of an old Africa and the emergence of a neo-colonial class.

In its modest way, *Borom Sarret* reveals the dilemma in which Africa is caught, showing the dangers which threaten its development and advocating a fight for survival away from the postcolonial corruption. The film does not attempt to follow Western aesthetic dictates; it combines Africa's oral tradition of storytelling with the camera's potential to show images. The film language thus developed also becomes representative of the urgent need for Africa to find her new self-image.

The fact that this film is in French may seem counter-productive as far as reaching the Senegalese is concerned – the majority have no knowledge of French – but it is more effective in appealing to a larger audience, investing the film with the quality of an allegory which is not culture specific but which extends its meaning to Africa at large and to the world beyond.

La Noire de . . . (1967)

The plight of the African woman is touched upon in *Borom Sarret*, through the quiet determination of Ly Abdoulaye's wife to survive. She is an African woman who appears to have had little contact with European or Western culture. In *La Noire de . . . (Black Girl)* Sembene examines the predicament of a young African woman who, lured by European images, falls victim to her false dreams.

The film, based on a true story, tells the story of Diouana, a young girl, who accompanies her white employers to France. Mistreated and humiliated by them, she eventually commits suicide. The French title, *La Noire de . . .* contains an ambiguity which is lost in the English title, *Black Girl*. The suspension after the preposition *de* leaves unspecified whether the word means *from*, that is to say, coming from a specific place, or the possessive *of*, indicating that the black girl is someone's property. The syntactic device evokes both meanings in French. The anonymity of the title strips the girl of every possible attribute of identity, other than being black.

The black-and-white cinematography provides the formal and semantic basis of the film. Everything is reduced to a black/white dichotomy: Diouana's dress, the apartment, the food prepared, even the whisky consumed generously by the Frenchman bears the label 'Black and White'. The opposition is enacted most dramatically when the camera focuses on Diouana's inert black body in the white bathtub. The obvious binary syntax of the film corresponds to the crude polarity that underlies any system of oppression and exploitation, a system that divides the world into two opposing categories, the oppressed and the oppressors – as was also the case in *Borom Sarret*.

If, in *Borom Sarret*, the poor cart driver had a dream of illustrious ancestors which elevated him above his modest status, Diouana's sense of self in *La Noire de . . .* is a fragile one, having absorbed the icons of 'white' models. The illiterate Diouana has no knowledge of France apart from that gained from the alluring verbal reports of the French women and the glossy pictures of an *Elle* magazine, bought by her boyfriend on one of their meetings in Dakar. Her image of life in France springs entirely from these commodified representations of women. Slowly, she begins to erect a self-image based on them. She expects that, when in France, her wages will allow her to buy elegant clothes in beautiful shops; the *Elle* women in bathing suits lead her to imagine her own picture taken on the beach and sent to Dakar, where 'they will be envious'. But instead, Diouana becomes a virtual prisoner in a French apartment. The France she dreamed of is replaced by the rooms she cleans, the noise of quarrelling neighbours upstairs, or the 'black hole' she perceives from the window as she looks out over the dark Antibes bay.

The more Diouana tries to enact the image represented to her in Dakar, the more she incurs the anger of the French woman who, nevertheless, contributes to Diouana's desire for that image. In her mistress's old clothes, Diouana is then scorned for looking too elegant; she is given an apron and required to take off her high-heeled, Western-style shoes. Her interior monologue conveys dismay, but she never utters a word besides,

'Oui, Monsieur' and 'Oui, Madame'. The most painful contrast between expectation and reality concerns 'her picture on the beach'. In fact, Diouana is never photographed by the sea. Instead, the viewer sees her lifeless body in the bathtub – and then a cut to holiday-makers in bathing suits on the beach, reading the account of her suicide, now a minor story in the local newspaper. Her life has been reduced to an anecdote in a paper.

But Diouana's death is not depicted as an isolated event: the film also evokes the death of other Senegalese people, the Senegalese soldiers who died in World Wars I and II and who also identified with white Europeans. This is seen in the sequence on the war memorial shortly before Diouana's departure for France, when she and her boyfriend are near the monument. A brief vision of veterans putting wreaths on the monument flashes through the friend's mind as Diouana, apparently unaware of the monument's importance and rejoicing over her imminent departure for France, dances barefoot on it. For her friend, dancing on this war memorial is tantamount to a sacrilege and he orders her to come down immediately.

The sequence has a twofold implication. First, the dance on a monument erected to commemorate the soldiers who went to fight in Europe may be seen as a prediction of Diouana's own death. Second, her departure for France and subsequent suicide become linked to the Senegalese political involvement in World Wars I and II. The friend's respect for the monument reveals the pride he takes in the courage and sacrifice of his Senegalese compatriots, and in one way Diouana's going to France parallels the Senegalese soldiers' participation in these wars. These soldiers had gone to fight for France's freedom and were honoured to die for the 'fatherland'. Similarly, Diouana's work frees the French woman, and her death, although self-inflicted, is not unlike that of the soldiers. Her belongings are returned to Dakar; her clothes, like the uniform of a slain soldier, are taken back to the mother with a sum of money offered in compensation. The linking of Diouana with the soldiers suggests that behind the overt exploitation lies another deeper, covert and political one. Both exported female domestic labour and male military service based on an identification with France, emerge as tantamount to suicide.

Camp de Thiaroye (1988)

Like *La Noire de* . . . , *Camp de Thiaroye* (*The Camp at Thiaroye*) is based on a true story concerning the massacre of a group of rebelling Senegalese *tirailleurs* (infantrymen). When the *tirailleurs* return from fighting in World War II, the French fail to pay them their demobilisation allowance and refuse to exchange their French money at the going rate. The soldiers have already endured appalling racist treatment from the French and suddenly realise that their own country is occupied, just as France was during the war. Now they have only one thought: 'we helped free France from the Germans, we must now free Africa'.

The film opens showing soldiers on stretchers being carried off the plane. On their return to their native Africa all the marks of French domination await them: cries of 'Vive la France' and French songs resound. Military discipline is maintained as white officers and black sergeants shout orders in French. One officer addresses the men: 'Worthy successors of your fathers of 1914–1918! It is thanks to your courage and devotion . . . that our cherished mother country still stands. France,' he adds, 'has been reborn from its ashes.' Ironically, the soldiers are wearing uniforms borrowed from the American army. One officer comments that they 'would have returned in rags' otherwise.

The film concentrates on three specific individuals who each embody different aspects of the war's legacy: Pays, mentally damaged and mute as a result of his imprisonment at Buchenwald; Diatta, the Westernised sergeant-major, with a French wife and French values, who discovers that his parents have been killed and their village destroyed by the French; and Corporal Diarra, who feels loyal to both France and Africa and has an unwavering respect for humanity and justice. These three characters constitute a microcosm of post-war colonised Africa. Pays is the defenceless victim of violence, Diatta the African intellectual elite, and Diarra the authentic human being, whose integrity transcends race, colour and nationality.

Before the French renege on the agreed arrangements for demobilisation, Sembene depicts the African soldiers being subjected to a multitude of dehumanising attitudes and actions. For example, when Diatta, in his borrowed American uniform, goes into a popular Dakar bar, the 'Coq Hardi', the bartender is told to 'charge double because he is American'. But when he reveals himself to be African by speaking French, she exclaims, 'A nigger!' and has him thrown out on the street. This is a humiliating moment for the refined sergeant-major, who discovers that his blackness would have been acceptable had he been an American with money. Upon leaving the bar, Diatta is exposed to further humiliation when he is stopped by a black American military policeman for not wearing the badges on his 'American' uniform. Kicked and beaten, he ends up in hospital. In retaliation Corporal Diarra authorises the kidnapping of an American soldier.

The 'Coq Hardi' sequence brings out the complexity of the dichotomy of black and white: not only is Diatta's 'African black' more objectionable than 'American black', his rank in the French army and his education, which qualify him for French citizenship, are nullified by his colour. In a parallel way, the kidnapping of the American soldier is an exceptionally serious offence because the victim is 'white', even though, unlike the hospitalised Diatta, he incurs no injury whatsoever. Meanwhile, with the exception of Captain Raymond, the white officers are guilty of the worst racism imaginable.

Through numerous incidents of this kind a dramatic crescendo builds to the Thiaroye massacre. Having been constantly humiliated and denied decent food and compensation, the *tirailleurs* finally rebel when the French decide to change their money at half the going rate. They kidnap a French general, who is placed under Pays's mute surveillance in the barracks. Eventually the general regains his freedom by promising to change the money at the official rate. The soldiers rejoice and proclaim victory but Pays knows that the general is lying. He is the only one to doubt the word of a French general.

From that moment, Pays knows no peace and keeps watch while the other soldiers celebrate into the night. When tank headlights appear out of the darkness, Pays tries to warn the others, but they fail to understand him. In the ensuing massacre Pays, Diatta and Diarra are killed.

The final sequence is set in the officers' mess where the general is told that his order has been executed. He approves and confirms that the Minister of Colonies and the Governor General in Dakar have also endorsed the action. The film closes with long shots of departing recruits and superimposed close-ups of the smiling faces of the Camp de Thiaroye soldiers.

Camp de Thiaroye is an outstandingly powerful film depicting the most outrageous colonial violence. It is also a biting satire on France's 'assimilation' policy, which called on Africans to 'feel French'. Offering France as the homeland of the French empire and French 'citizenship' as a reward for having reached a sufficiently high standard of 'civilisation' are mere deceits aimed at providing maximum gain for France. Sembene sees the hypocrisy behind the propagation of French ideals for France's benefit alone.

All three films, then, are a plea for Africa to find a modern self-image which is not modelled on that of the coloniser. In *Borom Sarret* it was necessary to turn away from traditional customs to gain access to the Western district of the city; in *La Noire de . . .* the alluring images disseminated from France lead to an African woman's development of a false self-image which proves suicidal. Then in *Camp de Thiaroye*, made with financial backing from Senegal, Tunisia and Algeria, but none from France, Sembene makes his strongest indictment of France's exploitative manipulation of the colonised through the principle of 'assimilation'. Here, as elsewhere in his work, it is clear that Sembene sees cinema as one way to resist the cultural assimilation France has so strongly promoted and which many Africans have so readily accepted. Doing this, he goes some way towards the creation of an African cinema and an African identity.

Djibril Diop-Mambéty

The 1999 FESPACO programme included a tribute to this much-loved Senegalese director, who died in July 1998 and whose films remain among the most original in the history of African cinema.

Mambéty's oeuvre, though limited, is diverse. In his early film, *Contras City* (1968 – *A City of Contrasts*), he gives a satirical and amusing picture of Dakar's cosmopolitanism. Those films which focus on an individual, such as *La Petite Vendeuse de soleil* (1998), *Badou Boy* (1970) and *Le Franc* (1994), reveal Mambéty's love of people, his sense of humour and his belief in positive qualities of humankind. *Badou Boy* relates the adventures of a young delinquent boy while *Le Franc* depicts everyday African life by focusing on a poor man, harassed by his landlady for not paying his rent. In burlesque mood, *Le Franc* follows the poor man's complicated efforts to claim his lottery win. In order not to lose his winning ticket, he glues it to the door of his room. When he arrives with the door at the office to claim his reward, he learns that a ticket glued to a door is invalid. He attempts to retrieve the ticket by taking the door to the sea and soaking it in the water, hoping it will come loose. The mood shifts from despair when he loses the ticket to elation at retrieving it when the waves return it and deposit it on his forehead.

Mambéty's subsequent two films, *Touki-Bouki* (1973) and *Hyènes* (1992 – *Hyenas*), both use the same animal metaphor of the hyena to portray African society. According to Pfaff, the West African oral tradition includes many stories involving the hyena, 'an animal accused of greed and mischievousness' who has 'an unpleasant odour and repulsive physical characteristics' and who 'also symbolises trickery and social marginality' (1988: 220). *Hyènes*, inspired by the story of Swiss writer, Friedrich Dürrenmatt's *The Visit* (1955 – *Der Besuch der alten Dame*), is set in a small fictional town, Colobane, now struck by poverty but priding itself on past glory. One day the news spreads that Linguère Ramatou, a woman who used to live in Colobane, is returning on a visit to the town. Linguère has become a millionaire and the inhabitants hope that she will save their town. Her former lover, Draman Drameh, is the first to welcome the visitor, but it transpires she has come back to avenge herself against him for abandoning her when she became pregnant by him. She offers the town an inordinate amount of money on condition that Draman be put to death. The film portrays the resulting moral dilemma: on the one hand, the town's inhabitants are moved by sympathy for the woman who, disgraced by a fatherless child, had to leave the town and became a prostitute; on the other, they are reluctant to give in to blackmail and accept Linguère's money in exchange for the death of a popular inhabitant of the town.

Mambéty transposes the Swiss narrative material to Africa and thereby draws attention to the fact that the African matter in cinema can be circumstantial and that themes such as love and betrayal are universal. The film thus emphasises the fact that the label 'African' may be applied all too readily to films produced in Africa, when many of them actually deal with subjects that are fairly common the world over but that have a specific relevance in each country.

Touki-Bouki (1973)

Mambéty's most memorable film is undoubtedly Touki-Bouki (Journey of the Hyena) the story of two Senegalese university students, Mory and Anta, who dream of going to France. They manage to find the money for the trip through various dubious and unscrupulous means but, on the point of setting off, Mory cannot bring himself to leave his country and only Anta sets out to fulfil the dream.

This film has been discussed extensively by critics. For Ukadike, Touki-Bouki typifies 'a trend dedicated to total decolonisation of both content and style of movies' (Ukadike 1994: 172). For Pfaff, the film 'requires the viewers' ceaseless participation in the reconstruction of a deconstructed reality, a device also found in Western literature and cinema (e.g. Jean-Luc Godard's films)' (Pfaff 1988: 222), while Brahimi argues that in this film Mambéty 'invents a rhetoric of the image which moves from medieval allegory to surrealist collage' (Brahimi 1997: 53, trans.).

Touki-Bouki is an avant-garde film in a highly personal style. The linear narrative is constantly interrupted by symbolically charged inserts and vignettes that are semantically and emotionally related to the unfolding story, suggesting multiple readings. Mambéty has found a cinematic language hitherto unknown to African cinema that is indisputably his own. While earlier film-makers have used inserts, none has used them with such frequency. Moreover, these images are unusually powerful, even shocking.

Touki-Bouki opens in pastoral mood: a young boy on a dark bull is guiding a large herd to the accompaniment of an African reed instrument. But the mood changes abruptly with a cut to a slaughterhouse, into which one of the animals is being dragged. The slaughtering process that follows is shown at length and in considerable detail, accompanied by cavernous bellowing. The episode is hard to watch, full of close-ups of animals' staring eyes and body parts still moving while being slaughtered. Then the pastoral mood returns. The boy rides towards the camera and the noise of a motorbike is heard superimposed on the reed music. There is a sudden cut to reveal a bull's horns attached to the motorbike and the houses and people along the road as the rider speeds by.

The cut from Mory on the bull to Mory on the motorbike makes a leap in time and space, from childhood to adolescence, from countryside to city, exemplifying the rural exodus. Next we see Mory's girlfriend, Anta, writing, in the midst of the hustle and bustle of daily life.

High-rise city buildings are seen in the distance, accompanied by the mingled sounds of crying babies, trains and sirens. Then Anta's mother is shown selling food at the market and grumbling about people who leave for France: 'They return changed and all they bring are a French wife and disease.'

These opening sequences encapsulate the context against which Anta and Mory build their dream of escaping to France and returning rich and famous. For Ghanaian-British director, John Akomfrah, *Touki-Bouki* was a revelation that convinced him that African cinema is political by nature, 'being born out of the process of cultural and postcolonial renewal'. For him Mambéty's film 'cuts through the pedagogical imperative: straight to this guy and his girlfriend who wanted to leave Africa' (Akomfrah 1995: 19).

African cinema is often seen as expressing the dichotomy between tradition and modernity, between Africa and Europe, and as emphasising the erosion of 'authentic' African identity for an adulterated identity where traditional values are lost. But the differing values of traditional and modern life are by no means limited to Africa; instead, as Akomfrah states, they are 'the kind of youth traumas that have been a stock-in-trade of cinemas all over the world' (Akomfrah 1995: 37). What is specific to the dream of the two young heroes is the 'Frenchness' of their dream: the myth of France and Paris, which spins a web of dreams made of ambition, hope, nostalgia and despair.

It is this dream that Mambéty emphasises, as when he cuts from Anta and Mory on the motorbike ride to a baobab tree, then to Mory, surrounded by cattle, trying to throw a rope around a bull's horns, all to the sound of Josephine Baker singing 'Paris, Paris . . . c'est sur la terre entière le paradis' ('Paris, Paris . . . it is paradise on earth'). When Mory finally succeeds in tying the horns, they turn out to be attached to the motorbike. This burlesque and playful sequence is typical of Mambéty's cinema, where narrative intertwines with childhood memories, familiar figures, images recorded, stories told, and early sexual experiences.

Finally, when the dream is about to become reality and Mory and Anta are near the ship, Mory hesitates, then suddenly turns and runs off at speed. A long sequence shows the fragmented pictures he perceives as he races away, interspersed with inserts of the cattle in the slaughterhouse and cuts to Anta on the ship.

Mory's race ends when he sees his horned bike wrecked in an accident. 'Has he', Brahimi wonders, 'had an impulse to flee the "slaughterhouse" of Paris? Or is he returning to the past?' (Brahimi 1997: 53). The film ends with the postman, the symbolic link between France and Africa, descending the steps on which Mory is sitting, in Western dress and holding the bull's horn, intercut with images of the ship sailing to France. The opening shot of the boy and herd returns and closes the film.

All this could be interpreted as the conflict between two lovers, Anta and Mory. She stands for Western values and, in an attempt to shed her African persona, decides to go to France; he, at the last moment, rejects the escape to France and chooses Africa. The film may also be seen as a socio-political allegory or postcolonial fairy-tale, in which Africa allows itself to be seduced by Western values and constructs a dream of false happiness in whose name it embraces corruption, theft and betrayal. The film-maker does not specify how the film should be read but, by finding his own innovative cinematic language, aesthetically integrates the many contradictions and conflicts inherent in African society.

La Petite Vendeuse de soleil (1998)

La Petite Vendeuse de soleil (The Little Girl Who Sold the Sun) was shown at the FESPACO tribute ceremony in 1999 and moved the audience deeply. It tells the story of a little disabled girl who wishes to become a newspaper street vendor, traditionally a boy's prerogative. She thus faces the two obstacles of her gender and her disability. But nothing will deter her; she walks resolutely to the distribution centre on her crutches and succeeds in convincing the agent to let her try to sell a few copies of the newspaper *Le Soleil (The Sun)*. The hurdles to be overcome are considerable, the most painful of which is the boys' hostility. The girl's success is met with increasing aggression on their part, and at one point the boys

13 Djibril Diop-Mambéty, *La Petite Vendeuse de soleil.*

push her over violently and make her lose a crutch. One boy, with whom the girl has already struck up a friendship, now lends her his support.

It is a moving story of resilience and motivation, of determination, friendship and solidarity. As the smiling girl cries out 'Le Soleil, Le Soleil!', the viewer cannot but see the literal meaning of the paper's title – a little girl selling warmth and happiness. It also suggests an allegorical transfer of the girl's story to the continent of Africa and its crippling poverty, so much in need of the qualities the girl displays. The optimism conveyed by the girl's victory over natural and social adversities may be read, on an idealistic level, as Mambéty's dream for his country and his continent; a programme promoting social equality, economic policies and a belief in change for Africa.

Safi Faye

Like Sembene and Mambéty, Safi Faye has succeeded in developing a personal cinematic language demonstrating that cinema offers a medium to the African artist in which a new language, and hence a new identity, can be created. The technical requirements and visual dimension of cinema inevitably force the film-maker to transcend Africa's oral traditions and the expertise of African artisans. Film-makers are also aware that cinema overcomes the problem of illiteracy – which is still high in many African countries – reaching a far wider audience than literature.

Safi Faye, hailed as the first 'active independent female Black African-born film-maker' (Pfaff 1988: 115), first entered cinema as an actress through the French anthropologist film-maker, Jean Rouch, who chose her to act in his 1968 film *Petit à petit*. Although Rouch is recognised as having had a positive influence on the development of African cinema, he has also been charged with having promoted an 'exotic', Western view of the African. In retrospect, Faye says she dislikes Rouch's film, although through him she discovered the world of cinema and, in particular, *cinéma vérité*, whose initial aim was to film in a direct and unobtrusive way with non-professional actors, no staging and little or no editing.

Faye started her career as a teacher before going to Paris to study ethnology. Her first short ten-minute film *La Passante* (1972 – *The Passerby*), is about a woman walking down a street who realises that she is an attraction to the men around her. Faye focuses on two men, one white, one black, and explores their fantasy world as triggered off by the woman, acted by Faye herself. No one speaks in the film – other than a few lines of poetry being read, only music is heard. A personal experimental style is already apparent, but it was Faye's first long feature film, *Kaddu beykat* (1975 – *Letter From My Village*), that drew international attention to her talent as a socially committed, ethnographic African film-maker.

Kaddu beykat (1975)

Kaddu beykat is Wolof for 'The Voice of the Peasant'. The film, an attack on the imposition of monoculture for cash crop production, is structured in the form of a letter written to a friend. It gives a moving account of village life and adopts a slow, lyrical pace to show the daily routine and the rituals of the farming families, the evening meetings under the tree, the songs and games.

The focus is on two characters from a small agricultural Senegalese village, Ngor and Coumba, who have been wanting to get married for two years. But once again, the rains have been insufficient and irregular with disastrous consequences for the annual harvest of groundnuts, the sole crop on which the village depends. They will have to delay the marriage again, and Ngor, in order to earn his fiancée's dowry, is forced to go to Dakar where he is exploited by Senegal's new middle class.

Faye's concerns are not only individual, relating to the couple waiting to get married, but also profoundly socio-political in a larger sense. The story deals with colonial farming practices, still upheld by present-day governments, which have had disastrous consequences for the farming families. When working for themselves, Africans could generally provide for their families, but when colonialism introduced the culture of cash crops for export, in this case groundnuts, less and less food could be grown for local use. Moreover, the prices were fixed by the foreign companies that controlled the export trade. Most of the returns went to these traders, who made large profits from the differential between what they paid to the Africans and what they charged to European and American markets.

The personal tone Faye adopts in this film lends it an increased sense of authenticity. The voice-over, that of the letter writer (Faye), is part of the village though she is at the same time both an insider and an outsider: she belongs to the village but is able to observe it from a distance.

Fad'jal (1979)

In Faye's later film, *Fad'jal*, the camera again becomes the witness of village life, this time in Faye's own village, which lends the title to the film. The camera shows farmers working in fields, women singing, a tam-tam being played, children dancing, men wrestling. At the heart of it all, the elders of the village gather with young boys under the baobab tree where they talk about the origin of Fad'jal, founded by a woman, Mban Fadial.

The film is about collective memory, about ritual and about birth and death. When a descendant of Fadial is born, celebrations take place and different lines of descent are explained, while the elders also point out the ancestors' places of burial. The village is a harmonious place, a place of continuity, where birth and death are communal events in which the entire village participates.

14 Safi Faye, *Fad'jal.* In Faye's village.

But whereas in *Kaddu beykat* monoculture destroyed the traditional food supply, in *Fad'jal* another calamity threatens the village, that of land development. A voice-over announces in French that on 1 May all land is declared 'national domain'; from then onwards all the land will belong to the state. Later the woman's voice-over reports that one October afternoon in 1977 the developers arrived with tools and equipment. Faye's lyricism poeticises the harsh realities of Senegalese farming as caused by government policies.

Faye's originality lies in her intertwining of narrative and documentary, fiction and social history. Here is an ethnologist and storyteller at work, speaking for her people, for their memories, for the land on which the ancestors are buried, for the elders who ensure that knowledge is transmitted and collective memory and identity are preserved.

Mossane (1996)

Set in a Senegalese village, *Mossane* is about the transition from adolescence to adulthood. Mossane, a young and very attractive fourteen-year-old girl, had been promised at birth in marriage to Diogoye, an emigrant who lives in France. All the financial arrangements have been settled and Diogoye, who has regularly sent presents to Mossane's parents, has now sent the dowry for the marriage. The plan is for Mossane to marry him by proxy in her village and then join her husband in France. However, when Fara, a poor student in agronomy, returns home because of a strike at the university, he and Mossane discover that their feelings of fondness have grown into love.

An inevitable confrontation ensues, when the parents insist on Mossane marrying Diogoye, who earns a good living and will solve the family's financial problems. But Mossane feels she should be free to marry whoever she wants. In spite of her threat to throw herself down a well, the marriage is arranged and the guests admire the lavish presents sent by Diogoye. Mossane, in despair, runs away. When she is found dead, the village goes into mourning.

While the film focuses on one particular person, its impact transcends that of the individual. Mossane's mythic beauty and unusual qualities lend her a symbolic quality that makes her representative of womanhood as well as of the village itself. Her parents, in forcing their daughter to emigrate to France, rob the village of one of its most admired and beloved women. This 'robbing' may be read as the threat to the identity of this old village, which was founded by a king in the fourteenth century: its inhabitants, enticed by gifts from Diogoye, fail to see that they are contributing to the decline of the village. This also may be seen on a deeper level, referring to France's and other countries' neo-colonial practice inherent in Third World aid.

Moussa Touré

While the film-makers so far considered may constitute the core of Senegalese cinema, a new generation of film-makers is emerging. Moussa Touré, for example, whose film *TGV* was entered for competition at the 1999 FESPACO and at several other festivals, is undoubtedly a promising new talent. From the age of fifteen he had an interest in cinema and worked as an electrician with Sembene and Flora Gomès (Guinea-Bissau) before becoming a film-maker himself.

Toubab-Bi (1991)

Toubab-Bi tells the story of the thirty-year-old cinema technician, Soriba, who has never left Senegal. He has acquired a lot of knowledge about France, through school books that date from pre-independence days, through the cinema and through French people with whom he has worked. When the opportunity arises for an apprenticeship in a Parisian film laboratory, conflict emerges: he must choose between the warmth and values of the African family with its strong presence of women – his mother, his sister and his wife – and a hostel for male foreigners in a Paris suburb. Soriba leaves for Paris, however, with two further missions: to take Idi, the young son of his cousin, to his father who has not seen him for years, and to find his old friend Issa N'Doye, who left seven years ago and has not been heard of since.

The film operates on more than one level. On the level of film-making, it reveals how much French images have dominated the African film world and Soriba's leaving to train in France points to the lack of opportunities in Senegal. On the social level, the film shows the effects of the postcolonial erosion of society where families are separated, children are deprived of their fathers and wives are left to await the return of their husbands from France. The film shows the ongoing struggle of African society to preserve its own social cohesion and create an African cinema.

TGV (1997)

TGV, referring to the French high-speed train (*train de grande vitesse*) is the name given to a bus service between Dakar in Senegal and Conakry in Guinea. The film begins at the bus station where a group of people are getting on the bus. Shortly before departure Rambo, the driver and his passengers are warned that, at the Guinea border, the Bassari have risen up against the authorities and are seeking the return of their birth totem, kept in a European museum. On hearing the news a number of passengers cancel their trip, only a dozen or so being willing to take the risk.

The programme of the 1999 London Film Festival called *TGV* 'a road movie which combines drama and comedy with ease' (47). Susan Hayward states that in a road movie, generally speaking, 'the purpose of the trajectory is to obtain self-knowledge' (Hayward 1996: 301). *TGV* may well be seen as a road movie where the journey is undertaken by a heterogeneous group of people with a specific destination, who constitute a microcosm of society. The modern means of transport brings together an arbitrary group of people. The 'society' they form has neither ethnic nor ideological coherence. It is a new society having to overcome great difficulties to reach its destination. The viewer observes the dynamics of this newly constituted society, but also follows, from the travellers' points of view, the Africa the TGV travels through. Good humour and irony, rather than political commitment or ideology, underlie this film, although political events and manipulations are among the many facets of the African society *TGV* reveals.

Senegal was the first African country to produce African films and to understand that cinema could play a vital role in a people's understanding of their identity. While Vieyra emphasises the estrangement of the Africans in Paris, Sembene shows the plight of postcolonial Africa and examines the specious models that the white coloniser imposed upon Africa. Mambéty also deals with that influence and reveals the conflict this creates but he further resorts to putting forward positive models that encourage Africa in its building of an independent identity. Safi Faye locates the notion of identity in the village: the village itself has an identity, founded in the collective memory of a rich historical past. Finally, Moussa Touré adds to the depiction of cross-cultural experiences the use of cinema as an expression of a particular identity and of humorous fiction as a means of exploring facets of African society.

10 Mali

Like most African countries, Mali was keen to set up its own cinema production. Vieyra reports that a weekly news bulletin on film, made in collaboration with the federal republic of Yugoslavia, was launched in 1963 (Vieyra 1975: 123). Mali, then known as French Sudan, had already attracted the attention of important French anthropologists, in particular Marcel Griaule, who first revealed the Dogon people of the Bandiagara Plateau to the Europeans on his 1931 Dakar-Djibouti expedition, financed by the French government. The aim of that expedition was to acquire ethnographic knowledge and material for the Trocadéro museum in Paris. It led to Griaule's life-long study of and admiration for the Dogon. Griaule's work stimulated the ethnographic interest of French colleagues, including Jean Rouch and Germaine Dieterlen, many of whom took to filming the Dogon and neighbouring peoples in the late 1950s and 1960s (Bonte & Izard 1992: 309).

Malian directors did not start making films in Mali until the late 1960s, when Souleymane Cissé completed his cinematographic training in Moscow. Not only did Cissé found Malian cinema, this remarkable film-maker of unfailing political commitment is also a major figure in African cinema as a whole. Two other film-makers, Cheick Oumar Sissoko in the 1980s and Adamo Drabo in the 1990s, are equally dedicated to the urgent social needs of Africa at large and of Mali in particular.

Mali is located on what were once major caravan routes across Africa and it still occupies an important strategic position on the continent's north/south and east/west axes. It was a country of great renown in the thirteenth century, especially under the Muslim King Mansa Kankou Moussa, who subjugated the Songhai, Bambara, Mossi and Touareg peoples. Reminders of its great past still exist. The cities of Timbuktu and Djenné, which are linked by the Niger river, were prestigious centres of culture and commerce until the fifteenth century, when Songhai power became dominant. When the Europeans colonised Africa at the end of the nineteenth century, the great African divide (Berlin 1884–85) incorporated Mali into French Sudan. In 1960, with independence, the old country of Mali was restored and its illustrious name reinstated after the collapse of a two month long political union with Senegal.

Mali exemplifies the diversities, mutations and intersections of cultures that characterise the whole of West Africa. This mosaic structure works against the notion of a national identity or even an African identity, so it is not surprising that Cissé should remark: 'at the moment it is still impossible to pinpoint the cultural identity of our films' (*Cinécrits* October 1998: 5, trans.). Cissé's comment highlights the complexity of the struggle for identity characterising African cinema. It also expresses the new opportunity presented by such a convergence of cultures, which excludes any notion of a monoculture. For all three Malian film-makers a notion of film committed to Africa dominates. Writing for *Africa and the Centenary of Cinema*, Sissoko states: 'All African film-makers have the duty to transfer on to the screen the African way of life which has practically been banned from the international screen. In doing so, they cannot afford to be anecdotal' (FEPACI 1995: 356). In telling specific stories, Cissé, Sissoko and Drabo are addressing larger African issues.

Souleymane Cissé

According to Françoise Pfaff, Souleymane Cissé 'is, together with Ousmane Sembene, now widely considered to be one of the leading figures of African cinema' (Pfaff 1988: 51). Cissé's roots are Mali Muslim. Born in 1940 in Mali's capital, Bamako, he discovered film at an early age in open-air cinemas. After a spell in Dakar, where his parents had moved, Cissé returned to the newly independent Mali in 1960, where his interest in film intensified. Both Pfaff and Bachy record how, in 1962, Cissé saw a film showing the tragic death of Patrice Lumumba, leader of the National Congolese Movement. This marked Cissé profoundly. It made him realise the effect film can have upon an audience and prompted his decision to become a film-maker. After six years at Moscow's State Institute of Cinema, he returned to Mali in 1969 and was appointed film director at SCINFOMA (*Service Cinématographique du Ministère de l'Information*), for which he made a number of short films and many newsreels and documentaries between 1965 and 1972 (Pfaff 1988: 51–67 and Bachy 1983a: 39).

L'Aspirant (1968)

While still in Moscow, Cissé made several short films, including the fifteen-minute film, *L'Aspirant* (*The Aspirant*), in 35 mm and colour. This film is representative of his later film-making in two ways: firstly, it deals with specifically African material and, secondly, it already reveals the cinematic characteristics that Cissé was to display throughout his career. It shows a young doctor delivering a lecture to colleagues about traditional healing methods. As he is speaking the film cuts to Africa, where his father, a traditional healer, is trying to cure a little boy. The structure of the film and the reconstruction of African dancing and singing in the Moscow studio reveal an unusual technical assurance and display a Cissé style, even at this early stage (Vieyra 1975: 123–4).

Cinq jours dans une vie (1972)

After a few further short films, Cissé made *Cinq jours dans une vie* (*Five Days in a Life*), a forty-minute film that raises the problem of education in the traditional Koranic schools. When the main protagonist, the young N'Tji, leaves school, he speaks only Bambara and cannot read French. He fails to secure a job and ends up leading a vagrant life in town. After robbing a farmer, who has come to earn money during the rainy season, he is imprisoned. On his release the boy's uncle persuades N'Tji to return to his village.

The film was awarded the bronze medal at the Carthage Film Festival in Tunisia for its skilful technique and sensitivity. These early short films reveal Cissé's twofold concern: on the one hand he wishes to preserve valuable traditions but, on the other, he sees the danger of upholding traditions without questioning them.

Den Muso (1975)

In 1974 Cissé obtained the support of the French Ministry of Cooperation for his first feature length film, in the Bambara language, *Den Muso* (*The Girl*). The film had a great impact on the Malian public and, as Cissé comments in *The Guardian* (10 May 1984: 15), confirmed his view that Africans 'were anxious to see more films mirroring their own existence and preoccupations'. Although made in 1974, *Den Muso* was not released until 1978 because of legal wrangling over copyright (Pfaff 1988: 53).

The film tells the tragic story of a young mute girl, Ténin, the daughter of a well-to-do industrialist, who meets a worker recently sacked from his job at her father's factory because he asked for a wage increase. The boy rapes Ténin at a party, not knowing that she is the daughter of his former boss. When Ténin discovers she is pregnant and is rejected by her parents, she turns to her baby's father, but finds him with another woman and unwilling to recognise his child. In despair she sets fire to the hut, then, realising she has caused the death of two people, takes her own life. Cissé wanted to expose the problems of many young single mothers who are rejected by society. Ténin's muteness is a powerful representation of women's lack of power in a country where they have no voice.

Den Muso, which received a prize at the Three Continents Film Festival in Nantes, was followed by three major films, *Baara*, *Finyé* and *Yeelen*, all three of which won most prestigious awards. Both *Baara*, in 1978, and *Finyé*, in 1982, were awarded the Yennenga Stallion at FESPACO, making Cissé the only film-maker to have won it twice, while *Yeelen* was awarded the Jury Prize at the Cannes Festival in 1987. Cissé has become a key figure in African cinema, admired for both his political commitment and cinematic talent. The complexity of the stories in all three films require a fair amount of narrative guidance.

Baara (1978)

Baara (*Work*) opens with three brief sequences that precede the credits. The first shows close-ups of a young man from the front, back and sides, rather like police identification photos, posing the question of his identity. In the second, two people are seen walking very slowly from behind a fire in the foreground towards the camera. As they approach, the scene shifts to a room where a number of men are sleeping; then the action begins and the credits appear.

The man who appears in all of these sequences turns out to be Balla Diarra, a porter recently arrived in Bamako. On his way to work with his pushcart he takes on a pregnant woman and her four children, who are being brutally evicted by her husband. Balla refuses to let her pay. This sequence is reminiscent of Ousmane Sembene's portrayal of African daily life in *Borom Sarret*, where the film-maker depicts a carter who transports people to various places – including a pregnant woman to the maternity hospital, a man and his dead baby to the cemetery.

Balla's next customer is a textile factory engineer called Balla Traoré. Their shared first name establishes a link between the two men, but the different last names denote their class difference. Balla's last name, Diarra, conveys his inferior, servant class, while the engineer's last name, Traoré, denotes an upper class. The man to whom we were introduced in the opening sequences has now been identified and set in a social context. Though the engineer dismisses this distinction and also tries to do away with colonial terminology by urging his workers to address him as Traoré rather than boss, the evidence of social background remains in the names. In such narrative details of identity, Cissé refers to the larger social context that continues to affect individual lives beyond social changes.

Sometime after meeting the engineer, Balla Diarra is imprisoned because he cannot produce identity papers for the police, but is freed by Traoré, who finds him employment in the factory, where Balla's inadequate mask barely protects him against the harmful gases. In this way the viewer is introduced to working conditions in industrialised Mali and the workers' efforts to unionise.

At the same time the film also focuses on the powerful, corrupt factory owner and his entourage. The owner often appears centre screen, acting dictatorially both in the factory and in his family. His idle wife, who has secretly taken a lover, responds aggressively to his abusive comments; however, when he discovers her affair and she counters by revealing her knowledge of his corrupt dealings, he ensures her silence by strangling her.

In the dramatic finale the factory workers find Traoré murdered, also at the owner's instigation. Only the arrival of the police, who know about the first murder, prevents them from killing the owner. The film closes with the early shot of the now-familiar figures of the two Ballas walking towards the fire. Their friendship is not just a fortuitous encounter but the necessary solidarity which must occur between the factions in Mali and other African societies.

Finyé (1982)

Finyé (*The Wind*) deals with corrupt military and political power through the love story of two young students. The boy, Bah, is the grandson of Kansaye, a descendant of illustrious chiefs of the region; the girl, Batrou, is the daughter of Sangaré, the military governor, representing the new power. This opposition has led many critics to see the tradition/modernity dichotomy as the film's main theme. It has also been suggested that the title, in the context of the film, symbolises not only political and social renewal but also cinematographic renewal (Bachy 1983a: 51).

After the opening credits the screen is filled with rippling water through which a young boy is seen walking slowly towards the camera, while the sound of the wind is heard. He stops and looks off right, then his image fades as if he had returned to the water. The water/boy opening is followed by two long tracking shots, the first across a sun-burnt landscape and the second showing a green landscape after rain, with superimposed Bambara ideograms giving the film's title and a text translated as: 'The wind awakens the thoughts of man.' The presence of ideograms is an endorsement of the Bambara language and civilisation, especially since they express a mystical dimension and are considered to be emanations of reality, and not random representations of it.

As in *Baara* the opening sequence poses the question 'Who is this boy?' Tahar Chikhaoui suggests that the superimposing of water on the boy's face, accompanied by the sound of the wind, seems 'to integrate the boy into the elements and link him to the mythical origins of mankind' (*Cinécrits* 1998: 21). Certainly, the two tracking shots suggest the cycles of nature and give meaning to the symbol of the wind and so intimate a link between the elements, seasonal change and the story about to unfold.

At first, the story offers no overt connection to the opening images. As in *Baara*, it intertwines several social spheres and focuses on specific relationships: between the students Bah and Batrou, between Bah and his grandfather Kansaye and between Batrou, her father Sangaré and his third wife. Through these relationships, Cissé exposes the disintegrating social structures of African cities. The film reveals the drug addiction of the young, the corruption of the military government, the abusive power of men in their polygamous households and the waning of traditional values. When the high school results are announced and Bah learns that he has failed, he resorts to taking drugs with friends, but a close-up shows tears rolling down his cheeks. Then there is a shift to the vision he has at that moment, in which the boy of the opening sequence returns: Bah and Batrou are seen, both dressed in white; they smile at each other, then the child from the opening scene appears carrying a gourd, goes to the water, fills the gourd and offers it to the lovers who take turns drinking from it. Close-ups of the smiling faces are followed by a shot of the gourd floating on the water. The vision is accompanied by the earlier sounds which Amna Guellali poetically calls 'broken echoes' (*Cinécrits* 1998: 28). This moment lends a mythical tone to the film, suggesting that characters in the story refer to larger, deeper African and human values.

The love of Bah and Batrou is set against the enmity of the traditional chief, Bah's grandfather, and the military governor, Batrou's father. The students' imprisonment, following a protest over falsified exam results, leads to Batrou openly opposing her father. Sangaré renounces her while Kansaye, dressed in his chief's clothes, consults the spirits near the sacred trees on the land of his ancestors which his opponent, Sangaré, has acquired through corruption. When the two chiefs meet, the military governor attempts to kill the traditional chief; but the latter is protected by the spirits and the bullets do not penetrate his body. The camera shows him walking away, his colourful African garment filling the screen.

At home Kansaye's wife tells him – wrongly, as we learn later – that Bah has been killed. Kansaye, realising and accepting that his world is over, burns his robes and amulets and joins the students in their protest. In so doing he alters the manifestation of his power, but remains an authority that has always been more spiritual than political. Meanwhile, the military governor, who was about to exile the imprisoned students, is summoned by the governmental authorities and ordered to release them. The initial authority of both chiefs has clearly come to an end. The film then cuts to the closing sequence in which the little boy returns, thus framing the film: he offers a gourd filled with water to an off-screen receiver located top-right, the direction in which the child was looking in the opening sequence.

Although the film has developed characters, it is clear that this is the language of allegory. The poetic elements, the images of the child, the 'broken echoes' of the soundtrack and the ancestral trees all allegorise identities. The particular characters depicted by Cissé are ways of expressing the general phenomena of Africa's social problems.

Yeelen (1987)

Yeelen (*The Light*), widely acclaimed at the Cannes Festival when it won the Jury Prize, has become a landmark in African and Francophone cinema. The time and space of the story precede those of Francophone Africa, referring to a Mali of the past, well before the colonial era and its territorial divisions. Cissé strips away the many layers of identity formation that burden modern Africa and returns to the struggle for identity of a particular family, the Diarra, who belong to the Bambara, part of the Mande group. Though the geography of the film is confined to a region in south-east Mali which can be travelled on foot in a relatively short time, the incursions of neighbouring ethnic groups on horseback evoke a much wider area and recall the struggles for power which have characterised West Africa throughout the ages and which led to the creation of the prosperous and culturally rich thirteenth-century Mali empire.

The memory of Mali's past, recorded in myth, stories and ritual, is embodied in a moment of crisis, when the survival of Diarra values is endangered because of a father's decision to withhold the knowledge of the Komo (the secret society of blacksmiths), from his son. Soma Diarra rejects his son Niankoro at birth and so the mother takes her son into exile to protect him. The only reason suggested for the father's behaviour is given later when the mother says to her son: 'Will you ever become somebody? That's what your father feared.' This conflict between father and son reflects a much wider and older one; the son's search for affirmation signifies the restoration of the Diarra family and survival of the Bambara people.

The film opens with two graphic signs translated as 'produces fire' and 'the worlds of both earth and sky exist through light'. These are followed by the title *Yeelen*, meaning light, and by explanatory texts providing knowledge the viewer needs to understand the spiritual background against which the story will unfold. These texts emphasise the timeless Bambara spiritual values and introduce the Komo or society of blacksmiths, who possess magical powers.

As in most of Cissé's work, the film's opening and closing moments echo each other and form a framing device for the narrative. Here the opening sequence, which follows the written texts, anticipates the story and foretells the ending. It shows a young child (Niankoro's son) leading a goat to an ancestral statue and the symbolic objects referred to in the written texts, the Wing of Kore and the Magic Pestle. These symbolic objects, signifying knowledge and power, are the tangible expressions of the secrets Niankoro's father wishes to withhold from his son. Following this opening sequence, the film juxtaposes two sequences which, in combination with the first, stage the central conflict of the film. The first shows the father invoking the power of the god Mari to help him find and kill his son, while the second shows Niankoro – now twenty years old – with his mother, carrying out a ritual to see what awaits him. The vision he is granted reveals the father's hatred, malevolence and determination to find the son by means of the Magic

Pestle and kill him. These first sequences thus reveal, in triptych fashion, three generations of the Diarra family and how the old man, by withholding his knowledge, also holds the generations apart, hence making the group impotent.

The Komo traditionally holds the supreme position among the various secret societies in Mande culture and plays an important role in Mande political life. The father's abuse of power represents the moral decline of the Diarra family, while the son's refusal to continue fleeing from his father and determination to challenge him offer the chance to reverse the moral decline and renew the spiritual authority of the Bambara.

Relying on his mother's wisdom and advice, Nianankoro agrees to wear a fetish around his neck and to take a special fetish to his father's twin brother, who lives beyond the Peul country. He earns the protection and friendship of the Peul king but, when asked to use his magical powers to end the barrenness of the king's youngest wife, Attu, he has sexual intercourse with her, and both he and Attu are exiled.

Two different dramatic scenes, reminiscent of the father/son/grandson triptych at the beginning of the film, are then juxtaposed: in the first, the father is seen at a secret Komo initiation ceremony during which the danger posed by Nianankoro and his punishment are discussed; and in the second, the son and Attu are seen undergoing a purification ritual before meeting the uncle. The uncle, though blinded by the Komo's evil powers, is still able to prophesy the birth of a son who 'will shine as a bright star' and he passes on knowledge of the Diarra family to Nianankoro known only to himself and Nianankoro's mother.

So, while the Komo meeting plans the destruction of the son, the meeting with the uncle is about freeing the Diarra family from the curse which rests upon them. Both sides add to their magic powers; the father holds the Magic Pestle while the blind uncle has the Kore Wing whose missing eye is the fetish entrusted to Nianankoro by his mother. The restored Wing gives Nianankoro power equal to his father's. Nianankoro sets off, entrusting his robe to Attu to be given to his as-yet unborn son.

The encounter between father and son is a dramatically powerful scene: Soma and Nianankoro face each other across the Pestle and the Wing. Confident of his power, the father declares the son already dead from the effect of the Magic Pestle, but the son's fervent need to be recognised by the father whom he has never seen is such that he declares: 'Even dead, I want to speak to you.' Although rejected, he asserts his Diarra origins and Bambara affiliation, pleading for Soma's recognition, for a father's denial is a Bambara's greatest fear and humiliation. The father refuses.

A solemn voice is heard stating that Soma and other ancestors have abused power. At this point the opening shot of the boy with the goat is

15 Souleymane Cissé, *Yeelen*. Nianankoro's son is given the Wing of Kore.

repeated, reiterating what was already foretold. The film then returns to the scene of the confrontation between father and son, in which both die. Close-ups of the men's faces reveal their emotions and the visions they have of wild animals, conveyed through dissolves between man and animal. As tears trickle down the son's face, the Wing and the Pestle begin to emit rays. Earth and sky seem to merge and screeching and roaring sounds are heard. The son does not waiver, the father screams; finally, both fall to their knees and fade away into a nebulous landscape where white steam escapes from the earth's crevasses.

Attu then appears wearing Nianankoro's robe. She takes the Wing, gives it to her son and puts the robe on his shoulder. The film closes with the boy walking alone towards the horizon carrying the robe and Wing. The succession of events and scenes transcends geography and time as the story takes on a cosmic dimension.

In this Bambara epic, stretching across three generations, Nianankoro's search brings to light two social phenomena which lie at the heart of his Diarra identity and contribute to the survival of the Bambara. These are the role of women and the function of exile. The importance of the Diarra in Bambara society has been expressed through female metaphors: they are its 'placenta and umbilical cord'. However, what is metaphor in Diarra cosmology is reality in the safeguarding of the family. By rejecting the son 'when he left his mother's womb', the father, in effect, creates a womb-like situation in which mother and son live isolated and hidden from the outside world. During this time the mother's integrity and ethical values have marked her son and made him into a true Bambara, different from his evil father. In spite of the suffering inflicted upon her by Soma, she still wishes for a reconciliation between father and son and sacrifices to the water goddess. Suzanne MacRae remarks that 'Cissé's choice for this role of an 83-year-old woman – much too old to be the mother of a young man about twenty – indicates that he intends her to be an icon of wisdom rather than a realistic portrait of a biological mother' (MacRae 1997: 19).

Attu, exiled from the Peul country, is to be another link in the Diarra family. She safeguards the symbols left by the father in order to pass them on, intact, to the son. Both women are also repositories for important segments of Diarra history. The mother was the only one to know the uncle's story; Attu is the only one to carry that story with her. The camera accentuates her listening presence by focusing on her while the uncle narrates Diarra history. The fact that these two women and Nianankoro are all exiled reveals another facet of Diarra history and of social identity in general. The secret society of the blacksmith sorcerers has become so closed and impenetrable that they no longer function as a viable and just political force in Bambara society. However, Nianankoro's exile with his mother protects him from corruption. In this story, then, exile distances the hero from his people as an act of purification, preparing him for the sacrifice he will be called upon to make.

In his earlier films, *Den Muso*, *Baara* and *Finyé*, Cissé examines and denounces Mali's major social problems: class divisions, sexual immorality, the condition of women, the corruption of those in power, the marabouts (a religious authority who also possesses healing powers and is able to cast spells), the condition of the workers. He does not propose solutions but exposes problems, leaving the viewer to reflect on them. Various critics have highlighted the dichotomy of tradition and modernity that underlies the films and Gardies expands this idea, considering a number of oppositions through which this dichotomy is expressed: modernity is linked to Europe, the present, the town, money and knowledge, while tradition stands for Africa, the past, the village, barter and ignorance (Gardies 1989: 31). Pfaff shows how *Finyé* illustrates this conflict: 'the problems faced by urban youth in a changing African social milieu, corruption, the abuse of military power, polygamy, and the overall status of women in the Sahelian areas of Africa' (Pfaff 1988: 60).

Baara and *Finyé* can be seen as sociological documents 'of the dynamic kind', as Victor Bachy wrote (Bachy 1983a: 50). *Baara* deals with the emerging working class and their attempt to unionise, *Finyé* with corrupt political power. Such major social messages may underlie the films, but Cissé's strategy of focusing on the specific identity of one or several individuals allows the viewer to relate to the main character in the story. The social problems are shown as problems of specific people whose lives are represented on the screen.

In *Yeelen*, however, the hero's quest for identity has wider implications: this is one of the first African films to use technical sophistication to develop a specific African style. Cissé achieves this style through the cultural iconography, with its emphasis on African values and beliefs, and by foregrounding the oral tradition. Finally, Nianankoro's struggle for a Bambara identity evokes Cissé's search for an African identity in film-making.

Waati (1995)

If *Yeelen* is an entirely black film in which the story precedes colonialism and where, therefore, no reference to colonialisation or the presence of white people is either visible or inferred, Cissé's subsequent film, *Waati* (*Time*) deals with colonialism in its most extreme form, South Africa's apartheid. Unlike *Yeelen*, *Waati* covers a vast part of the African continent, allowing the film-maker to evoke different colonial systems. Here, too, an initiation journey takes place. This time it is a girl, Nandi, who undertakes a transnational journey from the arbitrary brutality of the settlers' South African colony, where her father and brother are shot for their black presence on a 'white' beach, to the former French colony, now independent Côte d'Ivoire, where she receives a university education, and then to the drought-stricken Sahara, where she rescues a child in the desert whom she then adopts. While Nianankoro's struggle in *Yeelen* concerned his Bambara identity and affiliation to the Diarra family, Nandi's struggle in *Waati* is an African one, arising from her attempt to find a unified image of Africa. This is not the Africa of ethnic conflicts but of fragmentation through settlers' appropriation and natural catastrophes.

Nandi's journey is one of discovery, a growing awareness of Africa's plight and a determination to play her part in fighting injustice and to work for a better Africa. Confronted with so much injustice and disaster, she slowly develops a new identity built from her family background, her many memories, the dramas she has witnessed, and, finally, the education she receives. This new identity is neither national nor ethnic, instead it transcends cultural identity and connects with some greater reality or story.

The linguistic dimension which is inevitably connected to identity formation also looms large in Nandi's life: there is the imposed shift from teaching in English to Afrikaans in Nandi's school; her father's experience of being denied his wages and told to speak English when questioned by his Boer 'bass' about his lost sheep; Nandi's adaptation to French in Côte d'Ivoire and her doctoral dissertation on African culture written in French; her need to have an interpreter to communicate with the Touareg and, finally, her choice to educate her adopted daughter, Aïcha, in French.

Inherent in the new African identity that Nandi develops is also a new power, reminiscent of that which Nianankoro obtained from his blind uncle; however, here this power also relates to that of the film-maker. It concerns Nandi's gaze and voice, which have a power that may be compared to that of the camera. In Nandi's case, the power of the gaze is given to her by her grandmother in a mysterious dream, in which she hears the voice of her grandmother say: 'Nandi, be careful. No animal can resist your anger or your stare.' This prophecy is fulfilled on two occasions, the first time when the farmer's dogs threaten her, then halt their aggressive attack when she stares fixedly at the lead dog; the second instance occurs on the beach when a white patrolman on a horse kills her father and brother and is about to shoot her too. The film juxtaposes close-ups of Nandi's eyes and those of the horse. The animal cannot resist Nandi's stare, bolts and throws the white man off, allowing her to get hold of the gun and kill him. In both cases, Nandi protects herself by staring at the animal auxiliaries of the oppressive system of the whites.

The film ends with a similar sequence, where Nandi's voice protects her in another threatening situation. On her return to South Africa with Aïcha, the immigration officials refuse to accept Aïcha's identity documents and are about to deport her forcefully. However, Nandi screams so fiercely that the officials stand immobile, frozen in time as it were, while a haze blurs the image. This time it is not the stare that gives her force but the voice: the scream is at once an act of power but also the ultimate lament for the endless recurrence of injustice.

Image and voice also constitute the language of film, and the power for change that they confer on Nandi is also that of the camera, which has the potential to expose injustice and thus to contribute to abolishing injustice and the abuse of power. The acquisition of identity brings responsibility: in this film the responsibility accepted by Nandi is also that for which Cissé pleads in African film-making.

Cheick Oumar Sissoko

At the 1999 FESPACO, Sissoko's film *La Genèse* was selected to be shown at the festival's opening ceremony in the stadium. The film-maker's well-established reputation almost made it a foregone conclusion that his ambitious biblical epic would be awarded the much-coveted Yennenga Stallion. The success of Sissoko's earlier films, *Nyamanton* (1986), *Finzan* (1990) and *Guimba* (1995) – which won the Stallion in 1995 – contributed to this expectation. The award of a second Stallion to Sissoko would have meant he had matched the success of his fellow-countryman, Cissé, who remains the only film-maker to have won the Stallion twice. This was not to be: the Stallion went to the Congolese film, *Pièces d'indentités*, by Mweze Dieudonné Ngangura. But not winning the 1999 Stallion does not take away from the film's success.

Like Cissé, Sissoko is a prominent figure in African cinema, not only because he has himself an impressive film record but also because he is highly committed to the development of Malian and African cinema and is actively involved in audio-visual media. Unlike Cissé, who was trained in Moscow, Sissoko was trained in France, where he obtained a post-graduate degree in Cinema and History at the EHSS (*Ecole des Hautes Etudes en Sciences Sociales*). He became Managing Director of the *Centre National de la Production Cinématographique au Mali* and is president of the independent radio station Kayira, for which he produces a weekly programme, *L'Afrique en Question*. He is also administrator of the audio-visual company, Kora. He has made a number of documentary films, but gained his reputation mainly from his feature films. What is striking in these films is the range of subjects and styles, which reaches its zenith in *La Genèse*.

Poverty and a lack of education and health care loom large in African society as depicted in *Nyamanton*. In his subsequent films, *Finzan* and *Guimba*, Sissoko addresses other destructive calamities: the intolerable oppression of women and the flagrant abuse of power. The corrupt tyrant in *Guimba*, who lives only to dominate men, to be cruel and merciless, is an allegory of today's political events. Sissoko uses the film 'to denounce all the African dictators and all those who have hindered Africa's development' (Sissoko 1995: 11, trans.).

Nyamanton (1986)

Nyamanton (*Lessons from the Garbage*) depicts the tragic situation of the children in Mali's capital city Bamako. The film depicts the many difficulties of a poor family of four in a society where health and education are hardly catered for. The two children, Kalifa and his sister Fanta, are sent to school, but nine-year-old Kalifa is sent home because there is no desk for him.

Determined to have their children educated, the parents borrow money in order to buy the desk, but at the same time they also hire a cart with which the boy can find work. He uses his cart to carry rubbish in the area where his mother works as a maid, while Fanta sells oranges in the street where her father is a driver. Work becomes such a necessity for survival that all hope of becoming educated has to be abandoned, as for so many other children for whom, as Patrick Ilboudo puts it, 'the marks left by "lessons about rubbish" are stronger than those left by the lessons about things' (Ilboudo 1988: 130, trans.). But it is not just the lack of education that affects the lives of these children. The death of a pregnant woman adds to the despair of the little girl, Fanta, who utters these words: 'Nous aurions dû mourir petits' ('We should have died when we were little').

Before making this film, Sissoko had made a documentary on the rural exodus to the city caused by the desertification of the country. Here, in this first feature film, his social commitment remains a priority. For him, African children have a right to an identity but the fact that their lives are entirely devoured by material needs makes the notion of identity sound like a Western luxury.

Finzan (1990)

Finzan (*A Dance for Heroes*) deals explicitly with the situation of African women. The film is set in the Bambara region of Mali, and the dialogue is in Bambara. Two main narrative strands intersect: the first concerns taxes and the government's requisition of millet; the second deals with a woman who is forced into marriage and with female excision. These different stories are interconnected and unfold in parallel, signifying that the socio-political and economic progress of society can succeed only with the active involvement of women. The crisis that occurs in the village is not only linked metaphorically to the struggle of women but also intricately related to the place accorded to women in that society.

From the very beginning of the film, femaleness and motherhood are prominent. Images of a donkey giving birth and tethered goats are followed by a French text revealing the tone and the intentions of the film. In translation it reads:

> A world-wide study of women reveals their dual oppression due to their sex and place in society. Whilst they represent half the world's population, and do two-thirds of its work, women receive only one-tenth of the world's income and own one per cent of its property. World Conference of the United Nations Decade for Women. Copenhagen 1980.

The scene then shifts to a death-bed. A man is dying, leaving three wives. The third and youngest wife, Nanyuma, says she has lived eight years of hell with her aged husband. However, his death will not leave her free, since tradition dictates that she marry his brother, Bala, a most unattractive, buffoon-like character.

Nanyuma tries to run away, but can find no one to take her in; with the exception of her independent young niece Fili, everybody sides with tradition. When Nanyuma tries to escape she is tied up with thick ropes and transported back to her prospective husband. Eventually she flees into the bush at night and a search-party of villagers goes after her. Several critics have suggested that this night scene lacks cinematographic logic and therefore fails to have a powerful effect upon the viewer. Yet, in spite of its echoes of 'Tarzan jungle melodrama films' (Ukadike 1994: 273), it is effective in its representation of the 'taming' of the rebellious female in the tying-up scene, where ridiculously thick ropes are used. The same hyperbolic treatment is used for the brutal imposition of the marriage, when Nanyuma is physically forced to put her thumb print on the certificate.

Although the film's themes are dramatic, various narrative strategies de-dramatise them, such as Bala's excessive buffoonery and the tricks the children play on him. Even the couple's wedding night is played for entertainment value. Having refused to let her husband consummate the marriage and about to be raped, Nanyuma produces a knife and threatens to kill him – even this Sissoko presents in a semi-humorous way. There are many such crude or burlesque moments which lighten the tone without making the viewer oblivious to the issues at stake.

Nanyuma's struggle is paralleled by the problems faced by the villagers. The new economic system forces the villagers, who are already suffering the effects of a drought, to sell a large part of their millet production to the District Commissioner's official buyer at a very low price. The chief is arrested for refusing to levy excessive taxes and requisition the required tons of millet. But while the villagers' public fight is carried out peacefully, their private fight against the unarmed women is of a more violent nature.

The most tragic aspect of this private struggle concerns Fili, Nanyuma's niece. It is discovered that she has not been excised. Although not central to the film, this is by far the most dramatic episode and is treated without any of the burlesque touches which surround the Bala/Nanyuma drama or the District Commissioner's threat to the community. Fili is teased by the young girls, who call her 'unclean', and shunned by the other women. Even her boyfriend, who has a long-standing sexual relationship with her, states that he cannot marry a non-excised woman. As men proclaim that excision is the essence of Bambara society, Fili is captured and held down by the women. The excision is not seen but Fili's screams are heard, as are the comments of the women witnessing it. The excision ends badly when Fili's bleeding does not stop and her father has to rush her to hospital.

The film ends didactically with Nanyuma's words: 'The world comes from our wombs. It mistreats us. We give life, and we're not allowed to live. We produce the food crops, and others eat without us. We create wealth, and it is used against us . . .' Her final words explicitly link the separate narrative strands: 'The progress of our society is linked to our emancipation.'

Of all Sissoko's films, *Finzan* has received the most critical attention. This may be because it is one of the few African films to question

16 Cheick Oumar Sissoko, *La Genèse*.

traditions concerning the position of women in African society. Tradition is often seen as the framework which provides security to the members of a given society, guiding, and sometimes compelling individuals to adopt particular forms of social behaviour. However, progress cannot occur if accepted traditional norms or practices are never challenged. Identity is thus not static but involves the continual refashioning of the self and of culturally received frameworks.

La Genèse (1999)

Sissoko's *La Genèse* (*Genesis*) marks a turning point in African cinema in its creation of an African biblical fresco, linking the particular to the universal and illustrating the idea that the problems besetting modern societies are not new, but began with the beginning of humankind. Inspired by the first book of the Bible, it shows the destructive rivalry of two clans, the Hebrew cattle breeders and the sedentary agricultural farmers. In transposing the Judeo-Christian story to rural Africa it anchors African reality in an archetypal myth which the film's French scriptwriter, Jean-Louis Sagot-Duvauroux, sees as a story expressing a kind of collective unconscious (Sagot-Duvauroux 1999: 2).

The film shows how fundamental relationships both unite and separate the rival clans and traces the problem back to a fratricidal tendency that lurks in families and in society in general. In drawing a parallel between the conflicts depicted in the Bible and those of a specific African society, the Bambara, this film in the language of the Bambara shows how the culture-specific dimension veils universal human characteristics.

The elaborate costumes and rich decor, unexpected in an African film, evoke both the biblical atmosphere and that of ancient Mali, with its rich civilisation. This indirect reference to Africa's past, combined with the direct reference to the Judeo-Christian past, raises the question of humankind's origins and distinctive characters, which, as Kwame Anthony Appiah notes, are explained in the Bible 'by telling a story in which an ancestor is blessed or cursed' (Appiah 1992: 12). But while this blessed or cursed opposition might feed people's imaginations concerning the differences between races or peoples, it cannot explain how a curse might affect a whole lineage.

The film does not deal explicitly with these issues, although they are inevitably raised in the viewer's mind, but instead aims to provide a familiar historical setting for an explanation of social conflicts such as racism, nationalist claims, ethnic rivalries and religious intolerance in Africa and other societies. For Sissoko, film is 'a tool for awakening people's consciousness' (Sagot-Duvauroux 1999: 2, trans.). It is clear from *La Genèse* that Sissoko is an accomplished and talented filmmaker for whom, as for Cissé, social concerns are of the uppermost importance.

Adamo Drabo

While honouring the cultural heritage of Mali, Adamo Drabo also uses his films to reflect on the role of women in society.

Ta Dona (1991)

Ta Dona (*Fire*) intertwines several themes: it deals with environmental issues, exposes corruption and presents the mystical healing power of women. The main protagonist, Sidy, a young agricultural engineer, unites these three themes. He works for the Ministry of Rivers and Forests and favours environmental agricultural development but he is confronted with government corruption. He is determined to use his expert knowledge for the communal good and while in a small village, undertakes the search for a Bambara secret, the recipe for a herbal remedy, the seventh canari. He eventually finds Mother Coumba, the woman who knows the secret. She is a midwife who has delivered nineteen babies but has no children of her own. An outsider to society, who has much arcane knowledge she tells Sidy what he wants to know. 'Through Mother Coumba, Drabo honours elderly women as guardians of life's most profound mystery' (MacRae 1997: 249).

The film is a thinly veiled indictment of Malian dictator Moussa Traoré. Whether the film had any influence on the coup that happened shortly

17 Adamo Drabo, *Taafe Fanga*.

after the film was released (25 March 1991), is difficult to assess. It is clear though that it calls openly for political awareness.

Taafe Fanga (1996)

Taafe Fanga (*Skirt Power*) was entered for the 1997 FESPACO. Drabo seeks to pay tribute to the women's participation in the 1991 uprising, which started as a student demonstration and ultimately led to the overthrow of the Traoré regime. The story is set in an eighteenth-century village where the women have had more than enough of men's arrogance. Using Dogon cosmology the women gain access to a mystical mask. Using the mask, they reverse traditional gender roles, redistributing the tasks that are carried out. This gender reversal emphasises the difficulties that confront women in developing their own identity. The film is a feminist allegory that combines myth, history, culture and social issues; it is also a vindication of sexual equality.

Malian cinema combines the development of two major themes. One presents African tradition and values against a Western background and opposes tradition to modernity. The other traces the roots of identity in biblical times or in Mali's rich civilisation. But above all, Malian film-makers distinguish themselves by the power of their narratives. In their films a level of allegory is present where the story told suggests a double-ness of intention: Cissé focuses on specific social dramas of African society, Sissoko, attempts to reach non-African viewers and embraces larger themes or vast legends, while Drabo expresses his concern for social justice.

11 Mauritania

Although Mauritania, located in north-west Africa, is a sub-Saharan country, it is culturally and ideologically more akin to the Maghreb. It came under French influence after 1900 and became part of French West Africa in 1920, though heavy Arab resistance to French colonial rule was not suppressed until 1934. Mauritanian society has been characterised since colonial times by ethnic tensions between a well-educated black-African minority and an under-privileged majority of Moors, a Muslim people of north-west Africa.

Med Hondo

Mauritania's foremost film-maker, Med Hondo, is a self-taught man who has held a great variety of jobs and lived in Paris for the past thirty years. In his films he combines different ethnic strands: Mauritanian, Berber and Arab. He is a militant film-maker whose films are critical of both colonialism and neo-colonialism. Hondo took drama courses under the well-known French actress Françoise Rosay in 1965, but, according to Françoise Pfaff, he soon felt the need 'to express himself' rather than interpret parts in classical theatre. He decided to create his own theatre troupe and then started acting in films. Fascinated by the camera, he began to make films in the late 1960s.

Hondo's early films were two short black-and-white films, *Balade aux Sources* (1969), portraying an African immigrant, disenchanted with his living conditions, and *Partout ou peut-être nulle part* (1969 – *Everywhere or Maybe Nowhere*), about two white couples seen through the eyes of an African.

In 1973, Hondo completed *Les Bicots-Nègres, vos voisins* (*Arabs and Negroes, Your Neighbours*). A mixture of documents and sketches which also portrays African immigrant labour in Europe, the film reveals Hondo's genuine concerns for the lot of Africans in Paris. Two colour documentaries followed, *Nous aurons toute la mort pour dormir* (1977 – *We'll Sleep When We Die*) and *Polisario, un peuple en armes* (1979 – *Polisario, a People in Arms*), which depicts the freedom fighters of the Western Sahara.

West Indies (1979) presents the mechanisms of colonisation and slavery. The dialogue is in Creole and French and based on *Les Négriers* (*The Slavers*), a play by Daniel Boukman. The film is a musical epic which illustrates the main stages of the history of the French West Indies. In 1986, Hondo brought out *Sarraounia* – discussed more fully below – which *Le Monde* referred to as 'the first great epic of Black African cinema'. Finally, in 1994, *Lumière noire* (*Black Light*) appeared – an adaptation of Didier Daeninckx's thriller *Lumière noire*.

Soleil O (1969)

Soleil O examines the life of black and Arab workers in France. It attracted international fame and won many prestigious awards. Its memorable opening sequence poignantly renders the efforts made by the French during the colonial period to ensure the acceptance and transmission of their language and civilisation. Set in colonial Africa, the film begins with a Catholic baptism scene, in which a group of young African men are shown standing together, from the waist up, facing the camera. A male voice-over speaks about Africa's past:

> We had our own civilisation. We forged our own iron. We had our own songs and dances. We knew how to carve wood, make baskets, pottery, knives and utensils, bronze, brass and ivory. We had our own culture, our literature, our legal terms, our religion, our science and our methods of teaching.

In the course of this statement, all the men on the screen close their eyes. A Christian cross appears on screen, followed by a cut to the baptism ceremony of these young Africans. First, each one asks forgiveness for having spoken his own language: 'Father forgive me for having spoken Peul', 'Father forgive me for having spoken Bambara'. The requests continue: forgiveness for having spoken Creole, Bamum, Kikongo, Swahili, Kissonghi, Sambe. . . . Each African is then baptised individually and given a Christian name, after which he says his new name aloud, then spits while walking away, symbolically spitting out evil and the old name.

This powerful sequence gives dramatic expression to the Christian missionaries' exorcism of African identity at the most personal level, by obliging individuals to reject their names, native languages and African beliefs. All these new Christian Africans, united by a new language and a new faith, are now ready to embrace a new identity. The overt principle of including these new Christians in the church, which apparently underlies the white priest's mission, only thinly veils the European rejection of African beliefs and culture.

There is a similarity between inclusion in the church and the principle of assimilation which characterises France's colonial policy: both require the abandonment of African identity for a 'higher ideal': Francophone Africa has a history of surrendering identity. The Europeans hardly had a notion of a 'black' self, thinking instead in terms of the principles of civilisation, religious conversion, emancipation and assimilation.

It is clear that missionaries and colonisers were aware of the process of identity formation through language, as shown in Med Hondo's sequence. Since language laid the foundation for their 'civilising' work, it is not surprising that French was seen as the means to instil the new commitments and identities that were to underpin Francophone Africa.

Sarraounia (1986)

Shot in Burkina Faso, Med Hondo's most ambitious historical film, *Sarraounia*, was co-produced by his own film company, 'Soleil O', and the government of Burkina Faso. At the 1987 FESPACO in Ouagadougou it was awarded the Yennenga Stallion, the festival's most coveted award, and has since become a much quoted landmark as an African historical epic.

The film is adapted from a novel by Abdoulaye Mamani of Niger and depicts the heroic resistance of a West African queen, Sarraounia, in the face of invading French colonial troops in the late nineteenth century. In an interview with Françoise Pfaff, Hondo explains that in this film he 'wanted to illustrate historical facts to show that the African continent was not easily colonised and that it had a history of resistance to colonialism' (Pfaff 1997: 152).

The film opens with a long tracking shot showing a seemingly endless line of people walking through a dry and hazy Sahel landscape. The camera moves along the line from back to front, revealing first men and women carrying pots and baskets, then warriors with spears, then soldiers on horses with ammunition. Towards the front the viewer recognises the French flag. A text on screen states that the film is based on actual events that happened in Niger in 1898–99. This opening sequence is accompanied by singing in praise of queen Sarraounia, who foiled the French army's attempt to crush her and subjugate her people.

The image and sound thus reveal the paradox underlying the film: the image shows the familiar history of France's colonial conquest of West Africa, while the singing voices tell the forgotten story of French defeat by the Aznas and their queen. The film closes with a parallel scene, yet now image and sound are one. Again, a long line of people is seen, but this time moving towards the camera: this is Sarraounia's victorious return to her palace in Lugo, accompanied by her own people and others who have fled from the French invaders. This time the singing on the soundtrack emphasises rather than contradicts the meaning of the image. As well as praising Sarraounia, the song also pays tribute to the musicians and singers who preserve history and memory, endowing the people with an awareness of their identity.

The film starts in a Manichean way opposing French to Africans through two specific individuals, Captain Voulet, representing French colonial rule, and Queen Sarraounia, representing African freedom and independence. French and African identities are clearly defined at the beginning of the film, when African soldiers – mostly Sudanese – are made to adopt French culture, while Sarraounia resists all external infiltration and instils a notion of ethnic identity in her people. The film is divided into three main parts: the first shows Sarraounia's education and early life as Queen of the Aznas; the second shows the colonial army pillaging African villages and advancing towards Sarraounia's stronghold of Lugo; the final part shows the defeat of the French, the rallying of different African ethnic groups around Sarraounia and her return to Lugo.

Sarraounia's education is entirely focused on her task as future leader. Her people become her priority and she has to renounce motherhood for their sake. However, although Sarraounia is queen, in this early phase of her reign she is also a woman with a lover. It is only when she becomes aware of her lover's growing ambition that she ends the relationship and from that moment lives entirely for her people and her ideals.

The transition to the second part of the film, the French colonial conquest, occurs through the metaphor of a torn map of Africa, where boundaries appear in red streams while a voice-over tells how, in Berlin, the Europeans are dividing up the African continent and preparing to occupy it. French military music is heard and French soldiers on horseback appear on the horizon. They are followed by African soldiers singing 'The beautiful country of France. Long live France. She is our mother and our father. We are happy for France.' The viewer experiences their forced identification with France – a country they have never seen – and the singing in French – a language they do not understand – as a deeply disturbing caricature.

The film gives a harrowing and graphic account of the cruelty of the colonisers and their mercenary African soldiers. Colonial invasion is a brutal business, but what is perhaps most painful is the way that the African soldiers treat their fellow men and women in the same loathsome manner as the white colonisers do. Ukadike reports that at the 1987 FESPACO Hondo was asked 'whether he had not exaggerated the atrocities committed by the French soldiers, such as playing polo with the decapitated heads of Africans' (Ukadike 1994: 294). Hondo replied that he had obtained his information from respected historians. Another example of an 'African' atrocity, juxtaposed with the 'polo playing', involves a rape. This is carried out by African soldiers and happens off screen, while the head of the French forces, Captain Voulet, is seen watching with amusement. Although initially accepted for French distribution, not surprisingly the film was very swiftly withdrawn because of its depiction of the French colonial forces.

As the film progresses the apparently clear opposition between coloniser and colonised, with strictly defined identities, turns out to be a complex network of African differences and European divisions. The

Sudanese soldiers are called upon to identify with the French, in whose name they commit rape and pillage African villages, while their campaign reveals a wide variety of African ethnic groups, all with specific identities, who try to save themselves by compromise or surrender. All are in awe of Sarraounia and they are divided about the desirability of joining her to fight the French.

As Africa's diverse identities become more and more apparent, increasing divisions also appear among the colonisers. Firstly, Voulet becomes increasingly unable to identify with France. Victory over Sarraounia becomes his personal ambition. Not only is she African, she is also a woman and this twofold insult on his French manhood leads to his fixation on her defeat. This personal ambition becomes more important to him than colonial conquest and he refuses to be replaced by Colonel Klobb, his compatriot instructed to take over from him. His subordinates are also divided; they realise that promotion and honours from the French army are now lost. Then there is Voulet's rivalry with the British, whom he refuses to help in their attack on the Aznas and Sarraounia.

When the French finally reach Sarraounia's palace, they find it deserted. The queen has strategically retreated to the forest. At this point Colonel Klobb arrives and informs Voulet that he has come to take command of the campaign. Voulet refuses to let anyone steal his victory. As Klobb's entourage prepares to shoot, the colonel shouts, 'Don't shoot, they're French!', while Voulet gives his Sudanese soldiers the opposite order: 'Shoot! – aim at the whites!' But no African can take it upon himself to kill a white officer and it is Voulet himself who shoots and kills Klobb. He then turns to his troops and announces that he is no longer a French soldier, but will continue to lead them to Chad, where 'treasures and gold and women await them'. Then, when one of Klobb's officers prepares to shoot Voulet, some women suddenly dash up behind Voulet, plunge an arrow into his back and disappear. Their ululation resounds as the Frenchman's body fills the screen.

Throughout the film, women have been abused, killed or distributed as booty after a victory. They have been deprived of all identity, except that of belonging to someone, but in the end they are the ones who muster the courage to kill the white coloniser. The scene then shifts to show Sarraounia addressing the people gathered around her and calling for tolerance; she welcomes all peoples, expressing her respect for their different languages and beliefs. They are united as brothers and sisters in the fight to defend their freedom and resist oppression.

The identification process has thus developed in inverse ways for Voulet and Sarraounia. From an Aznas identity, Sarraounia has moved towards considering herself a Pan-African, while Voulet has abandoned all identification with France, substituting his own person for the country he was meant to serve.

Watani, un monde sans mal (1998)

Hondo's *Watani, un monde sans mal* (*Watani, a World Without Evil*) is a portrait of two men, one white and one black, who both lose their jobs. The white bank executive, who lives in an affluent suburb, takes to drinking and meets a gang of fascist youths. Together they drive around the streets of Paris at night and kill lone black people. The black street cleaner seeks refuge in a church where he finds support from other immigrants. Upon learning about her husband's crimes, the wife of the executive commits suicide. With this film Hondo attempts to establish a parallel between, on the one hand, the atrocities of slavery and colonialism and, on the other, present-day fascism and racism.

Hondo's three films discussed here develop a powerful picture of identity: in *Soleil O* Africans are robbed of their identity, in *Sarraounia* there is a proclamation of a far-reaching African identity that transcends ethnic differences and, finally, in *Watani*, Hondo questions the identification of the individual with causes such as fascism and racism that call for revenge and destruction.

12 Niger

The land-locked republic of Niger, north of Nigeria, was brought under French control between 1896 and 1900. It became an autonomous republic in 1958 and fully independent in 1960. It has very limited resources and has suffered from severe droughts. Images of Niger entered the world of cinema with Jean Rouch, whose films set in the country attained international fame. Rouch, whose influence on Senegal's Safi Faye has already been mentioned, is a controversial film-maker. Although revered in France and in many Western countries as the embodiment of ethnographic cinema, Rouch has been criticised by Africans for his biased and, as Ukadike records 'wrongful portrayal of Africa' (Ukadike 1994: 50).

Despite these criticisms, Rouch's use of African actors and assistants was a significant factor in the promotion of cinema. Senegal's Safi Faye is one example, but Rouch's influence is even more noticeable in Niger, whose two pioneering film-makers, Mustapha Alassane and the late Oumarou Ganda, both collaborated with him. Rouch often detected talent, encouraging Alassane, for example, to study animation for nine months under Norman McLaren at Canada's National Film Bureau.

Mustapha Alassane

Alassane is a unique and versatile director who has attempted various film genres. As well as making traditional narratives, he was also the first African to make cartoon films, a genre he learned while in Canada and for which he seems to have had an inborn talent. Martin records that, even before he knew what cinema was, Alassane organised a show in which he projected coloured drawings using transparent cellophane wrappers from cigarette packets (Martin 1982: 86). He was making films as early as 1962 and has remained one of Niger's most productive directors.

Alassane is first and foremost a storyteller, as is revealed in such films as *Aouré* (1962), *La Bague du roi Koda* (1962) and *La Mort de Gandji* (1965). *Aouré* (*The Wedding*) is a thirty-minute film that tells the simple story of a boy and a girl in a Djerma village who meet, like each other and get married; *La Bague du roi Koda* (*The Ring of King Koda*) recounts a legend of loyalty rewarded. King Koda, hoping to seduce the beautiful wife of a fisherman, sends the husband on a mission with a ring, with which he must return. However, the wife remains deeply faithful to her husband and the king's plan to seduce her fails. The king, impressed with her unshakable fidelity, recompenses the couple.

La Mort de Gandji (The Death of Gandji) is a cartoon that presents an allegory of toad-courtiers who live at the court of a toad-king. These are films rooted in African tradition and contribute to the creation of an African cinema based on its own past.

In 1970, Alassane brought out Deela ou El Barka le conteur (Deela or El Barka the Story-teller) which Vieyra considers one of Alassane's best works. This is a striking film, both technically and stylistically, whose narrative is conveyed on three levels, oral storytelling in the Hausa language, visual illustration of the story, and finally an explanation of the story in French. The film shows the innovation which established Alassane as Niger's most original film-maker. In 1972, he brought out his first full-length feature film, FVVA (Femmes, villa, voiture, argent – Women, Villa, Car, Money), a satire depicting the fate of a young and modest clerk who is lured away from honesty by the promise of material wealth, falls into a life of corruption and is finally imprisoned. Although Vieyra has misgivings about the choice of actors, Ukadike remarks that the 'wit and eloquence displayed here and in other films by Alassane obviously earn him recognition as Niger's foremost film-maker and one of Africa's most prolific' (Ukadike 1994: 171).

Alassane is clearly in search of original and personal forms of expression. While using traditional themes and emphasising oral storytelling, he has developed a very specific and unique film style, which combines African tradition with new artistic expression.

Oumarou Ganda

Oumarou Ganda, a talented actor and one of the main actors in Rouch's film Moi un noir also went on to become one of Niger's most celebrated film-makers, even though he had no formal film training. Unfortunately, his premature death in 1981 at the age of forty ended a promising film career which had lasted little more than ten years. Ganda was a sensitive film-maker who focused on the social issues that threaten Africa's progress, arising from the legacy of colonialism, neo-colonialism or ossified structures within African society itself. In Cabascabo (1969) he deals with the plight of the African soldier who has to reintegrate into his own society; in Le Wazzou polygame (1972 – The Polygamist's Moral), he looks critically at the tradition of polygamy; Saitane (1972) denounces the abuses perpetrated by the marabouts, and his last film, L'Exilé (1980 – The Exiled), features a diplomat who, while in exile, rediscovers African values, in particular the sanctity of the given word.

Cabascabo (1969)

Ganda's first film, *Cabascabo*, partially financed by the French Ministry of Co-operation and distributed internationally, brought him international fame. It captures one of the major problems besetting many former French colonies: the return home to his country of a soldier who has been fighting in the French army. *Tirailleur* (infantryman) Cabascabo has fought in the Indochina war (1951–55), in which France tried to reassert control over its former colony, but was defeated by strong communist-dominated Vietminh forces at Diên Biên Phû in 1954.

The film opens with the ceremony in which the soldiers from Niger are discharged and thanked for having contributed to 'vanquishing the enemy'. Convinced that returning from Indochina will make him an important man, Cabascabo proudly goes back to his home village with a strengthened identity. But he soon finds himself caught between his memories of the war and the disillusion he experiences on discovering that the village's admiration for him is only short-lived. Flashbacks show scenes that he remembers, some of killing people, others reflecting social issues related to the war – drinking, smoking and women. The villagers frown upon his smoking and drinking, considering them evil practices, but Cabascabo declares that, if they had been at war, they too would drink.

He is much appreciated in the village for as long as he has money and presents to lavish upon his friends. But once his resources run out, his prestige declines. He soon finds himself impoverished and jobless. Cabascabo becomes demoralised because of the illusory nature of his identity as a soldier who has fought in the war, especially when it emerges that this status does not entitle him to any job, not even one in the police force. Cabascabo ultimately realises that all he can do is return to the fields. The end of the film shows him accepting an axe and a gourd from farming women and walking away from his war experience (and the camera) into agricultural Africa.

The story told by this film is a simplified version of Ganda's own. After fighting for the French in Indochina for four years, Ganda returns home, changed and marked by the war experience, and has to face a society from which he has been torn away. Cabascabo's story, which stands out as a struggle to recover a lost identity, is also that of Africa itself which, like him, has to strive to redefine itself.

Alassane's main endeavour, with regard to identity, concerns film-making itself. His eclectic approach to film-making is a means to develop his own style and find his own artistic identity. Ganda, on the other hand, deals with the problem between Western and African identity. In *Cabascabo* the character realises that his European/Indochina traumatic experience has distanced him from his people and that he must reaffirm his African identity.

13 Côte d'Ivoire

Côte d'Ivoire is probably the most Europeanised country in West Africa and its capital, Abidjan, is a modern city (Bachy 1983b: 11). It opted to be part of the French Union in 1958 with de Gaulle's referendum and gained independence in 1960 under the presidency of Félix Houphouët-Boigny, who remained in power for more than thirty years. Although in favour of independence, he agreed with French leadership. He represented Côte d'Ivoire in the French Constituent Assemblies and the National Assembly, where he was instrumental in obtaining the abolition of all forced labour throughout the French colonies. There are numerous ethnic groups in Côte d'Ivoire and some hundred languages are spoken, but none became the dominant language of the country – which may explain the continued widespread use of French, especially in film.

The French – among them Jean Rouch – had been making films in Côte d'Ivoire since the 1940s. But it was not until the early 1960s that three African film-makers, Timité Bassori, Désiré Ecaré and Henri Duparc, established a national cinema. All three were trained at the IDHEC in Paris, reflecting the extent to which Côte d'Ivoire remained steeped in French culture.

In his survey of Ivoirian cinema, Victor Bachy distinguishes three different periods: an intellectual one, represented by the three film-makers just mentioned, a social one and a popular one (Bachy 1983b). The main representative of the last period, the popular group, is Fadika Kramo-Lanciné, who has had a fair amount of success. The social film-makers Bachy mentions, Roger Gnoan M'Bala and Vodio Etienne Ndabian, have both worked mainly for Ivoirian television. Their films explore social problems or depict socially deprived milieux, as M'Bala does in *Ablakon* (1984).

Ablakon is set in a large African city where poverty, corruption, abuse of power, crime and delinquency proliferate. A group of abandoned street children roam around together, replacing the family that rejected them or simply ignored them. The people who come to the city from the villages are confronted with the problems of the city. They finally return to the village while the children are dispersed by the police. Despite adopting a humorous tone, the film denounces the city's social pestilence.

M'Bala's 1993 film, *Au Nom du Christ* (*In the Name of Christ*), emphasises how development, religion and tradition are often associated. The film denounces how power is often taken by force and how the people's belief in God is manipulated to endorse that power.

Timité Bassori

In 1966, Timité Bassori brought out a twenty-two-minute film in black and white entitled *Sur la dune de la solitude* (*On the Dune of Solitude*). It is a well-known legend of a water goddess, Mama Wata, who seduces men and takes them into captivity deep beneath the water. The heritage of a specific African narrative underlies the film but the IDHEC experience has clearly influenced Bassori in his attempt to find a film language. Critics agree that the film suffers from this dichotomy but Bassori's talent nevertheless transpires. He clearly wishes to recast the African legend into a modern setting and explore a new way of filming.

Bassori's first full-length feature film, *La Femme au couteau* (*The Woman with a Knife*), made in 1968 with an entirely Ivoirian crew, deals with the recurring nightmare of a man, played by Bassori himself, who dreams he is being threatened by a woman brandishing a knife. The image prevents the man from forming a normal relationship with a woman until one day on the beach, when the image reappears, he recognises the face of his mother, and this frees him from the unconscious trauma that underlies his visions. It is worthwhile pointing out that this is the first time in African cinema that images borrowed from European neurosis appear, and the film reflects Côte d'Ivoire's 'Europeanness' and the new aspect of identity this proposes.

Désiré Ecaré

Désiré Ecaré's films also introduce the viewer to an Africa strongly marked by the European experience. His 1968 *Concerto pour un exil* (*Concerto for an Exile*) could be seen as a continuation of Vieyra's 1955 film *Afrique sur Seine* in that it also depicts the community of African exiles in Paris. The film was made with non-professionals and focuses on the Africans who have come to Paris to study and are torn between the desire to return home and the greater possibilities offered by France. The very title of the film expresses a European musical mode of structuring: as instruments appear in a concerto in various forms and combinations, so characters come and go and convey different aspects of their exile in Paris.

A nous deux, France (1970)

Ecaré's second film, *A nous deux, France* (*Take Care France*) – France being symbolically both the name of the main female protagonist and the host country – uses comedy to explore the Ivoirian presence in Paris. This time the protagonists are women from Côte d'Ivoire who are sent to Paris to meet – and possibly marry – educated Ivoirian men destined to be the future elite of their country. However, under the influence of the host country these women adopt Parisian attitudes, and the film itself develops a type of verbal wit unknown in Africa. It is difficult to imagine, as Victor Bachy writes, the echoes such a film could have in Africa (Bachy 1983b: 42).

The film draws attention to the emerging identity of African women, but Ecaré's decision to portray the African woman in a European context gives an ironic character to the film, for the 'African' woman who emerges is one imbued with European coquettish behaviour. 'The beautiful young women that Côte d'Ivoire sends to Europe to seduce these men into returning are themselves seduced by the West, and by which part of it?' Vieyra asks. 'The decadent West, represented by the luxurious old bourgeoisie, who spend the fruits of their financial manipulations on futilities. And one such futility is precisely these beautiful women, who are bitterly aware of their mission and have been chosen for their virtue' (Vieyra 1990: 85, trans.). However, the French title of the film, *A nous deux, France* (literally, 'the two of us, France'), suggests a confrontation between two people. Is it between France the woman and France the culture, or between Côte d'Ivoire and France? More is needed, Ecaré implies, than the charms of women to resist the spreading of this Western world.

Visages de femmes (1985)

In the mid-1970s, Ecaré embarked upon his long feature film, *Visages de femmes* (*Faces of Women*), a film set in Africa, again about women with a Western approach to sexuality. The film remained unfinished for ten years due to lack of funding: when it was finally released in 1985, the French daily newspaper *Libération* wrote: 'Enfin un porno africain' ('Finally, an African porn movie'). The mild scandal the film caused eclipsed its innovative aspect. *Visages de femmes* juxtaposes two women, one from a village, Koffiko, and one from the city of Abidjan. The first refuses to be objectified by her husband and claims her own right to love; the second, having to shift from barter economy to market economy, experiences the resistance of bankers to financing women in business. Failing to obtain a loan, she sends her attractive young daughter to the manager because, as she says, if women wish to succeed they 'should be twenty years old and beautiful'. While African women strive to find their identity and gain freedom and independence, they exploit all the means available to women for centuries, but these 'weapons' contradict the objectives they set out to achieve.

Henri Duparc

The third member of the Ivoirian trio, Henri Duparc, established himself in Côte d'Ivoire after three years of training, one in Belgrade and two at the IDHEC, where he was a contemporary of Ecaré, in whose film, *Concerto pour un exil*, he played a part. In his early film, made in 1969, *Mouna ou le rêve d'un artiste* (*Mouna, an Artist's Dream*), Duparc takes up the subject of the reproduction of African art. It continues in the vein of Alain Resnais and Chris Marker who, in *Les Statues meurent aussi* (*Statues Also Die*), dealt with the effects of colonialism on African art.

In his 1972 film *Abusuan* (*The Family*), Duparc addresses a social problem, the degeneration of African hospitality, which frequently turns into parasitism. In this case, villagers come to live with relatives in the city, but as delinquency sets in, the family decides to return to the village. The film was extremely well received in Abidjan and, Bachy writes, it is supposed to have heralded a trend of return to the village (Bachy 1983b: 45–6).

After *Abusuan* Duparc set up his own production company in Abidjan, Focale 13, and brought out several films. Both his 1988 *Bal Poussière* and his more recent *Une Couleur café* (1997) dealt with polygamy. The latter film, set in France, tells the story of an immigrant working as a janitor in a Parisian hospital, who is married and childless. When back in Africa for a holiday he decides to take a second wife, Kada. However, unable to obtain a French visa as a second wife, Kada has to be declared as his daughter. The film highlights the acculturation problems of Africans in Paris and intimates the predicament of women in polygamous households, although there is no overt political statement concerning polygamy.

Bal Poussière (1988)

The earlier film *Bal Poussière* (*Dancing in the Dust*), set in Africa, also posits the problem of women's identity but, according to Ukadike, does so 'at the expense of the changing role of African women or women's liberation, although that is exactly what it supposedly argues for' (Ukadike 1994: 288). The main character in the film, who calls himself 'Demi Dieu' (Demi God) is obsessed with power; though he has five wives already, he wants a sixth, a high-school student whose parents agree to the marriage. However, the girl, Binta, behaves in very untraditional ways – bathing naked, dressing Western style – and is not at all the traditional wife Demi Dieu had hoped for. In the end Binta is allowed to leave and marry the man she loves.

While the story introduces a new womanhood, a wife who refuses to conform, the film itself establishes a new liberty in African film-making. The indulgence of lingering close-ups of Binta's naked body is an explicit break from traditional African sexual mores, as is Binta's behaviour. Hence both film-maker and character (and actress) proclaim a new style and a new morality. The characters in these films, while distancing themselves from traditional African values, are not portrayed as having specific personal problems; they represent a situation rather than a human subject in search of specific values. It makes identification between spectator and character difficult and highlights the many contradictions in which the African man – and in this instance, the African woman – is caught.

Fadika Kramo-Lanciné

In 1981 Fadika Kramo-Lanciné won the Yennenga Stallion with his first feature film, *Djeli*.

Djeli (1980)

Started in 1978, *Djeli* was not completed until 1980 due to financial problems (the director himself and friends financed the film). Except for the two main protagonists, all the actors are villagers from Kouto, a village in the north of Côte d'Ivoire. The film features the Ivoirian students Fanta and Karamoko, who are in love with each other and plan to marry. Both were born in the same village and the parents know each other well. But Fanta is the direct descendent of one of the outstanding families of the Mandingue, while Karamoko is the son of a griot. The film highlights the problem of caste divisions which still prevail in the country and which prevent the two from marrying. In flashback Kramo-Lanciné explores the traditional origins of this distinction. The marriage proposal splits the village and the opposing parties engage in endless discussions, then resort to threats. In despair Fanta attempts to commit suicide. The film closes with a shot in the hospital corridor where Fanta's father and fiancé meet each other and exchange a long look. While the film-maker does not take a stand in this division, he nevertheless reveals how traditions regarding caste, status and profession affect a person's life and freedom. An individual's identity seems pre-ordained by the family's traditional background.

Wariko, le gros lot (1994)

Fadika's 1994 film, *Wariko, le gros lot* (*The Lottery*) is a humorous film about a man who unexpectedly wins a lottery ticket which his wife bought because she needed change. However, the ticket has disappeared. By means of the amusing situation, the film-maker gives an insight into daily life in Côte d'Ivoire and the many problems that beset its society.

At the 1999 FESPACO two Ivoirian films were entered for competition: the feature film *La Jumelle* (*The Twin Sister*) by Diaby Lanciné, about the relationship between a sister and her twin brother, and the documentary *N'gonifola* by Idrissa Diabaté, which deals with traditional music. Present film production in Côte d'Ivoire is promising. The noticeable presence of Côte d'Ivoire at FESPACO and other festivals signals an increasing presence in African cinema.

Ivoirian cinema, it seems, cannot avoid the mark of Europe's legacy on Ivoirian identity. In most cases the characters in the films have distanced themselves or become alienated from their African identity. While they opt for European life, they continue to maintain certain aspects of African life, such as polygamy, which leads to conflict. With the exception of Kramo-Lanciné, who gives insight into the association between identity and the African caste system, the Ivoirian film-makers present characters with Europeanised identities. This may well confirm Bachy's assertion that Côte d'Ivoire is a highly Europeanised country, which is also supported by the more Western approach to sexual mores that some of these film-makers adopt.

14 Guinea

Of all the sub-Saharan countries, Guinea was the first to show a determination to become independent. When de Gaulle returned to power in 1958, he realised that the sub-Saharan countries could no longer be kept under direct French rule, but he hoped that indirect control could be retained and proposed a referendum on membership of the newly created French Community (*Communauté Française*). This new body would give a great deal of local power to the different countries, but decisions relating to finance, foreign policy and military affairs would remain in the hands of France. As Basil Davidson succinctly puts it: 'The horse would certainly be African; but the rider, just as surely, would be French' (Davidson 1997: 126). It was at this point that the people of Guinea showed their determination to get rid of the French and become independent. Under Ahmed Sékou Touré, leader of the Democratic Party of Guinea, 95 per cent of the votes went against de Gaulle's plans, making Guinea the first colony to obtain independence in 1958. De Gaulle was infuriated and immediately cut off all aid.

It would be difficult to compare Guinea's film output to that of other African countries. When the country was receiving economic support from the USSR, censorship prevailed and few original features were produced, though there were several short films and documentaries. However, more recently, and since the break-up of the USSR, less censorship has been exercised and in 1995 the country held its first free elections. Guinea has also become eligible for funds from France and Europe. Recent films touch on socially sensitive issues, as can be seen in the work of Mohamed Camara.

Mohamed Camara

Camara, having trained in Germany, began his film-making career in 1975 with a number of documentary shorts; only in 1990 did he make his first significant film, *Sere* (*The Witness*), about the consequences of arranged marriages in contemporary Guinea.

Denko (1992)

Camara's prize-winning short *Denko* made with production funding from Europe and with French technicians in key roles, was shot in Burkina Faso. The film is a sensitively shot tale of a mother who, in accepting the help of an albino to restore her blind son's eyesight, has committed herself to satisfying the albino's desire 'to know a woman before he dies'. Although he can now see, the son remains blind to the sacrifice his sight has required from his mother, a sacrifice that violated her integrity.

Dakan (1997)

Camara's *Dakan* (*Destiny*) was shown in the 1999 FESPACO, where it was entered in the category of 'first feature'. Where *Denko* depicts the sensitive subject of an African mother paying for her son's sight with her body, *Dakan* introduces the taboo subject of homosexuality. It opens boldly with two boys, Manga and Sory, kissing each other in a red car. The film then goes on to depict the many difficulties that face the couple and to focus on the inability of their two families to reconcile themselves to the reality of their homosexuality.

The parents are torn between fondness for their sons and their own difficulty in accepting homosexuality. Deep down, the families still hold the belief that, once their sons form a family, these homosexual tendencies might vanish. The illness of Sory's mother adds to his difficult predicament since he experiences a conflict between his filial duty and his homosexual love. *Dakan*, now heralded as the first film on homosexuality by a black African, reveals the conflict experienced by parents and, above all, by two young people in a society where homosexuality is taboo.

Camara introduces sensitive issues surrounding individual identity. In both his films there is a conflict between society's norms and individual desire – in *Denko* the desire to restore a son's eyesight and in *Dakan* homosexual love.

15 Cameroon

Having first been occupied by Portuguese settlers, then passed on to Germany in 1911, Cameroon was subsequently invaded by the Allied armies. This succession of occupiers, each imposing a new culture and a new value system on to a country that itself counted a great number of different ethnic groups and had its own civilisation, left little sense of identity for its peoples. The last coloniser, France, was to instil and try to safeguard a Francophone heritage. French Cameroon finally gained its independence in 1960 after being placed under trusteeship, first of the League of Nations, then of the UN, but France did not withdraw fully after independence. Cameroon, like many of the other African neo-colonial states, had to enter into agreements with France. As Davidson remarks, 'France remained their "heart of civilisation"' (Davidson 1997: 128). It is not surprising that Cameroon's colonial history, being divided into three parts and governed by two colonial powers, led to internal conflicts when independence was granted. In 1961 northern Cameroon voted to become part of Nigeria, while the south opted for a federation with French Cameroon, creating a bilingual French/English Republic, although French is more widely spoken.

Jean-Marie Teno

Jean-Marie Teno started making documentaries in 1984 and was already an experienced film-maker when he brought out his 1991 *Afrique, je te plumerai*.

Afrique, je te plumerai (1991)

A well-known French song, in both the French- and English-speaking world, *Alouette, gentille alouette*, is often sung by children and adults alike as a game. The singers address the *alouette* or skylark, 'Lark, kind lark', but then go on to sing *je te plumerai* (I'll pluck you). The song continues by listing the various parts of the lark's body to be plucked: 'I'll pluck your head, your tail' and so on. The refrain, *gentille alouette* returns after the addition of each new body part and the song gets longer and longer, reminding the singers not to leave any parts out.

The title of Jean-Marie Teno's film, *Afrique, je te plumerai* (*Africa, I Will Pluck You Clean*) refers unmistakably to this song, which is also heard in the film. It is a very French song and, therefore, plays on Frenchness. The irony of it is that the song is sung by an African in a self-referential way: the lark that the African is plucking is Africa. The African is referring not only to the 'plucking' that goes on after independence, but also to the slow killing perpetrated by the French coloniser over a long period of time.

Set in 1991, thirty years after independence, Teno dedicates the film 'To all the people who have given their life for liberty' ('A tous ceux qui ont donné leur vie pour la liberté'). Written, narrated and directed by Teno, it surveys the preceding thirty years and denounces the ongoing 'plucking'. It opens with Teno's memories of his childhood, when he was told to study because that would allow him to grow up into a *monsieur*, instead of a black man. 'Study, my son', his father would say: 'You'll become like a white person.' White was the colour of success, black of despair.

The film takes a documentary approach for its critical exploration of the early years after independence. It is critical of the one-party system and of the lack of democracy. In reaction to and transgression of the prevailing censorship which banned freedom of speech, a voice-over reads a letter published in the national newspaper, *Le Messager*, but then had to be withdrawn. It was printed on the front page of the paper, under the heading *Lettre ouverte au Président de la République* and was written in response to the presidential address by President Paul Biya. The author and newspaper editor were both accused of insulting the President and the General Assembly.

The letter-writer asks President Paul Biya what 'democracy' he was referring to in his presidential address. All there is, says the writer, is a fake democracy (*démocratie truquée*). The film shows an enlarged close-up of the withdrawn issue of the newspaper, and the text is read in voice-over, while ironic images of the so-called democratic Cameroon Republic unfold showing poor children looking for scraps of food in rubbish bins and people queuing for water. The film shows how Cameroon, and by extension Africa at large, is in a way still being colonised. For many Africans, political independence has meant greater poverty and further decline in the quality of life. As Mbye Cham writes in *African Experiences of Cinema*:

> The undemocratic and even brutal methods that were formerly employed to establish, maintain and control such hegemonic structures before political independence are the same methods that have been fine-tuned, updated and employed by the postcolonial state to maintain and control these same structures. (Bakari and Cham 1996: 6)

Teno goes on to illustrate some of the methods of oppression: the killing of three participants in a demonstration held to free the newspaper's editor; the television policies which systematically rule out African programmes because, as the Director General of television explains, programmes such as *Dynasty, Dallas* and *Château Vallon* are transmitted free of charge; the book dealers, librarians and directors of cultural centres supported by their governments (French Cultural Centre, British Council, Goethe Institute), who emphasise and import Western cultures and do nothing to promote Africa's cultural independence.

The film also takes the viewers back to Cameroon's past and to Cameroon's involvement in World War I. A visit of de Gaulle is shown. 'I know what happened here', he proclaims, referring to Cameroon's heavy losses in World War I and to the division of the former German colony between the British and the French. At this point the *Alouette, je te plumerai* tune is heard, alluding to Cameroon's succession of occupiers and conveying bitterness about the country's colonial history. The film also evokes the earlier attempts at unification, the efforts of the nationalist trade union leader, Reuben Um Nyobé, who in 1948 formed the UPC (Union of the Populations of Cameroon), aimed at fighting both direct colonialism and also its indigenous result of neo-colonialism.

Non-African cinema also stands as an obstacle to true Cameroonian/African cultural identity. *Afrique, je te plumerai* shows a clip of the performance of a black stand-up comedian who tells the audience that he does not go the cinema any more: 'Because when I see Belmondo or Alain Delon killed in a film, they reappear in the next film . . . it is the white people's scam.' He ends by saying that he'll return to the cinema when there are films 'de chez nous' ('from home').

Chef (1999)

Eight years on, little had changed in Cameroon and Teno's film *Chef* (*Chief*) provides a bitter and biting criticism of Paul Biya's government. The film opens with an incident Teno had witnessed, which occurred on 21 December 1997. A young boy, in danger of being beaten to death for having stolen a hen and four chicks, is taken to the local chief who sends him to the police. This incident made Teno realise that the violence it triggered off exemplifies that which occurs on a national level. He goes on to reflect on the status of 'chief': in a marriage ceremony, the man is installed as chief of the family, and at every level of society there seems to be a chief, *chef de famille* (head of the family), *chef de bureau* (head of the office), *chef de service* (head of the department). Cameroon is a country where 70 per cent of the people are oppressed, controlled by 'chiefs' who abuse their power.

The highest chief, Paul Biya, the President, is the prime example of such abuse. Teno tells the story of how in 1997 the President attended a

18 Jean-Marie Teno, *Chef.*

football match from which he was absent for some time. Njawe, a journalist with *Le Messager*, speculated on this and wondered whether the President was ill. This led to Njawe's arrest. Without trial, he was condemned to a two-year prison sentence and a fine of $1,000. The sentence and fine were ultimately reduced to one year and $600, an indulgence which only revealed that Biya wants to be seen as sole 'captain of the ship', the 'chief' who holds the power over life and death. Teno is bitter about his country: each country has the government it deserves, he claims. People are fascinated by authority and this, he states, is the case the world over.

Both films are a kind of mosaic in which Teno blends numerous images – fiction, documentary footage and various reconstructions. He attempts to find a film language that will allow people to understand Africa and the many different facets of its history. He once described a sultan who created and refined a written language in the late nineteenth century. Teno's film-making and his attempt to find ways to express what he has to say are not dissimilar to this sultan's invention of a language. However, it is difficult for Teno to identify with his country in the present political climate. Though he is proud of its pre-colonial past, he deplores and denounces the postcolonial abuses and pleads for an Africa in touch with its own values and history.

Jean-Pierre Dikongué-Pipa

Jean-Pierre Dikongué-Pipa worked in theatre before coming to cinema. Starting in amateur theatre, he then founded his own company. He studied film-making at the Independent Conservatoire of French Cinema in Paris.

Muna Moto (1976)

While Teno's *Afrique, je te plumerai* sets its critique of colonialism and neo-colonialism against the background of Cameroon's history, Dikongué-Pipa's *Muna Moto* (*Somebody Else's Child*) exposes the abuses within traditional culture, denouncing the exploitation of the dowry system, the misuse of polygamy and the abuse of paternal authority.

The story focuses on two young people, Ngando and Ndomé, who love each other and want to marry. However, Ngando is an orphan; he lives with his uncle and does not see how he could possibly find the dowry to marry Ndomé. The usual means of acquiring a dowry are unavailable to him – especially since the fish stock, on which he and his uncle depend, has dwindled as a consequence of the white people's unrestricted fishing, as condoned by the Cameroonian government. Unable to accumulate the required dowry, the only course of action Ngando can think of is to run away with Ndomé. However, the implication of this, as Ndomé is aware, would be that not having paid the dowry, Ngando could not be recognised as the father of the child she wishes to conceive.

The situation becomes more complicated when it emerges that the uncle, who already has four wives but no children, wishes to marry Ndomé himself. Her refusal unleashes the anger of her father who uses physical violence to force the marriage upon her. Ndomé is not about to give in to her father and she asks Ngando to collude with her by taking her virginity and so making her ineligible to be his uncle's wife. Despite this the uncle pursues his plan, rapes Ndomé and so succeeds in acquiring her as his fifth wife. A complex family situation arises, the child born to Ndomé is Ngando's and not her husband's, which eventually leads to Ngando's attempting to flee with his child but instead being arrested and sent to prison.

The film has an experimental style involving unexpected and daring editing in which dreams, sudden visions and fantasies are inserted into the narrative. The structure leaves the viewer questioning the meaning of specific sequences, such as one early on in the film when a ritual celebration is taking place and a young man suddenly snatches a young child from a mother and flees with it. The viewer is left to query the link between the title of the film *Someone Else's Child*, and this event. The film also makes bold use of close-ups to emphasise the psychological strife that underlies society's expectations. For example, when Ngando introduces his hoped for future wife to his uncle, there is a series of brief close-ups of Ndomé, revealing the different parts of her body which the uncle is visually devouring, then a lingering close-up of Ndomé's enlarged abdomen, which the uncle fantasises as pregnant with his child.

The many fantasies, dreams and thoughts interspersed in the narrative reveal the film-maker's political convictions and social concerns. Ngando's reflective mood dominates the film, giving voice to his awareness of the ossified, traditional culture from which he is unable to distance himself. He reflects on the injustice of the dowry system and the failure of anyone, including himself, to attempt to bring about change.

The film also powerfully addresses the link between identity and paternity. The uncle, having scolded his first four wives in the harshest way and accused them of barrenness, then claims paternity of his nephew's child. When Ngando hears his uncle criticise his wives for their assumed infertility, he asks him whether having a child is all that important. It is the only thing that matters, his uncle replies. What emerges here is the uncle's conviction that to be a father is more important than to have one. Traditionally, the identity of the child is given by the father but here a corruption occurs. The real father, too poor to pay a dowry, is robbed of his fatherhood by his uncle and the uncle becomes the recognised father only through the lavish dowry he is able to pay. The child then becomes the necessary confirmation of the uncle's identity even if that child is, in fact, 'someone else's child'.

Jean-Pierre Bekolo

Quartier Mozart (1993) is an erotic comedy that questions the relative power of men and women. It offers a playful myth about gender identity and gender change. The sorceress Mama Thecla instructs a young freespirited girl about sex and female power. To the question, would she prefer to be a man or a woman, the sorceress replies that she would prefer to be a woman in a male body. She introduces the girl to various rituals and conjures up a mysterious yellow car which transforms the girl into a boy, My Guy, destined to seduce Saturday, the most desirable girl in the neighbourhood. The girl's aim is to discover what male sexuality is like. But Mama Thecla also transplants herself into a male body, that of Panka, who can make a man's penis disappear by shaking his hand. Through all these comical devices and scenes, the film-maker explores identity in relation to gender.

These Cameroonian films, all from the 1990s, expose the political and social problems which beset Cameroon. Against this background, they raise the question of identity: Teno by exploring racial context, Dikongué-Pipa by addressing the link between identity and fatherhood, while Bekolo playfully questions the link with gender.

16 Burkina Faso

It may seem paradoxical that a state believed to be the poorest country in Africa, Burkina Faso, formerly Upper Volta, should occupy a key position in African cinema. Its capital Ouagadougou, the venue of the most prestigious biannual African film festival, FESPACO, makes a vital contribution to the development and promotion of African cinema.

Burkina Faso has had a troubled history, and at one point nearly disappeared from the map. It was colonised by the French in 1896 and, as Upper Volta, became integrated into French West Africa, the French colonial territory created in 1904. In 1932 it was divided up and its components added to the colonies of Sudan, Côte d'Ivoire and Niger, only to be reconstituted in 1947 as a unified territory within the French Union, the short-lived organisation created to strengthen France's links with its colonies. In 1958 it joined the French Community, the successor to the French Union, as the autonomous Republic of Volta. It was re-named Upper Volta in 1959, before achieving independence in 1960. In 1983 the new president, Thomas Sankara, changed the country's name to Burkina Faso, which means 'country of upright (righteous) men'.

President Sankara inaugurated an extensive reform programme aimed at improving the living standards of the under-privileged people in society, particularly women and peasants. He also fought vigorously against corruption and dramatically reduced expenditure on salaries in the public sector. This measure alienated many interest groups: in 1987 a coup was mounted against him in which he was assassinated. Besides his commitment to social reform, Sankara also lent unfailing support to African cinema. Manthia Diawara records how, at the 1985 FESPACO, Sankara gave a press conference 'not only to address film issues but also to explain the domestic and foreign policies of the country' (Diawara 1992: 137). For Sankara film was an important means to express the aims of the OAU (Organisation of African Unity) in art. According to Ukadike, Sankara 'must be remembered for being the only African leader who was wholeheartedly committed to the development of African cinema' (Ukadike 1994: 199). Sankara confirmed the importance of an African cinema in which the politico-economic and cultural development of Africa would be stressed, an aim which had been voiced by film-makers themselves at the second FEPACI meeting in 1975 held in Algiers, and also at the meeting in 1982 in Niamey.

Burkina Faso remains one of the driving forces behind the development of African cinema. The country played a key role in celebrating cinema's centenary in 1995, by publishing a volume of articles assessing African cinema, under the auspices of the FEPACI. The book's general editor, Burkinabè film-maker Gaston Kaboré, reminds the readers of the FEPACI's aim, which is 'to develop a film industry that will serve the needs of the continent and play an active role in communication, education, investigation' (FEPACI 1995: 23). Kaboré also warns against the danger of losing one's African identity in a society constantly subjected to foreign images. 'The ability to picture oneself is a vital need', he argues; film-makers want to shoot pictures 'to serve as a catalyst for the full development of the African personality' (FEPACI 1995: 23).

If Burkina Faso has been at the forefront of the struggle for an African cinema, since the 1980s it has also created a strong Burkinabè cinema. According to Denise Brahimi, use of the term 'Burkinabè School' is justified because there is a continuity that underlies Burkinabè films; they share a common aim and proceed in a similar way (Brahimi 1997: 89). Indeed, the Burkinabè films of the 1980s and 1990s, represented especially by Gaston Kaboré, Idrissa Ouedraogo and Pierre Yameogo, reveal African images and emphasise themes such as the search for one's origins, the African village, entry into life, exclusion and escape to the city.

Gaston Kaboré

Gaston Kaboré, a pioneer of African cinema and former secretary of the FEPACI, is an innovating force in Burkinabè cinema. He raises the question of identity by exploring its articulation and necessary spatial context and by addressing the search of individuals for their origins and destiny. In an interview for *Le Film Africain* he emphasises that a single aspect dominates all his films: 'My films always touch upon memory. A kind of active memory. I not only ask who I am and where I come from, I also try to imagine what I could be tomorrow' (Kaboré 1999: 3a, trans.)

Kaboré's films attempt to locate an origin, to preserve the link with ancestral values, to understand who or what one is and to explore the moral obligation of contributing to the good life of the community. In interviews and in writing production notes about his films, Kaboré expresses these beliefs in an explicit and powerful way: 'My films speak of the transmission of a heritage, and of the duty to pursue a task' (Kaboré 1999: 3b, trans.). It is this very view which underlies his four films, *Wend Kuuni* (1982), *Zan Boko* (1988), *Rabi* (1992) and *Buud Yam* (1996).

Wend Kuuni tells of a mute child found in the bush by a traveller; *Zan Boko* is about ancestral land threatened by the onset of modernisation; *Rabi* shows a boy's growing up through his attachment to a turtle; *Buud Yam* depicts the search for individual roots. The titles *Wend Kuuni* and

Rabi are the names of the children in the film, while *Zan Boko* is a place and *Buud Yam* in Moré language refers to heritage in the spiritual and moral sense, that is to say, the legacy that comes from one's ancestors and the collective memory of a people.

Wend Kuuni (1982)

Wend Kuuni (*God's Gift*), the touching story of a mute boy, remains the landmark of Kaboré's oeuvre. The film opens with a sequence showing a grieving woman whose husband is missing. An elder of the clan tells her that he is certainly dead and that her son can become a man only if she remarries. Faithful to her husband, whom she believes to be alive, the woman decides to flee with her son. The next scene shows the mute boy being found by a passing traveller, who entrusts him to a man in a nearby village. Having failed to find the boy's family the villager adopts the child, now called Wend Kuuni, 'the gift of God'. The boy is raised lovingly by his foster parents, who do not have a son and whose only daughter, Pogneré, develops a close relationship with him in spite of his muteness.

According to French film critic and theoretician Michel Chion, a mute person in a sound film has a precise function. Unable to say who he is or where he comes from, he harbours an unspoken secret and the viewer has to wait until he regains his speech to learn the truth. He adds, moreover, that to meet a mute person is to encounter 'the question of identity, origin and desire' (Chion 1982: 82). Because Wend Kuuni is the main protagonist, muteness and its association with identity are located at the very heart of the film. However this 'body without a voice', as Chion calls the mute, also has its counterpart in the film: the voice without body, namely the voice-over which comments upon events or conveys characters' feelings and premonitions.

Wend Kuuni's silent movements and the peaceful atmosphere in which he lives are shown in minute detail, creating a scene of African pastoral harmony. However, the viewer is unable to forget the beginning of the film, and narrative tradition suggests that the missing link, contained in the temporal and spatial ellipsis, will eventually be provided. This does indeed happen when one day the boy sees a man hanged from a tree, because he could not tolerate being publicly rejected by his much younger wife, Timpoko. The trauma of this discovery makes him scream, and recover his speech. Only then does his adoptive family learn where Wend Kuuni comes from, and he can tell the story to Pogneré and, through her, to the viewer.

Up to this moment the story has been presented from the point of view of an omniscient narrator. Once the boy recovers his speech, the story shifts to his first person narrative, beginning with the words 'I remember . . .' Then his telling gives way to an entirely visual rendering of events: the story is transformed into a cinematic narration which depicts more than the boy could ever have seen or known. There is a similarity between Wend Kuuni's regaining his speech and Kaboré's narrative strategy. As he says,

cinema is not simply the transposition of one genre, the oral narrative, into another, that of narrative images. A kind of fertilisation takes place and we invent a new language in which the viewer not only recognises familiar elements from the tradition of storytelling but also understands the enormous contribution made by the image. (Kaboré 1999: 3c, trans.)

The images that replace the boy's oral narrative are those of the film's opening sequence. But, whereas in that sequence only the mother was seen, in the second telling the boy is central to the image. Mother and son are together in their hut when irate villagers come to drive the mother out because they suspect her of being a witch. The mother runs away carrying her son until, too tired to go on, she lies down with him and dies of exhaustion. When Wend Kuuni wakes up and finds his mother dead, he screams, 'Mother, mother!' and starts running until he faints, after which he is discovered by the traveller.

Wend Kuuni's last word before becoming mute is his scream for his lost mother. It is this loss that causes his muteness. When he discovers the hanged man, the image of his dead mother returns and again he screams 'Mother!' He is then seen looking up at the man rather than down at the mother. In this way the boy's vision of his dead mother and of the dead man are shown to merge, resulting in his screaming the repressed name.

The boy's recovery of speech, which allows him to exorcise his memories, is comparable to the development of African cinema (and literature), which allows buried memories to be spoken. Just as violence and trauma caused the boy to be mute, so the violence inflicted upon Africa silenced Africans. Cinema is helping them to recall memory and tell their own stories.

Wend Kuuni is a lyrical film, especially in the way images of the landscape glide by, suggesting the healing process to the viewer. The film espouses the rhythm of African life: images linger, allowing the viewer to absorb the landscape, to feel with the boy and the girl and to observe. Yet it also contains the two tragedies of the mother and the hanged man.

Critics have discussed many of the film's secondary themes, such as feminism. The little girl Pogneré is aware of the link between gender and identity: 'If I were a boy', she says to Wend Kuuni, 'I could stay with you when you look after the sheep. Would you like to be a girl?' When he says 'Yes', she exclaims, 'You're just saying that to please me.' It is clear that there is a difference in perception of identity based on gender from childhood onwards. Meanwhile, two adult women, the mother and the hanged man's wife, rebel against the imposition of a husband. Although Wend Kuuni's mother dies because she refuses to live by the clan's rules, her death plays a crucial role in the formation of her son's identity.

Wend Kuuni's sequel, Buud Yam, came out in 1996. In Buud Yam Wend Kuuni leaves his adoptive family to find a healer for his dangerously ill sister and to look for his lost roots. This echoing between the first and the fourth film shows Kaboré's insistence on identity as not only being a point of arrival in a person's life but also a new point of departure. 'Life', Kaboré says, 'is not static, you cannot just be there and live' (Kaboré 1999: 3d, trans.).

Zan Boko (1988)

Zan Boko (Homeland) opens with the birth of a child. The delivery is difficult and Tinga, the father, is called upon by the midwife to perform a specific ritual that will assist his wife, Nopoko. In many black African cultures the birth of a child is accompanied by rituals that are designed to prepare the way for the introduction and acceptance of a new member into the community. Kaboré explains that the burial of the placenta is an important rite practised by the Mossi in West Africa; it consecrates the first bond between the newborn child and the nourishing earth. The place where the placenta is buried is called 'Zan Boko' and is considered to be the home of the ancestors and the spirits which protect the family and social group (from the production notes for Zan Boko, quoted by Ukadike 1994: 264).

The story is located in the peaceful surroundings of a traditional Mossi village, where most of the work is done communally. The village houses are made of mud brick with straw roofs. All have the same cylindrical shape. But this peaceful village is now threatened by new urbanisation plans which propose to extend Ouagadougou into the countryside. Moreover, a wealthy African, living with his family on the edge of the village, has asked for planning permission to build a swimming pool on his property, which would require expropriation of part of the village.

The urbanisation plans go ahead and all the huts in the village are scheduled for demolition. Tinga cannot come to terms with these changes and expresses his distress over the loss of their land, saying, 'we are treated as outsiders on the very land of our ancestors'. This forced relocation is tantamount to a loss of identity, which is strongly connected to the land.

The planned urbanisation of the community comes to the attention of a journalist, who decides to include it in his television programme on current affairs, to which experts, officials and Tinga are invited. When those with a vested interest in the expropriation of the village land recognise Tinga on television, they immediately contact the authorities to have the programme stopped before Tinga speaks. A female presenter apologises for the interruption 'caused by technical difficulties' and announces the feature to follow, a programme on the French Riviera. Ironically, Tinga, who has frequently debated the issue under the baobab tree, would not have been able to participate in the television debate even if the officials had not intervened, as he does not understand or speak French.

The censored television programme reveals how modern technology can be used not only to subvert traditional culture but also forcefully to exclude its people from participating in debates about issues which concern them directly. The film, while revealing how deeply people's identities are tied to the land inherited from their ancestors, also denounces governmental corruption, nepotism and the decadent affluence of Africa's *nouveau riche*, who ruthlessly destroy the land and culture of their own people.

Idrissa Ouedraogo

Like Kaboré, Idrissa Ouedraogo has succeeded in creating a truly African cinema of international importance. Often referred to as the 'doyen of the African new wave', he is in the first instance a 'village film-maker'. He looks at African village life, depicting its harmony and its conflicts. He does not set out to demonstrate a view or propagate an idea, but instead observes the villagers, listens to them and, in this way, also presents an analysis of African society. Ouedraogo's style of careful observation, invested with social commentary, was already present in his early short films, *Poko* (1981) and *Issa le tisserand* (1984 – *Issa the Weaver*). *Poko* presents the problem of villagers who, when faced with a medical emergency, do not have access to proper transport to the city. It concerns a pregnant woman who has developed complications and has to be transported by cart to get medical attention. The slow pace of the film reflects the tragic reality of such slow transport as the woman dies on the way. *Issa le tisserand* tells the simple story of a weaver who uses traditional artisanal methods. He is seen weaving, with genuine love, but ultimately, lack of demand for what he makes obliges Issa to abandon his African methods and sell Western garments instead. By focusing on individuals, the pregnant woman or the weaver, with whom the viewers can identify, Ouedraogo calls for recognition of social problems that affect the everyday life of Africans.

Ouedraogo's films display a specific Franco-African identity: the subject and style are African but at the same time the mark of a film-maker trained in Europe is evident. He studied at the *Institut de Cinéma de Ouagadougou*, obtained a research degree (DEA) in cinema from the University of Paris (Paris I), and finally, in 1984, graduated from IDHEC. He recognises that films made in Africa with exclusively African resources can never be profitable: if African film-makers wish to promote Africa and African film, they must make films that will appeal to Western viewers.

Yam Daabo (1986)

Ouedraogo's first feature film, *Yam Daabo* (*The Choice*), already revealed his use of a truly cinematic language. The film's peaceful rhythm, reminiscent of still photographs, contributes to a genuine cinematic experience. Before the credits appear, the film opens by showing details of African village life. The camera then turns to the barren land through which a lorry approaches, bringing food sent by foreign governments and aid agencies to a group of patiently waiting villagers. Instead of joining the queue, Salam leaves the village with his family and his donkey and cart.

The film follows the family in their unending search for more fertile land and their struggle to survive against countless obstacles and adversities. Tragedy strikes when the youngest boy, Ali, is hit by a car and killed while looking at a poster for a film called *Le Fleuve de la vengeance* (*The River of Revenge*), but the family have little time to mourn death as they must continue their struggle for life.

Ouedraogo emphasises the immense courage and perseverance of a family group united in their fight against the harshness of destiny. When they finally reach a river they decide to settle near it, elated by the sight of water. The film records their labours in a placid way: without hastening to tell a story, it aims to convey the family's immense effort to resettle. One day, another family arrives from their old village to join Salam. However, the son, Tiga, introduces hostility into the peaceful family because he is in love with Salam's daughter Bintou, and uncontrollably jealous of her lover. The film effectively blends the many strands of emotions and character traits underlying the little community.

This new village-like settlement seems marked by age-old laws of human agrarian society where the individual can survive only in a group. Both families work in the fields together. Only Tiga fails to identify with the group, finally leaving for a life of crime in the city. The film contrasts village with city and reveals the problems that occur in the long dry seasons, drawing attention to the conflict between self-reliance and foreign aid programmes.

Yam Daabo had, and still enjoys, considerable success, but it was with *Yaaba* (1989) – the real 'village film' – that Ouedraogo achieved international recognition.

Yaaba (1989)

Yaaba has rightly been hailed as exemplifying a genuine African cinema. In this film there is no reference to colonial or postcolonial politics; it is an African story, whose style, as Ukadike writes, 'not only inscribes African identity in African films but also renders the films competitive in the international market' (Ukadike 1994: 279).

Like *Wend Kuuni*, the film is set in West Africa before colonialism and there is no reference to white people. It has been called both a 'simple village story' and 'Ouédraogo's most mysterious film' (Diawara 1992: 160 and Guellali 1998: 13). Indeed, what seems at first to be a simple tale involves a complex set of relationships. The characters in the film are Mossi people, Ouedraogo's own ethnic group, and the language spoken is Moré. The actors are non-professionals, old people and young children, and the film exploits the oral storytelling tradition, using images to capture the characters' natural gestures and facial expressions. The story is told slowly in the African mode, with long takes allowing the viewer to observe characters walking through the sun-burnt landscape until they nearly disappear over the horizon. Ouedraogo's images are unusually telling and the viewer needs to look and listen attentively in order to feel and understand the emotional currents underlying the narrative.

Before the credits appear, there is a brief shot of a boy and girl, Bila and Nopoko, running away from the camera. After the credits, these children are seen standing in a cemetery, with an old woman in the background. Both the little girl, Nopoko, and the old woman, Sana, are visiting their mothers' graves. On leaving the cemetery the children decide to play hide and seek. When Sana tells Nopoko where Bila is hiding a bond starts to form between the three.

The action in the film takes place within and around the village, from which Sana is completely excluded, as the villagers believe her to be a witch. Despite her exclusion, Sana remains good-natured and is depicted with great dignity and pride. When village children throw stones at her, she is shown looking back calmly with a wound on her forehead. To a lesser extent Bila also has a difficult relationship with the villagers, who regard him as troublesome. It is he who gives Sana a sense of identity. One day he catches a chicken for her and, seeing her in the distance, calls out 'Yaaba!' ('Grandmother!').

This naming is a key moment, establishing a bond between Sana and Bila. But they must win each other's trust. Their meeting is presented in a very slow rhythm: the boy is seen holding the chicken and looking at Sana, whom he has just addressed as 'Yaaba'. They face each other, come closer, the boy then repeats, 'Yaaba', smiles and adds, 'I brought this for you'. Sana, fearing the boy might have stolen the chicken, accepts it only after he says that his uncle gave it to him. The camera now leaves the two characters to track slowly across the barren countryside, a solemn moment accompanied by indigenous string and reed instruments. Then, in the distance, Sana's house becomes visible, with smoke rising in front of it and Sana and Bila sitting outside. The camera moves closer to show them eating the roasted chicken.

It is a moment of intimacy where humour and emotion blend. The boy munches a chicken leg and says to Sana, 'This is very good', adding, 'A shame you don't have any teeth.' 'Don't mock me', she replies as they both laugh heartily. She looks at the boy in silence, begins slowly, 'You know,' pauses, then goes on, 'that's the first time anyone has called me Yaaba. That makes me really happy.' If filiation and territory are important markers in establishing identity, then, until this moment Sana has had none. In endowing her with a title, used to mark an important familial relationship, Bila has given her both an identity and a role.

Sana also has a spiritual bond with Nopoko. Both have lost their mother and, like Sana, Nopoko is injured by the village boys, although much more seriously. Sana is accused of causing Nopoko's life-threatening injury and the villagers set fire to her house, yet it is she who goes to find the healer. Her long, silent walk through the landscape is an important element in the film's aesthetic and meaning. It is filmed mainly in long shot, with spoken language replaced by gestures and a soundtrack of indigenous music. When Sana and the healer return to the village, Nopoko's condition has deteriorated. Bila's father dismisses the healer, but Bila secretly brings back his remedy, which restores the girl's health.

19 Idrissa Ouedraogo, *Yaaba*. Bila and the healer.

Some time later, Bila and Nopoko take Sana a gift of food to thank her and find her sitting dead under a tree. The frightened Nopoko rushes back to the village, while Bila stays near Sana's body, respectfully covering it with Nopoko's shawl. Nopoko returns with the village drunk, another marginalised person, who digs a grave. He carries Sana to it, covered with Nopoko's shawl and watched quietly by Bila and Nopoko.

The legacy 'Yaaba' leaves to the children is considerable. Throughout the film she has taught them her values of human kindness, dignity in the face of persecution and tolerance towards others despite their prejudices. Before they find Sana dead, Nopoko makes a judgemental remark about the drunk's adulterous wife, whom they see furtively hurrying to meet her lover. Bila repeats Sana's advice word for word, saying, 'Don't judge, they have their reasons.'

Through her moral guidance to Bila and by healing Nopoko, Sana fulfils her role as 'Yaaba'. Whereas her own mother died giving life to her, Sana now dies after restoring Nopoko's life. Bila has been the mediator between the two: it is he who gave 'Yaaba' her name and rushed to her when Nopoko was dangerously ill. Through these three characters Ouedraogo emphasises the importance of spiritual bonds. Like the traditional healer, Sana represents true values, which the villagers fail to appreciate. Only those on the margins of society, the village drunk and the mischievous Bila, see the truth.

The film interweaves questions of inclusion and exclusion, centre and margins and tradition and its rejection with the underlying theme of identity. By excluding the orphaned Sana, the village not only fails to give her a sense of who she is, but also loses a valuable element of its own. In this film, Ouedraogo challenges the collective, socially constructed identity upheld by the judgemental villagers, contrasting them with Sana, whose non-prejudicial, ethical responses suggest that identity has at its core a moral imperative. In this film it is the 'outsiders' who have vision and compassion. In spite of the villagers' unmerited hostility towards her, Sana retains her generosity and great moral integrity. The film ends with the hope that the new generation of Bila and Nopoko can be morally and spiritually transformed by Africa's oldest and soundest traditions.

Ouedraogo's subsequent films have added further to his remarkable success. *Tilaï*, made in 1990, was awarded the Jury Prize at Cannes and won the Yennenga Stallion at the 1991 FESPACO, and *Samba Traoré* (1992) obtained awards at the Carthage and Berlin film festivals.

Tilaï (1990)

Tilaï, like *Yaaba*, deals with relationships, exclusion, tradition and moral values. Several critics see a link between this film and Greek tragedy in its dramatic representation of fratricide and the conflict between father and son (Machta 1998: 19 and Brahimi 1997: 96). Unlike Greek tragedy though, here there is no reference to gods or religious beliefs. The film opens with Saga's return to his native village, where he hopes to find his fiancée, Nogma. However, during his absence his father has married her. Finding the situation unbearable, Saga decides to exile himself and builds a hut outside the village. Nogma, who is in love with him, secretly visits him in his place of exclusion.

When the village finds out about the couple it is decided that Saga must be put to death and that his own brother, Kougri, must carry out the sentence. Kougri, judging fratricide to be more terrible than adultery, devises a ruse to avoid killing his brother. He allows Saga to escape, if he promises never to return. Nogma joins him in exile, where they get married. But when some time later Saga learns that his mother has died he feels obliged to return to the village. On learning of his son's return the father exiles Kougri. Having earlier acted against tradition, Kougri is now confronted with, for him, a tragic reality. He takes a rifle and kills his brother.

The film deals with moral issues concerning the village traditions and the father's abusive power. Taking advantage of his son's absence, he sets in motion a series of events for which he takes no responsibility. The son's self-exclusion takes him away from the village but not from his father's wife, while Nogma's choice of adultery over marital fidelity also unleashes a series of tragic events. The film is thus an interplay of decisions made by individuals who make moral choices that break with prescribed, traditional values.

Ouedraogo's strength here lies in placing each individual in a specific 'moral space', to use Charles Taylor's phrase. The people in this film do not follow a prescribed pattern, they define their own opinions and draw up their own life plans (Taylor 1989: 25). Within the context of a non-individualistic and tradition-bound social order the individualism of Saga, Nogma and Kougri has tragic consequences.

Samba Traoré (1992)

In Samba Traoré, moral choices are equally paramount. Samba Traoré also returns to his village, but he is returning from the city where he has committed an armed robbery. The film opens with the robbery filmed in thriller style, then switches to the village where a peaceful narrative rhythm dominates and where Samba embarks upon a new life. Far from resembling a criminal, he is a positive character, liked by the people, and uses his money to promote the well-being of the entire village. He has kind parents, friends and enters a happy marriage. Though the villagers sense some discrepancy between the person from the past and the one who returns to the village, all could have continued in this peaceful fashion had he not needed to take his pregnant wife to the city. On the way his behaviour suddenly becomes strange and he runs away, leaving his friend to deal with his pregnant wife. Eventually, Samba's past catches up with him and the film closes showing him hand-cuffed, on his way to prison.

Here again Ouedraogo deals with an individual's moral choices. Samba seems to have no regret for his past conduct, nor has he any inclination to criminal behaviour once he is back in his village. He hides his crime, relegating it to the confines of his own sub-consciousness. But, unable to obliterate it, he has nightmares and makes careless errors which eventually lead to his father finding out what Samba has done. Past, present and future seem interwoven through the appearance of characters belonging to different periods in his life. The past that Samba was unable to obliterate does not, however, close the future for him. The villagers, quietly watching him being taken to prison, are ready to welcome him back after his prison sentence.

Pierre Yameogo

Pierre Yameogo studied cinema at the Conservatoire in Paris and Communication Studies at Paris VIII. His film *Dunia* (1987) was preceded by a short film made in 1984.

Dunia (1987)

In *Dunia*, Yameogo depicts the life of a sturdy ten-year-old girl, Nongma. Most of the time she is seen walking – walking from her parents' house to her grandmother's home or to school. The road to her grandmother's house is long and Nongma has to ask for directions several times. She walks bravely all by herself and, although this is not explicitly an initiation journey, it is nevertheless a learning experience on the road to adulthood. She encounters dangers and witnesses various aspects of social life, such as the lot of a childless woman, the lies people tell and her grandmother's unkindness. These scenes of simple daily life become metaphoric images – the kind from which, according to Denise Brahimi, the cinema of Burkina Faso draws its strength (Brahimi 1997: 100). The paths the little girl has to find and travel are the difficult roads that lead her to the uncertain life of adult, African womanhood. Without conveying any of her thoughts, she has seen women, lonely, barren – and therefore worthless – and always dominated by men.

One day her grandmother dies while Nongma is caring for her. On her long walk back alone along the sandy paths, Nongma comes to a cross-roads and wonders which road to take: should she go back to her parents in the village or to the city where her Uncle Paul lives and where she goes to school? The film closes with the question unanswered.

The viewer has followed Nongma walking barefoot down endless paths with unfailing courage, never knowing what awaits her. When the film closes with the image of Nongma hesitating at the crossroads, the viewer is left uncertain as to which direction she will take and what future there is for her and for African women.

Laafi (1991)

Laafi (All Is Well) also deals with the future of young people trying to find their identity and role in life. As in Dunia, Yameogo uses the predicament of an individual, Joe, to reveal the different social problems a young person has to face. The film depicts the high school graduation of Joe and his friends. Joe has done well and hopes to become a doctor, thus keeping the promise he made to his father before his death. However, at the 'orientation', a government scheme that allocates student places at university, he is told that there is no place for him in medical school.

Following the main character, as in Dunia, Yameogo follows Joe as he travels up and down observing the world around him, riding his moped through town, visiting his widowed mother, meeting friends and trying to approach those in power in order to gain access to university. For Joe, like Nongma in Dunia, it is a kind of initiation into adulthood that lies ahead of him. Yameogo shows how these young people, who are about to embark on their adult lives, are confronted with aspects of society which will shape their personalities. In these films, as in road movies, the characters are always moving; Nongma on foot, Joe on his moped. This meandering along roads or paths metaphorically parallels their search for adult identity as they prepare themselves for the future. Little Nongma, tending her dying grandmother and Joe vowing to his dying father that he will become a doctor for the people of his country, are promises for the future of Africa. In them lies the hope that Africa may find its own voice and its own worth.

Silmandé (1998)

In Silmandé (The Whirlwind), Yameogo uses comedy-drama to denounce the corruption that cripples Africa and which is comparable to a whirlwind blowing everywhere. In the film, the corruption is aggravated by the presence of Lebanese fortune seekers in Burkina Faso.

Whereas his two earlier films, in road-movie fashion, emphasised the endless travelling of two young people, this film explores the various paths of trafficking, making deals and accepting bribes, which prevail in African cities. The film deals with the newly implemented strategy of bonne gouvernance (good governing), with which the Burkina Faso government hoped to end the control exerted by foreign businessmen over national imports and exports. However, when the Finance Minister decides to take the national rice contract from Yacine Jabert, a Lebanese business man, and entrust it to an African, Mouni, Yacine and his son

Amoudé become involved in complex and shady negotiations. They are seen driving from place to place in their Mercedes cars attempting to regain the contract.

This is not the journey of young African people like Nongma or Joe, but the calculated and ruthless exploitation of Africa by foreign settlers. Yameogo has chosen to depict the prevailing level of corruption through comedy, as for example in his portrayal of the high-placed minister who has to travel to Geneva. Her abuse of position and power becomes a burlesque. She has countless oversized luxury offices; an inordinate number of shiny suitcases filled with gold to be placed in Geneva banks; an outspoken contempt for the poor ('I do not like poor people'); and is preoccupied with shopping rather than ministerial matters.

Although the accumulation of examples of injustice and corruption reach the level of caricature, this tone does not diminish Yameogo's damning criticism of the profound sores Africa endures: the racism of the settlers; the injustice of the courts which are on the side of the whites; and the lot of African women – represented by the African woman made pregnant by Amoudé Jabert and whose child is taken from her.

Yameogo does not take away all hope for the creation of a dignified Africa in which justice prevails and all people are equal. Several of the characters abandon their shady dealings: one of these, who bears the humorous name of 'Je m'en fous' (I don't care), spends all his time trying to find a book he has lost which, he argues, should be read. His concern for the book elicits derogatory remarks from the Lebanese – 'The more ignorant they remain, the better it is' – but these comments do not deter him from putting all his energy into retrieving the book. He finally finds it in a small snack bar where the sales woman is using the pages to wrap food. He takes it back and reads it aloud: it is the manifesto of the rights of man. Even read in Je m'en fous's humorous way, it remains a powerful plea addressed to Africans to shed all their false beliefs – not only those that have been imposed upon them but also their own.

The success of the biannual FESPACO had already placed Burkina Faso and more specifically Ouagadougou, on the map of world cinema, when in the 1980s several Burkinabè film-makers brought further renown to the nation's cinema. Starting in 1982 with Kaboré's *Wend Kuuni*, there has been a steady production of quality films dealing with African issues and addressing African as well as international audiences. The main representatives of Burkinabè cinema, Kaboré, Ouedraogo and Yameogo, all emphasise the African village, depicting its daily life and internal conflicts. Kaboré's films reveal the importance of the ancestors and the transmission of values and beliefs through them, for the development of both individual and group identity. Ouedraogo and Yameogo continue this village tradition, depicting the impact of daily life and social behaviour on individual identity formation. In their later films Ouedraogo and Yameogo also refer to the postcolonial situation and introduce Western elements and influences which inevitably have an impact upon African identity.

17 Democratic Republic of the Congo

The Congo was founded in 1885 as a personal possession of the Belgian King Leopold II whose aim was to let the cost of the economic development be borne by the Congo itself. This led to ruthless exploitation by European firms, who were allowed to force the Congolese to work for them. The international outcry when this became known led to the Belgian state annexing the country. The country gained independence in 1958 and renamed itself 'Zaire'. In 1997, after the departure of General Mobutu, the country renamed itself 'Democratic Republic of the Congo'.

Mweze Dieudonné Ngangura

Mweze Ngangura is no newcomer to cinema. He studied cinema at the *Institut des arts de diffusion* in Brussels and made a number of documentary and fiction films among which *La Vie est belle* (1985 – *Life is Rosy*), made with Benoît Lamy, is the best known. Ukadike calls it a 'raucous musical comedy' in which 'popular theatre and music are used to experience the Kinshasha boisterous night life' (Ukadike 1994: 197 & 284). His 1998 *Pièces d'identités* brought Ngangura fame. First presented at the Milan festival of African cinema in March 1998, it won the coveted FESPACO Yennenga Stallion in Ouagadougou in 1999.

Pièces d'identités (1998)

The film, dedicated to the African diaspora, is a comedy about heritage, identity and self-discovery. It is set in Brussels in 1998, where Mani Kongo, King of the Bakongo, has returned for the first time since 1958, year of the World Exhibition. Now, forty years later, he returns to find the daughter with whom he has lost contact. While adopting a comic tone, the film exploits the King's visit in order to expose the Belgo-Congolese relations.

The visit is fraught with difficulties which occur as soon as he reaches the airport. He arrives wearing his ancestral gear, symbols of his traditional power, a sculptured head piece, a finely carved stick and a beautiful necklace. However, the Belgian customs require an import tax for these valuable items and will not recognise them as pieces of his royal identity. For them identity is proven by ID cards and not by such attire. From here onwards, the film blends thriller and comedy techniques while

20 Mweze Dieudonné Ngangura, *Pièces d'indentités*.

following the King's search for his daughter, who was sent to Belgium to attend school. The search brings him into contact with various shady as well as kind-hearted individuals before he is finally reunited with his daughter. Although in the many years since she was last at 'home' her identity has changed and with that her general views on life, her goal is to return some day to her country and to set up a local medical clinic.

The film focuses almost entirely on the issue of identity: each person is in search of an identity in some way or other: Mani Kongo seeks knowledge of his family, while still holding on to the deep traditions that give him his own legacy; his daughter is secure in her newly found European world, but knows that she has an identity with the Bakongo people as well. The entire minority of Africans who are living abroad are searching for a compromise between the different European and African life styles.

The film interweaves the 1998 visit with scenes in black and white recalling the Belgium Mani Kongo knew as a student; it gives a sweet-sour discovery of postcolonial Belgium where former colonial administrators and Congolese immigrants live side by side, as do corruption and idealism, incivility and kindness.

The thriller genre, adopted by the film-maker, is used entirely for the purpose of identifying people. In this comic mode, the film raises important questions concerning immigration, integration and above all about the pieces of identity needed by the many asylum seekers. But the King himself had trouble establishing his identity, as *Pièces d'identités* puts it: 'Without your ID, you've no identity.'

Conclusion

Francophonia has proven to be a valuable concept for the study of film. It has brought together an unusually rich and varied body of films which all, in one way or another, express a struggle for identity. Film, as an accessible popular medium, has been regarded throughout its century-old history as a way of moulding a people's perceptions and assumptions about their own identity. Aware of this, France has actively promoted film in its own country and abroad. However, the systematic development of its own film style and star system has to be seen in the larger context of a world cinema dominated by Hollywood. In order to escape comparison with Hollywood or to avoid being marginalised within its empire, it was imperative that France develop a film style that would set it apart from the Hollywood canon. If it succeeded in creating a unique French style, it has had to fight hard for survival.

The same applies to the French language, around which an equally fierce, though largely illusory battle continues to be fought. France's interest in promoting French language and culture, under the aegis of Francophonia, is part of that battle. French is losing ground. This study has shown, for example, that the large African continent is abandoning the use of French in its films in favour of its traditional languages.

France continues to dream its 'family romance' of Francophonia at considerable cost. Its own identity is not only threatened by the Hollywood empire, but also by the demographic changes within its own society. While it bestowed identity upon the family members of Francophonia, it now appears that the situation is reversed and that it leans on a *multicultural* and *multilingual* Francophonia for the preservation of its own fragile identity.

French quotations

Arcand (1976: 21):
je ne suis pas un cinéaste militant parce que cela suppose que l'on sait vers où doit aller la société. Et, en s'en tenant à la société nord américaine, je n'ai aucune idée où il faudrait amener cette société. Un cinéaste militant, c'est quelqu'un qui indique le chemin . . . mes films sont des constats, des constats d'échec et d'aliénation.

Aubenas (1996: 63):
La famille devient la métaphore d'un peuple exterminé et sa diversité même permet au dramaturge de s'interroger sur les rapport des Juifs et de l'Allemagne, sur l'inextricable réseau de culpabilité qui a lié victimes et bourreaux et les sépare radicalement. Mais le choix central même, la famille, donne à ce psychodrame de la douleur historique une résonnance humaine qui prolonge cette réflexion sur l'holocauste par d'autre rhizomes tout aussi universels: les luttes fratricides d'Abel et Caïn, le nécessaire meurtre du père, les rivalités sororales.

Bachy (1978: 328):
en proie à ses contradictions internes, confronté à des problèmes cruciaux, en marche vers un mieux . . . mais dont il voit encore mal la nature.

Brahimi (1997: 53):
invente une rhétorique de l'image qui va de l'allégorie médiévale au collage surréaliste.

Brahimi (1997: 102):
des forçats ou s'ils sont des mystiques en prière marchant vers leur Dieu.

Chion (1982: 68):
Le point de cri est un point d'impensable à l'intérieur du pensé, d'indicible à l'intérieur de l'énoncé, d'irreprésentable à l'intérieur de la représentation . . . Ce cri incarne un fantasme d'*absolu sonore*, il est censé saturer la bande sonore, rendre sourd qui l'écoute.

Cinécrits (October 1998: 5):
pour le moment, il est encore impossible de determiner l'identité culturelle de nos films.

Copie Zéro (1980: 22):
sépare avec insistance le réel de l'imaginaire, mais à l'inverse de ce qu'on croit. Les vrais acteurs se définissent comme les artisans de l'illusion (mensonge), tandis que l'histoire qu'ils racontent aussitôt est *vraie*, puisqu'elle s'est produite dans les faits.

Coulombe & Jean (1991: 11):
un constat cynique du Québec postréférendaire, constat de la mort politique, 'de l'écroulement du rêve marxiste-léniniste' au profit des plaisirs immédiats.

Deleuze (1985: 196):
Ce que le cinéma doit saisir, ce n'est pas l'identité d'un personnage, réel ou fictif, à travers ses aspects objectifs ou subjectifs. C'est le devenir du personnage réel quand il se met lui-même à 'fictionner', quand il entre en 'flagrant délit de légender', et contribue ainsi à l'invention de son peuple.

Glissant (1996: 15):
Ce qui se passe dans la Caraïbe pendant trois siècles est littéralement ceci: une rencontre d'éléments culturels venus d'horizons abolument divers et qui réellement se créolisent, qui réellement s'imbriquent et se confondent l'un dans l'autre pour donner quelque chose d'absolument imprévisible, d'absolument nouveau et qui est la réalité créole.

Ilboudo (1988: 130):
les empreintes de 'la leçon des ordures' sont plus fortes que celles de la leçon des choses.

Jean (1991: 33):
Dans le développment du cinéma québécois, l'importance de l'ONF est telle que l'on peut affirmer que rares sont les cinéastes majeurs qui n'y ont pas séjourné, à titre d'employés à plein temps ou de pigistes.

Jean (1991: 63):
un conteur capable de poser un regard tendre et amusé sur la société.

Jutra (1980: 22):
est d'être québécois. C'est cette passion là qui sous-tend chacun de ses gestes, chacune de ses oeuvres.

Kaboré (1999: 3a):
Mes films touchent toujours un peu à la mémoire. Une mémoire active en quelque sorte. Je ne me demande pas uniquement qui je suis et d'où je viens, j'essaie aussi d'imaginer ce que je pourrais être demain.

Kaboré (1999: 3b):
Mes films parlent de la transmission d'un héritage, et du devoir de poursuivre une oeuvre.

Kaboré (1999: 3c):
le cinéma n'est pas la transposition pure et simple d'un genre, le récit oral, à un autre genre, le récit en image. Une sorte de fécondation s'opère au contraire, et nous inventons un nouveau langage dans lequel le spectateur reconnaît ce qui relève de sa tradition, le conte, mais aussi comprend l'apport formidable de l'image.

Kaboré (1999: 3d):
La vie n'est pas statique, on ne peut pas être juste là et vivre.

Lever (1995a: 89):
voulait établir dès le départ que la lutte des Québécois minoritaires en Amérique est sans espoir.

Lever (1995a: 252):
Marcel, qui ne le méprise plus, n'a plus besoin de lui pour s'inventer une nouvelle vie.

Lever (1995a: 267):
Bernadette, née Bonheur, devenue Brown par mariage catholique, sera prise pour une Bernadette Soubirous puis pour la militante Bernadette Devlin, dont on parle à la radio au moment de la manifestation finale.

Lever (1995a: 258):
a su s'inventer une vie à la mesure de ses ambitions, qui ne sont pas très grandes. Il ignore probablement qu'on parle de Révolution tranquille dans les milieux instruits. C'est son fils qui en profitera.

Lever (1995b: 211):
le public n'aime pas toujours reconnaître la même facette de lui-même.

Lever (1995b: 486):
Quand je fais un film, je suis à la chasse . . . Il y a des pistes . . . et je me laisse inspirer par ces pistes . . . Au bout, il y a une bête ou il n'y en a pas.

Marcorelle (*Le Monde*, 22 January 1976):
Certainement le premier chef d'oeuvre au féminin de l'histoire du cinéma.

Nysenholc (1985: 28):
Le sujet, héros jadis sûr de lui, est ébranlé par les philosophies du soupçon (Marx, Nietzsche, Freud). . . . 'Je' ne sait plus s'il existe, s'il est lui.

Sagot-Duvauroux (1999: 2):
un merveilleux outil pour contribuer à l'éveil des consciences.

Silou (1991: 52–3):
Je me refuse à établir une version dite internationale, car je veux que le monde entier entende parler créole.

Sissoko (1995: 11):
dénoncer tous les dictateurs d'Afrique et tous ceux qui on bloqué son developpement.

Sojcher (1999 II: 162):
Ma vie est devenue le scénario d'un film qui lui-même est devenu ma vie.

Sojcher (1999 II: 185):
Adrien nous amène subtilement dans une problématique identitaire, dans un jeu de miroirs passé-présent, la mémoire du père devenant une quête existentielle.

Sojcher (1999 III: 77):
les différences font peur à tellement de gens, alors qu'elles expriment nos richesses d'êtres humains.

Suchet (1986: 83a):
de ces citoyens, groupes ou classes dont on dit qu'ils véhiculent avec une culture minoritaire (culture de pauvreté, culture rurale, culture hippie etc.), la culture majoritaire étant exprimée par les gouvernements.

Suchet (1986: 83b):
permettre aux femmes de briser leur isolement et d'acquérir un sens de la solidarité, d'apprendre à assumer une identité propre et à se redéfiner.

Tadros (1972: 18):
j'ai reçu, moi, toutes les ideés religieuses. J'ai voulu aussi que mes enfants les reçoivent, car je crois que c'est là une part importante du Québec. . . . Je suis, comme tous les Québécois, quelqu'un qui a subi tous les assauts de la religion. J'en porte en moi les traces; je ne veux pas les cacher ou les camoufler.

Tadros (1972: 19):
si j'essaye par exemple de traiter d'un sujet qui n'a plus aucune réalité au Québec, à ce moment-là la vie se charge un peu de l'éliminer.

Vieyra (1990: 85):
Ces belles jeunes femmes, que la Côte d'Ivoire envoie en Europe pour récupérer ses hommes par la séduction, sont elles-mêmes récupérées par cet Occident, et quel Occident? La partie décadente, représentée par cette vieille bourgeoisie jouisseuse, qui dépense le fruit de ses manipulations financières en futilités. Et l'une de ces futilités est précisément ces belles femmes, apparemment conscientes de leur mission et choisies pour leur vertu.

Filmography

Key: dir: director; scr: screenplay; ph: photography; ed: editing; mus: music; p.a.: principal actors; p: production

A nous deux, France/Take Care France
Dir: Désiré Ecaré (Côte d'Ivoire); p.a.: Fabienne Fabre, Pierre Garnier, Marie-Gabrielle N'Guipie; p: Argos Films; 60 min; black and white; 1970.

A tout prendre/Take It All
Dir: Claude Jutra (Canada); scr: Claude Jutra; ph: Michel Brault, Jean-Claude Labrecque, Bernard Gosselin; ed: Claude Jutra; mus: Maurice Blackburn, Jean Cousineau, Serge Garant; p.a.: Johanne Harelle (Johanne), Claude Jutra (Claude), Victor Désy (Victor), Tania Fédor (the mother), Monique Mercure (Barbara); p: Claude Jutra, Robert Hershorn; 99 min; black and white; 1963.

Ablakon
Dir: Roger Gnoan M'Bala (Côte d'Ivoire); p.a.: Matthieu Attawa, Kodjo Eboucle, Joel Okou; p: Radio-TV Ivoirienne; 84 min; colour; 1984.

Abusuan/La Famille/The Family
Dir: Henri Duparc (Côte d'Ivoire); scr: Blaise Agui; ph: Christian Lacoste; ed: C. Marsollier; p.a.: Léonard Groguhat, Naton Koly, Jean-Baptiste Tiemele; p: Société Ivoirenne Cinema-Sceme; 95 min; colour; 1972.

L'Acadie, l'Acadie
Dir: Pierre Perrault, Michel Brault (Canada); ph: Michel Brault; ed: Victor Jobin; mus: Eldon Rathburn; p: Roger Blais; 118 min; black and white; 1971.

Afrique, je te plumerai/Africa, I Will Pluck You Clean/Africa, I Will Fleece You
Dir: Jean-Marie Teno (Cameroon); scr: Jean-Marie Teno; ph: Robert Dianoux, Louis Paul Nisa; ed: Chantal Rogeon; mus: Ray Lema; p.a. Jean-Marie Teno (narrator), Narcisse Kouokam, Marie Claire Dati, Essindi Mindja, Aboubakar Toine, Ange Guetouom; p: Films Du Raphia; 92 min; colour; 1991.

Afrique sur Seine
Dir: Paulin Vieyra, Mamadou Sarr (Senegal); 21 min; black and white; 1955.

L'Age de la machinpe/The Age of the Machine
Dir: Gilles Carle (Canada); scr: Gilles Carle; ph: Pierre Letarte; ed: Avdé Chiriaeff; p.a.: Gabriel Arcand, Sylvie Lachance, Willie Lamothe, Jean-Pierre Bernier; p: Jacquet Bobet, ONF/NFB (Canada); 28 min; colour; 1978.

Album I
Dir: Boris Lehman (Belgium); 60 min; colour; 1974.

Alger-Beyrouth pour mémoire/Algiers-Beirut: a Souvenir
Dir: Merzak Allouache (Algeria); scr: Merzak Allouache; ph: Laurent Machiel; ed: Claude Fredèche; mus: René-Marc Bini; p.a.: Fabienne Babe, Hocine Choutri, Georges Corraface; p: Joëy Faré, Fabienne Servan-Schraiber, Cineteve, Djinn House Productions; 95 min; colour; 1998.

Algérie en flammes/Algeria in Flames
Dir: René Vautier (Algeria); ph: René Vautier; ed: René Vautier; p: René Vautier, La Defa; 23 min; colour; 1957.

Alyam Alyam/Oh les Jours/The Days, the Days
Dir: Ahmed el Maanouni (Morocco); scr: Ahmed el Maanouni; ph: Ahmed el Maanouni; ed: Martine Chicot; mus: Nass al-Ghiwane; p.a.: Abdelwahab Ben Abdelkrim; p: Rabii Film (Morocco); 80 min; colour; 1978.

Anne Trister
Dir: Léa Pool (Canada); scr: Léa Pool, Marcel Beaulieu; ph: Pierre Mignot; ed: Michel Arcand; mus: René Dupéré, Daniel Deshaime; p.a.: Albane Guilhe (Anne), Louise Marleau (Alix), Lucie Laurier (Sarah), Guy Thauvette (Thomas), Hugues Quester (Pierre); p: Roger Frappier, Claude Bonin, Films Vision 4 Inc.; 102 min; colour; 1986.

Les Années lumière/Light Years Away
Dir: Alain Tanner (Switzerland); scr: Daniel Odier (novel), Alain Tanner; ph: Jean-François Robin; ed: Brigitte Sousselier; mus: Arié Dzierlatka; p.a.: Trevor Howard (Yoshka Poliakeff), Mick Ford (Jonas), Bernice Stegers (Betty); p: Pierre Héros; 107 min; colour; 1980.

L'Arche du désert/The Ark in the Desert
Dir: Mohamed Chouikh (Algeria); scr: Mohamed Chouikh; ph: Mustapha Belmihoub; ed: Yamina Chouikh; mus: Philippe Arthuys; p.a.: Myriam Aouffen, Meddaouda Adami, Hacen Abdou, Shyraz Aliane, Amin Chouikh; p. Nadjet Taibouni, Sandrine Vernet, Atlas Films, K. Films, Vulkan, ENIPA; 90 min; colour; 1997.

L'Aspirant/The Aspirant
Dir: Souleymane Cissé (Mali); 15 min; colour; 1968.

Au Nom du Chirst/In the Name of Christ
Dir: Roger Gnoan M'Bala (Côte d'Ivoire); scr: Roger Gnoan M'Bala; ph: Mohammed Soudani; ed: Djangoye Amoussy; mus: Paul Wassaba; p.a.: Pierro Gondo; p: Films Abyssa; 81 min; colour; 1993.

Au Pays de Zom/In the Country of Zom
Dir: Gilles Groulx (Canada); scr: Gilles Groulx; ph: Alain Dostie; ed: Gilles Groulx; mus: Jacques Hétu; p.a.: Françoise Berd (Mme Zom), Joseph Rouleau (M Zom); p: Jean Dansereau, ONF/NFB (Canada); 77 min; colour and black and white; 1982.

Avec Dieric Bouts/Met Dieric Bouts
Dir: André Delvaux (Belgium); scr: Marcella Grawet; ph: Charlie van Damme; ed: Jean Reznikov, Monique Lebrun; mus: Frédéric Devreese; p: Ludo Bekkers, BRT Télévision Flamande; 30 min; colour, 1975.

Baara/Le Travail/Work
Dir: Souleymane Cissé (Mali); ph: Etienne Carton de Grammont, Abdoulaye Sidibe; ed: Andrée Davanture; mus: Lamine Konte; p.a.: Balla Moussa Keita (the director), Baba Niare (the porter), Boubacar Keita (the engineer), Oumou Diarra (the engineer's wife), Ismaila Sarr (the foreman); p: Cissé Films; 90 min; colour; 1978.

Bab el-Oued City
Dir: Merzak Allouache (Algeria); scr: Merzak Allouache; ph: Jean-Jacques Mréjen; ed: Marie Colonna; mus: Rachid Bahri; p.a.: Nadia Kaci (Yamina), Hassan Abdou (Boualem), Messaoud Hattou (Mess), Mohamed Ourdache (Said); p: Merzak Allouache, Jacques Bidou, Jean-Pierre Gallepe, Les Matins Films (France), Flash Back Audiovisuel (Algeria), La Sept Cinéma (France), ZDF (Germany), Thelma Film AG (Switzerland); 93 min; colour; 1994.

Babel, Lettre à mes amis restés en Belgique
Dir: Boris Lehman (Belgium); scr: Boris Lehman; ph: Michael Sander, Antoine-Marie Meert; ed: Daniel de Valck; mus: Edouard Higuet, Fernand Schirren; p: Marilyn Watelet, Paradise-Films (Belgium), Boris Lehman, Dovfilm; 380 min; colour; 1991.

Babel Opéra, ou la répétition de Don Juan de Wolfgang Amadeus Mozart
Dir: André Delvaux (Belgium); scr: Denise Debraut, Jacques Sojcher, André Delvaux; ph: Charlie van Damme, Walther van den Ende; ed: Albert Jurgenson; p.a.: Stuart Burrows (Don Ottavio), Christiane Eda-Pierre (Donna Elvira), Malcolm King (Leporello), Ashley Putnam (Donna Anna), Pierre Thau (Il Commendatore), José van Dam (Don Giovanni), Marcel Vanaud (Masetto); p: Jean-Claude Batz, La Nouvelle Imagerie (Belgium); 94 min; colour; 1985.

La Bague du roi Koda/The Ring of King Koda
Dir: Mustapha Alassane (Niger); scr: Mustapha Alassane; ph: Mustapha Alassane; p: Ministère de la Co-opération (France); 24 min; colour; 1962.

Bal Poussière/Dancing in the Dust
Dir: Henri Duparc (Côte d'Ivoire); scr: Henri Duparc; ph: Bernard Déchet; mus: Boncana Naiga; p.a.: Naky Sy Savane; p: Focale 13; 91 min; colour; 1988.

Les Baliseurs du désert/The Drifters/Al-haimoun
Dir: Nacer Khemir (Tunisia); scr: Nacer Khemir; ph: Georges Barsky; ed: Moufida Tlatli; mus: Fethi Zgonda; p.a.: Soufiane Makni, Noureddine Kasbaoui, Sonia Ichti, Abdeladhim Abdelhak; p: France Media, Latif Prods, Satpec (Tunisia); 95 min; colour; 1985.

Belle
Dir: André Delvaux (Belgium); scr: André Delvaux, Monique Rysselinck; ph: Charles Van Damme; ed: Emmanuelle Dupuis, Pierre Joassin; mus: Frédéric Devreese; p.a.: Jean-Luc Bideau (Mathieu), Adriana Bogdan (Belle), Roger Coggio (Victor), Danièle Delorme (Jeanne); p: Jean-Claude Batz, Albina de Boisrouvray, Albina Productions (France), La Nouvelle Imagerie (Belgium), Ministère de la Culture de la République Française; 93 min; colour; 1973.

Bent Familia/Tunisiennes
Dir: Nouri Bouzid (Tunisia); scr: Nouri Bouzid, Khaled Joulak; ph: Armand Marco; ed: Kahena Attia; mus: Nasser Shama; p.a.: Amel Hedhili, Nadia Kaci, Leila Nassim; p: Ahmed Attia; 105 min; colour; 1997.

Benvenuta
Dir: André Delvaux, Jean-Claude Batz (Belgium); scr: André Delvaux; ph: Charles Van Damme; ed: Albert Jurgenson; mus: Frédéric Devreese, Armando Marra; p.a.: Fanny Ardant (Benvenuta), Vittorio Gassman (Livio Carpi), Mathieu Carrière (François), Claire Wauthion (Inge), Françoise Fabian (Jeanne); p: UGC (France), France 3 Cinéma, La Nouvelle Imagerie (Belgium), Opera Film Produzione; 106 min; colour; 1983.

La Bête lumineuse/The Shimmering Beast
Dir: Pierre Perrault; ph: Martin Leclerc; ed: Suzanne Allard; p: Jacques Bobet; 127 min; colour; 1982.

Bezness
Dir: Nouri Bouzid (Tunisia); scr: Nouri Bouzid; ph: Alain Levent; ed: Kahena Attia; mus: Anouar Braham; p.a.: Abdel Kechiche (Roufa), Jacques Penot (Fred), Ghalia Lacroix; p: Isabelle Fauvel, Mokhtar Lahidi, Cinétéléfilms (Tunisia), Flach Films (France), Transméditerrannée; 100 min; colour; 1991.

Les Bicots-Nègres, vos voisins/Arabs and Negroes, Your Neighbours
Dir: Med Hondo (Mauritania); scr: Med Hondo; ph: Jean Boffety, François Catonné; mus: Mohamed Ou Mustapha, Louis Xavier, Frank Valmont, Catherine Leforestier; p.a.: Bachier Touré, Jacques Thébaud, Armand Aplanalph, Sally N'Dongo; p: Med Hondo; 160 min; black and white; 1973.

Les Bons Débarras/Good Riddance
Dir: Francis Mankiewicz (Canada); scr: Réjean Ducharme; ph: Michel Brault; ed: André Corriveau; mus: Bernard Buisson; p.a.: Charlotte Laurier (Manon), Marie Tifo (Michelle), Germain Houde (Guy), Louise Marleau (Mrs Viau-Vachon), Roger

Le Bel (Maurice), Gilbert Sicotte (Gaetan); p: Marcia Couëlle, Claude Godbout, Les Productions Prisma (Canada); 114 min; colour; 1980.

Borom Sarret
Dir: Ousmane Sembene (Senegal); scr: Ousmane Sembene; ph: Christian Lacoste; ed: André Gaudier; p: Ousmane Sembene; 18 min; black and white; 1963.

Les Brûlés (The Promised Land)
Dir: Bernard Devlin (Canada); scr: Bernard Devlin; ph: Georges Dufaux; ed: Victor Jobin, Marc Beaudet, David Mayerovitch, Raymond Le Boursier; sound: Michel Belaieff; p.a.: Félix Leclerc, Jean Lajeunesse, Aimé Major; p. Guy Glover; 114 min; black and white; 1958.

Buud Yam
Dir: Gaston Kaboré (Burkina Faso); scr: Gaston Kaboré; ph: Jean-Noël Ferragut; ed: Marie-Jeanne Kanyala, Didier Ranz; mus: Michel Portal; p.a.: Colette Kaboré, Amssatou Maïga, Séverine Oueddouda, Boureima Ouedraogo, Augustine Yameogo, Serge Yanogo (Wend Kuuni); p: Bruno Hodebert, Bertrand Kabore, Pierre Roda, Caroline Production, Cinecom Production; 97 min; colour; 1996.

Cabascabo
Dir: Oumarou Ganda (Niger); scr: Oumarou Ganda; ph: Gérard De Battista, Toussaint Bruschini; ed: Danièle Tessier; mus: Kaka e Dan Baba Ali; p.a.: Oumarou Ganda, Zalika Souley, Issa Gombokoye, Balarabi, Kaka, Dan Baba Ali, Gerard Delassus, Djingarey Maiga; p: Argos Films; 48 min; black and white; 1969.

Caméra Arabe
Dir: Férid Boughedir (Tunisia); scr: Férid Boughedir; ph: Ahmed Zaaf; ed: Moufida Tlatli; p: Férid Boughedir; 62 min; colour and black and white; 1987.

Camp de Thiaroye/The Camp at Thiaroye
Dir: Ousmane Sembene, Thierno Faty Sow (Senegal); scr: Ousmane Sembene, Thierno Faty Sow; ph: Ismael Lakhdar Hamina; ed: Kahena Attia; mus: Ismaïla Lo; p.a.: Sijiri Bakaba, Ibrahima Sane, Mohamed Dansogho Camara, Ismaïla Cissé, Ababacar Sy Cissé, Moussa Cissoko, Eloi Coly, Ismaïla Lo, Jean Daniel Simon, Gabriel Zahon, Pierre Orma, Gaston Ouedraogo; p: Mustafa Ben Jemja, Ouzid Dahmane, Mamadou Mbengue; 152 min; colour; 1988.

La Chambre/The Room
Dir: Chantal Akerman (Belgium); 11 min; colour; 1972.

Le Charbonnier/The Charcoal Burner/Al Fahham
Dir: Mohamed Bouamari (Algeria); scr: Mohamed Bouamari; ph: Daho Boukerche; ed: Ali Mehdaoui; mus: Ahmed Malek; p.a.: Fehouma Ousliha, Youssef Hadjam; p: ONCIC (Algeria); 100 min; black and white; 1972.

Charles, mort ou vif/Charles, Dead or Alive
Dir: Alain Tanner (Switzerland); scr: Alain Tanner; ph: Renato Berta; ed: Silva Bachmann p.a.: François Simon (Charles), Marcel Robert (Paul), Marie-Claire

Dufour (Adeline), Maya Simon (Marianne), André Schmidt (Pierre), Michèle Martel (Germaine); p: Alain Tanner; 93 min; black and white; 1969.

Le Chat dans le sac/The Cat in the Bag
Dir: Gilles Groulx (Canada); scr: Gilles Groulx; ph: Jean-Claude Labrecque; ed: Gilles Groulx; p.a.: Barbara Ulrich, Claude Godbout, Manon Blain, Véronique Vilbert, Jean-Paul Bernier, André Leblanc; p: Jacques Bobet; 74 min; black and white; 1964.

Chef/Chief
Dir: Jean-Marie Teno (Cameroon); ph: Jean-Marie Teno; ed: Christine Badgley; mus: Brice Wassy; p: Jean-Marie Teno; 61 min; colour; 1999.

Les Chemins de l'exil/Roads of Exile
Dir: Claude Goretta (Switzerland); scr: Claude Goretta, Georges Haldas; ph: Philippe Rousselot; ed: Joele van Effenterre; mus: Arie Dzierlatka; p.a.: François Simon (Rousseau), Dominique Labourier (Thérèse), Corinne Colderey, Didier Haudepin, Roland Bertin, Monique Mélinand, Maurice Jacquemont; p: Etienne Laroche; 165 min; 1978.

Chroniques Algériennes/Algerian Chronicles
Dir: Jean-Pierre Lledo (Algeria); scr: Jean-Pierre Lledo; p: Jacques Gary, Henri Jacob; 52 min; colour; 1994.

Chronique des années de braise/Chronicle of the Years of Embers
Dir: Mohammed Lakhdar-Hamina (Algeria); scr: Tewfik Fares, Mohammed Lakhdar-Hamina; ph: Marcello Gatti; p.a.: Mohammed Lakhdar-Hamina, Leila Shenna, Yorgo Voyagis; p: ONCIC (Algeria); 177 min; colour; 1975.

Chronique d'un été/Chronicle of a Summer
Dir: Jean Rouch, Edgar Morin (France); ph: Raoul Coutard, Roger Morillière, Jean-Jacques Tarbès; p: Argos; 1961.

Cinq jours dans une vie/Five Days in a Life
Dir: Souleymane Cissé (Mali); scr: Souleymane Cissé; mus: Artistes Maliens; p.a.: Falaye Dabo, Myriam Thiam; p: SCINFOMA (Mali); 40 min; black and white; 1972.

La Citadelle/The Citadel/Al-qal'a
Dir: Mohamed Chouikh (Algeria); scr: Mohamed Chouikh; ph: Allel Yahiaoui; ed: Yamina Chouikh; mus: Jawad Fasia; p.a.: Khaled Barkat, Djillali Aim-Tedeles, Fettouma Ousliha, Momo, Fatima Belhadj, Boumédienne Sirat, Nawel Zaater; p: Centre Algérien pour l'Art et l'Industrie Cinématographique (CAAIC); 95 min; colour; 1988.

Coco la fleur, candidat/Coco-the-Flower, Candidate
Dir: Christian Lara (Guadeloupe); ph: Jean-Claude Couty; mus: Expérience 7; p.a.: Robert Liensol (Coco la fleur), Greg Germain (Gaston Monbin), Félix Marten (Denis Pauvert), Jennifer (Marie-Ange); p: Claude Guedj; 90 min; colour; 1979.

Concerto pour un exil/Concerto for an Exile
Dir: Désiré Ecaré (Côte d'Ivoire); p.a.: Sokou Camara, Claudia Chazel, Hervé Denis, Henri Duparc; p: Films de la Lagune, Argos Films; 42 min; black and white; 1968.

Une Couleur café
Dir: Henri Duparc (Côte d'Ivoire); scr: Henri Duparc; ph: Bernard Dechet; ed: Kahena Attia; mus: Jacob Desvarieux, Jocelyne Berroard; p.a.: Jean-Marie Adiaffi, Gabriel Zahon, Awa Sene Sarr; p: Henri Duparc, Focale 13; 105 min; colour; 1997.

La Cuisine rouge
Dir: Paule Baillargeon, Fréderique Collin (Canada); scr: Paule Baillargeon; Fréderique Collin; ph: Jean-Charles Tremblay; ed: Babalou Hamelin; mus. Yves Laferrière; p.a.: Michèle Mercure, Han Masson, Catherine Brunelle, Marie Ouellet; p. Claude Des Gagné, Renée Roy; 82 min; colour; 1979.

Dakan/Destiny
Dir: Mohamed Camara (Guinea); scr: Mohamed Camara; ph: Gilberto Azevedo; ed: Dos Santos; mus: Kandia Kouyate; p.a.: Cécile Bois, Koumba Diakite, Mamady, Aboucar Touré; p: René Feret; 93 min; colour; 1997.

Dans la Ville blanche/In the White City
Dir: Alain Tanner (Switzerland); scr: Alain Tanner; ph: Acacio de Almeida; ed: Laurent Uhler; mus: Jean-Luc Barbier; p.a.: Bruno Ganz, Teresa Madruga, Julia Vonderlinn, José Carvalho, Victor Costa; p: Paulo Branco, Alain Tanner, Antonio Vaz da Silva; 108 min; colour; 1983.

De Mère en fille
Dir: Ann Claire Poirier (Canada), 1967.

Le Déclin de l'empire américain/The Decline of the American Empire
Dir: Denys Arcand (Canada); scr: Denys Arcand; ph: Guy Dufaux; ed: Monique Fortier; mus: François Dompierre; p.a.: Dominique Michel (Dominique), Dorothée Berryman (Louise), Louise Portal (Diana), Geneviève Rioux (Danielle), Pierre Curzi (Pierre), Rémy Girard (Rémy), Yves Jacques (Claude), Daniel Brière (Alain), Gabriel Arcand (Mario); p: Roger Frappier, René Malo; 102 min; colour; 1986.

Deela ou El Barka le conteur/Deela or El Barka the Story-teller
Dir: Mustapha Alassane (Niger); 10 min; colour; 1970.

Den Muso/The Girl
Dir: Souleymane Cissé (Mali); p.a.: Omou Diarra, Balla Moussa Keita; 90 min; black and white; 1975.

Denko
Dir: Mohamed Camara (Guinea); scr: Mohamed Camara; ph: Mathieu Vaudepied; ed: Agnes Bruckert; mus: Mamady Mansare; p: Movimento Productions; 21 min; colour; 1992.

La Dentellière/The Lacemaker
Dir: Claude Goretta (Switzerland); scr: Claude Goretta and Pascal Lainé; ph: Jean Boffety; ed: Joëlle van Effenterre, Nelly Meunier, Martine Charasson; mus: Pierre Jansen; p.a.: Isabelle Huppert (Pomme), Yves Beneyton (François), Florence Giorgetti (Marylène); p: Yves Gasser, Action Films, Citel Films, Filmproduktion Janus; 107 min; colour; 1977.

Les Dernières Fiançailles/The Last Engagement
Dir: Jean-Pierre Lefebvre (Canada); scr: Jean-Pierre Lefebvre; ph: Guy Dufaux; ed: Marguerite Duparc; mus: Andrée Paul; p.a.: Marthe Nadeau (Rose Tremblay), J.-Léo Gagnon (Armand Tremblay); p: Marguerite Duparc, Bernard Lalonde, Les Productions Prisma (Canada), Cinak Compagnie Cinématographique (Canada); 91 min; colour; 1973.

Djeli
Dir: Fadika Kramo-Lanciné (Côte d'Ivoire); scr: Fadika Kramo-Lanciné; p.a.: Fatou Ouatara, Joachim Ouatara; p: Ministère de l'Information de Côte-d'Ivoire; 90 min; colour; 1980.

Dunia
Dir: Pierre Yameogo (Burkina Faso); scr: S. Pierre Yameogo; ph: Issaka Tiombano; ed: Jean Dubreuil; p.a.: Sylvie Ouadba, Adama Kaore, Appoline Zongo, Elizabeth Ouedraogo, Marie Yameogo, Flore Yameogo, Claudine Kabre, Adama Ouedraogo; p: Les Films de l'Espoir (Burkina Faso), Archibald Films; 52 min; colour; 1987.

Dust
Dir: Marion Hänsel (Belgium); scr: J. M. Coetzee (novel), Marion Hänsel; ph: Walther van den Ende; ed: Susana Rossberg; mus: Martin St. Pierre; p.a.: Jane Birkin (Magda), René Díaz (Jacob), Trevor Howard (the father), John Matshikiza (Hendrick), Nadine Uwampa (young Anna), Tom Vrebus (Piet); p: Jean Daskalidès, Jacques Dubrulle, Marion Hänsel, Jean-François Lepetit, Daska Films, Flach Film (France), France 3 Cinéma, Man's Films (Belgium); 88 min; colour; 1985.

Emporte-moi/Set Me Free
Dir: Léa Pool (Canada); scr: Léa Pool; ph: Jeanne Lapoirie; ed: Michel Arcand; p.a. Karine Vanasse (Hanna), Pascale Bussières (Hanna's mother), Miki Manojlovic (Hanna's father), Alexandre Mérineau (Paul, Hanna's brother); p: Lorraine Richard, Louis-Philippe Rochon, Carole Scotta, Alfi Sinniger, Haut et Court (France), Catpics AG (Switzerland), Cité-Amérique Cinéma Télévision Inc.; 95 min; colour; 1999.

Entre la Mer et l'eau douce
Dir: Michel Brault (Canada); scr: Denys Arcand, Michel Brault, Marcel Dubé, Gérald Godin, Claude Jutra; ph: Bernard Gosselin, Michel Brault, Jean-Claude Labrecque; ed: Michel Brault, Werner Nold; mus: Claude Gauthier; p.a.: Claude Gauthier (Claude Tremblay), Geneviève Bujold (Geneviève), Paul Gauthier (Roger Tremblay); p: Pierre Patry; 85 min; black and white; 1967.

D'Est/From the East
Dir: Chantal Akerman (Belgium); scr: Chantal Akerman; ph: Raymond Fromont, Bernard Delville; ed: Claire Atherton; p: Paradise-Films (Belgium); Radio-télévision Belge (RTBF), Centre de l'Audiovisuel à Bruxelles; 110 min; colour; 1993.

Fad'jal
Dir: Safi Faye (Senegal); p: Jean-Serge Breton, Safi Film; 108 min; colour; 1979.

Falsch
Dir: Luc Dardenne and Jean-Pierre Dardenne (Belgium); p.a.: Bruno Cremer, John Dobrynine, Christian Crahay, Gisele Oudart, Andre Lenaerts; p: Derives, Arcanal, Théâtre de la Place, Belgian Ministry; 82 min; colour; 1986.

La Femme au couteau/The Woman with a Knife
Dir: Timité Bassori (Côte d'Ivoire); p.a.: Timité Bassori, Mary Vieyra, Danielle Alloh, Emmanuel Diaman; p: Société Ivoirienne de Cinéma; 116 min; black and white; 1968.

La Femme de l'hôtel/A Woman in Transit
Dir: Léa Pool (Canada); scr: Léa Pool, Michel Langlois, Robert Gurik; ph: Georges Dufaux; ed: Michel Arcand; mus: Yves Laferrière; p.a.: Louise Marleau (Estelle David), Paule Baillargeon (Andréa Richler), Marthe Turgeon (singer); p: Bernadette Payeur, Marc Daigle; 89 min; colour; 1984.

La Femme de Rose Hill/The Woman from Rose Hill
Dir: Alain Tanner (Switzerland); scr: Alain Tanner; ph: Hughes Ryffel; ed: Laurent Uhler; mus: Michel Wintsch; p.a.: Marie Gaydu (Julie), Jean-Philippe Ecoffey (Jean), Denise Péron (Jeanne), Roger Jandly (Marcel); p: Paulo Branco, Jean-Louis Porchet, Alain Tanner, Westdeutscher Rundfunk (Germany), Airone Cinematografica (Italy), Filmograph (US), GPFI (France), Gémini Films (France), Télévision Suisse-Romande (Switzerland); 95 min; colour; 1989.

Femme entre chien et loup/Woman in a Twilight Garden
Dir: André Delvaux (Belgium); scr: André Delvaux, Ivo Michels; ph: Charlie van Damme; ed: Pierre Gillette; mus: Etienne Verschueren; p.a.: Marie-Christine Barrault (Lieve), Roger van Hool (François), Rutger Hauer (Adriaan); p: Productions La Guéville; 111 min; colour; 1978.

Le Fils d'Amr est mort! Amr's Son is Dead!
Dir: Jean-Jacques Andrien (Belgium); scr: Jean-Jacques Andrien; ph: Giorios Arvanitis, Georges Barsky; ed: Philippe Gosselet; mus: Motets de Claudio Moneverdi; p.a.: Pierre Clémenti, Claire Wauthion, Malcom Djuric; p: Les Films de la Drève (Belgium), Unité Trois (France), Satpec (Tunisia); 80 min; colour; 1975.

Finyé/Le Vent/The Wind
Dir: Souleymane Cissé (Mali); ph: Etienne Carton de Grammont; ed: Andrée Davanture; p.a.:Fousseyni Sissoko (Bah), Goundo Guissé (Batrou), Balla Moussa

Keita (the governor), Ismaela Sarr (Bah's grandfather), Oumou Diarra (third wife), Ismaela Cissé (Seydou); p: Cissé Films; 100 min; colour; 1982.

Finzan/A Dance for Heroes
Dir: Cheick Oumar Sissoko (Mali); scr: Cheick Oumar Sissoko; p.a.: Oumar Namory Keita, Koti, Diarrah Sanogo; p: Kora-Film; 113 min; colour; 1990.

Le Franc
Dir: Djibril Diop-Mambéty (Senegal); scr: Djibril Diop-Mambéty; ph: Stéphan Oriach; ed: Stephan Oriach; mus: Dieye Ma Deiye, Issa Cissoko; p.a.: Demba Bâ (dwarf), Dieye Ma Dieye (Marigo), Aminta Fall (landlady); p: Silvia Voser, Waka Films; 36 min; black and white; 1994.

FVVA, Femmes, villa, voiture, argent/Women, Villa, Car, Money
Dir: Mustapha Alassane (Niger); p.a.: Sotigny Kouyaté, Djingareye Maiga; p: Ministère de la Co-opération (France); 75 min; colour; 1972.

La Genèse/Genesis
Dir: Cheick Oumar Sissoko (Mali); scr: Jean-Louis Sago-Duvauroux; ph: Lionel Cousin; ed: Ailo Auguste; mus: Pierre Sauvageot, Michel Risse; p.a.: Sotigui Kouyaté (Jacob), Salif Keita (Esau), Balla Moussa Keita (Hamor), Fatoumata Diawara (Dina), Maimouna Helene Diarra (Lea); p: Jacques Atlan, Chantal Bagilishya, Kora-Film; 102 min; colour; 1999.

Gina
Dir: Denys Arcand (Canada); scr: Denys Arcand, France Lachapelle; ph: Alain Dostie; ed: Denys Arcand; mus: Michel Pagliaro, Benny Barbara; p.a.: Céline Lomez (Gina), Claude Blanchard (Bob Sauvageau), Frédérique Collin (Dolorès), Serge Thériault (the assistant cameraman), Gabriel Arcand (the director), Louise Cuerrier (Carole Bédard), Paule Baillargeon (Rita John); p: Pierre Lamy, Luc Lamy; 94 min; colour; 1975.

Golden Gloves
Dir: Gilles Groulx (Canada); ph: Guy Borremans, Michel Brault, Claude Jutra, Bernard Gosselin, Gilles Groulx; ed: Gilles Groulx; mus: Les Jérolas; p: Victor Jobin, Fernand Dansereau; 28 min; black and white; 1961.

Le Grand paysage d'Alexis Droeven
Dir: Jean-Jacques Andrien (Belgium); scr: Jean-Jacques Andrien, ph: Georges Barsky, p.a.: Jerzy Radziwilowicz (Jean-Pierre), Nicole Garcia (Elizabeth), Maurice Garrel (Alexis), Jan Decleir (Jacob); p: Les Films de la Drève (Belgium), Radio-télévision Belge (RTBF); 90 min; colour; 1981.

Le Grand Voyage/The Big Journey/Ibn al- Sabil
Dir: Mohamed Abderrahmane Tazi (Morocco); p.a.: Ali Hassan, Nadia Atbib, Mohamed Bouanani, Ahmed Saari; p: Noureddine Sail; 75 min; colour; 1981.

La Grande Allure
Dir: Pierre Perrault (Canada); ph: Martin Leclerc; ed: Claire Boyer, Monique Fortier; p.a.: Christine Prud'homme (narrator); p: Louisette Neil, Hélène Verrier, ONF/NFB; 133 min; colour; 1986.

La Guerre de libération/The War of Liberation
Dir: Ministère de l'Information et de la Culture (Algeria), a remake of Farouk Beloufa's *L'Insurrectionnelle*; ed: Hamid Djellouli, Lyazid Khodja; mus: Piccioni; 90 min; black and white; 1972.

Guimba
Dir: Cheick Oumar Sissoko (Mali); scr: Cheick Oumar Sissoko; ph: Lionel Cousin; ed: Kahena Attia, M. Ouob; mus: P. Sauvaget, M. Risse; p.a.: T. Issa Traoré, B. Moussa Keita, H. Drembele, L. Diallo; p: Kora Films; 93 min; colour; 1995.

Halfaouine
Dir: Férid Boughedir (Tunisia); scr: Férid Boughedir, Nouri Bouzid; ph: Georges Barsky; ed: Moufida Tlatli; mus: Anouar Braham; p.a.: Selim Boughedir (Noura), Helena Catzaras (Aunt Latifa), Mohamed Driss (Salih the cobbler), Rabia Ben Abd; p: Cinétéléfilms (Tunisia), Scarabée films (France), France Media, La Sept Cinéman (France), Radio-télévision Tunisienne, Westdeutsche Rundfunk (Germany); 98 min; colour; 1990.

L'Homme au crâne rasé/The Man Who Had His Hair Cut Short
Dir: André Delvaux (Belgium); scr: André Delvaux, Anna de Pagter; ph: Ghislain Cloquet; ed: Suzanne Baron; mus: Frédéric Devreese; p.a.: Senne Rouffaer (Miereveld), Beata Tyszkiewicz (Fran), Hector Camerlynck (doctor), Hilde Uitterlinden; p: Ministerie van Nationale Opvoeding en Kultuur (Belgium); 94 min; black and white; 1966.

L'Homme de cendres/Man of Ashes/Rih Essed
Dir: Nouri Bouzid (Tunisia); scr: Nouri Bouzid; ph: Youssef Ben Youssef; ed: Mika Ben Miled; mus: Salah Mahdi; p.a.: Imed Maalal, Khaled Ksouri, Mouna Noureddine, Yacoub Bihiri; p: Cinétéléfilms (Tunisia); 109 min; colour; 1986.

L'Homme sur les quais/The Man by the Shore
Dir: Raoul Peck (Haiti); scr: Raoul Peck, André Graill; ph: Armand Marco; ed: Jacques Comets; mus: Amos Coulanges, Dominique Dejean; p.a.: Jennifer Zubar (Sarah), Toto Bissainthe (Camille Desrouillere), Patrick Rameau (Gracieux Sorel), Jean-Michel Martial (Janvier); p. Pascal Verroust, Blue Films (France), Frouma Films International, Velvet Film, Les Productions du Regard; 101 min; colour; 1993.

Hotel Monterey
Dir: Chantal Akerman (Belgium); scr: Chantal Akerman; ph: Babette Mangolte; ed: Geneviève Luciani; p: Chantal Akerman; 63 min; colour; 1972.

Le Huitième Jour/The Eighth Day
Dir: Jaco Van Dormael (Belgium); scr: Jaco Van Dormael; ph: Walther van den Ende; ed: Susana Rossberg; mus: Pierre van Dormael; p.a.: Daniel Auteuil (Harry),

Pascal Duquenne (Georges), Miou-Miou (Julie); p: Pan Européenne Production; 118 min; colour; 1996.

Hyènes/Hyenas
Dir: Djibril Diop-Mambéty (Senegal); scr: Djibril Diop-Mambéty; ph: Matthias Kaelin; ed: Loredana Cristelli; mus: Wasis Diop; p.a.: Mansour Diouf (Draman Drameh), Ami Diakhate (Linguère Ramatou), Mahouredia Gueye (the mayor), Issa Ramagelissa Samb (the teacher), Kaoru Egushi (Toko); p: Thelma Film AG (Switzerland), ADR Productions, MK2 Productions (France), Maag Daan; 110 min; colour; 1992.

L'Invitation/The Invitation
Dir: Claude Goretta (Switzerland); scr: Claude Goretta, Michel Viala; ph: Jean Zeller; ed: Joële Van Effenterre; mus: Patrick Moraz; p.a.: Jean-Luc Bideau (Maurice), François Simon (Emile), Jean Champion (Alfred), Corinne Coderey (Simone), Michel Robin (Rémy), Lucie Avenay (Mme Placet); 100 min; colour; 1973.

Issa le tisserand/Issa the Weaver
Dir: Idrissa Ouedraogo (Burkina Faso); ph: Sékou Ouedraogo; ed: Arnaud Blin; mus: Mustapha Thiombiano; p.a.: Ernest Ouedraogo, Assetou Sanfo; p: Films de l'Avenir; 20 min; colour; 1984.

J. A. Martin, photographe
Dir: Jean Beaudin (Canada); scr: Jean Beaudin, Marcel Sabourin; ph: Pierre Mignot; ed: Jean Beaudin, Hélène Girard; mus: Maurice Blackburn; p.a.: Marcel Sabourin (Joseph Albert Martin), Monique Mercure (Rose-Aimée Martin); p: Jean-Marc Garand, ONF/NFB (Canada); 101 min; colour; 1976.

Je pense à vous/I Think of You
Dir: Jean-Pierre Dardenne and Luc Dardenne (Belgium); scr: Jean Gruault; ph: Yorgos Arvanitis; mus: Wim Mertens; p.a.: Fabienne Babe, Suzanne Colin, Vincent Grass, Gil Lagay, Pier Paquette, Pietro Pizzuti, Stephane Pondeville, Robin Renucci, Nathalie Uffner; p: Jean-Pierre Dardenne, Luc Dardenne, Jean-Luc Ormières, Claude Waringo; 93 min; colour; 1992.

Je, tu, il, elle/I, You, He, She
Dir: Chantal Akerman (Belgium); scr: Chantal Akerman; ph: Bénédicte Delesalle, Charlotte Szlovak, Renelde Dupont; ed: Luc Frechté; p.a.: Chantal Akerman (Julie), Claire Wauthion (Julie's friend), Niels Arestrup (lorry driver); p: Chantal Akerman, Paradise-Films (Belgium); 86 min; black and white; 1974.

Jeanne Dielman, 23 Quai du Commerce 1080 Bruxelles
Dir: Chantal Akerman (Belgium); scr: Chantal Akerman; ph: Babette Mangolte; ed: Patricia Canino, Catherine Huhardeaux, Martine Chicot; p.a.: Delphine Seyrig (Jeanne Dielman), Jan Decorte (Sylvain), Henri Storck (first customer), Jacques Doniol-Valcroze (second customer), Yves Bical (third customer); p: Corinne Jénart, Evelyne Paul, Paradise-Films (Belgium); 200 min; colour; 1975.

Jésus de Montréal/Jesus of Montreal
Dir: Denys Arcand (Canada); scr: Denys Arcand; ph: Guy Dufaux; ed: Isabelle Dedieu; mus: Jean-Marie Benoît, François Dompierre, Yves Laferrière; p.a.: Lothaire Bluteau (Daniel), Catherine Wilkenig (Mireille), Rémy Girard (Martin), Robert Lepage (René), Johanne-Marie Tremblay (Constance); p: Roger Frappier, Pierre Gendron, Gérard Mital, Gérard Mital Productions (France), Max Films Productions Inc. (Canada); 120 min; colour; 1989.

J'me marie, j'me marie Pas
Dir: Mireille Dansereau (Canada); 1973.

Jonas et Lila, à demain
Dir: Alain Tanner (Switzerland); scr: Alain Tanner, Bernard Comment; ph: Denis Jutzeler; ed: Monica Goux; mus: Michel Wintsch; p.a.: Jérôme Robart (Jonas), Aïssa Maïga (Lila); p: Jean-Louis Porchet, Gérard Ruey, Alain Tanner; 120 min; colour; 1999.

Jonas qui aura 25 ans en l'an 2000/Jonas Who Will Be 25 in the Year 2000
Dir: Alain Tanner (Switzerland); scr: Alain Tanner, John Berger; ph: Renato Berta; ed: Brigitte Sousselier, Marc Blavet; mus: Jean-Marie Sénia; p.a.: Jean-Luc Bideau (Max Stigny), Rufus (Mathieu Vernier), Miou-Miou (Marie), Jacques Denis (Marco Perly), Dominique Labourier (Marguerite), Roger Jendly (Marcel Certoux), Myriam Boyer (Mathilde Vernier); p: Yves Gasser, Yves Peyrot; 115 min; colour; 1976.

Kaddu beykat/Lettre paysanne/Letter From My Village
Dir: Safi Faye (Senegal); scr: Safi Faye; ph: Patrick Fabry; ed: Andrée Davanture; p: Safi Faye; 98 min; black and white; 1975.

Kamouraska
Dir: Claude Jutra (Canada); scr: Anne Hébert, Claude Jutra; ph: Michel Brault; ed; Renée Lichtig; mus: Maurice Le Roux; p.a.: Geneviève Bujold (Elisabeth), Richard Jordan (Georges Nelson), Philippe Léotard (Antoine); p: Pierre Lamy, Mag Bodard, Les Productions Carle-Lamy, Parc Film (France); 124 min; colour; 1973.

Laafi/All Is Well
Dir: Pierre Yameogo (Burkina Faso); scr: Pierre Yameogo; ph: Sekou Ouedraogo, Jurg Assler; ed: Loredana Cristelli; p.a.: Yolande Belem, Laure Kaho, Cheick Kone, Denis Yameogo, Aline Hortense Zoungrana; p: Les Films de l'Espoir (Burkina Faso), Thelma Film AG (Switzerland); 98 min; colour; 1991.

Lorsque le Bateau de Léon M. descendit la Meuse pour la première fois/When Léon M.'s Boat Sails Down the Meuse for the First Time
Dir: Jean-Pierre Dardenne and Luc Dardenne (Belgium); 40 min; black and white; 1979.

Magnum Begynasium Bruxellense
Dir: Boris Lehman (Belgium); scr: Boris Lehman; ed: Roland Grillon; mus: Philippe Boesmans; p: Boris Lehman; 145 min; colour and black and white; 1979.

Maria Chapdelaine
Dir: Gilles Carle (Canada); scr: Gilles Carle, Guy Fournier; ph: Pierre Mignot, Richard Leiterman; ed: Avdé Chiriaeff, Michel Arcand; mus: Lewis Furey; p.a.: Carole Laure (Maria Chapdelaine), Nick Mancuso (François Paradis); p: Murray Shostak, Robert Baylis, Harold Greenberg, Astral Bellevue Pathé (Canada), Société Radio-Canada, TF1 Films Productions (France); 107 min; colour; 1983.

La Mémoire fertile/The Fertile Memory/Al Dhakira al Khasba
Dir: Michel Khleifi (Belgium); ph: Marc-André Batigne, Yves van der Meer; p.a.: Farah Hatoum, Sarah Khalifeh; p: Michel Khleifi; 99 min; colour; 1980.

Messidor
Dir: Alain Tanner (Switzerland); scr: Alain Tanner; ph: Renato Berta, Hugues Ryffel, Carlo Varine; ed: Brigitte Sousselier; mus: Arié Dzierlatka; p.a.: Clémentine Amouroux (Jeanne), Catherine Retouré (Marie); p: Yves Gasser, Yves Payrot; 123 min colour; 1979.

Le Milieu du monde/The Middle of the World
Dir: Alain Tanner (Switzerland); scr: Alain Tanner, John Berger; ph: Renato Berta; ed: Brigitte Sousselier; mus: Patrick Moraz; p.a.: Olimpia Carlisi (Adriana), Phillippe Léotard (Paul); p: Action Films; colour; 117 min; 1974.

Les Mille et une mains/A Thousand and One Hands/Alf yad wa yad
Dir: Souheil Ben Barka (Morocco); ph: Girolamo Larosa; ed: S. Hanou; p.a.: Elgazi Aissa, Abdou Chaibane, Mimsy Farmer, Si Ahmed; p: Euro-Maghreb Films; 80 min; colour; 1972.

Misère au Borinage
Dir: Henri Storck, Joris Ivens (Belgium); scr: Henri Storck, Joris Ivens; ph: Henri Storck, Joris Ivens; ed: Helen Van Dongen; p: Education par l'Image; 36 min; black and white; 1933.

Mizik rez-de-chaussé' neg'/Musique au rez-de-chaussée des nègres
Dir: Michel Traoré (Martinique); 60 min; black and white; 1981.

Mon Oncle Antoine/My Uncle Antoine
Dir: Claude Jutra (Canada); scr: Claude Jutra, Clément Perron; ph: Michel Brault; ed: Claire Boyer, Claude Jutra; mus: Jean Cousineau; p.a.: Jean Duceppe (Oncle Antoine), Olivette Thibault (Tante Cecile), Jacques Gagnon (Benoît), Claude Jutra (Fernand), Hélène Loiselle (Madame Poulin), Lionel Villeneuve (Jos Poulin), Monique Mercure (Alexandrine); p: Marc Beaudet, ONF/NFB (Canada); 104 min; colour; 1971.

Mossane
Dir: Safi Faye (Senegal); scr: Safi Faye; ph: Jürgen Jürges; ed: Andrée Davanture; mus: Yandé Codou Sène; p.a.: Alioune Konare (Fara), Magou Seck (Mossane); p: Atriascop; 105 min; colour; 1996.

Mourir à tue-tête/A Scream from Silence
Dir: Anne Claire Poirier (Canada); scr: Anne Claire Poirier, Marthe Blackburn; ph: Michel Brault; ed: André Corriveau; mus: Maurice Blackburn; p.a.: Julie Vincent (Suzanne), Paul Savoie (Philippe), Monique Millier (the director), Micheline Lanctôt (the film editor); p: Jacques Gagné, Anne Claire Poirier, ONF/ NFB (Canada); 96 min; colour; 1979.

Muna Moto/L'Enfant de l'autre/Somebody Else's Child
Dir: Jean-Pierre Dikongué-Pipa (Cameroon); scr: Jean-Pierre Dikongué-Pipa; p.a.: Philippe Abia, Arlette Din Beli, Gisèle Dikongué-Pipa, David Endene; p: Avant-Garde Africaine; 89 min; black and white; 1976.

Nice Time
Dir: Alain Tanner, Claude Goretta (Switzerland); ed: Alain Tanner, Claude Goretta; mus: Chas McDevitt; 17 min; black and white; 1956.

No Man's Land
Dir: Alain Tanner (Switzerland); scr: Alain Tanner; ph: Bernard Zitzermann; ed: Laurent Uhler; mus: Terry Riley; p.a.: Hughes Quester (Paul), Myriam Mézières (Madeleine), Jean-Philippe Ecoffey (Jean), Betty Berr (Mali), Marie-Luce Felber; p: Westdeutscher Rundfunk (Germany), Channel Four Films (UK), Filmograph (US), Films A2 (France), MK2 Productions (France), Télévision Suisse-Romande (Switzerland); 110 min; colour; 1985.

Les Noces barbares/Cruel Embrace
Dir: Marion Hänsel (Belgium); scr: Marion Hänsel, Yann Queffelec (novel); ph: Walther van den Ende; ed: Susana Rossberg; mus: Frédéric Devreese; p.a.: Marianne Basler (Nicole, the mother), Thierry Frémont (young Ludo), Yves Cotton (Ludo as a child), Marie-Ange Dutheil (Mademoiselle Rakoff); p: Marion Hänsel, Flach Film (France), Man's Films (Belgium), TF1 Films Productions (France); 90 min; colour; 1987.

La Noire de . . . /Black Girl
Dir: Sembene Ousmane (Senegal); scr: Sembene Ousmane; ph: Christian Lacoste; ed: André Gaudier; p.a.: Mbissine Thérèse Diop (Diousana), Anne-Marie Jelinek (Madame), Robert Fontaine Jr. (Monsieur), Momar Nar Sene (Diouana's Boy-friend); p: André Zwobada, Les Actualités Françaises, Filmi Domirev (Senegal); 59 min; black and white; 1966.

La Nouba des femmes du mont Chenoua/The Nouba of the Women of Mount Chenoa/Noubat nissa'Jabal Chnouwwa
Dir: Assia Djebar (Algeria); scr: Assia Djebar; ph: Ahmed Dedjane; ed: Arezki Haddadi, Nicole Schlemmer; p.a.: Sawan Noweir, Mohamed Haimour; 115 min; colour; 1978.

Nyamanton/La Leçon des ordures/Lessons from the Garbage
Dir: Cheick Oumar Sissoko (Mali); scr: Cheick Oumar Sissoko; ph: Cheick Hamala Keïta; ed: Vogislan Korijenac; mus: Sidiki Diabaté; Moriba Keïta; Mamadou Diallo;

Harouna Barry; p.a: Chaka Diarra Ada Thio Cary; Alikaou Kanté Koti; Diarrah Sanogo Macire Kanté; p: Centre National de Production Cinématographique; 94 min; colour; 1986.

L'Oeuvre au noir/The Abyss
Dir: André Delvaux (Belgium); scr: André Delvaux; ph: Charlie van Damme; ed: Albert Jurgenson; mus: Frédéric Devreese; p.a.: Marie-Christine Barrault (Hilzonde), Jean Bouise (Campanus), Mathieu Carrière (Pierre de Hamaere), Anna Karina (Catherine), Marie-France Pisier (Martha); p: Philippe Dusart Productions, Films A2 (France), La Nouvelle Imagerie (Belgium), La Sept Cinéma (France); 110 min; colour; 1988.

Omar Gatlato
Dir: Merzak Allouache (Algeria); scr: Merzak Allouache; ph: Smail Lakhdar-Hamina; ed: Moufida Tlatli; mus: Ahmed Malek; p.a.: Boualem Bennani (Omar), Farida Guenanèche (Selma), Rabah Bouchtal (Ali); p: ONCIC (Algeria), Arab Film Distribution (US); 88 min; colour; 1977.

L'Opium et le bâton/The Opium and the Baton/Al-afyum wal-'asa
Dir: Ahmed Rachedi (Algeria); scr: Ahmed Rachedi; ph: Rachid Merabtine; ed: Eric Penet; mus: Philippe Arthuys; p.a.: Mustapha Kaleb, Ahmed Rouiched, Mahieddine Bachtarzi; p: ONCIC (Algeria); 127 min; colour; 1970.

Les Ordres/Orders
Dir: Michel Brault (Canada); scr: Michel Brault; ph: François Protat, Michel Brault; ed: Yves Dion; mus: Philippe Gagnon; p.a.: Hélène Loiselle (Marie Boudreau), Jean Lapointe (Clermont Boudreau), Guy Provost (Dr Jean-Marie Beauchemin), Claude Gauthier (Richard Lavoie), Louise Forestier (Claudette Dusseault), Amulette Garneau (Mrs Thibault); p: Bernard Lalonde, Gui Caron, Les Productions Prisma (Canada); 108 min; colour and black and white; 1974.

La Passante/The Passerby
Dir Safi Faye (Senegal); 9 min; colour; 1972.

La Petite Aurore, l'enfant martyre/Little Aurore, the Child Martyr
Dir: Jean-Yves Bigras (Canada); scr: Emile Asselin; ph: Roger Racine; ed: Jean-Yves Bigras; mus: Germaine Janelle; p.a.: Yvonne Laflamme (Aurore), Lucie Mitchell (the stepmother), Paul Desmarteaux (the father); p: Roger Garand, L'Alliance Cinématographique Canadienne Inc.; 102 min; black and white; 1951.

La Petite Vendeuse de soleil/The Little Girl Who Sold the Sun
Dir: Djibril Diop-Mambéty (Senegal); scr: Djibril Diop-Mambéty; ph: Jacques Besse; ed: Sarah Taouss Matton; mus: Wasis Diop; p.a.: Lissa Balera (Sili), Tayerou M'Baye; p: Djibril Diop-Mambéty, Waka Films, Maag Daan; 45 min; colour; 1998.

Pièces d'identités/Identity Pieces
Dir: Mweze Dieudonné Ngangura (Democratic Republic of the Congo); scr: Mweze Dieudonné Ngangura; ph: Jacques Besse; ed: France Duez, Ingrid Ralet; mus:

Jean-Louis Daulne, Papa Wemba; p.a.: Gérard Essomba, Herbert Flack, Dominique Mesa, David Steegen; p: Isabelle Mathy, Mweze Ngangura, Films-sud (Belgium); 93 min; colour and black and white, 1998.

La Plage des enfants perdus/The Beach of Lost Children/Chati'al'Atfal al-Mafqudin
Dir: Jillali Ferhati (Morocco); scr: Jillali Ferhati; ph: Gilberto Azevedo, Jacques Besse; ed: Nathalie Perrey; mus: Djamel Allam; p.a.: Souad Ferhati (Mina), Mohamed Timod (Salam), Fatima Loukili (Zineb), Larbi El-Yacoubi, Mohamed Larbi Khazzan; p: Salim Fassi Fihri, Héraclès Production (Morocco); 88 min; colour; 1991.

Poko
Dir: Idrissa Ouedraogo (Burkina Faso); p: Idrissa Ouedraogo; 20 min; colour; 1981.

Une Porte sur le ciel/Gateway to Heaven/Bab al-Sama'maftuh
Dir: Farida Benlyazid (Morocco); scr: Farida Benlyazid; ph: George Barsky; ed: Moufida Tlatli; mus: Anouar Braham; p.a.: Zakia Tahiri; p: France Média, Satpec (Tunisia), Centre Cinématographique Marocain; 105 min; colour; 1988.

Poupées de roseaux/Reed Dolls
Dir: Jilalli Ferhati (Morocco); scr: Jilalli Ferhati; ph: Abdelkrim Derkaoui; ed: Jilalli Ferhati; mus: Zineb Alaoui; p.a.: Chaïb Adraoui, Souad Ferhati, Jilalli Ferhati, Souad Thami, Ahmed Ferhati; p: Héraclès Production (Morocco); 90 min; colour; 1982.

Pour la suite du monde/For Those Who Will Follow
Dir: Pierre Perrault, Michel Brault (Canada); scr: Pierre Perrault, Michel Brault; ph: Michel Brault; ed: Werner Nold; mus: Jean Cousineau, Jean Meunier; p: Fernand Dansereau, ONF/NFB (Canada); 105 min; black and white; 1963.

La Promesse/The Promise
Dir: Jean-Pierre Dardenne and Luc Dardenne (Belgium); scr: Luc Dardenne, Jean-Pierre Dardenne; ph: Alain Marcoen; ed: Marie-Hélène Dozo; mus: Denis M'Punga, Jean-Marie Billy; p.a.: Jérémie Renier (Igor), Oliver Gourmet (Roget), Rasmané Ouedraogo (Assita); p: Claude Waringo, Eurimages Fund of the Council of Europe, Films du Fleuve (Belgium), Radio-télévision Belge (RTBF), SAMSA Film, Touza Productions; 94 min; colour; 1996.

La Provinciale/The Girl from Lorraine
Dir: Claude Goretta (Switzerland); scr: Claude Goretta, Jacques Kirshner, Rosina Rochette; ph: Philippe Rousselot; ed: Joële Van Effenterre; mus: Arié Dzierlatka; p.a: Nathalie Baye (Christine), Angela Winkler (Claire), Bruno Ganz (Remy), Patrick Chesnais (Pascal); p: Gaumont (France), Phoenix Cinematografica; 112 min; colour; 1980.

Quartier Mozart
Dir: Jean-Pierre Bekolo (Cameroon); scr: Jean-Pierre Bekolo; ph: Régis Blondeau; ed: Jean-Pierre Bekolo; mus: Philip Nikwe; p.a.: Pauline Andela, Jimmy Biyona, Essindi Mindja, Sandrine Ola'a; p: Jean-Pierre Bekolo; 80 min; colour; 1993.

Rabi
Dir: Gaston Kaboré (Burkina Faso); scr: Gaston Kaboré; ph: Jean Noël Ferragut; ed: Marie Jeanne Kanyala; mus: René B. Guirma, Wally Badaru; p: BBC/Cinécom Production; 52 min; colour; 1992.

Les Raquetteurs/The Snowshoers
Dir: Michel Brault, Gilles Groulx (Canada); ph: Michel Brault; ed: Gilles Groulx; p: Louis Portugais, ONF/NFB (Canada); 17 min; black and white; 1958.

Le Règne du jour
Dir: Pierre Perrault (Canada); ph: Bernard Gosselin, Jean-Claude Labrecque; ed: Yves Leduc, Jean Lepage; mus: Jean-Marie Cloutier; p: Jacques Bobet, Guy L. Coté, ONF/NFB (Canada); 118 min; black and white; 1966.

Réjeanne Padovani
Dir: Denys Arcand (Canada); sc: Denys Arcand, Jacques Benoît; ph: Alain Dostie; ed: Marguerite Duparc, Denys Arcand; mus: Willibald Glück, Walter Boudreau; p.a.: Luce Guilbeault, Jean Lajeunesse, Pierre Thériault; p: Duparc; 94 min; colour; 1973.

Rendez-vous à Bray/Appointment in Bray
Dir: André Delvaux (Belgium); scr: André Delvaux; ph: Ghislain Cloquet; ed: Nicole Berckmans; mus: Frédéric Devreese; p.a.: Jean Bouise, Mathieu Carrière, Anna Karina, Bulle Ogier, Martine Sarcey, Roger Van Hool; p: Parc Film (France), Showking Films (Belgium); 93 min; colour; 1971.

Les Rendez-vous d'Anna/The Meetings of Anna
Dir: Chantal Akerman (Belgium); scr: Chantal Akerman; ph: Jean Penzer; ed: Francine Sandberg, Suzanne Sandberg; p.a.: Aurore Clément (Anna), Helmut Griem (Heinrich), Magali Noel (Ida), Hans Zieschler (man from train), Lea Massari (the mother), Jean-Pierre Cassel (Daniel); p: Alain Dahan, Paradise-Films (Belgium); 127 min; colour; 1978.

Requiem
Dir: Alain Tanner (Switzerland); scr: Alain Tanner, Bernard Comment, Antonio Tabucchi; ph: Hugues Ryffel; ed: Monica Goux; mus: Michel Wintsch; p.a.: Francis Frappat (Paul), André Marcon (Pierre), Alexandre Zloto (Father), Cécile Tanner (Christine); p: Paulo Branco, Jean-François Porchet, Gérard Ruey, Alain Tanner; 100 min; colour; 1998.

Le Retour d'Afrique/Return from Africa
Dir: Alain Tanner (Switzerland); scr: Alain Tanner; ph: Renato Berta, Carlo Varini; ed: Brigitte Sousselier, Marc Blavet; p.a.: José Destoop, François Marthouret, Juliet Berto, Anne Wiazemsky, André Schmidt; p: Alain Tanner, Filmantrope, VM Productions, CECRT Paris; 109 min; black and white; 1973.

Rosetta
Dir: Jean-Pierre Dardenne and Luc Dardenne (Belgium); scr: Luc Dardenne, Jean-Pierre Dardenne; ph: Alain Marcoen; ed: Marie-Hélène Dozo; mus: Jean-Pierre

Cocco; p.a.: Emilie Dequenne (Rosetta), Fabrizio Rongione (Riquet), Anne Yernaux (Rosetta's mother), Olivier Gourmet (the boss); p: Jean-Pierre Dardenne, Luc Dardenne, Laurent Petin, Michele Petin, Films du Fleuve (Belgium); 91 min; colour; 1999.

Rue Cases-Nègres/Sugar Cane Alley
Dir: Euzhan Palcy (Martinique); scr: Euzhan Palcy, Joseph Zobel (novel); ph: Dominique Chapuis; ed: Marie-Josèphe Yoyotte; mus: Groupe Malavoi; p.a: Garry Cadenat (José), Darling Légitimus (M'Man Tine/Amantine), Douta Seck (Médouze), Joby Bernabé (Monsieur Saint-Louis); p: Jean-Luc Ormières, NEF Diffusion, ORCA Productions, SUMAFA; 133 min; colour; 1983.

Les Sabots en or/Golden Horseshoes/Safaith min dhahab
Dir: Nouri Bouzid (Tunisia); scr: Nouri Bouzid; ph: Youssef ben Youssef; ed: Kahena Attia; mus: Anouar Braham; p.a.: Hichem Rostom, Hamadi Zarouk, Michket Krifa, Fathi Heddaoui; p: Cinétéléfilms (Tunisia), France Média; 104 min; colour; 1988.

La Salamandre/The Salamander
Dir: Alain Tanner (Switzerland); scr: Alain Tanner, John Berger; ph: Renato Berta, Sandro Bernardoni; ed: Brigitte Sousselier, Marc Blavet; mus: Patrick Moraz; p.a.: Bulle Ogier (Rosemonde), Jean-Luc Bideau (Pierre), Jacques Denis (Paul), Véronique Alain, Marblum Jéquier, Marcel Vidal; p: Svocine (Switzerland); 129 min; black and white; 1971.

Samba Traoré
Dir: Idrissa Ouedraogo (Burkina Faso); scr: Idrissa Ouedraogo; ph: Pierre Laurent Che; ed: Joelle Dufour; p.a.: Bakary Sangaré (Samba), Irène Tassembodo (Binta), Abdoulaya Komboudri (Salif); p: Sophie Salbot, Silvia Voser, Les Films de la Plaine (France); 85 min; colour; 1992.

Sarraounia
Dir: Med Hondo (Mauritania); scr: Med Hondo, Abdoulaye Mamani, Abdoul War; ph: Guy Famelhon; ed: Marie-Thérèse Boiché; mus: Pierre Akendengué, Abdoulaye Cissé, Issouf Compaore; p.a.: Ai Keita, Jean-Roger Milo, Fedor Atkine, Didier Sauvegrain, Roger Mirmont, Tidjani Ouedraogo; p: Med Hondo, Les Films Soleil O; 120 min; colour; 1986.

Saute ma ville/Blow Up My Town
Dir: Chantal Akerman (Belgium); ed: Geneviève Luciani; p.a.: Chantal Akerman; p: Chantal Akerman; 13 min; black and white; 1968.

Le Silence violent/The Violent Silence/El Chergui
Dir: Moumen Smihi (Morocco); scr: Moumen Smihi; ph: Mohamed Sekkat; ed: Claude Farny; p.a.: Leila Shenna, Abdelkader Moutaai, Aïcha Chairi, Kenza Fadhil; p: Aleph Film, Centre Cinématographique Marocain; 90 min; black and white; 1975.

Les Silences du palais/The Silences of the Palace/Coumt al-Quçour
Dir: Moufida Tlatli (Tunisia); scr: Moufida Tlatli, Nouri Bouzid; ph: Youssef Ben Youssef; ed: Moufida Tlatli, Karim Hammouda, Camille Cotte; mus: Anouar Braham; p.a.: Amel Hedhili (Khedija), Hend Sabri (Young Alia), Najia Ouerghi (Khalti Hadda), Ghalia Lacrois (Adult Alia), Sami Bouajila (Lofti), Kamel Fazaa (Sid' Ali); p: Eddine Attia, Ahmed Baha, Richard Magnien, Cinétéléfilms (Tunisia), Mat Films; 127 min; colour; 1994.

Silmandé/The Whirlwind
Dir: Pierre Yameogo (Burkina Faso); scr: Pierre Yameogo; ph: Jean Clave; ed: Jean Dubreuil; mus: Wasis Diop; p.a.: Amadou Bourou, Ali Guentas, Abdoulaye Komboudri, Anne Roussel, Saida Sallem, Halidou Sawadogo, Doua Sibide; p: Emmanuel de Soria, Les Films de l'Espoir (Burkina Faso), Afix Productions; 85 min; colour; 1998.

Un Soir un train/One Night a Train
Dir: André Delvaux (Belgium); scr: André Delvaux; ph: Ghislain Cloquet; ed: Suzanne Baron; mus: Frédéric Devreese; p.a.: Yves Montand (Mathias), Anouk Aimée (Anne), François Beukelaers (Val), Adriana Bodgan (Moira); p: Mag Bodard, Parc Film (France), Fox-Europa, Les Films du Siècle; 91 min; colour; 1968.

Soleil des hyènes/Sun of the Hyenas/Chams Dhiba
Dir: Reda Behi (Tunisia), scr: Reda Behi; ph: Théo van de Sande; ed: Ton de Graaf; mus: Nicolas Piovani; p.a.: Larbi Doghmi (Haj Ibrahim), Mahmoud Morsi (Lamine), Ahmed Snoussi (Tahar), Helene Catzaras (Mariem), El Omari (Omda), Tewfik Guida (Slim); p: Reda Behi, Fugitive Film, Z. Huisman; 100 min; colour; 1976.

Soleil O
Dir: Med Hondo (Mauritania); ph: François Catonné; mus: George Anderson; p.a.: Bernard Bresson, Robert Liensol, Théo Légitimus; p: Shango, Grey Films; 102 min; black and white; 1969.

Sonatine
Dir: Micheline Lanctôt (Canada); scr: Micheline Lanctôt; ph: Guy Dufaux; ed: Louise Surprenant; mus: François Lanctôt; p.a.: Pascale Bussières (Chantal), Marcia Pilote (Louisette); p: Pierre Gendron, René Malo, Corporation Image M & M (Canada); 91 min; colour; 1983.

Sud/South
Dir: Chantal Akerman (Belgium); scr: Chantal Akerman; ph: Raymond Fromont; ed: Claire Atherton; p: Xavier Carniaux, AMIP (France), Carré Noir, Chemah I.S., Radio-télévision Belge (RTBF), Finnish Broadcasting Company (YLE), INA, La Sept Cinéma (France), Paradise-Films (Belgium); 71 min; colour; 1999.

Sur la dune de la solitude/On the Dune of Solitude
Dir: Timité Bassori (Côte d'Ivoire); 22 min; black and white; 1966.

Ta Dona/Au Feu/Fire
Dir: Adamo Drabo (Mali); scr: Adamo Drabo; ph: Lionel Cousin; ed: Rose Evans-Decraene; mus: Banzoumama Sissoko; p.a.: Djeneba Diawara (Koro), Balla Moussa Keita (Fakoro), Diarrah Sanogo (Gnedjougou), Fily Traore (Sidy); p: CNPC, Kora-Film; 100 min; colour; 1991.

Taafe Fanga/Le Pouvoir des pagnes/Skirt Power
Dir: Adamo Drabo (Mali); scr: Adamo Drabo; ph: Lionel Cousin; ed: Rose Evans-Decraene; p.a.: Fanta Berete, Ramata Drabo, Ibrahim Koïta; p: Adamo Drabo, CNPC (Mali), ZDF (Germany); 95 min; colour; 1996.

Le Temps d'une chasse
Dir: Francis Mankiewicz (Canada); scr: Francis Mankiewicz; ph: Michel Brault; ed: Werner Nold; mus: Pierre F. Brault; p.a.: Guy l'Ecuyer, Marcel Sabourin, Pierre Dufresne, Olivier l'Ecuyer, Frédérique Collin, Luce Guilbeault, Monique Mercure; p: Pierre Gauvreau, ONF/NFB (Canada); 98 min; colour; 1972.

TGV
Dir: Moussa Touré (Senegal); scr: Moussa Touré, Alain Choquart; ph: Alain Choquart; ed: Josie Miljevic; mus: Wasis Diop; p.a.: Oumar Diop Makena (Rambo), Al Hamdou Traore (Demba), Bernard Giraudeau (Roger), Philippine Leroy-Beaulieu (Sylvia); p: Bernard Giraudeau, Jean-François Lepetit, Moussa Touré, Les Films du Crocodile, Flach Film (France), Les Films de la Saga; 90 min; colour; 1997.

Thèmes d'inspiration
Dir: Charles Dekeukeleire (Belgium); scr: Roger Avermaete; ph: François Rents; p: Production Dekeukeleire; 9 min; black and white; 1938.

Tilaï
Dir: Idrissa Ouedraogo (Burkina Faso); scr: Idrissa Ouedraogo; ph: Jean Monsigny, Pierre Laurent Chénieux; ed: Luc Barnier; mus: Abdullah Ibrahim; p.a.: Rasmane Ouedraogo (Saga), Ina Cissé (Nogma), Roukietou Barry (Kuilga), Assane Ouedraogo (Kougri); p: Films de l'Avenir, Waca Films, Rhea Films; 81 min; colour; 1990.

To Woody Allen, from Europe with Love
Dir: André Delvaux (Belgium); scr: André Delvaux; ph: Michel Baudour, Walther van den Ende; ed: Jean Reznikov, Annette Wauthoz; mus: Egisto Macchi; p: Danien van Avermaet, Pierre Drouot, Iblis Films (Belgium); 90 min; colour; 1980.

Toto le héros/Toto the Hero
Dir: Jaco Van Dormael (Belgium); scr: Jaco van Dormael; ph: Walther van den Ende; ed: Susana Rossberg; mus: Pierre van Dormael; p.a.: Michel Bouquet (Thomas as an old man), Peter Boehlke (Alfred as an old man), Didier Ferney (Alfred as an adult); p: Philippe Dusart Productions, Iblis Films (Belgium); 91 min; colour; 1991.

Toubab-Bi
Dir: Moussa Touré (Senegal); scr: Michèle Armandi; ph: Alain Choquart; ed: Josie Milievic; mus: Ali Wague; p.a.: Oumar Diop Makena (Soriba), Hélène Lapiower (Marie), Khalil Gueye (Prince), Cheikh Toure (Idi); p: Valérie Seydoux, Valprod; 96 min; colour; 1991.

Touki-Bouki/Journey of the Hyena
Dir: Djibril Diop-Mambéty (Senegal); scr: Djibril Diop-Mambéty; ph: Papa Samba Sow; p.a.: Al Demba, Dieynaba Diens, Assane Faye, Magaye Niang, Myriam Niang; p: CINEGRIT; 89 min; colour; 1973.

Tu as crié, 'Let me go'/You Shouted, 'Let Me Go'
Dir: Anne Claire Poirier (Canada); scr: Anne Claire Poirier, Marie-Claire Blais; ph: Jacques Leduc; ed: Monique Fortier, Yves Dion, Myriam Poirier; mus: Marie Bernard; p: Paul Lapointe, Joanne Carrière, ONF/NFB (Canada); 96 min; black and white; 1998.

Le Vent des Aurès/The Wind from the Aurès/Rih al-Awras
Dir: Mohamed Lakhdar-Hamina (Algeria); scr: Tewfik Farès; ph: M. Jovanovic; ed: Yazid Khoudja, Hamid Djelouli; p.a.: Keltoum, Mohamed Chouikh, Hassen el Hassani, Omar Tayane; p: Office des Actualités Algériennes (OAA); 95 min; black and white; 1967.

La Vie heureuse de Léopold Z/The Merry World of Leopold Z
Dir: Gilles Carle (Canada); sc: Gilles Carle; ph: Jean-Claude Labrecque; ed: Werner Nold; mus: Paul de Margerie; p.a.: Guy l'Ecuyer (Léopold), Paul Hébert, Suzanne Valéry, Monique Joly, Jacques Poulin, Gilles Latulippe; p: Jacques Bobet, ONF/NFB (Canada); 69 min; black and white; 1965.

La Vie rêvée
Dir: Mireille Dansereau (Canada); sc: Mireille Dansereau; ph: François Gill, Richard Rodrigue, Louis de Emsted; ed: Danielle Gagné; mus: Emmanuel Charpentier; p.a.: Liliane Lemaître-Auger, Véronique Le Flaguais, Jean-François Guité p: Guy Bergeron, 85 min; colour; 1972.

Une Ville à Chandigarh/A City at Chandigarh
Dir: Alain Tanner (Switzerland); scr: Alain Tanner; ph: Ernest Artaria; p: Alain Tanner, Ernest Artaria; BBC (UK); 51 min; colour; 1966.

Visages de femmes/Faces of Women
Dir: Désiré Ecaré (Côte d'Ivoire); scr: Désiré Ecaré; ph: François Migeat, Dominique Gentil; ed: Nicolas Barachin, Madame Djé-Djé, Gisèle Miski; p.a.: Sidiki Bakaba, Kouadou Brou, Albertine N'Guessan, Eugénie Cissé-Roland, Véronique Mahilé, Carmen Levry, Anny Brigitte, Alexis Leache, Victor Cousin, Fatou Fall, Traore Siriki, Désiré Bamba; p: Désiré Ecaré, Films de la Lagune; 105 min; colour; 1985.

Le Voleur/The Thief/El bouhali
Dir: Merzak Allouache (Algeria); ed: Reda Guenfoud; p: CNC, Institut National de Cinéma d'Algérien (INC); 20 min; black and white; 1966.

La Vraie nature de Bernadette/The True Nature of Bernadette
Dir: Gilles Carle (Canada); scr: Gilles Carle; ph: René Verzier; ed: Gilles Carle, Susan Kay; mus: Pierre F. Brault; p.a.: Micheline Lanctôt (Bernadette), Donald Pilon (Thomas), Reynald Bouchard (Rock); p: Pierre Lamy, Gilles Carle, Les Productions Carle-Lamy; 96 min; colour; 1972.

Waati/Time
Dir: Souleymane Cissé (Mali); scr: Souleymane Cissé; ph: Marano Vincenzo, Georgi Rerberg, Jean-Jacques Bouhon; ed: Andrée Davanture; mus: Bernard Coulais; p.a.: Sidi Yaya Cissé (Solofa), Mariame Amerou, Mohamed Dicko (Nandi at six years), Balla Moussa Keita (the teacher), Eric Miyeni (the father), Nakedi Ribane (the mother), Niamanto Sanogo (Rastas' prophet), Linèo Tsolo (Nandi), Mary Twala (the grandmother); p: Cissé Films, Carthago Films; 143 min; colour; 1995.

Wariko, le gros lot/The Lottery
Dir: Fadika Kramo-Lanciné (Côte d'Ivoire); scr: Fadika Kramo-Lanciné; ph: Lionel Cousin; ed: Cisse Salimata; mus: Cheick M. Smith; Abiba Kabore (Awa), Allassane Toure (Ali); p: Kramo-Lanciné Productions; 100 min; colour; 1994.

Watani, un monde sans mal/Watani, a World Without Evil
Dir: Med Hondo (Mauritania); scr: Med Hondo; ph: Olivier Drouot; ed: Laure Budin; p: M.H. Films Productions; 78 min; colour; 1998.

Le Wazzou polygame/The Polygamist's Moral
Dir: Oumarou Ganda (Niger); scr: Oumarou Ganda; p.a.: Goubokoye Issa, Souley Zalika, Dia Lam Ibrahim; p: Argo Films; 50 min; 1972.

Wechma/Traces
Dir: Hamid Benani (Morocco); scr: Hamid Benani; ph: Mohamed Aberrahmane Tazi; ed: Hamid Benani; mus: Kamal Dominique Hellebois; p.a.: Mohamed Kadan, Khadidja Moujabid, Abdelkader Moutaa; p: Sigma 3 (France); 100 min; black and white; 1970.

Wend Kuuni/God's Gift
Dir: Gaston Kaboré (Burkina Faso); scr: Gaston Kaboré; ph: Sekou Ouedraogo; ed: Andrée Davanture; mus: René B. Guirma; p.a.: Serge Yanogo, Rosine Yanogo, Joseph Nikiema, Colette Kaboré, Simone Tapsoba, Yaya Wima, Martine Ouedraogo; 75 min; colour; 1982.

West Indies
Dir: Med Hondo (Mauritania); p.a.: Roland Bertin, Robert Liensol, Hélène Vincent; 110 min; colour; 1979.

Yaaba
Dir: Idrissa Ouedraogo (Burkina Faso); scr: Idrissa Ouedraogo; ph: Matthias Kalin; ed: Loredana Cristelli; mus: Francis Bebey; p.a.: Fatimata Sanga (Yaaba), Noufou Ouedraogo (Bila), Roukietou Barry (Nopoko); p: Michel David, Freddy Denaës, Pierre-Alain Meier, Idrissa Ouedraogo, Films de l'Avenir, Arcadia Films (France), Thelma Film AG (Switzerland); 90 min; colour; 1989.

Yam Daabo/Le Choix/The Choice
Dir: Idrissa Ouedraogo (Burkina Faso); scr: Idrissa Ouedraogo; ph: Jean Monsigny, Sekou Ouedraogo, Issaka Thiombiano; ed: Arnaud Blin; mus: Francis Bebey; p.a.: Aoua Guiraud, Moussa Bologo, Assita Ouedraogo, Fatimata Ouedraogo, Oumarou Ouedraogo; p: Mario Gariazzo, Films de l'Avenir; 80 min; colour; 1986.

Yeelen/La Lumière/The Light
Dir: Souleymane Cissé (Mali); scr: Souleymane Cissé; ph: Jean-Noel Ferragut, Jean-Michel Humeau; ed.: Andrée Davanture, Marie-Catherine Miqueau, Jenny Frenck, Seipati Bulane; mus: Michel Portal, Salif Keita; p.a.: Issiaka Kane (Nianankoro), Aoua Sangaré (Attou), Niamanta Sanogo (Soma the father/Djigui the twin), Soumba Traore (Mah, the mother); p: Souleymane Cissé, Cissé Films, Les Films du Carrosse; 105 min; colour; 1987.

Youcef ou la légende du septième dormant/The Legend of the Seventh Sleeper
Dir: Mohamed Chouikh (Algeria); scr: Mohamed Chouikh; ph: Allel Yahiaoui; ed: Yamina Chouikh; mus: Khaled Barkat; p.a.: Mohamed Ali Allalou, Youcef Benadouda, Mohamed Benguettaf, Dalila Helilou, Azzedine Medjoubi, Selma Shiraz; p: Rachid Diguer, Centre Algérien pour l'Art et l'Industrie Cinématographique (CAAIC), ENPA; 105 min; colour; 1993.

Zan Boko/Homeland
Dir: Gaston Kaboré (Burkina Faso); scr: Gaston Kaboré; ph: Issaka Thiombiano; ed: Andrée Davanture, Marie-Jeanne Kanyala; mus: Henri Guédon; p.a.: Joseph Nikiema, Colette Kaboré, Pafadnam Mady, Jean-François Ouedraogo, Célestin, Zongo, Georgette Salambere; p: Gaston Kaboré; 92 min; colour; 1988.

Un Zoo la nuit/Night Zoo
Dir: Jean-Claude Lauzon (Canada); scr: Jean-Claude Lauzon; ph: Guy Dufaux; ed: Michel Arcand; mus: Jean Corriveau; p.a.: Gilles Maheu (Marcel), Roger Le Bel (Albert); p: Roger Frappier, Pierre Gendron, Louise Gendron, Les Productions Oz; 115 min; colour; 1987.

Bibliography

Akomfrah, J. (1995), Interview with June Givanni in *Sight and Sound*, Volume 5, Issue 9, pp. 37–9.

Allouache, M. (1995), Interview with Hadani Ditmars in *Sight and Sound*, Volume 5, Issue 9, pp. 34–5.

Andrade-Watkins, C. (1996), 'France's Bureau of Cinema – Financial and Technical Assistance 1961–1977. Operations and Implications for African Cinema', in *African Experiences of Cinema*, ed. I. Bakari & M. Cham, London, British Film Institute, pp. 112–27.

Appiah, K. A. (1992), *In My Father's House. Africa in the Philosophy of Culture*, New York/Oxford, Oxford University Press.

Arcand, D. (1976), Interview by J. Bouthillier-Levesque in *Positif*, No. 187, pp. 20–2.

Arcand, D. (1986), 'Le Confort après l'indifférence', Interview for *24 Images*, No. 28–30, pp. 28–32.

Armes, R. (1996), *Dictionnaire des cinéastes du Maghreb*, Paris, L'Association des Trois Mondes.

Armes, R. (1998), *Omar Gatlato*, Trowbridge, Wiltshire, Flick Books.

Ashbury, R., Helsby W. & O'Brien, M. (1998), *Teaching African Cinema*, London, British Film Institute.

Aubenas, J. (1995), *Catalogue des films de Chantal Akerman* (R. Dehaye ed.), Bruxelles, Commissariat Général aux Relations Internationales de la Communauté Française de Belgique.

Aubenas, J. (1996), 'Falsch, une adaptation', in *Revue belge du cinéma*, No. 41, pp. 63–7.

Bachy, V. (1978), *Le Cinéma de Tunésie*, Tunis, Société Tunésienne de Diffusion.

Bachy, V. (1983a), *Le Cinéma au Mali*, Bruxelles, OCIC/L'Harmattan.

Bachy, V. (1983b), *Le Cinéma en Côte d'Ivoire*, Bruxelles, OCIC/L'Harmattan

Bakari, I. & Cham, M. (1996), *African Experiences of Cinema*, London, British Film Institute.

Barette, P. (1999), 'Pierre Perrault. Un Passage vers le réel', in *24 Images*, No. 98–9, pp. 5–11.

Bénôt, Y. (1997), 'The European Conscience and the Black Slave Trade. An Ambiguous Protest', in *The Routes and Traces of Slaves*, Diogenes Number 179, Providence/Oxford, Berghahn Books, pp. 93–109.

Bonte, P. & Izard, M. (1992), *Dictionnaire de l'ethnologie et de l'anthropologie*, Paris, Presses Universitaires de France.

Boughedir, F. (1987), *Le Cinéma africain de A à Z*, Bruxelles, OCIC.

Bouzid, N. (1994), *Ecrans d'Afrique*, No. 9/10, pp. 14–23.

Brahimi, D. (1997), *Cinémas d'Afrique francophone et du Maghreb*, Paris, Nathan.

Buache, F. (1974), *Le Cinéma suissse*, Lausanne, L'Age d'Homme.

Burgin, V. (1996), *In/Different Spaces: Place and Memory in Visual Culture*.

Césaire, A. (1992), Interview with Marie-Line Sephocle (translation of 1988 interview), in *Ex-Iles. Essays on Caribbean Cinema*, ed. M. B. Cham, Trenton, N.J., Africa World Press, pp. 359–69.

Cham, M. B. (ed.) (1992), *Ex-Iles. Essays on Caribbean Cinema*, Trenton, N.J., Africa World Press.

Cheriaa, T. (1995), 'La FEPACI et nous', in *L'Afrique et le centenaire du cinéma/ Africa and the Centenary of Cinema*, ed. Gaston Kaboré, Paris/Dakar, Présence Africaine, pp. 253–68.

Chikhaoui, T. (1998), 'Au commencement était l'Afrique', in *Cinécrits 16* (special issue on Souleymane Cissé), Tunis, Maison de la Culture Khaldoun.

Chion, M. (1982), *La Voix au cinéma*, Paris, Etoile/Cahiers du Cinéma.

Cinécrits (October 1998), special issue on Souleymane Cissé.

Copie Zéro (1980), No. 5, special issue on Michel Brault, Montréal, La Cinéma-thèque Québécoise.

Coulombe M. & Jean, M. (1991), *Le Dictionnaire du cinéma québécois*, Montréal, Boréal.

Davidson, B. (1980), *The African Slave Trade*, Boston, Little Brown and Company, Back Bay Books.

Davidson, B. (1997), *Modern Africa. A Social and Political History*, London and New York, Longman.

de Gaulle, C. (1970), *Discours et messages*, Paris, Plon, Vol. 5.

Deleuze, G. (1985), *L'Image-Temps*, Paris, Les Editions de Minuit.

Diawara, M. (1992), *African Cinema: Politics and Culture*, Bloomington & Indianapolis, Indiana University Press.

FEPACI (1995), *L'Afrique et le centenaire du cinéma/Africa and the Centenary of Cinema*, ed. Gaston Kaboré, Paris/Dakar, Présence Africaine.

Fowler, C. (1995) Entry on Belgian cinema in *Encyclopedia of European Cinema* (ed. G. Vincendeau), London, Cassell and British Film Institute, pp. 37–8.

Gardies, A. (1989), *Cinéma d'Afrique francophone: L'Espace miroir*, Paris, L'Harmattan.

Glissant, E. (1996), *Introduction à une poétique du divers*, Paris, Gallimard.

Goyette, L. (1989), 'L'Insertion de la chanson dans le cinéma québécois des années 80', in *Le Cinéma québécois des années 80*, sous direction de C. Chabot, M. Larouche, D. Pérusse & P. Véronneau, Montréal, Cinémathèque Québécoise.

Guellali, A. (1998), 'La Transmission dans *Yaaba*', in *Cinécrits*, 15, pp. 13–15.

Hadj-Moussa, R. (1994), *Le Corps, l'histoire, le territoire. Les Rapports de genre dans le cinéma algérien*, Paris, Les Editions Balzac, Publisud.

Hall, S. (1992), 'Cultural Identity and Cinematic Representation', in *Ex-Iles. Essays on Caribbbean Cinema*, ed. M. B. Cham, Trenton, N.J., Africa World Press, pp. 221–36.

Hand, S. ed. (1989), *The Levinas Reader*, Oxford, Blackwell.

Harrow, W. K. (ed.) (1997), *With Open Eyes: Women and African Cinema*, Amsterdam/Atlanta, Rodopi.

Hayward, S. (1996), *Key Concepts in Cinema Studies*, London and New York, Routledge.

Hennebelle, G. (1972), *Les Cinémas africains*, Société Africaine d'Edition.

Ilboudo, P. G. (1988), *Le FESPACO 1969–1989. Les Cinéastes africains et leurs oeuvres*, Ougadogou, Editions La Mante.

Jean, M. (1991), *Le Cinéma québécois*, Montréal, Boréal.

Jones, B. (1993) 'La Rue Cases-Nègres (*Black Shack Alley*): From Novel to Film', paper delivered at the ICS Caribbean Societies Seminar.

Jones, B. (1998), 'Telling the Story of King Béhanzin', in Year Book 3 of the Association for the Study of Caribbean and African Literature in French.

Jones, B. & Dickson Littlewood, S. (1997), *Paradoxes of French Caribbean Theatre. An Annotated Checklist of Dramatic Works, Guadeloupe, Guyane, Martinique from 1900*, London, Roehampton Institute.

Judge, A. (1999), 'Voices and Policies', in *Francophone Voices*, ed. K. Sahli, Exeter, Elm Bank Publications, pp. 1–25.

Jutra, Cl. (1973), 'Une Espèce de joie dans la création', interview with J. P. Tadros in *Cinéma/Québec*, Vol. 2, No. 6/7, pp. 15–19.

Jutra, Cl. (1980), 'Au Québec, c'est sûrement Michel Brault qui est le cinéaste plus présent, le plus versatile, le plus prolifique, le plus constant', in *Copie Zéro* 5, pp. 20–2.

Kaboré, G. (1999). 'Entretien avec Gaston Kaboré', Garcia, J. P. & Laniesse C. in *Le Film africain*, No. 28, pp. 2–3.

Laverdière, S. (1983), 'Personnage symbolique ou film d'époque?', in *24 Images*, No. 17, pp. 36–7.

Lawless, R. I. (1995), *Algeria*, Oxford, Clio Press, World Bibliographical Series, Vol. 19.

Lever, Y. (1986), 'Les "Fondateurs"', in 'Aujourd'hui le cinéma québécois', Paris, *CinémAction*,

Lever, Y. (1995a), *Les 100 Films québécois qu'il faut voir*, Québec, Nuit Blanche.

Lever, Y. (1995b), *Histoire générale du cinéma au Québec*, Montréal, Boréal.

Lockerbie, I. (1991), 'Québec Cinema as a Mirror of Indentity', in *Canada on the Threshold of the 21st Century/Le Canada au seuil du 21ième siècle*, ed. C. H. W. Remie & J. M. Lacroix, Amsterdam/Philadelphia, John Benjamins Publishing Co.

Lockerbie, I. (1996), 'Regarder la mort en face', in *Cinébulles*, Vol. 15, No. 2, pp. 46–9.

Loiselle, M. C. (1994) 'Les Bons débarras: "Une fleur dans l'asphalte, pas écrapoutissable . . ."', in *24 Images*, No. 70, pp. 20–2.

Loomba, A. (1998), *Colonialism/postcolonialism*, London, Routledge.

Maalouf, M. (1998), *Les Identités meurtrières*, Paris, Grasset.

Machta, I. (1998), '*Tilaï*: La Tragédie des humbles', in *Cinécrits*, Octobre 1998, pp. 19–23.

MacRae, H. S. (1997), 'The Mature and Older Woman of African Film', in *With Open Eyes: Women and African Cinema*, ed. Kenneth W. Harrow, Amsterdam, Rodopi, pp. 241–54.

Maherzi, L. (1980), *Le Cinéma algérien*, Algiers.

Marsolais, G. (1994), 'Des Personnages en quête d'identité', in *24 Images*, No. 70, pp. 17–19.

Martin, A. (1982), *African Films: The Context of Production*, dossier no. 6, London, British Film Institute.

Massey, I. (1994), *Identity and Community*, Detroit, Wayne State University Press.

McDonald, C. (1998), 'Factoring the Father', in *Paternity and Fatherhood: Myths and Realities*, ed. Lieve Spaas, Basingstoke, Macmillan, pp. 49–61.

Ménil, A. (1992), 'Rue Cases-Nègres or the Antilles from the Inside', in *Ex-Iles. Essays on Caribbean Cinema*, ed. M. B. Cham, Trenton, N.J. African World Press, pp. 155–75.

Ngayane, L. (1993), 'For Africans, with Africans, by Africans', in *Africa at the Pictures*, ed. Keith Shiri, London, British Film Institute, pp. 12–26.

Nysenholc, A. (1985), *André Delvaux*, Editions de l'Université de Bruxelles.

Ostria, V. (1985), 'Terroriste d'amour, *Les Bons Débarras*', in *Cahiers du cinéma*, 378, pp. 54–5.

Pallister, J. L. (1995), *The Cinema of Québec. Masters in their Own House*, Madison Teaneck, Fairleigh Dickinson University Press.

Parker, G. (1978), Review of *The Lacemaker*, in *Film Quarterly*, Vol. 32, pp. 51–5.

Pazzanita, A. G. (1998), *The Maghreb*, Oxford, World Bibliographical Series, Vol. 208.

Petty, S. (1996), *A Call to Action. The films of Ousmane Sembene*, Bath, Flick Books.

Pfaff, F. (1988), *Twenty-five Black African Filmmakers: A Critical Study with Filmography and Bio-Bibliography*, Westport, Connecticut, Greenwood Press.

Pfaff, F. (1997), 'Sarraounia: An Epic of Resistance. Interview with Med Hondo', in *With Open Eyes: Women and African Cinema*, ed. K. W. Harrow, Amsterdam/Atlanta, Rodopi, pp. 151–8.

Piemme, J. M. (1996), 'Usage de la blessure', in *Revue Belge du cinéma*, No. 41, pp. 7–9.

Pool, L. (1986), 'Une Simple Question de déplacement. Rencontre avec Léa Pool', in *Cinéma du Québec. Au Fil du direct*, dossier composé par P. Leboutte, Liège (Belgium), Editions Yellow Now.

Reclus, O. (1883), *France, Algérie et colonies*, Paris, Hachette.

Rousseau, J. J. (1959), *Le Persiffleur*, in *Oeuvres complètes*, Tome I, Paris, Editions Gallimard, pp. 1103–12.

Sagot-Duvauroux, J. L. (1999), 'Déplacer le regard', in *Le Film africain*, No. 31, pp. 2–3.

Shafik, V. (1998), *Arab Cinema: History and Cultural Identity*, Caïro, The American University in Caïro Press.

Silou, O. (1991), *Le Cinéma dans les Antilles françaises*, Bruxelles, OCIC.

Sissoko, O. (1995), 'Rencontre avec le réalisateur', J. P. Garcia, in *Le Film africain*, No. 18/19, pp. 10–11.

Smihi, M. (1994) Interview with Guy Hennebelle on *El Chergui*, in *Le Film africain*, No. 14, p. 26.

Sojcher, F. (1999), *La Kermesse héroïque du cinéma belge*, 3 vols, Paris, L'Harmattan.

Suchet, S. (1986), 'L'Oeil au féminin', in *Aujourd'hui le cinéma québécois*, CinémAction 40, dossier réuni par Louise Carrière.

Tadros, J. P. (1972), 'Rejoindre le mythe par le quotidien', in *Cinéma Québec*, Vol. 1, No. 9, May–June, pp. 17–21.

Taylor, C. (1989), *Sources of the Self. The Making of the Modern Identity*, Cambridge, Cambridge University Press.

Ukadike, N. F. (1994), *Black African Cinema*, Berkeley/Los Angeles/London, University of California Press.

Vieyra, P. S. (1975), *Le Cinéma africain des origines à 1973*, Paris, Présence Africaine.

Vieyra, P. S. (1990), *Réflexions d'un cinéaste africain*, Bruxelles, Editions OCIC.

Index

064 L2 FM 3685 ∏Group
07/26/10 44400

9 780719 058615